Patents, Inventions and the Dynamics of Innovation

Patents, Inventions and the Dynamics of Innovation

A Multidisciplinary Study

Roger Cullis

Senior Visiting Fellow, Queen Mary Intellectual Property Research Institute, University of London, UK

Edward Elgar
Cheltenham, UK • Northampton, MA, USA

Published by
Edward Elgar Publishing Limited
Glensanda House
Montpellier Parade
Cheltenham
Glos GL50 1UA
UK

Edward Elgar Publishing, Inc.
William Pratt House
9 Dewey Court
Northampton
Massachusetts 01060
USA

A catalogue record for this book
is available from the British Library

Library of Congress Cataloguing in Publication Data

Cullis, Roger, 1938-
    Patents, inventions and the dynamics of innovation : a multidisciplinary study / Roger Cullis.
        p. cm.
    Includes bibliographical references and index.
    1. Technological innovations. 2. Inventions. 3. Electronic industries–Technological innovations. I. Title.
    T173.8.C85 2007
    621.38109–dc22
                        2006103544

ISBN 978 1 84542 958 4

Printed and bound in Great Britain by MPG Books Ltd, Bodmin, Cornwall

Contents

Preface

We are apt to consider that invention is the result of spontaneous action of some heavenborn genius, whose advent we must patiently wait for, but cannot artificially produce. It is unquestionable, however, that education, legal enactments, and general social conditions have a stupendous influence on the development of the originative faculty present in a nation and determine whether it shall be a fountain of new ideas or become simply a purchaser from others of ready-made inventions.

Sir Ambrose Fleming

An inventor is an opportunist, one who takes occasion by the hand; who, having seen where some want exists, successfully applies the right means to attain the desired end. The means may be largely, or even wholly, something already known, or there may be a certain originality or discovery in the means employed. But in every case the inventor uses the work of others. If I may use a metaphor, I should liken him to the man who essays the conquest of some virgin alp. At the outset he uses the beaten track, and, as he progresses in the ascent, he uses the steps made by those who have preceded him, whenever they lead in the right direction; and it is only after the last footprints have died out that he takes ice-axe in hand and cuts the remaining steps, few or many, that lift him to the crowning height which is his goal.

Sir Joseph Swan

The man of true genius never lives before his time, he never undertakes impossibilities, and always embarks on his enterprise at the suitable place and period. Though he may catch a glimpse of the coming light as it gildes the mountain top long before it reaches the eyes of his contemporaries, and he may hazard a prediction as to the future, he acts with the present.

Joseph Henry

Well, about ninety-nine per cent of it is a knowledge of the things that will not work. The other one per cent may be genius, but the only way that I know to accomplish anything is everlastingly to keep working with patient observation.

Thomas Edison

... At every stage promoters are thwarted by Parliament, by municipalities, by chaotic survivals from legislation passed before electric power was heard of, and by an equally chaotic overlapping of different jurisdictions. Add to all this the competition in our open market of firms enjoying a protected market at home, and ably assisted by Governments which call them into council instead of treating them as public foes, firms that have profited by our folly and obtained the commanding position of which ours have been robbed. Then the wonder will be, not that the British electrical industry is more backward than it ought to be, but that it is so forward as it is. When there is trouble of this kind all parties are vexed and irritated. Instead of looking to the common cause of their ills, they are often found hitting at one another merely because it is through one another that the ill effects reach them. The worried manufacturers blame the capitalists for not finding money, the men of science declaim against the manufacturers for not doing pioneer work, when they can hardly maintain the road to their own shops, and the educationists scold everybody for not building more technical schools. On the other hand, capitalists are blamed for overcapitalising because dividends are small, and the men of science are told that they do not know anything except theory, and are of no real use in the workshops. The truth is that all are placed in very unfavourable conditions.

Leading article in *The Times*, 20 October 1906

A roulette wheel is a deterministic system in which the ultimate resting place of a ball depends precisely on the physical parameters of its initial trajectory and those of the motion of the wheel. However, the financial returns are influenced by many other factors, such as the personality of the gambler, the management policy of the casino and the regulatory regime under which it operates, together with the success of a liaison with Lady Luck.

Likewise, the economic rent of engineering innovation is governed, *inter alia*, by the laws of physics, chemical properties of materials, the timing of inventions and the stimulus and countervailing action provided by intellectual property monopolies, competition law and direct regulation, as well as the idiosyncratic contribution of the inventor's personality, all leavened by the unpredictable advent of serendipity.

This work, which is based on my personal experience of inventing during research and development with the early silicon chips and of over forty years as a patent attorney protecting other people's inventions, employs the methodology of Schmookler and Jewkes to investigate the path of innovation in the electrical, electronic and communications engineering industries. Relational databases, derived mainly from Patent Office records, were used to construct chronologies which formed the basis for case studies that cover a period of two hundred years. The subjects included the incandescent lamp, the telegraph, wireless and the thermionic valve, the transistor and the relatively recent inventions of microprocessor and memory chips, personal computers and software. Examples were selected from these case studies to highlight microeconomic and macroeconomic factors of different determinants.

The stimuli and constraints which controlled the dynamics of the earlier innovations were identified and used to construct a black box model of innovation. This was then applied to an empirical consideration of an emerging technology (the erbium-doped fibre-optic amplifier), which underpins the embryonic information-based economy, to test the hypotheses that the determinants are both hierarchical and time-dependent in their influence and that it is possible to predict the likely success of an invention.

I started out with a series of answers and finished up with a series of questions. Along the way, I gathered many rosebuds and a few aphorisms. I savoured the ingenuity of the nineteenth century engineers and twentieth century physicists and was teased by a problem which exercised the ancient Greeks and Norse as well as modern theoreticians. I learned that what is new is sometimes old and that rogues may become deified through the agency of the cleansing fires of the passage of time. As with Molière's Monsieur Jourdain, it became apparent to me in many ways *'il y a plus de quarante ans que je dis de la prose sans que j' en susse rien.'*

I should like to express my thanks to Professor Gerald Dworkin who encouraged me to undertake this investigation, to Dr Noel Byrne and Professor Alison Firth, for their helpful comments and suggestions, to Elizabeth Woodruff, Eifion Jones, Elaine Watson and Steve Wall, librarians of BTG plc, for their skill in tracking down obscure documents and those long out of print, to the Institution of Electrical Engineers, whose archive of nineteenth century books and journals proved invaluable, to my colleague, John Gaskin, who lent me rare books from his personal collection, to British Rail and South West Trains, which provided me with a warm and comfortable travelling office, to Professor Michael Bailey, without whose surgical skills in removing a cancer I may not have had time to finish this work, to my daughter Gemma, who waded through the manuscript and, especially, to my wife Barly, whose extreme patience made it all possible and, particularly, for nursing me to recovery from brain injury suffered in a fall.

I dedicate this book to the patent attorney's profession which has, for over forty years, permitted me to be an invited guest for the 'one per cent inspiration' without requiring me to serve as a journeyman for the 'ninety-nine per cent perspiration'.

Roger Cullis, Fernhurst, March 2007

1. Prologue

Give me a child until he is seven and I will show you the man.
St. Ignatius Loyola

Tell me what you eat and I will tell you who you are.
Anthelme Brillat-Savarin

If the world gives you lemons, make lemonade.
Anon.

The only way of finding the limits of the possible is by going beyond them into the impossible.
Arthur C. Clarke, *Profiles of the Future* (1962)

When you are fat, balding and forty and have a lot of patents already, you don't have to try.
C. Steven Hannigan, Vice-President of Compaq,
Fortune, 15 February 1985

1.1 THE AUTHOR'S PERSPECTIVE

In his youth, the author's hobbies included photography and electronics. He participated in the growth of the semiconductor industry during its early development and acquired sixteen patents for his inventions relating to the early silicon chips. When the global economy in technology was in its embryonic stages, he worked for one of the pioneering multi-national conglomerates and helped to devise strategies to obtain competitive advantage. As a patent attorney, he has frequently encountered mould-breaking inventors, sophisticated inventions and the countervailing influences of intellectual property and competition laws. Analysis of his education, motivation and experience led to the following observations.

Innovation is strongly constrained by the physical and chemical properties of materials and much invention is aimed at overcoming these constraints. Whilst not acting as an absolute barrier, intractable materials frequently inhibit desired developments. An innovative mind can overcome or circumvent limitations (GB Pat 1028485). On the other occasions, the apparently adverse properties of materials may be turned to advantage (GB Pat 1023532).

Inventions are primarily subject to the laws of nature. Just as it is not possible to make a perpetual motion machine, so it is not feasible to realise certain desirable ideas. To give a detailed engineering example, it would be attractive to manufacture bipolar transistors which are capable of operating at high voltages with high current gain. To meet the latter requirement, the base region must be narrow so that the transit time of the minority charge carriers, and hence the probability of their recombination with majority charge carriers whilst they are traversing the base region, is low. To achieve high voltage operation, however, the starting semiconductor crystal must be of high resistivity. The direct consequence of using this raw material is that, when a high voltage is applied, there will be a wide depletion layer at the collector junction. Under these conditions, there is a risk that the depletion layer will extend completely across a narrow base region, giving rise to device failure by a mechanism known as 'punch-through'. Hence, high voltage and high current gain are mutually exclusive. However, difficulties of this type may often be circumvented by the application of creative thinking (GB Pat 1035727).

Most inventions are solutions to a problem, resulting from the application of the inventor's acquired knowledge (possibly from unrelated fields), for which a catholic education and an enquiring mind are productive attributes. Indeed, much invention arises purely from the recognition of the nature of problems to be solved.

Inventive activity therefore depends on the influx of problems. It exhibits a peak at the time of highest rate of incidence and falls off when there are alternative calls on the inventor's mind. The closer the inventor is to the problem, the more likely he is to devise fundamental solutions. Peripheral involvement implies that he will make improvements to others' ideas (GB Pat 1391270). Lateral or unconventional thinking and the ability to apply ideas from other fields (GB Pat 1035727) are significant facilitators.

Some people invent; others, with an apparently similar background, do not. The propensity to invent depends on the breadth of the inventor's knowledge base and is enhanced by efficiency of two-way communication with others. Motivation is another essential feature. The culture of some organisations tends to favour invention by placing a high value on patents and the dissemination of technical information, and also by encouraging employees to make themselves aware of what others are doing.

Some inventions are ephemeral, either a temporary fix for an urgent problem which is blocking progress (GB Pat 1023532) or a technical advance which is useful but is superseded by later developments (GB Pat 1027550). They have only a limited window of opportunity in which they can be exploited. The use of epitaxial deposition techniques to make field-effect transistors with sub-micron channel lengths (GB Pat 1084937) was superseded by improvements in photolithography, the process by which the transistors were fabricated.

The adage 'Time is money' is never more true than when it is applied to inventions. Many good ideas are not developed because of limited resources and the need to concentrate on those ideas with the quickest payback. These inventions may be exploited independently by those who are not subject to the same constraints (GB Pat 1010404).

Enabling events trigger consequential innovations. The development of a method of deposition of a graded composite metallic film of gold and chromium gave rise to a family of flip-chip devices.

The quality of an invention is unpredictable. Some are good; some mere paper ideas. It is not necessarily apparent at the time of creation which ones are dodos and which are simply ugly ducklings. Even those which are swans *ab initio* may not be recognised as such – the launch of a pioneering, plastic-encapsulated transistor was vetoed by a senior engineer who stated that nobody would purchase a transistor unless it was hermetically sealed in a metal enclosure.

In an industry which is growing at 30 per cent per annum, there is a strong incentive to innovate as the potential rewards can be out of all proportion to the effort involved. The incentive is magnified by the globalisation of the industry. Volatile market dynamics increase the propensity to patent, not only to protect market share, but also to put up the entry price to competitors.

There may be a second-order effect due to the latent influence of economic determinants on the activities of entrepreneurs. Because of his experience of the thermionic valve cartel of the 1930s, C.O. Stanley, Chairman of Pye Ltd., set up Newmarket Transistors and Cathodeon Electronics in a challenge to established oligopolies (Geddes 1991, p317).

Competition law can change the balance of an entire industry. Because it was precluded from making electronic components for re-sale, the Bell System decided to license potential transistor manufacturers. The balance of advantage between US national manufacture and foreign manufacture was further biased by a Consent Decree ([1965] RPC 335 at 344).

Domestic manufacturers may also be favoured by covert subsidies given through government contracts for development and supply.

At the inventor level, the propensity to invent does not appear to be inhibited by financial considerations.

Consideration of these disparate tenets engendered a curiosity about the dynamics of innovation and led to the study which is set out in the following pages.

2. Setting the Scene

.... of all the potential ways of improving the performance of modern economies, technological change is probably the most important. Without invention and innovation it is highly likely that improvement in living standards would occur at a much reduced rate.

J.E.S. Parker, *The Economics of Innovation*, (London 1978) p3

Barring indivisibility or lumpiness, the physical marginal productivity of every factor must, in the absence of innovation, monotonically decrease. Innovation breaks off any such 'curve' and replaces it by another which, again except for indivisibility, displays higher increments of product throughout, although, of course, it also decreases monotonically.

Joseph Schumpeter, *Business Cycles*, p88

It is innovation, the exploitation of new technologies as marketable products or solutions, which brings the real benefits. Innovation is the end product of a complex process of development and testing of which invention is only the initial component. The globalisation of markets, shorter product life cycles, decline in demands for the products of traditional industries and competition from east Asia have led industry to recognise the opportunities which innovation can bring.

Peter Watson, CEO of AEA Technology, *Financial Times*, 22 March 1996

2.1 INTRODUCTION

Ignoring artificial semantic distinctions, this study is concerned with all types of innovation capable of generating an economic rent. Taking the electrical, electronic and communications engineering industries as a model, it examines factors which contributed to the success of innovations. Starting from an historical perspective, this chapter commences with a consideration of the nature of innovation and the mechanics of changing technological paradigms. It seeks to identify which determinants are potentially significant. It then poses hypotheses concerning their relationship and their impact on the success of developing innovations, both on a microeconomic and on a macroeconomic time scale. The methodology and assumptions made by previous researchers are considered in order to provide criteria for the selection of a vehicle by means of which the present investigation may be performed. The nature of information which may be derived from the analysis is discussed. Subjects for investigation are then selected and the reasons for the choice are set out.

2.2 THE NATURE OF INNOVATION AND THE MECHANICS OF CHANGE

Many writers (Wyatt 1986, p19) have drawn distinctions between scientific discovery, invention and innovation on the basis of artificial benchmarks, such as definitions set out in patent legislation or criteria applied by the courts. However, scientific discoveries may be applied commercially and technical advances may fail to satisfy statutory tests for quantum of inventive step, with the result that there are no distinct boundaries and one category flows into another to form a continuum. No practical advantage, therefore, is to be gained by creating semantic barriers, so this investigation will span all technological developments which are capable of being exploited for economic gain. Such an approach entails making value judgements on scientific and technical matters, a factor that has been notably absent from previous examinations which have, in the main, been based on legal or economic criteria.

   Can we predict the trend of invention and, if so, under what circumstances? Is there a set of conditions that will enhance the process of innovation? How do we make the best of what we have got? Are there some conditions that will yield better financial returns from investment in inventions? Is the *phasing* of the factors that influence innovation relevant, critical or unimportant? Could we, indeed, develop a technique for making successful inventions or predicting those which will be 'winners'?

These and similar questions arise from a consideration of the reasons for innovation. Answers to them would lay the foundation for organisations to use innovation as a strategic tool in the battle for supremacy in the world of commerce and for governments to devise legislation which acts as a catalyst rather than as a constraint. Economic and technical advancement does not proceed smoothly. Rather it takes the form of a series of iterations – invention and supersession, innovation and obsolescence, introduction and abandonment. History has shown that exogenous invention – the unpredictable breakthrough which presages a major advance – is sporadic and therefore will not necessarily be the product of economic influences whereas endogenous invention, which results from attempts to improve efficiency to maximise profits (Wyatt 1986, p30), will be more predictable and amenable to control.

Schumpeter stated that the path of economic development is one of evolution, with innovation providing discontinuities in the physical marginal factor productivity (Schumpeter 1939, p87). Koestler argued that the new ideas which formed the springboard for innovation, arose from the intersection of logically separate matrices (Koestler 1964), whilst Shockley (1957, p286) suggested that invention was the result of the concatenation of distinct modes of thought. These theories lead to a socio-deterministic view and favour a proposition that invention is an inevitable consequence of the felicitous conjunction of technological and economic events. The corollary is that, although an invention may emerge at any time, the propensity for it to succeed will exhibit maxima determined by the current ambient environment. This would imply that an invention could emerge on a number of occasions before the juxtaposition of physical and financial parameters is favourable (Mokyr 1990, p291). If a chronology reveals that an invention does appear a number of times, it should be possible to identify *which* factors are important.

This study adopts Kuhn's concept of the scientific paradigm (the very general conception of the nature of the endeavour within which a development occurs) (Kuhn 1970) and expands the evolutionary theme, first proposed by Marx in *Das Kapital* (Mokyr 1990, p273) and subsequently developed by Nelson and Winter, (Nelson 1982) Saviotti (Saviotti 1991) and others, in order to analyse technological paradigms as phylogenetic tree structures. Put another way, the significance of individual scientific frameworks, within which inventions are made, may be expected to wax and wane as changes take place in the macroenvironment. If this is so, there will be periods of steady progression interposed with discontinuities (Mokyr 1990, p291). As with living organisms, innovations will emerge, flourish and become extinct. For example, improvements in lighting technology which led to the bats' wing and fishtail gas burners arose when the luminous flame was the principal source of artificial light; further development along this line was curtailed by the invention of the gas mantle and eliminated completely when the electric lamp became the main source of night-time illumination.

2.3 THE INFLUENCE OF THE DETERMINANTS

Hitherto, most authors have approached the subject of innovation from a unilateral viewpoint, typically with an economic perspective. Wyatt (1986, p4), for example, states

> There are, of course, many factors that determine how much inventive activity is carried out and in what directions, but the basic supposition is that among these, importantly, are economic factors. This means that, for the most part, the scientific, technological, sociological, political, psychological and cultural determinants of inventive activity are subsumed in an implicit *ceteris paribus* clause. The present analysis, in other words, takes them as given.

However, such an assumption should be questioned. Since it would appear likely that *many* of the factors listed by Wyatt will exert a significant influence on the success of the process, an investigation of the dynamics of innovation needs to be multidisciplinary. Although a purely economic analysis may be more *tractable*, it clearly is not reasonable to sweep all of the other elements under the carpet with just a nod in the *ceteris paribus* direction. Amongst the determinants which may be important are the nature and process of invention, the logistics of, and agencies for, change, interaction with the economy, the influence of official policy and the role of the inventor. An initial empirical investigation of the part played by these elements will permit the identification of response patterns, the establishment of benchmarks for comparison and ultimately provide a basis for the extraction of strategies for optimisation of a technological paradigm.

As Schumpeter states, the motivation for change will, in general, be some form of economic influence. This may be a primary innovation – which creates intrinsic growth of a mainstream nature and generates its own returns – or a secondary innovation, which is not only ancillary to a primary innovation but is also dependent on its progress (Mokyr 1990, p293). Need may be real – either extant or latent – or apparent, giving rise to the phenomena of market pull and production push, but in the end, there must be a dominant factor which creates, at least, a *perceived* prospect of innovation rent.

The course of innovation is subject to various modifiers or influencers. Some may have a positive and some a negative effect. Typically, marketing will attempt to stimulate demand, whilst the need to raise finance and create an infrastructure could be an inhibiting factor. The action of some influencers will be progressive, whilst that of others will approach an asymptote. For instance, Moore's Law states that miniaturisation doubles the complexity of an integrated circuit every eighteen months. (Moore 1965, 1975, 1995). Increased finance provision, on the other hand, cannot overcome the physical barriers introduced by nature and their bearing on the time delays in developing new processes, although it may ameliorate an adverse situation. It will, however, be subject to diminishing returns.

Technological development is frequently the engine which drives innovation (Nishi 1995). A new material or process may act as a stimulus, but do the laws of physics and properties of materials act universally in support of innovations? It is to be expected that, whilst they may open up fresh avenues or create a prejudice in favour of a particular paradigm, they will equally make advance in some directions difficult, or simply impossible. Case studies can demonstrate whether or not this is so.

An economic motivation for innovation would imply that an opportunity-cost threshold must be surmounted before a transition between technological frameworks will take place. At many points during the evolution, alternative courses of action will present themselves. Those options which offer the greatest *perceived* net return are likely to be taken. In consequence, technological development will follow a path in which a binary decision process is controlled by current values of the anticipated innovation rent (Mokyr 1990, p276, Schumpeter 1934, p6). It is this constraint, the economic equivalent of the survival of the fittest, which will give rise to the dynamic similarity between innovation and biological evolution mentioned above.

One major unknown factor in the progress of innovation will be the role of the inventor, since people are, by nature, unpredictable. Rossman, a US Patent Office examiner, found that some environments will be more conducive to invention than others (Rossman 1931). If these can be identified, it will enable a business to set up the right conditions for propitious management of its inventors.

When disparate skills are required, inventors will have to be polytechnic to succeed unless complementary resources are made available. Inventors are faced, in their task, with unique problems which cannot necessarily be solved by conventional methods. It will therefore be an advantage if they are lateral thinkers.

Since mental faculties change over a lifetime, it is unlikely that the propensity to invent will be age-invariant. Older men may be liable to be distracted by other pursuits, or simply become less active, whilst youth may be more single-minded. Could, therefore, inventors be expected to be more prolific when they are young? A study of the inventions profile over the lifetimes of prolific inventors will confirm or disprove this contention. Inventors will also need to be motivated and persevering, and possess the vision and faith to persist when others tell them that their baby is not beautiful.

Second-order vectors, such as cartels or the statutory intellectual property monopolies, are determinants of market structure. Free market dynamics are also changed by war and military procurement, whilst physical regulation, competition law and international treaties will create constraints.

The magnitude of the influences, and possibly also the qualitative effect, of the components of change will vary with their temporal phasing (Kingston 1984). Thus factors, such as patent monopolies, which exert major control early in the innovation cycle may be relegated to a subsidiary role at a later stage, whereas the marketing power created by a trade mark will increase with continuing use. Temporal variations may also take place over a longer term with, for example, changes in the attitudes of society, cyclic variations in world trade or simply an improvement in communications.

2.4 INITIAL HYPOTHESIS

It is improbable that the influences of the factors of invention will be uniform. One may postulate that they fall into an hierarchical structure categorised by the nature and timing of the change they induce and by their interaction with the technical and economic environment. Thus the physical properties of a newly-discovered material might make feasible the manufacture of a new electrical device which overcomes a problem in telecommunications. If the anticipated commercial return appears attractive, manufacture will be commenced. Initially, patent protection might shield the embryonic industry which makes the device, whilst, in due course, competition law could be invoked to prevent the original manufacturer from exercising undue market power. The second of these statutory vehicles exerts a countervailing force against the former, but neither of these two factors will come into play if, firstly, the physical properties of the material are not apposite and, secondly, the financial incentive is insufficiently large – fire burns paper (but only if oxygen is present) and water quenches fire (but the fire brigade will only be called to deal with large fires).

2.5 RESEARCH METHODOLOGY AND ANTICIPATED UTILITY OF RESULTS

As a precursor to his study of invention, Schmookler attempted to formulate an objective definition. He identified the joint determinants of invention as wants, which the inventors satisfy, and the intellectual ingredients of which the inventions are made. Actual inventions were the intersection of the set of possible inventions and the set of desirable inventions. He and his co-workers investigated four different industries using a chronology of inventions, derived from patent office records, as a starting point (Schmookler 1966). They found that, in a chronology, it is unimportant whether an invention is ranked according to its economic or technological significance or whether items in the chronology are weighted or unweighted. This is because inventions which are economically significant will be sources of further invention and because no one invention is likely to stand on its own.

Chronologies (Cullis 2004) also provide the foundation for the present study. They are derived mainly from patent office records and from patent specifications, which establish an accurate date for each invention, since a requirement for patentability (except in the USA) is that the specification of the invention shall be filed at the patent office before the invention is disclosed elsewhere or put to commercial use.

Although patent offices provide prolific statistics about inventions, this information does not distinguish between ideas which make a significant contribution to scientific and economic progress and those which are mere paper proposals. In consequence, a study of invention based on patent office data needs to be supplemented by value judgements on the significance of the inventions. It is, furthermore, essential to approach the subject from more than one viewpoint, if only to be in a position to be able to compensate for the prejudices of different observers. Additional information may be drawn from papers published in journals of learned societies, contemporary reports in books and newspapers, from biographies and, most importantly, from autobiographical writings of inventors. (Of course, in the last case it is necessary to apply a critical eye to discount the effects of a skewed viewpoint.)

Analysis of the influence of various parameters on the progress of a range of innovations over an extended time interval will permit conclusions to be drawn, not only about their relative importance, but also the temporal variation. Furthermore, if innovations selected for case studies are separated by several decades, an opportunity to examine the effects of a changing macroeconomic environment is presented. It therefore becomes feasible to highlight those factors which have an altered significance at different points in history. For example, in the nineteenth century the individual inventor was the norm, whereas, at the present day, joint inventorship is common and we have the concept of corporate invention, which will have the effect of expanding Schmookler's cohort of possible inventions.

The technologies selected for study and comparison were artificial lighting and, in particular, the incandescent lamp, the thermionic valve, telecommunications, the transistor and a group of modern developments – the microprocessor and the memory chip, software and the personal computer. These innovations possess a common characteristic in that, potentially, they were capable of spawning an almost entirely independent expansion of the economy.

The methodology to be followed in each case was first to construct a series of relational databases, primarily from Patent Office records and journals of learned societies. A chronology was, next, prepared from these databases. On the basis of (mainly) contemporary commentaries, this was then fleshed out into narrative descriptions describing the evolution of key technological paradigms. Each case study was analysed to identify the factors which contributed to the success of the various innovations. In the following chapters, examples are selected from the case studies to highlight the contributions of the individual input factors. Often, an individual example drawn from a case study will illustrate the influence of more than one determinant or different aspects of the influence of a particular determinant. The results of this analysis are used to construct a black box model of the process of innovation. This model is then deconstructed and presented as a questionnaire which may be used to derive the set of empirical relationships which are significant in any specific case. Finally, the empirical rules are applied to an exemplary emerging technology, the fibre optic amplifier and laser, in order to appraise its future progress as a contributor to the transition from a manufacturing- to an information-based economy.

2.6 CONCLUSION

Historical experience shows the sporadic nature of paradigm-changing invention and its uneven evolution under the control of a multiplicity of determinants. This leads to the hypothesis that the influence of the factors of invention is both hierarchical and dependent on the timing of their incidence. In consequence, although a given invention may appear on one or more occasions, it will have a limited window of opportunity for successful development and will not achieve a critical mass if conditions are unfavourable.

Adoption of Kuhn's concept of the scientific paradigm will enable developing technologies to be viewed as phylogenetic trees, which highlights their transient nature. Due to the variable characteristics and incidence of the factors, the study must be multi-disciplinary, rather than follow the methodology of many previous authors who assumed that only one factor at a time need be considered.

Typical of the contributory determinants is the inventor's role, which has its own sub-set of influences. It may, for example, be postulated that *when* an inventor makes his invention is significant, since the corollary of the concept of a variable propensity to invent is that certain stages of life will be more fruitful than others.

Second-order vectors are cartels, statutory monopolies, war and government regulation. The temporal phasing of their influence will vary both on a microeconomic and a macroeconomic scale.

Case studies of major innovations, based on chronologies derived from patent office records, provide a framework for the identification of response patterns, the creation of comparison benchmarks and the extraction of paradigm optimisation strategies. This will permit, firstly, the main hypothesis concerning the importance of the hierarchical nature and significance of its temporal context for the success of invention to be tested and, secondly, a challenge to be made to the contention that it is reasonable to investigate the dynamics of innovation from a purely economic viewpoint. It will also lay a foundation for maximising the advantages of innovation in the business environment and for possible changes in public policy to increase the efficiency of industrial change.

3. Placing the Research in Context

…large industrial institutions have both an opportunity and a responsibility to provide for their own life insurance. New discovery can provide it.
Willis R. Whitney, First Research Director of General Electric

Indeed, they are lucky to live in such a problem-rich environment.
John Poate, Head of Silicon Processing, Bell Laboratories, *Physics World*

To describe the difference between basic and applied research, it has been suggested that the former is after discoveries, the latter after inventions. There is much to be said for this suggestion; as I see it, the concepts of 'inventive activity' and 'applied research' overlap to a large extent.
Fritz Machlup, *The Supply of Inventors and Inventions*, p148

Technological possibilities are an uncharted sea. We may survey a geographical region and appraise, though only with reference to a given technique of agricultural production, the relative fertility of individual plots. Given that technique and disregarding its possible future developments, we may then imagine (though this would be wrong historically) that the best plots are first taken into cultivation, after them the next best ones and so on. At any given time during this process it is only relatively inferior plots that remain to be exploited in the future. But we cannot reason in this fashion about the future possibilities of technological advance. From the fact that some of them have been exploited before others, it cannot be inferred that the former were more productive than the latter. And those that are still in the lap of the gods may be more or less productive than any that have thus far come within our range of observation.
Joseph Schumpeter, *Capitalism, Socialism and Democracy*, 1950

3.1 INTRODUCTION

The previous chapter has introduced the hypotheses that the factors which contribute to the success of an innovation will have an hierarchical structure and that the nature and magnitude of their influence will vary with time. It identified determinants likely to be significant and proposed a methodology for investigating their relationship. Amongst the matters considered likely to be important were the stimuli which give rise to inventions, the actual mechanism by which they are conceived, the logistics of development, the incidence of serendipity, personnel, including inventors and those who work with them, business and communications, market structures, intellectual property rights, government regulation and last, but not least, finance. This chapter reviews the literature to identify significant factors, with a view to assembling these elements into a framework for their contextual examination in case studies.

3.2 THE EMERGENCE OF INVENTIONS AND DISCOVERIES

> Our minds are cast after a common pattern, in substantially the same mould. While in particular cases, we must necessarily admit the existence of finer texture, of better hereditary peculiarities, of higher development, and of grander possibilities, yet, after all, thoughts conceived by one mind are apt to be common to many, if not the majority of minds.
>
> At certain times in the world's progress the environment may cause so rapid a development of the germs of great ideas, the incentive to unusual effort may be so great, the necessity for a new combination of ideas so urgent, and the encouragement of an age ripe for the birth of such ideas, so marked, that substantially the same ideas may be conceived simultaneously in different parts of the world.
>
> At other times the peculiarities of the environment may be so unfavorable, the incentive to unusual effort so small, the necessity for new ideas so apparently limited, and the encouragement so feeble, that although the idea may be born, yet it may fail to meet with recognition by the world, and so be passed by and forgotten, only, in some later, riper time to be again independently conceived, and offered to the world.
>
> E.J. Houston, *Electricity – One Hundred Years Ago and Today*, p8

It was with these words that Houston, writing during a period of frenetic industrial growth towards the end of the nineteenth century, epitomised the process of invention. Surveying the hundred years or so which had elapsed since the development of the voltaic pile, the first practical application of electricity, he classified inventions in three groups: (a) immature or incomplete, (b) untimely and therefore unfruitful and (c) fruitful because

mature and timely.   Such an analysis is too broad-brush to permit the
extraction of useful information.   Half a century later, Jewkes *et al*, in a
study of over fifty major inventions, recognised that it was necessary to
adopt a less simplistic approach and take into account historic, scientific,
technological, economic and legal viewpoints (Jewkes 1969, p24).   To this,
other authors have added personal psychology (Rossman 1931), social
needs (Schmookler 1966, p194), communications (Kingston 1977, p147),
finance and marketing (Kingston 1984, p37).

What will be the expected pattern for the emergence of inventions in a
new paradigm?   According to Jewkes the timing and reasons for the
emergence of new ideas elude prediction.   He summarised the process in the
following terms.

> Inventors have often started from different points and reached much the same
> results or, starting with a common problem, adopted widely varying means of
> solving it.   Emerging ideas have proved intractable, been dropped and, when
> apparently forgotten, been subsequently picked up and used to effect.   Inventions
> in one field have lain dormant until some ingenious inventor has seized the old
> idea, combined it with a notion gleaned from another apparently unrelated field
> and produced a new and fruitful combination.   Inventions have been born before
> their time; either the public refused to accept them or a practical model could not
> be built because the rest of the technical art was backward.   Identical or nearly
> identical ideas have emerged independently many years apart.   Inventions not
> infrequently have been simultaneous or so near together in time that the
> determination of priorities has stretched the power of judgment even of the
> Courts with all the facts at their disposal.   Useful products and processes have
> arisen from reasoning which subsequently proved to be fallacious.   The simple
> route to the solution of a problem has sometimes seemed to be almost perversely
> overlooked by the cleverest inventors and the most tortuous path followed to a
> point to which there has all the time been an easy and direct line.   Inventors,
> groping for solutions along complicated and expensive roads, have missed the
> target completely, while an individual entering the field with a fresh approach,
> crude equipment and a generous smattering of common sense has achieved
> success along a path which, in retrospect, looks perfectly simple.   Chance and
> accident seem often to have played an important part in discovery, but so, too,
> has brilliant and disciplined thinking and a persistence amounting almost to
> obsession.
>   J. Jewkes (1969, p71)

Schumpeter recognised that innovation is an extended process which is
characterised by a brief, discontinuous genesis (the A-phase) followed by a
longer development period (the B-phase), in which consolidation takes
place.   After the initial discovery, many others may follow, and often appear
as a linked chain of events.   Kingston explained that the reason inventions
emerge in this way is that acceptance of the initial idea reduces the

perceived risk of innovation in that area, with the result that others will be attracted to work on it – increase in the number of inventions is a direct consequence of the increase in activity (Kingston 1977, pp21-27)· There will also be a similar effect in peripheral technologies as participants see opportunities of rewards from associated or niche markets. Much technical progress is the result of collective effort.

Schmookler (1966, p87) looked further ahead and considered the characteristic ultimate decline in the number of inventions in a field. His view was that this reflected the exhaustion of the field's technical possibilities. This idea, which owes its origin to Julius Wolf (Wolf 1912, p336), was developed by Kuznets, who suggested that the rate of technical progress in an industry will fall with the passage of time:

> The stimulus for technical changes in other processes of the industry is thus present from the moment the first major invention is introduced. ... While the stimulus for further inventions appears early, the number of operations to be improved is limited and gradually becomes exhausted. In a purely manufacturing industry technical progress consists mainly in replacing manual labor by machines. When all the important operations are performed by machines which have reached a stage of comparative perfection, not much room is left for further innovations. If in addition to that, the chemical processes are perfected to a point allowed by modern machinery, no great new improvements may be expected. As inventions take over one process after another, a very limited field is left to the later periods of an industry's history, and the rate of progress in terms of separate inventions declines. ... Improvements, which come with an ever-extending practical use, are minor in character, and the field for them is limited, since there comes a time when the machine or the process is practically perfect. The same rule of exhaustion operates here as within the larger field of the industry itself. Improvements tend to come at a faster rate during the early periods of use, immediately after the faults are indicated by the practical operations of the innovation. They tend to diminish because there is less to improve.
> (Kuznets 1930, p31).

Salter, (1960, p133) reverted to the theme some thirty years later, explaining differential rates of growth of disparate industries on the basis that, after an industry is born around a new scientific principle, there is a great potential for improvements around that principle. New technology arises and, for a period at least, spawns a continuous flow of significant improvements and modifications. At any given time, some industries are in this stage of rapid improvement, whilst others, more mature, find significant advances less frequent and less rewarding.

Schmookler postulated that inventors approach the natural physical limits of processes (Schmookler 1966, p90). He deduced that this would give rise to an asymptotic reduction in the rate of invention. Such a proposition is, however, a very broad generalisation and should be challenged. For instance, the automobile industry has not ceased to innovate, although the manufacturing techniques it employs have their origins in the nineteenth century. The silicon chip industry is another example of an industry which uses mature technology.   (The basic manufacturing processes were introduced at the end of the 1950s and have remained essentially unchanged ever since.) This industry is ripe for study, as the time within which it will reach the limits of miniaturisation is already within view (Wong 2005). It will provide an excellent example of how an expanding industry reacts when it reaches a point of inflection towards the end of one of the periods of stasis highlighted by Mokyr (1990, p291).

Another influence which moderates the rate of progress of an innovation was observed by Kingston. He commented that new technology frequently contains an element which may be used to improve the old and hence delay introduction of the new (Kingston 1977, p67). This is a sub-set of the well-known 'sailing ship effect' where many of the major improvements in sail technology were introduced after the advent of steam power.

Clearly there are many factors which influence the emergence of inventions and it might be questioned whether or not they fall into a general pattern. Case studies might provide an answer, but, logically, can only confirm the negative. If the positive proposition is true, they will only yield evidence in support.

3.3   THE SOURCE AND NATURE OF THE INVENTIVE PROCESS

Great discoveries belong not so much to individuals as to humanity; they are less inspirations of genius than births of eras. As there has been a definite intellectual progress, thought has necessarily been limited to the subjects successively reached. Many minds have been thus occupied at the same time with similar ideas, and hence the simultaneous discoveries of independent inquirers, of which the history of science is so full.

E.J. Youmans, *The Correlation and Conservation of Forces*, p xv

This spark of intellectual incandescence, in the form of a rare creative genius, shot like a meteor into the midst of human society in the latter decades of the last century; and he lived almost until today. His name became synonymous with magic in the intellectual, scientific, engineering and social worlds, and he was recognized as an inventor and discoverer of unrivaled greatness.

J.J. O'Neill, *Prodigal Genius – the Life of Nikola Tesla*, p4

How do inventions arise?   The quotations above reflect opposing explanations of the genesis of invention.   The first represents the sociological deterministic view, which arose as a reaction to an attempt to explain invention and discovery primarily in terms of the men who made them. The latter tendency is identified by Schmookler as merely a particular expression of the 'great man' theory of history which was an explanation for invention popular in the early part of the twentieth century. The alternative sociological-deterministic theory, by contrast, attributes little value to the contribution of individuals – discoveries and inventions become virtually inevitable as requisite knowledge accumulates and as the attention of a sufficient number of investigators is focused on a problem by emerging social needs or by developments within the particular science. Investigation of the cause and effect of inventions arising during the evolution of a new technological paradigm will provide evidence in favour of one theory or the other. The emergence of identical inventions simultaneously or the relative success of the same invention in different macro-environments would serve as a simple litmus test.

3.4 THE STIMULUS FOR INVENTION

Industrial research is profit-motivated and will therefore be strongly oriented towards demand. Population growth, accumulation of capital, urbanisation, war, laws and use of new technology create environmental changes and consequent aspirations which result in new 'desired inventions'. According to Schumpeter, (1950) innovators gain market advantage by innovation and the resulting temporary monopoly permits them to recover economic rents. However, whilst the process of invention is cheap, the consequent development necessary to bring a product or process into manufacture is costly and affects the commercial returns, and hence the effort entrepreneurial inventors are likely to put into the improvement of their inventions. This, in turn, will alter the direction of inventive evolution. Secondary inventions are generated by socio-economic needs rather than as a consequence of earlier inventions – after the stimulus of the original invention, the most important innovations are likely to arise from the exposure of the mind to technical and economic factors.

Will the *timing* of the response to a stimulus be important? It is conceivable that many inventions made possible by the great growth of science in modern times are not made because those who are familiar with the problems or opportunities may not know the science, and those who know the science may not be aware of the problems or opportunities. By the time either group learns what it lacks, the problems or opportunities may have vanished. An invention may therefore have only a limited window when the socio-economic conditions are favourable. Although the gas mantle was an immense improvement on the previous methods of lighting based on a luminous flame, it required a distributed gas supply which, for technological and safety reasons, was not as acceptable as the distributed electricity supply which was the alternative.

3.5 THE LOGISTICS OF INVENTION

3.5.1 Effect of Random Events

> After a period of preparation, in which the creator has explored the difficulties in his path, the analogies to be explained, and the real or apparent connections that he must elucidate, directive ideas are slowly firmed and organized more or less consciously in his mind. Then, quite suddenly and generally with a jolt there occurs some kind of crystallization, and the research worker perceives instantly and very clearly, and from then on perfectly consciously the main outlines of the new concepts that were latent in him, and at a stroke he arrives at the absolute certainty that the implementation of these new concepts will allow him to solve most of the problems posed, and to elucidate the entire question by revealing clearly those similarities and harmonics that were previously unknown.
> Poincaré, *Science and Method*

The conception of new ideas is a sporadic process (Taton 1957). One reason for this is that *Geistesblitz* (the 'flash of inspiration') occurs in a random manner. Another is that, although invention frequently follows a sequence, steady progress is, at times, inhibited by the need for some enabling process or other event, such as the discovery of a suitable material for construction (Jewkes 1969, p100).

3.5.2 Analogy with Biological Evolution

The discontinuous nature of innovation has led many authors to draw an analogy with biological evolution, which is also characterised by sharp transitions separated by periods of continuous adaptation to the ambient environment. Mokyr summarised the similarity in the following terms.

> Like mutations, new ideas represent deviations from the displayed characteristics, and are subjected to a variety of tests of their performance against the environment. Like mutations, most are stillborn or do not survive infancy. Of the few that do, a number of ideas are actually reproduced, that is, are transferred to other specimens. Natural selection may well operate through changes in gene frequencies without mutation, simply by more adaptive species dominating the processes of Mendelian inheritance. Yet the stationary state in which a single superior species dominates the environment may not ever be observed. By the time the new species has replaced the old one, new mutations may have occurred

creating an even more successful form. ...Technological change follows a similar dynamic. At any given time, we observe a best-practice (most up to date) technique, as well as an average-practice technique reflecting older practices still extant. For a one-shot innovation, the competitive process will, under certain circumstances, eventually eliminate the obsolete technologies, and produce uniformity in production methods. But if novel techniques are continuously 'born,' no single best-practice technique will ever dominate the industry
(Mokyr 1990, p277)

Nelson and Winter, in a seminal exposition of the theory of the firm, based on an evolutionary model, stated that possible developments are determined by the starting point (Nelson 1982, p142). When a traveller needs to go from New York to Paris, it is of no significance that the journey would be easier if the embarkation point were London. In such a journey, some routes will be preferred to others.

Mayr drew attention to resistance to change as a characteristic of path dependency. Innovation is constrained by its environment because the greater the departure from the norm, the greater will be the costs (Mayr 1988, p424). However, if the apparent advantages of a new technology are sufficiently attractive, it will be adopted (Basalla 1988, p190). The criteria for success are that the new idea must be technically and economically feasible and it must be conceived in a socially sympathetic environment (Mokyr 1990, p291).

At any given point in time, the future path of innovation will depend on economic choices. The portents will, furthermore, change as time passes – decisions made in the past will constrain the extent of future options (Arthur 1989). An abandoned route will not be retraced, even though subsequent technological developments might have made previously rejected options feasible, or even attractive. The binary-decision nature of the selection process gives rise to innovation patterns which resemble biological phylogenetic trees.

Another hypothesis that has been borrowed is that, just as geographical isolation allows more primitive forms to survive (i.e. survival of the fittest is not universal), less efficient producers can survive if they possess property rights which permit them to avoid competing head-on with other producers.

In biological evolution, Goldschmidt distinguished between micromutations, which accounted for changes within a species and were continuous and cumulative, and macromutations, which gave rise to new species (Goldschmidt 1940). The technological analogue is the concept of secondary innovation or microinvention, which extends the existing technology, and primary innovation or macroinvention, which is responsible for a major paradigm shift, either replacing an existing technology or making possible a completely new development. Gould has cast aspersions on the analogy (Gould 1987) but Goldschmidt's dichotomy provides a useful tool for modelling the innovation process.

Cavalli-Sforza and Feldman (Cavalli-Sforza 1981, p66) argued against the use of the analogy on the grounds that biological adaptation was of a passive nature and did not involve intentionality. With technological paradigms, ideas are frequently transferred from other, quite unrelated, disciplines, a process regarded as important by Sahal (1981, p71-74) and Basalla (1988, p137-138). Biological hybridisation, on the other hand, takes place naturally, only between closely related species. However, the recently developed, and controversial, techniques of genetic modification involving the isolation, alteration and implantation of gene sequences has negated this criticism since biological information may be thus transferred in either direction between unrelated species. Although this development means that what were points of distinction have now reinforced the similarity between the concepts, the argument remains that it is still an analogy and should therefore not be regarded as an absolute parallel.

3.5.3 The Role of Chance

> I don't know when I'm going to stop making improvements on the electric light. I've just got another one that I've found by accident. I was experimenting with one of my burners when I dropped a screwdriver on it. Instantly the light was almost doubled, and continued to burn with increased power. I examined the burner and found that it had been knocked out of shape. I restored it to its original form, and the light was decreased. Now I make all my burners in the form accidentally given to that one by the screwdriver.
> Thomas A. Edison (Clark 1977, p104)

Occasionally errors of observation, commission or interpretation lead to felicitous results. For example, the interpretation of differences between theory and experimental results may give rise to the development of new and better explanations of the observed phenomena. Limitations of measuring instruments often prevent investigators from achieving an expected result.

Taton (Taton 1957, p79) distinguished between psychological chance, the fortuitous juxtaposition of two ideas, and external chance, a serendipitous combination of events which leads research workers in a particularly fruitful direction. Statistical analysis of inventions will provide the best evidence of the role that chance plays in the overall picture.

3.5.4 The Personality and Motivation of the Inventor

Inventors are agents for change and their personalities may be expected to influence advances in innovations. Most inventions are made by practical men rather than men of science. Scientific discovery is more a permissive than an active factor in the inventive process. A test for this contention is to query whether the invention could have been made earlier.

Taton classified scientists as intuitive or logical, the latter preferring to follow a more rigorous and systematic path. He highlighted perspicacity in choice of subjects and a more or less direct intuition of the results to be obtained, the obstacle to be surmounted and the particular means to be employed, and perseverance and method in the presentation of the definite solution as contributing to deductive attitude. According to Hademard (Taton 1957, p47), some of the other factors distinguishing between the various types of minds are the degree of precision in approach, the degree of apparent mental order, auxiliary mental pictures supporting mental progress, and finally the extent to which the difficulty of making fruitful use of theories or algorithms is developed (Taton 1957, pp28-29). Paul Souriau, a psychologist, regarded vanity, manifest as 'attracting public attention' or with 'establishing a pleasant and independent position for himself' as a major source of creative activity (Souriau 1881).

Observation plays a major role in the intellectual process. Jewkes recognised that the exceptional and largely intuitive powers of individuals to identify unexpected variations have been the source of much individual discovery and invention (Jewkes 1969, p99). However, many claims to authorship of a discovery are based on *ex post facto* arguments and are not justified. Often a major discovery occurs as a result of painstaking preparation by others. In cases of simultaneous discovery, the principals are usually men of unquestionable merit. It is their disciples or national vanity that generate disputes. Many discoveries belong to an epoch as much as to individuals. Missed inventions or discoveries may, only with hindsight, be seen as such.

Some potential inventors lack the right theoretical background, or simply have a closed mind (Taton 1957, p145). An untutored or uncommitted mind, however, may often be an advantage to an inventor, since he will not be trammelled by the prejudices and traditions of those already working in the field. For the same reason it may also be fruitful to bring together men from disparate backgrounds and disciplines, as variety of experience often stimulates the fresh or unconventional approach which gives rise to invention (Jewkes 1969, pp96-97).

Innovators need to be persistent in order to overcome establishment prejudice and resistance to change. This is a particularly inhibiting factor for young inventors or scientists who may be browbeaten by their seniors (Taton 1957, pp147-148) or simply overawed.   Spencer, the nineteenth century sociologist and engineer, experienced many frustrations in his attempts to exploit inventions. Charles Kettering, Head of General Motors, epitomised this hostility with the statement 'Inventors must not bruise easy.' Successful innovation, therefore, often needs a product champion.

Some inventors have succeeded in industrial research laboratories, whilst others have taken an entrepreneurial route.   The financial rewards of corporate inventors may be substantially less than those of the successful individual, but there are other compensations, such as the security of working for an employer who provides a regular salary, the prestige which accompanies recognition, and the absence of a need to engage in ancillary activities in order to develop their ideas. In the modern high-tech society, the individual worker will rarely possess the resources necessary to make successful inventions. The threshold is high for individuals – as it is for firms.

Everyday life has changed significantly over the centuries. Although, within this time-scale the genetic make-up of *homo sapiens* will have remained constant, macroeconomic changes to the environment within which an inventor operates may have altered his potential contribution to the innovation process.

3.6 CORPORATE STRATEGY

Personal attitudes of peripheral players often play a major role in determining the progress of an invention. A corollary of this is the 'NIH' (Not-Invented-Here) syndrome. This is a special case of a more general phenomenon, in which a desire for personal security, manifest in a lack of willingness to take risks, inhibits the take-up of new ideas (Jewkes 1969, pp119-122). There is some justification for this attitude, as inventions which are offered by individuals to corporations are rarely of value. On the other hand, non-core inventions may be a fruitful resource, since they may be licensed to generate an incremental income.

There is a strong incentive for firms in a technically advancing industry to innovate (Mokyr 1990, p281). Large firms may buy up smaller firms in order to acquire ideas or men of promise, even in the research fields in which they themselves are active.

Certain types of invention favour the larger firm, but it is difficult to find a correlation between size of firm and its propensity to engage in research. All other things being equal, the greater the amount of research, the greater will be the chances of making inventions. Nevertheless, a barn-storming approach does not necessarily guarantee success.

It is difficult to exploit a monopoly position unless there is a tangible embodiment. Know-how on its own also presents problems because, once transferred, it cannot be taken back.

Cross-licensing is of great value since there is prospect of returns from serendipitous developments which bring fresh products into a firm. The ultimate expression of cross-licensing is the patents pool.

The culture of cross-licensing varies from industry to industry. Is this merely an historic accident, or is it somehow related to the technology? When cross-licensing does take place, are there benefits beyond straightforward cash transfer? Again, answers may be revealed by case studies.

3.7 COMMUNICATIONS AND THE INTRODUCTION OF CHANGE

Houston (1894, p89) identified the difficulty of communication and gaining acceptance of new ideas as part of the general attitude of the public of resistance to change. Individuals play a key part in the dissemination of knowledge, taking the role of prophet and teacher. Innovations are spread by imitation. Companies that are good at learning from others are successful in the Schumpeter B-phase of development (Kingston 1977, p60).

Von Hippel discussed the phenomenon of informal know-how trading, the converse of maintenance of trade secrecy, as a mechanism for diffusion (von Hippel 1988, p76). He treated it as a case of the Prisoner's Dilemma problem and concluded that this paradoxical concept was not irrational because, in most cases, proprietary know-how is not vital to a firm and it can be developed independently, given competence, time and money. He surmised that the arrangement succeeds because a favour granted – know-how disclosed – creates an implied obligation to reciprocate. One could take this analysis further and speculate that time gained by the interchange of knowledge will more than compensate for the increased competition. Indeed, the presence of other participants may expand the market and take it earlier to the critical mass necessary for success.

3.8 THE INFLUENCE OF INTELLECTUAL PROPERTY MONOPOLIES

> It is to be observed that the statute of James gives no right to the inventor. The statute is a statute for the abolishing and forbidding monopolies, and the sixth section, under which the Crown acts in these matters, is a mere proviso excepting from the operation of that Act certain patents or grants of privileges, which are to be of such force as they should be if that Act had never been made, and of none other.
> Observations of James, *LJ* on the 1623 Statute of Monopolies
> *Von Heyden* v. *Neustadt* 50 L.J. N.S. Ch. 126

Received wisdom is that innovation is encouraged by grant of temporary monopolies which generate an enhanced return to compensate for the initial investment and risk involved. The oldest of such monopolies are copyright and patents, but, in recent years, further monopolies, in the form of *sui generis* rights, have been created for emerging technologies to prevent reproduction, *inter alia*, of semiconductor masks and of novel databases.

With regard to patents, the basis for this contention is of doubtful provenance. The origins of the modern patent system are to be found in the 1623 Statute of Monopolies, which was drawn up on the grounds of political expediency. Its primary objective was to curtail the ability of the monarch to grant monopolies, which had been abused, in turn, by Elizabeth I and James I, who both issued patents for the supply of staple commodities such as salt, iron and coal (Johnson 1890, p2). It also had to avoid impinging on the lucrative overseas trade of merchants such as the East India Company, which imported necessities such as silk and spices. When these conflicting criteria had been satisfied, what remained was merely the right to grant a monopoly for the introduction of new methods of manufacture into the realm. With the passage of time, the underlying reasons for the legislation have faded into obscurity and the residual monopoly is now regarded as meritorious.

Given the above genesis, it is not surprising that assessments of the contribution of patents to the development of inventions have been somewhat equivocal. Jewkes stated that, whilst there are conflicting arguments on whether a monopolist will (by nature) innovate, it is commonly held that a patent monopoly is an essential accompaniment to successful innovation. He then went on to conclude that the patent system is an ineffective and inefficient stimulus to invention. This finding was supported by Taylor and Silberston (Taylor 1973), who found that only five per cent of research and development by the firms surveyed would *not* have been carried out if there were no patent system.

Although the mantra is that patents are a stimulus to innovation, when rigorous accounting principles are applied, the costs of the process cannot be justified on the basis of the expected return. The cost of obtaining patent protection in the global market place will range from £200,000 to well over £1 million, according to the technology, and this sum excludes the cost of the litigation which is sometimes necessary to enforce the rights. Since, maybe, one in ten thousand inventions generates a significant return, expenditure on patents is akin to the venture capitalists' 'Friday-afternoon punt' – it is justified retrospectively if the invention is successful and the rewards are very high.

Kingston indicated that patent protection was an important factor in industrial development during the latter part of the nineteenth and the early part of the twentieth centuries. Following international discussions and conferences in 1873, 1878 and 1880, the International Convention for the Protection of Industrial Property, the Paris Convention, was signed in 1883. This provided the basis for the expansion of the patent system, underpinning the second stage of the industrial revolution (Kingston 1984, pp83,100).

Jewkes (1969) expressed surprise that the patent system continues largely unchallenged, likening it to an august political institution and not an economic device directed to a specific economic end. Kingston's explanation was that, with the growth in cross-licensing, patent pools and similar reciprocal arrangements, patents have developed into a form of currency for technology marketing.

It is difficult to make an objective evaluation of the influence of the patent system since there has been effective patent legislation at all material times in most significant territories in which industrial development has taken place. However, there were brief interludes in the Netherlands, Switzerland and, under special circumstances, during hostilities, in the USA, when patent laws were actually or effectively abandoned. It may be possible to gain an insight by studying what happened during these periods.

By analogy, conclusions may be drawn as to the influence of other statutory monopolies. The impact of intellectual property rights also varies from industry to industry and with the nature of the technology. For instance, in the pharmaceutical industry, a patent can create an absolute monopoly, ring-fencing the ability to manufacture a particular drug, whereas in electronic engineering, industry-wide standards mean that inventions must be shared because patent monopolies intersect. Trade marks are of major significance in advertising products to the domestic consumer, but they play no significant part in a market where the technical specification is dominant, such as that for fibre optic cables. Due to the idiosyncracies of development of the law, literary copyright has been adopted for the protection of computer programs. As might appear obvious, a process devised in the Middle Ages to respond to the introduction of the printing press is likely to have shortcomings when it is applied to what is quintessentially a problem of twentieth century technology.

3.9 MARKET STRUCTURE

The structure of an industry is likely to have a profound influence on the way the participating companies treat innovation (Cullis 1973). Whilst it may be argued that some form of monopoly is a pre-requisite to innovation, possession of a monopoly is not necessarily an incentive to innovate. Jewkes proposed a number of tests for the contention that firms in a monopoly or oligopoly will possess this tendency, but after applying those tests concluded that it is not possible scientifically to correlate monopoly and invention. It has also been argued that a price-fixing ring will foster innovation (BEAMA 1927), but again the evidence is inconclusive.

Kingston demonstrated that successive industrial revolutions each had a form of monopoly associated with it; the first, capability, the second, patent, and the third, marketing. An oligopoly based on market power is, in effect, a covert cartel (Kingston 1984, p128).

Sylos-Labini found that it was not fewness of numbers in itself, but concern with rivals, which is the heart of oligopolistic behaviour. In a concentrated oligopoly, prices tend to settle just above the entry-preventing level of the least efficient firm and will be determined by the size of the market. This implicit collusion between firms acts as a barrier to market entry by small competitors. Product differentiation is of major significance; patents are unimportant (Sylos-Labini 1957).

In an oligopoly, initiative by one firm, be it in cutting prices or introducing changes in marketing strategy, will stimulate a matching response from the other participants. If one player innovates, the others will also need to innovate to keep up. This is the equivalent of what biologists have called the Red Queen hypothesis – the need of a species to evolve to respond to the evolutionary changes of their ecosystem (Maynard Smith 1988, p183).

It is to be expected that market dynamics will exhibit a degree of inertia. Evidence in support of this proposition will be the persistence of the patterns of trade generated by patents or market power beyond the expiry of the monopoly.

3.10 MARKET POWER

It is characteristic of market-oriented firms to be international, either actually or potentially ... to have fewer products but longer production runs for them, and to be slower to change direction and to take a longer view in their planning for the future, than product-oriented firms are. All this is because of the nature of the 'uncertainty-reducing' process, which has become a major activity of this type of firm. ... Marketing power can therefore be more expensive to maintain, and may give a lower level of barrier against entry by newcomers for a given capital cost, than 'capability'. Against this, however, marketing power contributes to the efficiency of the plant, because it is a force tending towards the realization of whatever scale economies in operation are available; it reinforces the firm's capability market power also. Capability market power works in the opposite direction, by attempting to conform the plant's output to the range of objectively different requirements of the market, resulting in short production runs.

   W. Kingston, *The Political Economy of Innovation*, pp43,48

Kingston highlighted the importance of market power as a driving force of innovation (Kingston 1984, p5). Market power can be created by an individual firm's own efforts and brings the ability to inhibit the actions of others. It has its origins in Josiah Wedgwood's pottery and W.H. Lever's use of a trade mark to create brand differentiation following enactment of the 1883 Trade Marks Act. During the first stage of the Industrial Revolution (1780-1880) capability power protected markets. From 1880 to around 1914, patents were the main vehicle. After 1920, marketing power was dominant.

   The importance of marketing is that it reduces uncertainty in purchasing decisions. Persuasive market power is used to reduce the countervailing power of buyers. Marketing requirements are a primary stimulus for R&D. Consumer-oriented innovations possess both a physical and a psychological component.

   Brand identity has traditionally been associated with consumer products, but could it also be used as a tool to stimulate demand for technological products? Certainly companies such as IBM and Hewlett-Packard have built a strong corporate image, but promotion of individual products has been much more low key. Is it feasible to use the skills of marketing to change the dynamic of innovation? There is no reason to suppose that what is successful in the domestic market could not, with advantage, be translated into a technological environment. Why, then, do the producers of technological products not avail themselves of this tool? Marketing patterns could be tested to determine whether or not there is advantage to be gained by the product differentiation that trade marks offer.

3.11 *DE FACTO* AND RESPONSE-TIME MONOPOLIES

Trade secrecy is a well-established alternative to patenting under appropriate circumstances. For the strategy to be successful, it must be possible to restrict access to the product or process and to proscribe communication by employees.

Another factor which distorts markets is the *de facto* standard. So that multiple suppliers can service demand, their products must be interchangeable – all light bulbs must be capable of being plugged into a universal socket; personal computers need a common operating system, such as Microsoft Windows, which will interface with any applications program which may be installed on the computer.

Von Hippel identified response time, which he defined as the period an imitator requires to bring an imitative product to market or to bring an imitative process to commercial usefulness once he has full and free access to any relevant trade secrets or patented knowledge in the possession of the innovator, as a further informal temporary monopoly (von Hippel 1988, p59). Response time arises from the need to overcome barriers such as the design of engineering tooling, ordering of components, setting up manufacturing plant or the creation of a sales force. During the response-time period an innovator may capture rent from his innovation-related knowledge without fear of competition.

One may hypothesise that in industries in which there are universal standards, the organisation which established those standards will also be able to use response time to manipulate the market and steal a march on its competitors.

3.12 EXTERNAL AGENCIES – GOVERNMENT POLICY; REGULATORY CONTROL; ECONOMIC CYCLES

For political reasons, governments attempt to manipulate the economy. They are in a position, either by way of direct procurement or by placing of research contracts, to inject cash into the coffers of an innovator. It is anticipated that this will act as a positive stimulus for invention and may exert a Keynesian effect elsewhere in the economy.

As well as pressing on the accelerator in this way, authority has the brake of competition laws to curb excesses of monopoly. This is, however, an unwieldy tool, involving, as it does, a government agency and possibly judicial action. By definition, competition laws are used only when a participant in a market is able to exert undue power. At that stage, control will be difficult because of the immense resources the offender is able to command. For this reason, one might expect the remedy to be ineffective.

Other forms of control, such as the direct regulation of public utilities or the requirement to comply with national or industry standards, may also hedge certain activities.

In the absence of competition laws, the effect of market power is to increase the concentration of an industry with the passage of time. However, in most markets, behaviour moderates with increasing size so that oligopolies rather than monopolies are the asymptote (Kingston 1984, p43).

3.13 FINANCE

That access to sources of finance is an essential factor in the development of invention may be regarded as *sine qua non*. Innovations confer market advantage, but the cost of bringing them to fruition is high. Innovation is associated with negative cash flow and this must be balanced by a compensating influx of capital. Rational financial criteria militate against investment in inventions; the risks are too great.

At the beginning of the nineteenth century, investment in innovation was even more speculative than it is now. However, the social innovations of the joint stock company (1856) and limited liability (1855) laid the basis for the expansion of finance required for the capability marketing stage of the Industrial Revolution (Kynaston 1994). This, in turn, led to the expansion of the patent system as a basis for protecting investment.

Schumpeter has highlighted the effect on finance of the cyclic nature of business and, in particular, the influence of Kondratieff economic cycles:

> These revolutions periodically reshape the existing structure of industry by introducing new methods of production – the mechanized factory, the electrified factory, chemical synthesis and the like; new commodities, such as railroad service, motorcars, electrical appliances; new forms of organization – the merger movement; new sources of supply – La Plata wool, American cotton, Katanga copper; new trade routes and markets to sell in and so on. This process of industrial change provides the ground swell that gives the general tone to business: while these things are being initiated we have brisk expenditure and predominating 'prosperity' – interrupted, no doubt, by the negative phases of the shorter cycles that are superimposed on that, ground swell – and while those things are being completed and their results pour forth we have elimination of antiquated elements of the industrial structure and predominating 'depression.' Thus there are prolonged periods of rising and of falling prices, interest rates, employment and so on, which phenomena constitute parts of the mechanism of this process of recurrent rejuvenation of the productive apparatus.
> (Schumpeter 1950, p67)

Cash flow may be improved if a firm has access to the R&D of another, possibly by way of a licence agreement. Such a strategy will reduce the cost of market entry by removing duplication and reducing lead times. It avoids or postpones expenditure and permits resources thus released to be deployed elsewhere.

3.14 MAIN POINTS FROM THE LITERATURE SURVEY

Schumpeter revealed that innovation is characterised by a short, disruptive conception, in which discrete and random advances occur spontaneously, followed by a longer period of consolidation, in which improvements are of a steady and asymptotic nature. There is no clear picture of which factors contribute to success, but modern observers consider that, in order to provide useful information, a study needs, at least, to take into account historic, scientific, technological, economic and legal viewpoints, personal psychology, social needs, communications, finance and marketing.

Jewkes examined details of the history of different innovations, but discovered no common pattern. One suggestion by Julius Wolf, later taken up by Schmookler and others, was that, ultimately, the possibilities for innovation in a technological field become exhausted. This may be because the physical limits of processes are reached. Kingston noted that cross-fertilisation of ideas may postpone any reduction in the rate of innovation, as does the 'sailing-ship effect'. However, Wolf's theory is contradicted by the example of the automobile industry, which is based on mature technology but continues to innovate. Integrated circuit manufacture could provide a test for the proposition, since the limits of current technology are only about three technological generations (about ten years) away.

Opposing views of the origins of invention are that either they are the conception of great men or they are the inevitable product of socio-deterministic pressures – a consequence of the needs of an époque. Under the latter theory, they will just have a window of opportunity during which the socio-economic environment is favourable for their exploitation. This polarisation of ideas needs to be investigated further.

Various authors have observed that progress by fits and starts, initiated by sporadic flashes of inspiration and inhibited by obstacles such as the need to develop new materials, finds a parallel in biological evolution. The opportunity cost of re-working an abandoned idea is greater than that of developing the current technology. This is manifest in the binary nature of technological choices and gives rise to innovation paths which resemble phylogenetic trees.

A significant corollary of the biological analogy is that Goldschmidt's distinction between micromutations and macromutations leads to a corresponding dichotomy between microinventions and macroinventions, a concept which may be useful when modelling innovation dynamics. However, whilst the comparison provides useful analytical tools, it should not be regarded as set in stone.

Occasionally inventions will be made purely by chance – erroneous observations may have felicitous consequences, a newly discovered material may have ideal properties for a particular application or an unplanned discussion between two individuals may resolve an apparently insuperable problem.

Taton noted that, even if inventions do not require great men for their genesis, they will be influenced by the personal characteristics of individual inventors. The ability to observe is one significant quality. Perseverance and attention to detail are others. The inventor's path is hard and he needs strength of purpose to act as product champion. An inventor also needs to have the right sort of mind, which may be stimulated by cross-fertilisation of ideas from other disciplines. Different environments suit different inventors – some prosper in institutional environments, whilst others like to plough a lone furrow.

Innovation is, at times, inhibited by the need for some enabling invention or other event, such as the development of a material having suitable physical characteristics or the enactment of legislation which removes regulatory barriers. Is scientific discovery more a permissive than an active factor in the inventive process, or could it, perhaps, perform both roles?

Firms need to innovate to keep up with competitors. Often, however, resistance to change – a universal trait – manifests itself in the Not-Invented-Here (NIH) syndrome, in which it is difficult for an outsider to get his ideas accepted. Skills are not always home grown. Sometimes their acquisition takes the form of such predatory activities as hiring inventors employed by rivals or taking over companies to gain access to their technology. Information sharing by cross-licensing is an alternative means. This brings incremental revenue and there may be other benefits. Informal know-how trading also spreads the knowledge base and may take innovation to its critical mass or speed a company's progress up the learning curve.

Is the process of intellectual property law making designed to produce effective results? The nature and extent of the monopoly provided by intellectual property rights vary from industry to industry. This is due partly to the particular way monopoly impinges on the technology and partly to the haphazard way the law develops. The established view is that statutory monopolies provide a temporary respite from competition to enable innovation to become established. However, the origins of the modern patent system, for instance, militate against the proposition that it will be an effective tool to foster innovation. Empirical evidence gathered by Taylor and Silberston supports this contention, as does a rational financial risk analysis. However, Kingston pointed out that patents do serve a useful purpose as a form of currency for technology marketing. Isolated periods, when certain countries abandoned patents, may provide a vehicle for study of the utility of the system.

Market structure exerts a dominant effect on the propensity to innovate. For instance, inertia in market dynamics may create opportunities for an innovator and market power, which can be generated intrinsically by a firm's own efforts, may be used to reduce the countervailing power of buyers. Informal distortions of a market may be generated by trade secrecy and *de facto* standards. Response-time delays, which were highlighted by von Hippel, create a temporary monopoly which can assist an innovator in controlling a market. Marketing requirements, which possess both physical and psychological components, are a stimulus for research and development and, hence, invention.

Governments may be a major influence in controlling the progress of innovation. On the one hand, they can stimulate it by direct procurement or fiscal incentives, whilst, on the other hand, they can control the power of innovators by competition laws or direct regulation or the application of national or international standards.

Finally, finance is important because innovation is accompanied by the absolute certainty of negative cash flow, whereas the prospect of an innovation rent is highly uncertain. The anticipated return will depend on risk assessment, which is also a very imprecise procedure. Why then should capital be forthcoming? Comfort for the capitalist may be supplied by intellectual property rights, but cyclic variations in the economy will also affect the magnitude of the income. The cost of market entry may be reduced by using others' R&D through the medium of a licence which will usually be obtained at marginal cost.

3.15 CONCLUSION

In an evolving economy, firms need to innovate in order to survive. A steady flow of obstacles to be overcome will provide an opportunity to do this. The literature survey confirmed that to produce meaningful results, a study of the dynamics of innovation needs to be multi-disciplinary. Jewkes searched for a universal pattern but this proved fruitless. Other authors attempted to explain this failure, but their assumptions are open to question.

There are opposing views on the origins of invention. It may be the inevitable consequence of the environment, the product of great minds or, simply, serendipity. Market structure is a dominant factor in shaping the evolution of innovation and this may be distorted by influences, some of which can be controlled by the innovator. Intellectual property is not necessarily the stimulus that it is usually held out to be. Government intervention, particularly at the early stages, may promote or inhibit it, as may the laws of physics and the properties of materials. Good communication, however, is an essential component. The role of finance is significant because cash is a consumable and, if the rate of consumption is constrained by the rate of supply, it can inhibit progress or even stifle the innovation completely.

One school has used biological analogies as a tool for analysis. In the present study, it is likely to be helpful to represent technological paradigms as phylogenetic trees because technological innovation involves a succession of paradigm shifts which fulfil the role of biological mutations. Case studies (Cullis 2004) which examine the reasons for the choices made will therefore, by corollary, throw light on the hierarchy of the factors of invention. They are to be found on the internet at

http://www.hm-treasury.gov.uk/media/51A/54/queen_mary_ip_research_institute_043_8080kb.pdf

They may also be found on the website of the Chartered Institute of Patent Attorneys

http://www.cipa.org.uk/pages/successfulinnovation

under the title *What Makes a Successful Innovation?*

4. Analysis of Technological Innovation Case Studies

I ... bought all the transactions of the gas engineering societies, etc., all the back volumes of the gas journals. Having obtained the data and investigated the gas-jet distribution in New York by actual observations, I made up my mind that the problem of the sub-division of the electric current could be solved and made commercial.

Thomas A. Edison, 1878

Inventors were few in those earliest years of the century. Invention was easy, the soil exceedingly fertile, and the Patent Office not yet clogged with thousands of pending applications on insignificant, or hardly distinguishable, details. Consequently the incentive to strike out and pioneer on paths radically new, and therefore wondrously attractive, was intense. In rapid succession followed the auto-detector (self-restoring, electrolytic, and crystal types), the telephone receiver, the alternating current transmitter, the two-tuned circuits at sender and receiver, the high frequency spark, the quenched-spark gap, the Poulsen arc and tikker, the direction finder, the series selective circuits of Stone, the heterodyne principle of Fessenden, the Audion as detector and as radio-frequency and telephone amplifier, the Alexanderson high-frequency generator, and the Audion oscillator (first as regenerator for heterodyne reception, then as transmitter for telegraph and telephone). All of these kaleidoscopic changes were accomplished in less than eighteen years – from 1900 onward.

Lee de Forest, *Father of radio – the autobiography of Lee de Forest*, p249

Brattain's *24 December* notebook entry continues after the report of the 23 December demonstration to record that an oscillator was constructed on 24 December and did, indeed, oscillate. The birth of the point-contact transistor was a magnificent Christmas present for the group as a whole.

William Shockley, *IEEE Trans Electron Dev* **ED-23** (No.7), July 1976, p597

We had been the first to introduce the product and build the business. Even as we were losing market share hand over fist, we clung to the idea that we'd come back. DRAM was taking a third of Intel's R&D dollars and contributing only 5% of its revenues. Pulling out freed resources to go into microprocessors. It was one of the toughest and the best decisions we ever made.

Andy Grove, CEO of Intel

4.1 INTRODUCTION

To test the hypothesis that the factors which underpin and control the progress of innovation have an hierarchical structure and an influence which depends on the temporal context, a first case study (Cullis 2004) considered the humble light bulb, the invention which laid the foundation for the explosive development of the electricity industry in the last two decades of the nineteenth century. Following a broadly chronological path, it surveyed the evolution of the incandescent filament lamp, which was to become the dominant artificial light source for the next hundred years. Using the knowledge base at the beginning of the nineteenth century as a starting point, it examined milestones along the way to the 'subdivision of the light', a problem which was, in the 1870s, considered by established scientific experts of the time, to be insoluble.

A chronology of key events (Cullis 2004, Appendix 2) was expanded and then analysed, paradigm by paradigm, to determine the relative significance of the factors which contributed to the success of this major innovation. Many of the components were common to the sister industries of communications and electronics and were also included in the chronology to facilitate comparison with a second case study which was considered subsequently.

In order to lay the technological foundations, the narrative looked at early sources of artificial light – those based on a chemically generated flame and the electrically powered precursors of the incandescent filament. This was important because it set out the technological context and economic motivation for the key inventions which set the paradigm changes in train and subsequently ensured their success.

Brief biographies of the inventors were presented to draw out factors which may have contributed to their achievements. Amongst this cohort were two (Göbel and Swan) who made the invention before conditions were apposite, two (Swan, on his second attempt, and Edison) who brought the innovation to a successful conclusion, and five (Farmer, Maxim, Lane Fox, Sawyer and Man) who were capable of similar achievement, but either arrived too late on the scene or lacked one or more of the attributes necessary to drive the innovation onwards.

A description of the creation of the industrial infrastructure provided an indication of latent technical, financial, social and legislative problems associated with the development of the innovation. Subsequent technological developments were also considered, to illustrate how physical properties of materials were responsible for success and failure in carrying the paradigm forward to the ultimate substitution of refractory metals for carbon in the fabrication of a lamp filament.

The case study also investigated the role played by secondary vectors in changing the structure of the market from free competition, first into a monopoly, and subsequently into an oligopoly which persisted for the next hundred years or so. Amongst these influences were the divergence of national patent laws and key litigation which the innovators used as part of their commercial strategies.

The play and counter-play of cartels, competition law and physical regulation were interwoven, as were the various aspects of finance, including raising of capital and use of intellectual property rights as collateral, marketing strategies and advertising techniques. A description of communications showed how knowledge was diffused at the relevant time. Finally, the key steps in the evolution of the technological paradigms were extracted to complete the picture.

4.2 INFLUENCES ON THE DEVELOPMENT OF THE INCANDESCENT LAMP INDUSTRY

The stimulus for the development of the incandescent lamp industry was Volta's invention of the voltaic pile which, for the first time, provided a reliable source of continuous electric current. Humphry Davy, during his tenure of the Royal Institution, was provided with a powerful battery composed of these cells and, with this, he demonstrated the electric arc, the incandescent filament and the luminous gas discharge, precursors of three main technological paradigms for conversion of electrical energy to light.

A latent demand for electric lighting had been created by the luminous flame. Before artificial lighting became economically viable with the development of coal gas and the bats' wing and fishtail burners and the portable kerosene lamp, the workman had been constrained by the availability of daylight. He rose with the sun and retired at dusk.

The gas flame was not an efficient source of light. It relied on incomplete combustion to create illumination – the gas mantle was not invented until towards the end of the nineteenth century. The gas itself was smelly and potentially explosive. There were therefore many incentives to replace it, provided a sufficiently cheap alternative could be found.

Although the battery provided a source of steady current, the primary cell consumed zinc, which was an expensive fuel (Houston 1894, p123). A cheaper alternative became available when Gramme and others invented dynamos for conversion of mechanical energy into electricity. The power of steam generated by combustion of readily available coal, or of water flowing from high reservoirs, could then be harnessed.

As soon as electricity was viable, it was used to drive the carbon arc lamp. Early developments, such as hard carbons, made this practicable and refinements such as a clockwork mechanism for automatically maintaining optimum spacing of the arc could be established using extant technology. Moving parts were eliminated when Jablochkoff introduced his 'Candle' and this might have proved to be a fruitful line of development had the arc not been displaced by the incandescent filament. Improvement to the arc lamp went on long after its successor was established – a manifestation of the well-known 'sailing ship' effect.

The arc lamp was noisy and it produced a huge amount of light – far more than was necessary for domestic purposes. 'The subdivision of the light' therefore became an objective for researchers in this field. Davy and others had experimented with incandescent wires as a source of light. Platinum was the most widely used because it did not oxidise when heated in air, although other noble metals were also pressed into service. These materials were, however, not satisfactory because the temperature at which they became white hot was very little below their melting points. With the poor regulation of early power supplies and non-uniformity of wires due to crude metallurgy, lamp filaments frequently fused and failed.

Heinrich Göbel was the first inventor to make a working light from a refractory material – carbon (Fürst 1926). His lamp exhibited many of the characteristics of the later devices of Swan and Edison. It had a glass envelope and a carbon filament glowing in a vacuum. However, Göbel lacked the skills of communication and commerce necessary to crown his invention with success. Edison and Swan, on the other hand, in their very different ways, were able to marry their skills with those of others to exploit the invention effectively.

The carbon filament lamp was the direct result of the combination of improvements in vacuum technology, effected by Sprengel and others, with the serendipitous discovery of the technique of 'running on the pumps' to remove adsorbed gases which had previously been a source of destruction of the carbon. Once Edison and Swan had shown the way, many others, including Lane Fox, Maxim, Sawyer and Man, were immediately able to tread the same path. Intellectual property rights were the tool by means of which the pioneers were able to suppress the competition. Edison and Swan demonstrated the truth of the adage 'United we stand, divided we fall' by combining their resources to turn a weak patent into one that was invincible. They exploited the common law system of precedent to establish a monopoly which remained absolute until their original patents expired. By this time patterns of trade had been firmly established and the market was closed to newcomers.

Swan demonstrated the truth of the statement that 'a little knowledge is a dangerous thing'. On the basis of his previous experience of the patent system, he delayed filing an application on the carbon filament lamp because he considered that his collocation of features was obvious and an insufficient inventive step to support a patent. As a result, his rival Edison, who operated on the principle of file first and enquire later whether the invention is patentable, pre-empted important aspects of Swan's patent.

Edison believed strongly in a vertically integrated manufacturing system. He set up plant to make all of the components of his lighting system, from generators to supply cables and meters. This philosophy persisted in his successor company, General Electric, up to the end of the twentieth century.

Patent protection bred complacency. The metal filaments which superseded the carbon filament were developed by third parties who were trying to break into this lucrative market. It was of little avail. The market power resulting from being first in the field permitted the original companies to purchase rights to the new technology, thus retaining their market dominance.

Swan and Edison represented opposite ends of the spectrum of the process of innovation. Swan would select his goal and work steadily towards it, picking off useful peripheral ideas such as the miners' safety lamp and artificial silk along the way. He believed in the *keiretsu* method, harnessing the independent resources of fellow workers including Crompton and C.W. Siemens (Crompton 1928). Edison, on the other hand, adopted a scatter-gun, bull-in-the-china-shop approach. He squandered the profits from his invention of the quadruplex telegraph on trying unsuccessfully to develop a sextuplex version. Although his initial attempt at subdivision of the light was based on a meticulous study of the economics of gas lighting, he financed expensive expeditions to seek natural sources of carboniferous fibres without any consideration of the likelihood of an adequate return. A large number of his inventions failed, lacking a sound technological foundation, whilst many of those which succeeded did so mainly because of manufacturing or market power. He failed to recognise the importance of alternating as opposed to direct current and was unsuccessful in developing wireless communications although he had all of the necessary inventions to hand. As well as being the inventor of the carbon filament lamp, the phonograph and the quadruplex telegraph, he was also the proponent of the odoroscope, the tasimeter, the pyromagnetic generator and vacuum 'preservation' of meat, all unworkable ideas. His most significant innovation was of the concept of the industrial research laboratory, although he viewed this merely as an extension of his personal skills, frequently taking the credit for the work of others. His career exhibited a classic Gaussian profile of the propensity to invent, peaking in his early thirties and tailing off with increasing age, with subsidiary peaks corresponding to new enthusiasms and troughs resulting from extraneous distractions.

Von Welsbach's invention of the rare-earth-charged gas mantle, with its vast increase in efficiency over the batwing and fishtail burners, delayed the universal adoption of electric lighting. One of his co-workers, Nernst, also adapted the process to use electrical power (Fürst 1926).

Evolving public attitudes to private monopoly were a major influence on the international structure of the electrical industry. The choice of an inappropriate precedent – the Tramways Act 1870 – for the first Electric Lighting Act (Bowers 1982) to control the installation of infrastructure for generation and distribution of electricity in the UK set back British industry ten years and allowed US and German rivals to gain a commanding lead. It was only the creation of international cartels and the existence of the imperial preference that permitted British companies to play a subsequent part on the world stage.

Finance was not an important influence. Although needs ranged from the modest requirements of experimenters like Swan to the social capital for the creation of the infrastructure necessary to establish the embryonic electricity industry, the greed of speculators ensured that resources were forthcoming. Marketing techniques were relatively unsophisticated, but the modern exponent of this art would recognise the use of public figures, exhibitions and learned societies to mould opinions. Some approaches, such as Edison's use of his rival Westinghouse's alternating current generator to power the electric chair, as a means of promoting the use of direct current, would now be regarded as unethical, but were effective in achieving publicity.

4.3 CONCLUSIONS FROM THE FIRST CASE STUDY

Early forms of artificial lighting, through the medium of discrete sources, such as the fire brand, tallow dip and candle, stretch back into pre-history. The motive force behind the first paradigm change, from the individual flame to the continuous illumination of the centrally produced coal gas, was purely economic. It used, in an entirely predictable manner, only those technological resources which were already available. Financial returns were assured and capital was therefore forthcoming. On two occasions, inventions reinforced this paradigm. The first was the dilution of coal gas using petroleum-vapour-enriched water gas, which reduced input costs, and the second was the introduction of the gas mantle, which delayed the move to electric lighting.

When limelight was invented, a decade after the introduction of coal gas, it provided the prospect of a great increase in luminosity, but this could not be harnessed because conventional gas burners did not give a hot enough flame, unless they were supplied with pure oxygen to aid combustion. No viable means of generating this oxygen was available. (At that time, pure oxygen was produced by relatively costly chemical processes rather than the present-day technique of fractional distillation of liquefied air.) In any event, pure oxygen when mixed with coal gas is potentially explosive and, for safety reasons, would probably not have been acceptable. Indeed, if modern safety criteria had been prevalent at the beginning of the nineteenth century, it is questionable whether gas would have been taken up as a universal energy source.

Sixty years elapsed from Drummond's invention of the limelight burner before a clever and resourceful inventor – Carl Auer von Welsbach – devised a means of harnessing the luminosity of refractory oxides. His gas mantle, which was impregnated with, *inter alia*, [radio-active] thoria, found immediate acceptance and remained in general use for another seventy years or so. There is no apparent reason why this invention could not have been made forty or more years earlier, if someone had decided to carry out research into improved burners to raise the temperature of refractory oxides in coal gas flames sustained by air rather than pure oxygen. The time and environment were ripe. It was only the invention that was lacking. The inference is that the problems of gas lighting technology did not attract sufficiently smart thinkers.

The genesis of electricity as a power source was serendipitous, but it required Volta's perspicacious interpretation of Galvani's observation to turn the discovery into a viable innovation. Volta's ideas, in turn, needed a receptive environment – which he sought in London rather than his native Italy – to provide the resources for the discovery, development and dissemination of basic forms of electric lighting.

The drawbacks of gas – including poor luminosity, hazardous operation and pollution – created a strong latent demand for a better alternative. The first to be developed was the arc, which could be made to operate reasonably satisfactorily using extant technology developed in a logical, extrapolative manner. The negative features were that it was noisy, that the level of light from an individual burner was very high, that the spacing of the electrodes required continual and precise adjustment and that it was very sensitive to variations in the electrical power supply.

The incandescent filament, the principle of which was established by Davy at the same time as the arc light, overcame these problems, but its immediate take-up was inhibited by the unsuitable properties of available materials – noble metals, such as platinum and iridium did not oxidise but melted if they were overheated; carbon did not melt but was oxidised, due to the presence of adsorbed oxygen, even when encapsulated in a sealed chamber. Early workers who tried carbon did not succeed until Sprengel's and Geissler's more efficient vacuum pumps for creating better vacua and the serendipitously discovered technique of 'running on the pumps' solved the latent problem of oxidation by occluded gases. This was the last step in the jigsaw. The floodgates opened and other potential makers were able to commence manufacture.

Patents were the key to control of the market. Combination of Edison's and Swan's resources to assemble a portfolio of key inventions created a dominant position. Patterns of trade established by this monopoly persisted after expiry of the patents. Innovation followed the classical Schumpeterian model. Eventually, a paradigm-changing invention came from without, but the market power of the original monopolists enabled them to acquire the substitute technology.

Once the way was created by Swan's and Edison's invention of the carbon filament lamp, there was no insuperable obstacle to the establishment of the massive infrastructure needed to support this innovation. Vertically and horizontally integrated business models were equally appropriate for this development. Problems were solved as they were encountered, over a very short time interval, by using adaptations of existing technology on an *ad hoc* basis. Sometimes this created long-lasting *de facto* standards, such as Edison's screw and Swan's bayonet lamp connector.

Swan worked selectively towards his goals but Edison adopted a random approach, throwing money at problems to find a solution. Edison's concept of an industrial research laboratory enabled him to maximise his efforts. He missed many opportunities through lack of focus, but created many more as a result of his free thinking. His propensity to invent changed through his life, following a skewed gaussian distribution.

Edison's and Swan's differing methodologies were equally successful in initiating innovation. Edison, however, did not hesitate to punch below the belt if it would help him to achieve his objectives. He also consumed more resources, both physical and mental. Swan, on the other hand, always adopted a strictly ethical approach. The former's more robust stance succeeded better in business. If one contestant adopts a 'no-holds-barred' attitude and the other is playing by the rule book then clearly the former will be at an advantage.

The conduct of litigation demonstrated another important plank of innovation strategy – the choice of the most suitable opponents and venue for litigation. Edison and Swan had both patented the important combination of elements in the manufacture of the carbon filament lamp –

the use of a vacuum, an all-glass enclosure and a thin carbonised filament. In opposition, the two patentees could have destroyed one another. They therefore settled their differences and combined to litigate against third parties. In common law jurisdictions, an increasingly invincible series of precedents was built up by initiating proceedings against weak opponents. A combination of deep pockets, multiple actions and retention of the leading advocates was employed to ensure victory. In jurisdictions where there was an inquisitorial system of justice, this strategy did not prevail and the market became more fragmented.

In most territories, markets evolved into oligopolies, often with overt cartels, such as the British Electric Lamp Manufacturers' Association. The Phoebus Organisation, controlled by the US General Electric Company, regulated international trade. Early competition law was ineffective against these trusts. Indeed, the strong industry which they engendered was viewed with favour in Germany and Britain. Absence of a patent system in Holland and Switzerland permitted small manufacturers to establish themselves, but, in the long term, they were either absorbed by larger businesses or joined them in an oligopolistic market.

Direct regulation can have a disproportionate influence on a developing industry. An infelicitous choice of legislative precedent, although reflecting public attitudes, did not take sufficient account of the need for adequate financial return and almost strangled the juvenile British electrical industry at birth. However, once the regulatory regime was structured satisfactorily, finance ceased to be an important influence.

The dissemination of Humphry Davy's findings stimulated research elsewhere and led to improvements in battery technology, but energy produced in this way could not supplant that produced by coal as it was three orders of magnitude more costly. In 1831, Faraday, Davy's successor at the Royal Institution, discovered a means of converting mechanical energy to electricity and hence of harnessing the low cost and ready availability of coal, but it was another forty years before a reliable dynamo was developed. The move from battery to generator as a source of electric current was analogous to the paradigm shift from the candle to the gas flame – the change from a discrete to centralised power supply.

Advances in power sources led to improvements in lighting. Better light sources created a demand for more electric power and the two paradigms advanced in a stepwise manner.

Von Welsbach's contribution to the improvement of gas lighting through the invention of the oxide-charged gas mantle, with its vast increase in efficiency over the bats' wing and fishtail burners, led directly to Nernst's development of an electrical analogue, which found commercial success in Germany and America. This could well have spawned an alternative train of development, a different phylogenetic tree, but another of von Welsbach's inventions, the extruded, sintered osmium filament lamp, set in motion the successive introduction of other refractory metals, vanadium, tantalum and tungsten, which exhibited a greater luminous efficiency and product life. Stanley Mullard's Point-o-lite bulb, a sealed tungsten arc lamp, might also have been the source of another fruitful line, had it appeared three decades earlier. Both Nernst's and Mullard's inventions demonstrate the need for felicitous timing as a component of success.

A major paradigm shift in ancillary technology, from direct to alternating current electricity supply, was conceived theoretically and reduced to practice by a 'great man' (Tesla). He combined with a 'man of vision' (Westinghouse) who had the resources to bring the idea to fruition and the experience to transfer the technology effectively (O'Neill 1944). Although it evoked a Luddite reaction in Edison, this negative response was no more effective in delaying progress than a similar reaction was in delaying the transition from a cylindrical to a disc-shaped sound recording medium some years later.

Two further conclusions may be drawn from this case study. Firstly, although it is not always possible to transfer technology between paradigms, the possibility of success justifies the attempt, and secondly, old technologies do not die, they just survive in niche applications.

4.4 THE BIRTH OF ELECTRONICS

The first case study traced the development of artificial illumination from the early light sources through to the incandescent tungsten filament lamp, which is still the most widespread method of lighting in use today. Although driven by socio-economic considerations, technological innovations were shown frequently to be initiated by serendipity and their development constrained by the physical properties of materials. A second case study followed the evolution of communications and electronics. This technological development was chosen to cover a similar period of history to that of the initial case study. Since they occurred in a similar socio-economic environment, many influences were common to both regimes. A comparison of the mechanics of the paradigm changes with that of those studied in the initial investigation therefore highlighted the effect of the differences. As many of the key events which shaped the evolution of communications were shared with the lighting and electrical industries, the two case studies were built around a common chronology (Cullis 2004, Appendix 2).

After looking at manually-operated, visual communication systems which were used almost exclusively for military purposes, this case study investigated how the technological innovation of the battery and the discovery of electromagnetism gave rise to different forms of the electric telegraph. It considered how nineteenth century commercial pressures led, first to land-based lines following the wayleaves of the railways, and then to submarine cables which linked continents. Finally, it traced the complementary innovation of radio and some of the inventions which made it feasible.

Although the national economies in which development took place were the very ones which provided the environment for the evolution of the electric light, the global nature of communications meant that international agreement was necessary to regulate the growth and operation of cable and its sister paradigm, wireless. The case study therefore illustrates the effects on innovation of this additional influence.

Due to the underlying military application of communications technology, ordnance procurement and two world wars were also expected to play a significant role. Furthermore, since a temporary suspension of the US patent system took place when the Americans entered hostilities in November 1917, an opportunity was presented to review the influence of the presence or absence of this statutory monopoly.

During the growth of these technologies, arrangements were set up for the pooling of patents. It was therefore possible to investigate how this reduction of competition impinged on the development of the industry.

4.5 INFLUENCES ON THE DEVELOPMENT OF THE ELECTRONICS INDUSTRY

Early communications were driven by military requirements. The semaphore held sway for many years and the advance of the electric telegraph was delayed by the cessation of hostilities between England and France (Jarvis 1955a). The advent of the railways provided a commercial incentive and also the wayleaves to lay cables from city centre to city centre. Once the cables had been installed, the explosion of commerce that accompanied the industrial revolution ensured their viability.

The telephone was invented in America. Edison and Bell both set up, in Britain, service companies which posed a threat to the General Post Office's monopoly of communications. Although the Telegraph Act was invoked in a landmark case, *Attorney-General v. Edison Telephone Co. of London* (6 QBD 244), to restore control to the state, the prospect of growth in the telephone system was not taken seriously because, in the words of the Chief

Engineer to the Post Office, 'We have a super-abundance of messenger boys.'

Starting with the modest beginning of a cable under the Thames, Britain pioneered underwater communications cables. As well as the burgeoning demand of trans-Atlantic commerce, there was a need to communicate with the outposts of Empire, which provided the political incentive to undertake the massive investment required. As a maritime nation, Britain had rope-making technology available and it was readily adapted, but cable construction was a new art. Suitable materials had to be discovered by trial and error. Gutta percha, a product of the rubber industry, proved to be a suitable insulator. This led to Britain, with its imperial sources of raw materials, becoming a leader in cable-based communications. This eventually inhibited the progress of wireless in Britain because, by the First World War, when wireless was beginning to expand, there had been a huge investment in the cable infrastructure and, it was thought, the power of the Royal Navy would prevent these cables from being cut, so there was no need for an alternative form of communication – an echo of the decision a century earlier on replacement of the semaphore. Even before the laying of the first trans-Atlantic cable, the telegraph companies had formed a price-fixing cartel. This remained effective throughout the latter half of the nineteenth century.

There were many pioneers of wireless communications, including Hertz, Lodge, de Forest, Marconi and Slaby. Even Edison had tried his hand and, indeed, had made the inventions which would have laid the foundations for a successful development. He, however, was fully occupied with the exploitation of the electric light and lacked the motivation to drive the inventions through to commercial viability. With wireless, Marconi was the man of vision. Lacking support in his native Italy, he emigrated to Britain, the home country of his wife, where he received the patronage which supported his early experiments.

The early detectors of wireless signals were many, various and crude, but were universally based on the creation of an audible signal which was translated by a trained operator. J.A. Fleming, scientific consultant to Marconi, suffered from progressive deafness and could not use these techniques and was forced to seek an alternative. He adapted apparatus on which he had worked two decades earlier to invent the thermionic diode detector. As a consequence of the English common law of master and servant, he assigned his rights to his employer, the Marconi Company. Lee de Forest, in the USA, extended Fleming's work and made a more sensitive detector by adding a third electrode to the diode. At the time, he did not realise that he had made an amplifier, but he later exploited the invention to the full. Wehnelt, von Lieben and Reiß in Germany mirrored the work of Fleming and de Forest to develop a thermionic relay valve.

De Forest was a difficult character, who fell out with his business associates. Shortly after his invention of the triode valve, he underwent a period of financial stringency, as a result of which he was unable to maintain his foreign patents. He became involved in litigation with Marconi and again, due to his personality, was unable to reach a settlement. This led to a stand-off in the US thermionic valve industry which was not resolved until the suspension of patent monopolies during the first world war. The Fleming diode patent was eventually held to be invalid by the US Supreme Court, but, by then, its role in shaping the structure of the industry had been fully played out.

The upheaval caused by the first world war allowed the lamp manufacturers to gain control of the manufacture of thermionic valves. The industry was ruled by cartels which paralleled those of the lamp manufacturers. The demarcation of national boundaries was enforced by the adoption of non-tariff barriers such as the use of mechanically incompatible valve bases for devices with similar electrical characteristics. In this regulated environment, the rate of technological development was slow.

The need to communicate with ships was the economic driver which stimulated the early expansion of wireless communications. Marconi adopted an aggressive commercial stance and threatened to gain a monopoly. Other nations were antipathetic and adopted countermeasures to prevent Britain gaining the degree of control of wireless which it enjoyed in cable-based telegraphy. Germany convened international conferences at which it fought for its national interests. Britain's support for Marconi was half-hearted, partly as a result of a desire to preserve the Post Office monopoly. In the USA, commercial interests closed ranks and set up the Radio Corporation of America (RCA) to prevent Marconi gaining access to the Alexanderson alternator which would effectively have given him a monopoly of trans-Atlantic wireless.

The broadcast entertainment industry was a by-product of the wireless communications revolution, but this was completely regulated by cartels. Patents were pooled and *de facto* standards created by a need for a *lingua franca*. There was therefore little incentive to innovate other than in response to consumer demand for advances, such as colour television.

4.6 CONCLUSIONS FROM THE SECOND CASE STUDY

Although Volta's battery made the electric telegraph feasible, existing technologies did not yield viable systems. The enabling step was Oersted's discovery of the magnetic effects of an electric current, but even so, the electric telegraph did not become widespread until there was a strong commercial demand initiated by railway mania.

In the nineteenth century, Britain had long been a maritime nation and possessed appropriate industries to service naval activities. British manufacturers became dominant in cable manufacture because they could adapt established rope-making techniques and had exclusive access to suitable raw materials through trade with the Empire. Commercial demands attracted many new suppliers, but, almost as soon as a regular service was established, the cable operators found it necessary to set up a price-fixing cartel to maintain profits.

As with limelight in the previous case study, technological limitations at the time of the invention of the telephone inhibited its immediate acceptance. It posed a potential threat to telegraphy, but lack of a means for compensating for transmitted signal degradation blocked an early paradigm shift. In the legal environment, statute law did not keep pace with technology, but judge-made law, based on the legal fiction that the telephone was a telegraph, enabled the government to retain its monopoly of operations.

Like the luminous flame before von Welsbach, cable construction techniques did not inspire successful lateral thought. Until the invention of the fibre optic light guide towards the end of the twentieth century, there was no fundamental re-appraisal of cable communications technology.

The evolution of wireless followed the *classical* path of theoretical proposal, followed by proof of concept, development of crude practical systems with commercial utility and, ultimately, supersession by more refined systems. As with the electric lamp, although many inventors were capable of making the enabling inventions, the one who succeeded (Marconi) also possessed the necessary business acumen. The new paradigm destroyed the economic viability of its predecessor (cable communications) and Marconi used this as a threat to gain access to the cable operators' local delivery network. Like Edison and Swan, he employed a domino strategy to eliminate or marginalise competition, picking off his opponents one by one. He used patents to control the market, whilst his contemporary Lodge, who had a similar command of the technology, was timid in enforcing his rights.

Development of long-distance wireless communications was frustrated by conflicting national interests and reluctance of governments to come to terms with private monopolies when they, themselves, were not prepared to commit to investment in infrastructure or write off outmoded cable systems. Political considerations over-rode technological ones.

A conflict of interest affected the British government's stance. On the one hand, it wished to encourage national commercial interests, but on the other it wanted to maintain the Post Office's monopoly of communications. Other nations fought their own corner vigorously.

For ship-owners, investment in wireless for safety purposes was a 'distress purchase' and compliance had to be enforced by diplomatic agreement – a very slow process.

The broadcast entertainment industry was a by-product of the wireless communications revolution. Radio broadcasting excited public interest. It grew organically over many decades (and is still growing), interrupted only by the precedence accorded to the demands of military communications for limited resources, particularly during periods of war.

When broadcasting got under way, Marconi repeated the strategy he had used with maritime wireless and set out to establish a dominant patent portfolio by original invention or by acquisition of other people's. As with cable, a cartel was established to further the interests of the principal suppliers. Patents were pooled and *de facto* standards created in response to a need for inter-working of products from different manufacturers. Pool licensing conditions created artificial constraints on receiver design and marketing. There was therefore little incentive to innovate other than to reduce manufacturing costs and to respond to consumer demand for novelties such as colour television. A radio receiver manufactured in 1955 differed little from one made in 1935, apart from the substitution of physically smaller valves with all-glass bases (albeit performing identical functions).

With the thermionic valve, there was considerable borrowing from incandescent lamp technology. Fleming's diode was a direct consequence of an unexpected (and ignored) observation by Upton and Edison two decades earlier. De Forest's discovery of the amplification by his Audion valve was also serendipitous – for a long time, he thought that he had merely made a more sensitive detector.

In the main, technological advance in valve construction techniques went hand in hand with progress in communications technology. The early innovations were empirically-based. One early paradigm shift was the result of a chance contamination of materials but, once the fundamental principles of the thermionic valve had been established, subsequent advances were made by developments in electrode materials and mechanical construction to enhance the electron emission characteristics and optimise the internal electric field topography.

Due to their relatively short lifetimes, the replacement market for valves was profitable. This influenced the pricing structure of component supplies to original equipment manufacturers, which was designed to gain access to these lucrative later sales. Non-tariff barriers were erected to protect national markets.

War provided increased focus and direction for innovation. In the British Empire, because there was a highly developed cable communications network which was not considered vulnerable, due to the strength of the Royal Navy, little effort was expended on radio. German cables, on the other hand, were constantly cut, so great strides were made there in transmitter and receiver design to improve long-distance wireless communications. War also encouraged long uniform production runs and standardisation. To this end there was exchange of know-how between manufacturers and suspension of patent monopolies. Eventually it created a vast post-war surplus market which fed pioneering amateur enthusiasts and entrepreneurs. War stimulated demand, but peace switched it off again, with wireless as it had done with the electric telegraph at the start of the nineteenth century.

Paranoia about freedom-to-use created a cross-licensing culture when monopolies intersected. This was often accompanied by an overt or implicit agreement to respect exclusive territorial rights to markets – Philips exchanged licences with RCA and kept out of the US market. There were also complementary cross-holdings of shares in competing companies. Personality conflict was a significant determinant of the structure of the electronics industry because this paranoia was a direct consequence of de Forest's lack of willingness to compromise in his conflict with Marconi, which created a hiatus in the industry's progress.

Valves made communications much more reliable. However, the thermionic valve was a technological dinosaur. It consumed huge amounts of power to achieve a modest amplification, had a short operating life and was mechanically fragile. These drawbacks provided a strong motivation in the search for a replacement. The two world wars were periods of rapid technological advance. Probably the most important innovation during this time was the introduction of the new semiconductor materials which led to the invention of the transistor, which was the subject of the third case study.

4.7   THE INVENTION OF THE TRANSISTOR

The first two case studies provided an opportunity to contrast the changes in two regimes. In the first, innovation rent was generated by the introduction and organic growth of electric lighting. The desire to remove the constraints imposed by the absence of natural daylight created a demand which grew continuously as economies of scale reduced input costs. Technological superiority provided the motivation for paradigm shifts, from the luminous flame to the arc discharge and then from the arc to the incandescent filament.

The second case study examined the course of communications engineering as it traversed changes of comparable magnitude. It illustrated the path from historical precursors, based purely on human sensory phenomena, to cable systems made possible by the discovery of basic electro-magnetism and then to radio, which was initially predicted theoretically and, subsequently, demonstrated practically and refined into a working system.

In contrast to electric lighting, the growth of which was limited only by socio-economic considerations, cable and wireless communications were subject to external constraints. Intrinsically, their use transcended national territorial boundaries and required common standards for inter-operability. Transmissions could interfere with one another, so wireless was regulated by diplomatic agreement. Efficient communications had a significant military application. They therefore created a demand, the impact of which varied with the incidence of war and peace. Commercial markets were, for many applications, inelastic, reducing the propensity to reduce input costs by way of economies of scale. For example, a ship would need only one wireless system and, hence, the total market was constrained by the number of ships and could expand only with an increase in maritime activity.

The events examined in the two case studies took place concurrently, permitting the effects of differing microeconomic factors to be highlighted. The paradigm changes were also sufficiently remote in time for them to be examined with an historic perspective, as their consequences are, by now, fully played out. A direct corollary of this, however, is that, as the innovations can only be studied using the information that is currently available, the conclusions clearly lack the insights which can be provided by observation at first hand.

The objective of the third case study was to investigate in greater detail the effect of technological considerations on the dynamics of paradigm shifts. This was achieved by examining a relatively recent, hi-tech innovation, the factors of which are within current experience. During the last fifty years or so there has been an explosive increase in the numbers of learned journals and technical newspapers, so contemporary thinking is well documented. The case study also acquired credibility both from knowledge gained by the author's direct participation in the relevant research and development during the early 1960s and from a personal acquaintance with many of the companies and individuals who were involved with decisions which shaped the industry and guided its transition from parochial to global organisation.

The investigation traced the development of the transistor through its entire Schumpeter A-phase. The example chosen was particularly important because, throughout the period in question, the industry was growing at an average rate of 30 per cent per annum. Initially, the cost of market entry was low but, even in the later stages, the magnitude of this growth meant that the payback time for investment in innovation was short and therefore cost considerations would not greatly inhibit a change of direction if technological indicators suggested that a paradigm shift was the right course to take.

Following the pattern of the two previous case studies, the development of the solid-state amplifier was traced from its nineteenth century origins, through early abortive attempts, to the Nobel prize-winning invention made just before Christmas 1947. The contributions of theoreticians, experimental physicists, materials scientists and applications engineers were documented, together with the battle against technological dragons which appeared to threaten the innovation in its early stages.

Of particular interest was the way in which the physical properties of materials, especially their metallurgy, were characterised and then harnessed to create device topographies with desired electrical parameters. The technology of fabrication techniques underpinned the entire development, but would other factors, notably inventors, patents and communications, have a significant impact? The legacy of the growth of the telephone had created a situation in which the company which fostered the invention of the transistor was constrained by US anti-trust law restrictions and could not exploit the invention directly by manufacture and sale of the components. This provided a unique opportunity to view the impact of competition law at the outset of an innovation, rather than when it has reached maturity, which is the more usual circumstance.

Although the thermionic valve had given good service as an electronic amplifying device since the turn of the century, it had a number of disadvantages. It was based on the physical phenomenon of thermionic emission of electrons which involved heating a cathode to around 1000°C. This process required a relatively large amount of energy and generated a high level of noise in the signals which were to be amplified. The heat also caused the degradation of the electrical characteristics of other components mounted in physical proximity.

The thermionic valve was a device which had a high failure rate. Constructed of fine wires and welded metal plates which were mounted in a geometrically critical relationship in a vacuum-sealed glass bulb, it was not robust. Furthermore, the cathode material exhibited a fall-off in efficiency with the passage of time, which set a finite limit on its service life.

When the transistor arrived it promised the same performance as the valve whilst consuming less than one thousandth of the power. Because the new device generated a much smaller amount of heat, it was potentially more reliable and could be installed in circuits at a much higher packing density. This was facilitated by the fact that it was very small. Mass production would lead to low cost and large volumes of uniform devices. A solid-state amplifier which exhibited these characteristics would therefore rank highly in Schmookler's tests for desired inventions (Schmookler 1966) and its success could be assured.

4.8 INFLUENCES ON THE DEVELOPMENT OF THE SEMICONDUCTOR INDUSTRY

A three-electrode semiconductor amplifying device was first invented in the 1920s by Julius Lilienfeld (Sweet 1988). He proposed device structures which were brought to practical realisation some 30 to 40 years later. His inventions were patented, but not developed commercially because the materials available to him were not capable of sustaining the minority carrier charge flow necessary for viable operation. Although his ideas were soundly based, Lilienfeld did not have the resources or perseverance to push them through to fruition.

Hilsch and Pohl revisited the concept of a solid-state amplifier in the 1940s (Hilsch 1938). They did not succeed because they tried to simulate a thermionic triode structure in an ionic crystal. Although they achieved a measurable current gain, the properties of the materials inhibited operation at frequencies which would have been commercially useful.

Wartime activity, in particular at Purdue University, was responsible for the development of the materials which provided the springboard for the discovery of the transistor effect. Another essential component was the existence of a culture in the Bell Telephone System which permitted the expenditure of substantial funds on a programme of fundamental research. Although such research could conceivably lead to the holy grail of a solid-state replacement for the unreliable thermionic valve, there was no requirement for it to be so targeted.

The Bell Telephone Laboratories were a centre of excellence, and the team which was assembled there was of the highest quality. It was also multi-skilled, including theoretical and applied physicists, chemists, metallurgists and electronic engineers. As befits a major US corporation, it was well briefed legally and performed a thorough job of protecting the intellectual property generated by the research.

Constraints which had arisen from anti-trust actions prevented the Bell System from exploiting the invention of the transistor in the most direct way – by making and selling the devices. An imaginative licensing programme was therefore introduced by seminars, which provided a taster of the significance of the invention. This was followed up by well-organised transfer of know-how to the licensee organisations. Success was further assured by inviting only companies of substance to participate ([1965] RPC 335).

An artificial situation existed initially as an anti-trust consent decree effectively forced Bell to pass on its semiconductor know-how to others. The transfer of know-how was soon reinforced by movement of personnel as Shockley and Teal, who were members of the original team, sought pastures new. Another early influence was Shockley's irascible personality. Scientists and engineers who had joined his Palo Alto start-up, found that he was impossible to work with, and left to create their own companies. This was the beginning of the 'Silicon Valley Effect' – technology transfer through the founding of new companies.

There was a great *cameradie* amongst the Californian semiconductor community, which shared technical knowledge, oblivious to the proprietary nature of the know-how. The semiconductor manufacturers possessed a vast core of technical skills. As soon as a new idea was made public, many rivals were in a position to exploit it, a factor which was confirmed by the short lead-time between seminal patents and daughter inventions. Patents were either cross-licensed or ignored (Cullis 2004, Appendix 1), so the lead-time advantage of innovation was negligible.

Although the first wave of manufacturers was drawn mainly from the ranks of those who made thermionic valves, the predecessor product, by the time the industry was ten years old, many of these had fallen by the wayside and newcomers, such as Texas Instruments and Fairchild, had taken their places. The Not-Invented-Here syndrome was probably playing a significant role.

Market growth of the order of 30 per cent per annum attracted many newcomers to the industry. Cyclic profitability and zero average net profit caused many of them to quit. Market leaders came and went with the introduction of new manufacturing methods.

During the fifteen years after the initial discovery, the dominant manufacturing technology changed every three to four years. The point contact electrode was superseded by the grown junction, which was more robust. The alloyed junction, which followed, reduced manufacturing waste and parasitic collector resistance. Silicon replaced germanium to make devices less sensitive to the effects of high temperatures, whilst the associated double-diffusion and mesa etching processes gave much better high-frequency performance. Planar surface passivation techniques introduced long-term stability and permitted the use of plastic encapsulation. Finally the materials processing technique of epitaxial deposition gave rise to flexibility in device topography and presaged the fabrication of complex integrated circuits.

Advances in device technology were governed by properties of materials and the materials scientists and metallurgists were the unsung heroes who made the industry viable (Petritz 1962). Silicon took over from germanium partly because it had a wider band gap, but mainly because it had a stable glassy oxide which provided surface passivation and immunity to contamination. Alloyed junction transistors were predominantly *pnp* devices, despite the fact that electron mobility was of the order of three times that of hole mobility, because indium, an acceptor dopant, was ductile and alloyed readily with germanium. Complementary *n*-type dopants, antimony and arsenic, were brittle and volatile at alloying temperatures. They had to be used in conjunction with an inert metal carrier such as lead, which did not wet the surface of germanium as well as indium did. The post-alloy-diffused transistor was made possible because donor impurities had higher diffusivities than acceptors, whereas the segregation coefficients, which were important for alloying, were higher with the *p*-type dopants. Gallium arsenide, a material which had a wider band gap and higher minority carrier mobility than silicon, both desirable characteristics from a device fabrication viewpoint, did not supersede it because it was difficult to fabricate from its volatile components. Eutectic bonding processes, such as bird-beak and nail-head or ball bonding, used for external lead attachment were a serendipitous consequence of the metallurgy of gold and aluminium. (A counter-influence, which caused many catastrophic failures until its mechanism was well understood, was 'purple plague', a brittle, non-conducting intermetallic compound of gold and aluminium which formed at high temperatures.)

The commercial potential of the transistor was apparent, even before a practical implementation was developed. It was a salesman's dream – a product capable of satisfying a huge latent need. In the early days, when the volume of sales was low, the cost of market entry was commensurate. Potential participants either possessed the skills and equipment necessary, or could acquire them with very little outlay. Later, as markets increased in size, specialist equipment suppliers emerged and device manufacturers relinquished in-house equipment construction. The industry was a technological meritocracy. Companies with the most efficient processes succeeded; those which did not adapt to change, went to the wall.

The transistor and the *pn*-junction diode were the mainstream components of the semiconductor paradigm, as the thermionic triode and diode had been during the first age of electronics. Other thermionic and gas discharge devices also had their semiconductor analogues. Thus the thyristor was the equivalent of the thyratron, whilst the unijunction transistor and the four-layer diode played the role of the gas discharge tubes. The vertical junction field-effect transistor was able to mimic the electrical characteristics of the pentode valve and the zener diode provided a voltage reference, as did the neon tube in valve circuits. The existence of so many comparable devices is indicative of the methodology of circuit design during the genesis of the semiconductor industry. The general approach was to attempt to translate the equivalent valve circuit by substitution of an appropriate semiconductor component. It was not until the invention of the integrated circuit and the move from analogue to digital electronics that engineers truly began to think in new terms.

4.9 CONCLUSIONS FROM THE THIRD CASE STUDY

As with the electric light and cable and wireless communications, the technological origins of the transistor may be traced to discoveries made some fifty to a hundred years earlier. Again, like the light and cable and wireless, it was invented at least twice before its time. The transistor finally got off the ground, mainly as a result of wartime research which produced new and suitable materials, but also due to the assembly of a polytechnic team of scientists of the highest calibre – analogous to Edison's laboratory at Menlo Park – by a company which allocated sufficient resources to a management which, in turn, had the creative vision to see the project through to a successful conclusion.

The transistor was developed as a result of a well-directed, broadly-based investigation, which was carried out from first principles by a high-calibre, multi-disciplinary team. The discovery of the point-contact transistor effect was a chance consequence of rigorous, comprehensive and thorough experimental procedure, but it provided a huge fillip to the project. The team leader, William Shockley, had developed the theoretical basis for the transistor over a long period of time and was annoyed when Bardeen and Brattain stole his thunder with the fortunate discovery, but the cognitive dissonance which this engendered resulted in the conception of a viable alternative by Shockley.

Production versions of the point-contact transistor were based on existing, well-established diode manufacturing technology developed in war time to provide radar detectors based on the early wireless 'cats' whisker', but they were soon replaced by the first junction transistors which were fabricated by a brute-force method and, like Edison's tar-putty incandescent lamp, were little more than a proof of the concept. This was, however, sufficient to stimulate enthusiastic work on circuit applications. As with the metallic incandescent-filament lamp, many major paradigm shifts came from without and were based on combinations of materials with felicitous physical, metallurgical and electrical properties.

The use of single crystal material rather than the polycrystalline germanium which was more readily available for the development work was an early, informed decision based on theoretical principles. Materials were chosen and their properties orchestrated to construct device topographies yielding desired electrical characteristics. Manufacturing paradigm shifts were the mechanism by which this procedure was optimised.

The key to the successful initial development of the transistor was a polytechnic research team. Contributions were often made by scientists from different disciplines bringing their particular heritage as a contribution to the feast. Materials scientists, chemists and metallurgists made major breakthroughs but received scant praise for their efforts. Many technological barriers were surmounted *ad hoc* as they were encountered. This did not require unduly creative thinking, merely meticulous attention to detail and mastery of the underlying scientific principles.

The combination of many companies, employing strong R&D teams and enjoying free exchange of information, meant that new advances could potentially come from any quarter. If successful, they would rapidly be adopted universally. Some new paradigms offered the prospect of commercial advantage but, after a brief period of exploitation by the single company that introduced them, they were abandoned and that company reverted to the technological roadmap being followed by the remainder of the industry. Not all technologically elegant solutions proved to be commercially viable. However, due to the underlying economic growth pattern of the industry, it was possible to try them and then abandon them if they were unsuccessful.

Electronic circuit applications for the new transistor expanded rapidly as new fabrication techniques yielded devices with ever improved characteristics. The result of the impact of the classic cash-flow J-curve associated with technological paradigm shifts was cyclic profitability and zero or negative average net profit. This caused many participants to quit – market growth of the order of 30 per cent per annum, easy access to know-how and low cost of market entry in the early days attracted many newcomers to the industry. Market leaders came and went with the introduction of new manufacturing methods. Research and development were also stimulated because the military potential of the new development attracted a large provision of funds by the US government.

The most obvious choice of materials for device manufacture, from the point of view of desirable electrical characteristics, was often *not* adopted because alternatives were either easier to fabricate or produced devices which exhibited greater reliability. Silicon, which became the universal material of choice for the mainstream semiconductor industry, was a compromise based on these alternative considerations.

As experience increased, opportunities evolved from threats. For instance, 'deathnium', which destroyed many early transistors, was found to be caused by deep-trap impurities introduced by contamination in the processing apparatus, and the property was harnessed to make faster switching transistors for computers. Planar integrated circuits arose from treatment of a threat (formation of a surface oxide layer to counteract pollution) as an opportunity (use of the oxide layer as support for interconnections). This methodology was applied twice in one company – Fairchild – which, as a consequence, became the dominant company in the industry.

The subject chosen for this case study provided a particularly apt example of change for technological reasons in the Schumpeter A-phase because there was always a strong demand for the end product and an extremely high rate of growth, year on year, which meant that the payback from paradigm shifts was quick and mistakes could be abandoned without significant penalty. Change was also facilitated by formal and informal exchange of know-how within the industry.

This case study also provided a unique example of the influence of competition law at the start of a new development rather than when it is mature (which is the usual situation). Because a Consent Decree was already in force when the transistor was invented, Bell Laboratories were forced to license all comers. To generate income, they provided know-how to permit the licensees to become established in the new industry. Potentially, this could have resulted in a completely different evolutionary characteristic because the sanction was applied from the outset. However, in the long run, the market leaders which emerged were those companies which were responsible for significant paradigm shifts. In the absence of this competition law influence, these actual market leaders may well have been different, but the overall structure of the industry would, in all probability, have been the same, because it was determined by innovations which offered a technological advance. New innovations came from without, possibly as a result of the 'Not-Invented-Here' syndrome. Absence of response-time monopolies, which would have permitted the advantages of technological paradigm shifts to be pressed home, and freedom-to-use paranoia, together with technological lead-times which were shorter than patent-granting procedures and therefore negated the effect of intersecting patent monopolies, allowed competitors to play 'catch-up' in characteristic oligopolistic fashion.

Ultimately, the universal adoption of planar diffusion and epitaxial deposition manufacturing techniques, and the transition from discrete devices to integrated circuits, marked the end of the gestation of the semiconductor industry. By this time the thermionic valve precursor was effectively dead, surviving in only a few niche applications and in price-sensitive markets where it still offered a financial advantage because it was a mature product and all costs had been fully amortised. The next springboard was very large scale integration (VLSI), the so-called silicon chip, which was the subject of the fourth case study.

4.10　THE SILICON CHIP

The development of the transistor in the middle of the twentieth century provided an example of innovation in its Schumpeter A-phase. By the beginning of the 1960s, however, its manufacturing process had stabilised – epitaxial deposition of semiconductor materials and planar diffusion of dopants were used universally for device fabrication. The concept of the integrated circuit had been demonstrated to be feasible. The path of development was clear. New devices would, for the foreseeable future, continue to become smaller and their complexity would increase (Moore's Law). As a result, unit costs would decrease and this would permit electronics-based industries to expand.

The final case study followed what may be regarded as the Schumpeter B-phase of the transistor, the development of the silicon integrated circuit, exemplified by the progress of the bell-wether company, Intel, which was responsible for the introduction of semiconductor-based memory circuits for computers and the microprocessor – two major innovations which resulted in massive expansion of the global economy.

The review started with the setting up of the company at a time when the manufacturing technologies were well-established industry standards. It followed Intel through the travails of free competition and marked the key events on the path to becoming industry leader. Initially, many companies – Texas Instruments, Fairchild, Motorola, Signetics, ITT and Philips are just a random selection – possessed the potential and the will to succeed in the industry. One by one they fell by the wayside on the path to the summit, as did the many individual entrepreneurs who participated in the development of the incandescent lamp.

Although many of the factors which contributed to Intel's success may be regarded as felicitous, the case study highlighted how chance events were turned to advantage by the 'prepared mind' of its management. Of particular note were the initial use of scarce resources, the treatment of threats as opportunities, the creation of luck, the transformation of finances, the change in utilisation of intellectual property rights, the exploitation of the legal process and the adroit political management of competition law.

4.11 CONCLUSIONS FROM THE FOURTH CASE STUDY

The development of very large scale integrated (VLSI) circuits was the inevitable consequence of Jean Hoerni's invention of the planar process and Bob Noyce's development of etched metallic film interconnections. As with many major breakthroughs, the basic ideas were also identified by others – notably Frosch and Derick at Bell Labs – but the successful company was the one which pushed them through to a logical conclusion. The received wisdom was to etch away the oxide diffusion mask. Fairchild left it on as a surface passivating layer.

There *were* changes in the fabrication technologies during the Schumpeter B-phase. Processes such as ion implantation and molecular beam epitaxy provided greater precision in the placing of impurities in the semiconductor wafers, but they achieved, in essence, the same end result as the less-refined, early processes of thermal diffusion and chemical vapour deposition. The principal economic consequences resulted from new applications of these fabrication technologies, notably to the memory cell and the microprocessor.

The personal computer was an obvious application of the microprocessor, but it was of major importance because it permitted bipedal advance. New software could be developed on old processors and migrated easily when a new processor was introduced, giving the innovation an immediate user base. Bill Gates succeeded because he was in the right place at the right time, listening to the emissaries of IBM and *not* flying his aeroplane over San Francisco bay, the distraction of his rival Gary Kildall.

Intel was founded by entrepreneurial characters who were not content to work for others. It set out to provide a product which the market needed (semiconductor memory). As with the incandescent lamp and the transistor, the decision to go for a latent market created by an alternative, but flawed, technology made the success of the memory chip inevitable, provided the product could be made satisfactorily. Backing three horses to be sure of being first to the winning post was the successful strategy adopted by Intel.

Its first leap forward was the dynamic random-access memory (DRAM) memory chip, the result of an enlightened trade-off – the addition of a cheap power supply gave an order of magnitude performance improvement. Another chip used by early computers, the electrically programmable read-only memory (EPROM), on the other hand, was the serendipitous recognition of the opportunities offered by a physical effect. The opportunity was, however, a manifestation of Pasteur's prepared mind syndrome, since both the initial discovery and the later development were identified as a result of painstaking investigation. The microprocessor, like the integrated circuit, was a logical extrapolation of a proven product (the DEC PDP-8 computer) – make it smaller, make it in one piece. The skill lay in reducing the idea to practice and this was driven by the need to make best use of scarce resources.

The success of Intel was founded on the lucky choice of its hybrid 8/16-bit 8088 microprocessor to power the first IBM PC. However, this was an example of the successful making their own good luck. The reason that the 8088 was chosen was that the necessary 8-bit peripheral chips were readily available and the next-generation 16-bit processor (the 8086) was already in prospect.

By definition, start-up companies are starved of resources. Intel lacked a cash cow which was sufficiently fruitful to meet the demands of the expansion engendered by the runaway success of the IBM PC. Fortunately IBM was in a position to play fairy godmother by taking an equity stake at the appropriate time. Fortunately, also, IBM was so frightened by the prospect of anti-trust proceedings that it failed to exact the full price of exclusivity, which it could reasonably have demanded.

Recognition of when to quit is an important component in achieving commercial maturity – Intel left the memory chip market when it became unprofitable and very quickly abandoned a foray into digital watches. Another reason that Intel succeeded was because it made full use of the legal process. Like the politicians who rejected Edison's vote counter, it recognised the importance of delay, which, for Intel, amplified the effects of response-time monopoly. Like Edison, too, Intel was not afraid to hit below the belt if that would achieve an appropriate result. The name of the game was domination and legal filibustering was one of the tools available. Intellectual property monopolies were another. *Sui generis* rights were created by exerting the right political influence. Market power coupled with the characteristics of the learning curve was used to control the cash flow of competitors and maintain a quasi-stable monopoly indefinitely.

However, either timidity engendered by lack of confidence or possibly naïvety regarding intellectual property matters in a start-up organisation resulted in failure to establish a dominant patent position with memory circuit chips. The consequence was that competition increased, these products became commodities and the markets ceased to yield viable returns. With the microprocessor, Intel failed to establish the absolute monopoly that patents would have provided. In that case, it succeeded because it won a captive market which would be created and supported by IBM. George Westinghouse laid the foundations for Tesla's alternating current machines in an analogous manner.

A positive management decision to go for a market- rather than a production-led approach resulted in the creation of a legacy-system evolutionary model, which maintained Intel's initial hold and locked customers into its products. This tactic, which was embraced as a result of failure of a proposed ground-breaking product to meet a critical development timetable, was supplemented by a willingness to exploit the legal process to enhance response-time delays, thereby emasculating competitors by controlling their cash flow. Not until the industry was well established did Intel turn to the use of patents and trade marks to reinforce its control of the market. It did, however, exhibit a prudent and opportunistic political attitude. It lobbied effectively to obtain enactment of *sui generis* intellectual property rights (semiconductor mask protection legislation) and, whilst its predatory techniques in the market place were not dissimilar to those of Microsoft, it reacted in a conciliatory manner and compromised with the authorities on anti-trust matters, whereas Microsoft was more confrontational and became involved in major litigation with the US Justice Department. It is too early to say whether this difference will have any long-term effect, but it did, in the short term, conserve resources and allow Intel's management to concentrate on the primary role of developing the business.

Intel succeeded because of the 'hare and tortoise' syndrome. Success comes not to those who make rapid advance, necessitating a fresh start each time, but to those who make an incremental change and build on an existing foundation – like Newton standing on the shoulders of giants. To some, the decision to make each generation a superset of its predecessor was reactionary, but for Intel it delivered a core of users who could be up and running immediately.

The rise of Intel was largely a matter of luck, albeit supplemented by a responsive and sometimes cynical management whose decisions, on balance, proved to be correct more often than they were wrong.

The case study demonstrated that the path of evolution of the industry was determined by specific events. The progress would clearly have been different without the influence of IBM, or if Intel had used patents to establish a monopoly over memory chips and the microprocessor.

Under the current paradigm, Moore's Law serves as a predictor of the growth of the semiconductor industry, but other factors will increasingly come into play. At present Keynesian influences drive suppliers along the path of technological development. Eventually, physical parameters, such as the magnitude of the charge on a single electron and optical limits on the ability of lithography to produce even smaller feature sizes, will provide an endpoint to further increases in packing density (Wong 2005). As time passes, economic constraints, due to escalating costs of plant for new generation products, will exert greater influence.

The case studies presented an overview of different aspects of the dynamics of innovation. The first and second provided contrasting perspectives of evolution over a relatively large period of time and under changing macroeconomic influences, whilst the third and fourth gave an insight into the differences between the Schumpeter A- and B-phase of a common innovation. The following chapters will extract the evolutionary elements and examine them in greater detail.

5. The Nature and Process of Invention

'There are no inventions,' he was wont to say, 'without a pedigree.' Critically examined and analysed, an invention is seen to be a derivative and composite thing, the result of successive and progressive accretions of knowledge. It may seem invidious, therefore, to single out any one person alone for the credit of an invention such as the 'carbon process' or the incandescent electric lamp. From the practical point of view, however, the essential requirement of an invention is its utility. In a certain sense no invention which involves an addition to previously existing knowledge can be said to be wholly useless. The failures of unsuccessful inventors often make admirable stepping-stones for those who come after. Nevertheless, an invention which fails to achieve the purpose for which it is designed, and so fails to provide the public with any useful addition to existing appliances (other than a 'stepping-stone') sinks not unnaturally into comparative oblivion, and it is the later experimenter, shrewdly perceiving the cause of failure in the work of his predecessors, and ingeniously discovering and providing the necessary additions or corrections to remedy the defect, who is usually and fairly entitled to the credit of the invention.
Sir Joseph Swan, *Sir Joseph Wilson Swan F.R.S.*, M.E. Swan and K.R. Swan, p30

Our software is fragile as well – if people built houses the way we write programs, the first woodpecker would wipe out civilisation.
Dennis Hall, quoted by Clifford Stoll in *The Cuckoo's Egg*

5.1 INTRODUCTION

The case studies (Cullis 2004) provided an empirical record of innovation under a variety of circumstances. In the following chapters, the individual factors are analysed to determine how they contribute to the final picture.

One element which might be expected to exert a fundamental influence is the process of conception of the invention, with the magnitude of the innovation rent exhibiting a degree of correlation with the nature of invention *per se*.

The characteristics of invention are not uniform. They may be classified by the magnitude of their interaction with the environment, by their origins and by the nature and timing of their inception. Schumpeter identified two stages of innovation – a preliminary step in which major changes take place, followed by a period of consolidation during which the innovation is refined. Invention in the Schumpeter's initial or A-phase is sporadic and may not be the product of macroeconomic influences, whereas the incidence of inventions in the B-phase will be more predictable since they will be the result of attempts to improve efficiency to maximise profits.

This chapter looks at the nature of inventions *per se* and of the corresponding innovation rents which they produce. It selects inventions from the case studies and separates them into different categories according to the mechanics of the process involved in their conception and then analyses their relative contribution to the subsequent economic development. The spectrum of inventions ranges from those dependent on pure chance on the one hand to those which arise from a carefully worked out theory at the other extreme. It may be postulated that each type will be characterised by an associated probability of occurrence and success.

5.2 CATEGORIES OF INVENTION

One scheme of classifying inventions would be according to the magnitude and character of the step they represent over their precursors. Such an analysis would take as its starting point the heroic or seminal invention, exemplified by the carbon filament lamp, the thermionic valve, the transistor and the microprocessor, since innovations of this nature are major stepping stones in the progress of techno-economic evolution. In this schema, seminal inventions are followed by a succession of derived inventions as the inventive mind is applied to refining the methods of manufacture, employing such techniques as value engineering to attain greater efficiency by reduction in the input costs or the use of new materials with improved properties. As production ramps up, economies of scale will also add their associated benefits.

What is the consequence of innovation? As a result of the invention of the incandescent lamp people were active for a greater proportion of the day; after the introduction of the valve, they communicated more; demand for computers rose from the total world market of five envisaged in the 1940s by Thomas Watson, Senior, President of International Business Machines, to one per desk when the invention of the microprocessor followed the introduction of the large-scale integrated circuit. Clearly, a major effect of innovation is an overall growth in consumption.

In addition to the magnitude of the prospective innovation rent, a significant determinant to be considered is the associated uncertainty. This will help to determine potential success, since it will influence the propensity of suppliers of capital to invest in a project. With many unknown factors, the risk associated with innovation will be high.

When the incandescent lamp was first developed, the characteristics of the carbon filaments were unpredictable. It was necessary to measure each one and ascertain the supply voltage for which it would be suitable, as many would fail at voltages well below the 100 volts at which electricity was delivered from the power station (Bright 1949). In modern production, testing at an early stage, associated with a demand for well-defined properties from materials suppliers, means that the coiled-coil tungsten filament lamp, which is the present-day successor of the carbon filament lamp, is produced to a predetermined specification, with very few failing to meet the required standard. The first junction transistors exhibited low current gains and transition frequencies (f_T) (Morton 1952). This was a consequence of the long charge-carrier drift distance between the collector and emitter electrodes. Desired high-gain, high-f_T devices were selected, at low yields, from the overall production spread. Later, when the planar process was developed, the physical geometry of the device was much more precisely defined. The electrical properties improved, and yields of the high-performance ones increased immeasurably. These examples confirm that early products are variable in characteristics. As a result, the magnitude of the prospective innovation rent is more uncertain in the initial phase but more accurately quantifiable later. It is therefore difficult to rationalise the decision to innovate which may, in many cases, be considered as an act of faith or a leap in the dark.

Seminal inventions are a source of economic growth rather than the product of it. They tend to be associated with the Schumpeter A-phase of an innovation, when volume of production is low. Derived inventions, on the other hand, follow later, when volume has increased. They arise as a consequence of economic pressures and their rate of growth is limited by factors outside the immediate control of their producers.

5.3 THE NEED TO CREATE AN INFRASTRUCTURE

All industrial production has an infrastructure associated with it. The supply of petroleum implies the existence of refineries, a transport system to carry the product to the consumer, a knowledge of geology and geophysical techniques to find the sources of crude oil, and so on. Although it might be expected that some innovations could build on the infrastructure of their precursors, others, particularly where there is a major advance, will require the infrastructure to be developed as the innovation moves forward. Problems associated with the creation of the infrastructure will have to be solved, and this will limit the rate of progress of the primary innovation.

Whilst the existence of artificial lighting by means of the luminous flame and the electric arc had already created a latent demand, and commercial sales of these products provided a benchmark pricing structure, the means of production and distribution of the carbon filament lamp, and even devices for measurement of consumption (electricity meters), had to be built up from scratch (Cullis 2004, Case Study 1). Edison, in keeping with his character, decided to do everything himself – the precursor to the technique of vertical integration, a philosophy still practised by General Electric, his successor company, at the middle of the twentieth century. Although this did not appear to slow down the introduction of incandescent lighting significantly, it curtailed his work on the electric railway simply because he was unable to devote sufficient time to the latter project. Swan, on the other hand, as his 1883 lighting catalogue shows (Cullis 2004, Appendix 5), was content to rely on a network of independent suppliers, a concept which is manifest today in the Japanese system of *keiretsu*. Since these suppliers would benefit from the innovation rents associated with infrastructure development, they were prepared to devote resources to this activity. It is a remarkable observation, and a tribute to the nineteenth century economy, that the gestation of the electricity industry took less than a decade.

At the outset, the thermionic valve was simply an incandescent lamp with an additional metal plate attached to a lead-in wire which protruded through the glass envelope (Fleming 1924). It was produced by lamp manufacturers using the same plant and skills as were required to produce lamps. There were, however, no established markets for the product. Wireless telegraphy was in its infancy and was essentially an experimental technique. User demand was therefore limited by extraneous factors outside the control of the valve suppliers. Radio telephony depended on the ability to amplify small electrical signals. It arose as a serendipitous consequence of the invention of the triode valve by Lee de Forest, who was attempting to make a more sensitive detector for the signals sent out by spark transmitters (de Forest 1950). The developments of the device and its applications were symbiotic – improvements in device characteristics gave rise to new applications, whilst increased production made it feasible to develop new variants or select those with optimal characteristics. Because the markets were new, they were dependent on the establishment of changes in consumer practices – communication by telephone rather than by telegram and messenger boy, broadcasting of concerts by radio rather than physical attendance at the concert hall.

These examples confirm that manufacture of a new artefact or the introduction of a new process is invariably associated with the creation of an appropriate infrastructure. The need to create this infrastructure will have a Keynesian effect on the overall returns from an invention, although the innovation rents of the infrastructure providers must be financed from those of the primary innovators. This effect is much more marked in the case of seminal inventions since the infrastructure exhibits a greater departure from its antecedents than that of a derived invention. The more infrastructure creation that is necessary, the slower will be the introduction of an innovation, since more processes will be introduced serially into the critical path.

5.4 THE SOURCES OF INVENTION

Another method of classifying inventions is by reference to their origin. Each type will have its associated probabilities of occurrence and success.

5.4.1 Invention by Chance Observation and Deduction – Serendipitous Invention

The least predictable innovations will clearly be those which arise purely through good fortune. It follows that the outcome of such innovations will also be uncertain. However, it is feasible that if an inventor knows what he is looking for, he will have a greater success rate. Furthermore, if this reasoning is taken a step further, he can also improve his chances by knowing *where* to look.

Edison was an empiricist. Whilst he was engaged in the development of apparatus for automatic transmission and reception of telegraphic communications, he connected a stylus from his automatic telegraph to a speaker which he had developed for the telephone. He shouted into the latter as the stylus traversed a band of waxed paper, creating indentations. When the stylus passed over these indentations again, a recognisable sound was emitted by the speaker. Edison realised that this phenomenon could form the basis of recording and reproducing sound and set to work to turn the crude response into a viable system (Cullis 2004, Case Study 1).

During the development of the incandescent lamp, Edison happened to drop a screwdriver on to the carbon filament. He observed that this particular lamp glowed more brightly. He applied this lesson and subsequently distorted filaments in the same way to increase their luminous efficiency.

Early glow lamps relied on the presence of a high vacuum to prevent attrition of the filament by 'air washing'. However, incandescent carbon has a relatively high vapour pressure and sublimes to form a deposit on the inside of the glass envelope. Upton and Edison noticed that the filament cast a shadow, a region where there was no deposit. By experimenting with a metal electrode, Edison discovered that he was able to pass a current through the vacuum in one direction, but not the other. He could not, however, envisage an application for the effect, other than the obvious one of measurement of electric current (for which there was already a more efficient electromagnetic instrument in existence). John Ambrose Fleming, the scientific adviser to his British lighting company, performed an experimental characterisation of these Edison-effect bulbs, and presented papers describing his results (Fleming 1883, Fleming 1896). He did not utilise the discovery immediately but realised its potential some twenty years later, when he encountered the problem of constructing a sensitive detector for wireless signals (Fleming 1924). This was just one of a number of significant inventions which were within Edison's grasp but which he failed to recognise. With the Black Box and the Grasshopper telegraph, he was on the verge of development of wireless communication; he patented a frame-sequential technique which would have given a viable system of colour cinematography (Cullis 2004, Case Study 1). He was extremely focused and would concentrate on the task in hand to the exclusion of all others. For this reason, and also because he was an empiricist and thus did not take many of his ideas to their logical conclusion, he missed opportunities which were subsequently identified and exploited by others.

Whilst experimenting with an electrolytic detector for radio waves, Lee de Forest noticed that his spark transmitter caused a dimming of the Welsbach gas mantle by the light of which he was working (Cullis 2004, Appendix 8). This phenomenon proved to be an acoustic artefact of the ambient environment in which he performed his experiments, but it set him off on an investigation which commenced by inserting two platinum electrodes into a Bunsen flame. He found that this acted as a detector for radio waves. Following the lead of Fleming's work on the Edison Effect, he constructed a two-electrode 'relay valve' based on a similar structure. Further experiments with the Bunsen flame revealed that a third electrode would enhance the detection efficiency, so he decided to determine whether a similar advantage could be obtained with a device based on the incandescent filament lamp. This device became the three-electrode Audion and was, at first, used merely as a sensitive detector. It was not until 1911-1912, some five years later, that its amplifying properties were recognised by von Lieben and Armstrong and it became the foundation of the electronics industry.

John Bardeen and Walter Brattain were members of a team working on the characterisation of semiconductors. When investigating the properties of germanium, they pressed a metal point on to the surface of the crystal, surrounded it with a drop of glycol borate and found that an electrical potential applied between the semiconductor and the electrolyte could control the current flowing from the germanium to the point electrode (Bardeen 1956). In a variant of the experiment, two closely spaced metallic points were applied to the germanium surface and amplification by the transistor effect was observed for the first time. The point-contact transistor, which was the immediate outcome of these experiments, was a fragile device and an inefficient amplifier, but it provided a huge stimulus which led to the development of the junction transistor and subsequently the integrated circuit.

Silicon is an elemental semiconductor with a band gap of 1.1eV. It forms a stable, glassy oxide, which acts as a barrier to the diffusion of impurities and creates a passivation layer on the surface of a crystal. Germanium, on the other hand, although it has a higher charge carrier mobility, does not form such an oxide. (Germania, GeO_2, is unstable in the presence of water.) In consequence, silicon rather than germanium became the semiconductor of choice for the fabrication of transistors and integrated circuits.

Serendipitous inventions may arise at any time. The talent lies in recognising their significance and nurturing them to fruition. In Pasteur's words, 'Fortune favours the prepared mind' but heroic inventors do not necessarily recognise heroic inventions. Although serendipitous inventions are sporadic in their appearance, the development of the transistor, for example, was the predictable outcome of setting a highly qualified team to work on the problem and giving them appropriate resources to carry out the task.

5.4.2 Practical Embodiment of Theoretical Principles

Another way of inventing is by application of thought and logic. The process begins with analysis and de-construction of a problem. The solution is conceived by application of existing and, possibly, new techniques. Finally, theory is put into practice by fabrication of a working embodiment.

It will be difficult to identify minor inventions which arise in this way because *ex post facto* examination will not be able to distinguish them from inventions derived by other methodologies. Major, theoretically derived inventions are likely to be rare because they will require a commensurately great intellect to identify and solve problems of great magnitude.

One example of a theoretically derived invention was when Tesla, as a young man in Budapest, developed a theory of electrical machines operated by alternating current (O'Neill 1944). He conceived generators for polyphase currents, and motors which could be driven by them. He devised high-voltage systems for the efficient transmission of power over large distances, a practice that was not possible with the direct current systems which were then in common use. When finance was eventually forthcoming (organised by A.K. Brown of Western Union), he designed transformers which were needed to perform the conversion between high and low voltage.

He read a paper describing his experiments before the American Institute of Electrical Engineers and, as a result, was approached by George Westinghouse, who had plans to exploit the new proposals. Westinghouse purchased Tesla's patents for $1m and set him to work for a year to bring the prototypes into a form suitable for production.

Another example is found in the development of the transistor. Whilst Bardeen and Brattain were investigating the surface of semiconductor materials, Shockley was studying the theory of conduction in crystalline structures. Between New Year's Eve 1947 and the end of January 1948, he devised the original junction transistor, although a practical working embodiment was not constructed for another two years (Shockley 1976).

Shockley's invention was part of a process directed at harnessing knowledge derived from practical observations and experiment. It also built on existing understanding of the theory of solids. Tesla's work, on the other hand, was derived from a more abstract consideration of the mathematics of the interaction between a magnetic field and a changing current flowing in a conductor. An invention conceived from theoretical principles may thus arise sporadically or it may be part of a logical train of development. Great inventions require the agency of correspondingly heroic inventors.

5.4.3 Invention by Extrapolation

An invention is a latent event awaiting its genetic stimulus. The development which represents the smallest step is an improvement invention. Such an invention can be devised by following an innovation from its origins and posing the question 'What is the next logical step?' This is the lowest common denominator, possibly even below the minimum level that the courts will accept in their test of patentability. Since the quantum of invention is small, the frequency of occurrence of innovations which result from extrapolations may be expected to be great. By corollary, the rents obtained from them will reflect their cost and will also be small.

Edison's original carbon filaments were prepared by rolling out a tar putty, made from lamp black and syrup, into a thread-like format ([1886] RPC 167). Whilst they demonstrated the feasibility of using carbon as a 'burner', the method would never have been amenable to mass production due to lack of consistency. Other raw materials which would give rise to the same end result were sought. Initially, cardboard, in the shape of a horse-shoe and, subsequently, thinly shaved bamboo fibres were used in the production versions of the lamp. Greater uniformity in the initial components was reflected in the properties of the final product.

The spacing of the carbons of the early arc lamps was adjusted manually. Staite, Petrie and other workers devised ever more elaborate clockwork mechanisms to perform this task mechanically, whilst Archerau employed an electromagnet to introduce a control loop into the process (Jarvis 1955a).

By mounting a second grid between the control grid and the anode in the triode valve, manufacturers were able to reduce the inter-electrode capacitance which inhibited performance at high frequencies. The penalty for this improvement was susceptibility to secondary emission – electrons, accelerated by the high field created by the new screen grid, struck the anode with sufficient force to cause the generation of a spurious electron current (Hull 1916). Using the principle underlying operation of the screen grid (local application of a potential to change the electric field profile in the path of the main electron beam), Philips's engineers inserted a further grid (the suppressor grid) between the screen grid and the anode and reduced the potential gradient in the vicinity of the anode by connecting this new grid to the cathode ([1933] RPC 333). This principle was also applied to the triode-heptode valve which was used for the oscillator-mixer stage in a superheterodyne radio receiver.

In a further development, the control grid was constructed in the form of a helix with a progressively variable pitch. This endowed the valve with a transconductance which could be controlled by the direct-current bias voltage applied between the cathode and control grid, thus making it amenable to automatic gain control in radio frequency amplifier circuits. These examples illustrate the rule that invention by extrapolation does not require a large inventive step. Indeed it is a progression which follows from consideration of the physical principles on which the original product or process was based.

5.4.4 Topological Manipulation

Certain innovations depend for their properties on the geometry of the components of which they are constructed. An inventor, with a thorough grasp of the relationships of the physical principles involved, should be able to modify the layout of the components and use the underlying characteristics to achieve different effects. This topological manipulation will only be possible in a limited number of instances. It will also require inventors with a particular aptitude.

The first fluorescent lamps were constructed using glass tubing coated internally with phosphorescent material which was stimulated to emit visible radiation by ultra-violet light generated in a low-pressure mercury plasma discharge. The tubes were typically around 40mm in diameter and between 450mm and 2400mm in length. Having an electrode at each end, they were unwieldy and provided a constraint on the architecture of the locations in which they were installed. When modern, so-called low-energy lamps were devised, they relied on the same principle for generation of visible radiation, but the tubes were much smaller and were bent back on themselves into a U-shape to permit contiguous mounting of the power-supply electrodes. This allowed the lamps to be installed using the same connectors and fittings which were employed for incandescent lamps. This factor was extremely important in ensuring their commercial acceptance, since they could be used simply as a plug-in replacement for existing incandescent lamps.

The author devised a transistor for flip-chip mounting by positioning all three of the electrodes on the same surface of the semiconductor wafer (GB Pat 1015588). In order to make an ohmic contact for the collector electrode, a low resistivity region was formed in a high-resistivity epitaxial layer by means of the diffusion process which was used to create the emitter electrode. By modifying the photolithographic mask design and performing the collector contact diffusion during the base diffusion stage, a flip-chip four-layer switching device was constructed (GB Pat 1039915).

Topological manipulation is a variant of extrapolation which may be utilised in the case of artefacts, the properties of which are determined by their physical layout. Its conception involves a certain degree of lateral thinking but, for a suitably trained mind, this does not present a significant difficulty.

5.4.5 Product Extension

Another variant of extrapolation is product extension. This is exemplified by the development of the bipolar junction transistor, a three-electrode device formed in a unitary body of an elemental semiconductor in which two regions of the crystalline body, extrinsically doped with substitutional impurities of one conductivity type, were separated by a thin layer extrinsically doped with substitutional impurities of the opposite conductivity type. Semiconductor device researchers also found that regions of a semiconductor body, accessed by ohmic contacts, behaved like resistors, whilst inversely biased *pn* junctions exhibited the characteristics of a voltage-dependent capacitor. Jack Kilby of Texas Instruments proposed, in 1958, that several of these simulated components should be combined, first as separate interconnected dice in a single encapsulation, and later, as manufacturing skills improved, as a monolithic block of semiconductor, to form an integrated circuit (US Pat 3138743).

At about the same time, Bob Noyce and Jean Hoerni of Fairchild developed the planar diffusion process to form contiguous regions of opposite extrinsic conductivity type, having a passivated surface and metallisation overlaying the insulator for external contacts (US Pats 2981877, 3025589). At that time, a number of manufacturers realised practical versions of the epitaxial deposition process which had been proposed earlier by Gordon Teal (Cullis 2004, Case Study 3). The combination of these new processes made the fabrication of more complex devices feasible.

Improved photolithography and clean-room facilities led to large-scale integration (LSI), the microprocessor and the memory chip. Successive iterations, with increased packing density and smaller component element geometry, permitted the manufacture of the computer on a chip and similarly complex devices.

Using the methodology of product extension, once a problem is posed, the solution is usually apparent.

5.4.6 Invention by Analogy

Yet another variant of invention by extrapolation is invention by analogy. This will demand knowledge and skills beyond those possessed by the run-of-the-mill inventor, since it requires the ability to translate a problem to a different framework.

Walter Nernst was working on the theory of light emission from the Welsbach gas mantle when he devised his lamp (Fürst 1926). The original version was simply an electrical analogue of his mentor's ideas. In the gas mantle, a cotton carrier was impregnated with rare earth and alkali metal oxides and heated to incandescence by a non-luminous flame. The fragile structure was protected by a transparent glass enclosure. In Nernst's lamp, a rod of metal oxides was heated by the passage of an electric current. In this structure, too, the fragile assembly was protected by a transparent glass enclosure.   The metallic oxides used for the radiator had a negative temperature coefficient of resistance.   The effect of this was that the rod acted as an insulator at room temperature and did not permit the passage of a current until it reached a high temperature.   An externally applied flame was required to perform the pre-heating.   Later versions addressed this weakness of the initial design by enclosing the radiator rod in an electrical pre-heater coil, which was disconnected from the circuit when the rod reached operating temperature. This lamp enjoyed a measure of success in Nernst's native Germany and its production was licensed in America. However, when the incandescent filament lamp went over to the use of malleable, hot-drawn tungsten, it was rapidly superseded, due to its successors' superior efficiency and lower production cost.

Edison attempted to make the incandescent filament analogue of the Jablochkoff Candle. He proposed a form of construction which used a thick 'bridge' element of a composite material which consisted of conductive particles buried in an insulating matrix. The element was mounted between lead-in electrodes in a glass enclosure. Although a US patent was granted for the idea, no actual practical embodiment was constructed (US Pat 219628). This demonstrates that mechanical translation of an idea to a fresh environment is not an automatic recipe for success.   The underlying physical principles must also be sound.

Swan, Powell and others prepared thin, non-structured carbon filaments by extrusion of carrier compounds which were then reduced to leave a thread of pure carbon (GB Pat 5978/1883). It was to a variant of this process that von Welsbach turned when faced with the problem of forming wires from non-malleable osmium. He mixed the metal powder with a hydrocarbon binder and extruded the mixture to form thin filaments which were then heated to a high temperature to drive off the binder and leave the pure filament material. The metal particles which had been heated in this way were bonded together by sintering ([1912] RPC 401).

When a scientist or engineer trained in one discipline is presented with a problem from another area of technology, he will often rely on the principles with which he is familiar. His solution may well differ radically from that produced by someone who has had training which is apparently more appropriate to that field. The unconventional solution may, however, not be a pragmatic one since, by the same token, he will not be familiar with all of the constraints. Paradoxically, he may, at times, succeed because he does not perceive some of these constraints.

5.4.7 Invention by Emulation

Invention by analogy substitutes the elements of an existing product or process with components which will perform the same task. If an alternative can be devised to do this by means of a different paradigm, there will be a prospect that it could produce a greater innovation rent.

When developing the incandescent electric lamp, Edison attempted to emulate the gas burner in order to reach an assured market. Indeed, he conducted a detailed survey of gas purchases in New York to ascertain benchmark technical performance and costings (Friedel 1986). These represented threshold values which, if achieved, would ensure financial success.

The entire radio and television industry had grown up around the thermionic valve. The transistor was a new product which could (at least in prospect) perform most of the electrical functions of the valve, but also brought additional benefits in the form of lower energy consumption, increased reliability and small size. Although its unique properties created new potential markets, it had immediate application as soon as reduced selling prices, which were a natural consequence of the manufacturing learning curve, made replacement of valves economically viable.

Emulation of a product or process may give rise to invention by substitution. Such an invention has the advantage that its potential market is already established, although it may require a different infrastructure. The substitute product is a variant of the analogue invention. An example is the incandescent lamp, the market for which was established by the gas burner and the kerosene lamp. Inventors had a clear picture of what their targets were.

The presence of an existing product provides a foundation for the establishment of the new industry, although it may create unnecessary constraints by pre-conditioning thinking and thereby inhibiting possible alternative developments.

Whilst products and processes may not be directly transferable, analogous inventions arise. Nernst designed his lamp using the principles developed by von Welsbach in constructing the gas mantle. US gas producers adapted Edison's method of calculating appropriate sizing for conductors to equalise voltage at the consumers' premises to permit the installation of pipes of appropriate diameter and thereby the achievement of uniform gas pressure at the delivery point. Transistor circuit designers embraced the concept of 'duality' to adapt valve circuit designs to operate with the new solid-state devices, whilst the thermionic valve amplifier replaced the intermediate telegraph operator in communications cables.

A substitute product or process, the apocryphal 'better mousetrap', has a greater chance of success than a virgin invention. However, it still needs to surmount an economic-advantage threshold in which the anticipated innovation rent exceeds the contemporary profits of the extant technology.

Where a new product or process is developed as a substitute for an existing one, symbiotic innovations may emerge as exponents of the old and new technologies learn from one another.

5.5 THE HALF-BAKED IDEA

It is a popular belief that motor omnibuses are likely to prove serious competitors to tramways, but this view is not shared by experts who have studied both sides of the question. The suggestion that motor omnibuses have an advantage over electric tramways by reason of avoiding the necessity for permanent way is effectively disproved upon examination. Calculations based on the *minimum* service for which the tramways would be constructed show that the figure representing the interest, depreciation, and sinking fund charges on the cost of permanent way is less per car mile than the cost per omnibus mile of flexible rubber tyres.
E. Garcke M.I.E.E., *The Times*, 26 September 1906

The tram's revival has been prompted by increasing traffic congestion and constraints on car use, their environmental acceptability and their popularity amongst potential travellers. Tram networks are, however, much more expensive to build and operate than buses and the government warned recently that there was very little money available for more to be built.
Financial Times, 13 March 1996

Thomas Edison devised a fluorescent lamp in which a calcium tungstate coating was applied to a glass envelope (US Pat 865367). An electrical discharge between electrodes within the enclosure was intended to generate x-rays, which would stimulate the coating to emit visible radiation. The overall efficiency of the process was such that it was not viable, a fact which would have been revealed by a straightforward calculation.

Edison also proposed a technique for the preservation of fresh meat and vegetables by placing them in a glass vessel, creating a vacuum and then sealing the container (US Pat 248431). A simple experiment would have shown that the process would not prevent anaerobic degradation.

The quotations above illustrate the fact that many inventions are not viable but are still put forward as serious propositions, either because they are based on a false premise or simply because the vanity or greed of the inventor drives him to increase his tally of inventions. A few basic calculations or simple experiments are all that is needed to demonstrate that the proposals are doomed to fail. Nevertheless, the innovators proceed, in ignorance, to file patent applications and perform other non-trivial tasks in an attempt to work the ideas.

5.6 CONCLUSION

The origin of some inventions is serendipitous, an opportunistic realisation that an observed phenomenon represents a viable solution to an extant problem. The observation may be made by pure chance, as with Edison's improvement in luminous efficiency of a lamp which was caused by a change in the shape of the carbon filament when a screwdriver was dropped on the bulb. Alternatively, it may arise as part of a directed effort – the point-contact transistor was a happy consequence of applying probes to a germanium crystal as part of a programme of study of the physics of the solid state. By contrast, Edison found no practical use for his eponymous effect, although it was subsequently to become the basis of the thermionic valve. Fortune may indeed favour the prepared mind, but eminence of the inventor is no assurance that he will recognise the merits of an idea. Indeed, such men may easily be blinkered by prejudice or channelled thinking or, simply, preoccupied with other matters.

Other inventions come into being through rational thought processes. At one extreme, this may be an abstract theoretical consideration of physical principles or mathematical relationships, as with Faraday's realisation of electromagnetism or Tesla's conception of alternating current machines, but, more usually, it will be some form of extrapolation of an existing product or process. The extrapolation may take the form of a reasoned progression along an established path, or it may require a lateral transposition, such as an analogy, a topological manipulation or the desire to produce a product or process which is currently effected in some other way. This type of lateral invention requires an untrammelled mind, a stipulation which may be met by transplanting an established inventor into an unfamiliar field. Invention by extrapolation is far more probable than invention based on an original theory and does not require such a highly developed mind.

The corollary is that inventions which are based on earlier building blocks usually involve a smaller inventive step. The propensity to invent increases with the number of precursors.

Although serendipitous inventions are sporadic, they are not necessarily unpredictable. The transistor was a direct consequence of the decision to provide appropriate resources and to direct a talented team to work in an area which was capable of producing a solid-state amplifier. A prolific harvest may be the inevitable consequence of the decision to cultivate a fertile plot.

Frequently, invention will be triggered by the identification of a problem. Indeed, many inventions are manifest simply as the formulation of a problem, the existence of which had not previously been recognised.

Embryonic innovations are 'fuzzy'. The early incandescent lamps, thermionic valves and transistors made by various processes did not exhibit consistent characteristics. It was necessary to select lamps which were capable of operating at high voltages (defined as greater than 100 volts) and valves and transistors which would provide a specified minimum level of amplification. As experience was gained, so the end products became more predictable.

Prospective innovation rents from seminal inventions are high – witness the incandescent filament lamp, the transistor and the microprocessor – but the risk factor is also high – high-temperature superconductors have only yielded limited returns, whilst buckminster fullerenes have, so far, filled only niche applications. Lilienfeld could not fabricate a successful transistor because materials technology was inadequate and de Forest failed initially to make money from the Audion, partly because his way was blocked by Fleming's patent on the diode detector. It is not feasible to discount the return because the risk factor is equally unpredictable at this stage of the innovation cycle.

Innovation rents are moderated by the need to create the infrastructure which is necessary to work an invention. With seminal inventions this penalty may be high since there will frequently be no infrastructure in existence. In consequence, one has to be created from scratch and financed from the rents of the initial innovation. On the positive side, this is a Keynesian influence, since there will be an opportunity for the infrastructure providers themselves to acquire innovation rents and hence they will, in turn, be motivated.

An analogue innovation has a lower credibility threshold than a virgin invention because the product or process for which it is substituted will already have established benchmarks for performance and infrastructure requirements.

Innovations which have their roots in another technology may well spawn improvements in the parent product or process, allowing the two to develop in a symbiotic manner.

Many futile ideas are put forward as a result of misplaced enthusiasm, lack of critical analysis or simply through overweening ambition.

This chapter has identified different mechanical processes which may be involved in the conception of inventions. It has shown that the nature of the inventive process involved in the inception of an innovation may be a significant factor in deciding the eventual return from an innovation. Fundamental inventions conceived from theoretical principles can create huge innovation rents, but their incidence is rare. Inventions conceived by chance observation or resulting from felicitous properties of materials may be equally fruitful but they are also equally unpredictable. A major determinant of success is the fertile ground of a prepared mind, possibly primed by exposure to a foreign discipline.

6. The Logistics of Innovation

The transition from a paradigm in crisis to a new one from which a new tradition of normal science can emerge is far from a cumulative process, one achieved by an articulation or extension of the old paradigm. Rather it is a reconstruction of the field from new fundamentals, a reconstruction that changes some of the field's most theoretical generalizations as well as many of the paradigm methods and applications. During the transition period there will be a large but never complete overlap between the problems that can be solved by the old and by the new paradigm. But there will also be a decisive difference in the modes of solution when the transition is complete, the profession will have changed its view of the field, its methods and its goals.

Thomas Kuhn, *The Structure of Scientific Revolutions*

Thirty years ago, Germany and America were following the lead of this country in theoretical developments, and until some years later Germany obtained machinery from England. Now we are behind other countries in pioneer work, in volume of manufacture, and in ability to compete in advantageous terms. The causes of this reversal have been indicated in previous articles, but the bearing they have on the manufacturing conditions requires elucidation. While British manufacturers were compulsorily inert during periods of impeded growth manufacturers in America and on the Continent of Europe, who were encouraged, rather than impeded, devoted their resources to the establishment of factories and electrical undertakings and to the development of efficient selling organisations at home and abroad. The result was that when adverse legislation was amended, and a demand for electrical machinery arose in this country, the foreign manufacturers took advantage of our system of free imports and secured the orders. The British manufacturers were not in a position to offer any effective resistance; they had to enlarge and re-adapt their factories, to procure experienced officers and to resuscitate their business organisations.

E. Garcke M.I.E.E, *The Times*, 10 October 1906

In hindsight, our work in x-ray lithography was done much too early.
Eberhard Spiller, *IBM J Res Dev*, 1993

6.1 INTRODUCTION

Heroic theory presents the process of invention in terms of great men thinking great thoughts. The socio-deterministic view, on the other hand, is that, if the timing and surrounding circumstances are right, invention will follow automatically, so it is the inevitable consequence of the felicitous conjunction of technological and economic space–time curves. The corollary of this proposition is that the propensity for an invention to succeed will exhibit maxima and minima which are determined by the current ambient environment. This leads to the hypothesis discussed in the opening chapters, that the path of innovation is analogous to biological evolution, with the technological paradigm playing the role of plants and animals. As with biological species, inventions will emerge and die out. There will be a steady progression interposed with discontinuities as a shift from one physical schema to another takes place.

An opportunity cost threshold will have to be surmounted before these paradigm shifts will take place. As a consequence, change will follow a locus determined by a time-dependent binary decision tree because the opportunity cost of a particular transition will vary with the passage of time. Within a paradigm, the innovations offering the greatest perceived net return will persist.

This chapter seeks to justify a socio-deterministic rather than an heroic viewpoint of the origins of invention. It also examines those factors, highlighted by the case studies, which exert a temporal influence on the progress of innovations.

6.2 THE INEVITABILITY OF CONCEPTION

The Edison Effect was first observed by Upton and Edison at Menlo Park in 1882. Having noted the phenomenon (and filed a patent application) (US Pat 307031), they consigned the idea to the trash can. J.A. Fleming made an experimental evaluation of Edison's concept shortly after its discovery, (Fleming 1883, Fleming 1896) but it was not until many years later, when he had a need for a sensitive detector of radio waves, that he returned to the idea and put it to practical use (Fleming 1905).

In 1875, with his Etheric Black Box (Jehl 1937, p81), and in 1885, with his Grasshopper-telegraph proposal for communication by induction, Edison was on the verge of development of radio. Again, the ideas were no more than a passing thought, although he did retrospectively take advantage of them when he sold his patent to Marconi. It was left to Hertz, Lodge,

Marconi and others independently to develop the concept of radio communication.

Göbel conceived most of the features of the carbon filament lamp at the end of the 1860s, well before Swan and Edison made their ideas public – he lacked only the crucial step of 'running on the pumps' (Fürst 1926). Coming from different starting points, Swan and Edison independently developed lamps with a thin carbon filament which was heated to incandescence *in vacuo* in a glass envelope with platinum lead-in wires to which an electrical generator was connected.

Julius Lilienfeld patented the structure of the bipolar transistor, the junction-gate field-effect transistor and the insulated-gate field-effect transistor in the period 1925-32 (US Pats 1745175, 1900018 and 1877140). Due to the lack of suitable materials' technology, he was not able to construct viable devices and abandoned the inventions to concentrate on the manufacture of electrolytic capacitors. A quarter of a century later, the economic motivation for the development of a solid-state amplifier was still pressing. Tractable materials in the form of single-crystal, elemental germanium and silicon were developed by Theurer, Pfann and Teal, opening the way for Bardeen, Brattain and Shockley to visit Lilienfeld's concepts anew and make them work.

These examples reinforce the view that successful innovation is a socio-deterministic rather than an heroic process. It arises to satisfy an immediate or latent need. However, the faculties of 'great men' are more acute and they are therefore more likely to be originators of inventions which are *per se* inevitable.

Fundamental to socio-deterministic theory is the premise that discovery is inevitable – if a need arises and economic circumstances are right, an invention will emerge to satisfy that need. Conditions must be favourable for the innovation to flourish or it will remain dormant or wither away and die.

6.3 THE PARADIGM SHIFT

> Often a new paradigm emerges, at least in embryo, before a crisis has developed or been explicitly recognized.
> Thomas Kuhn, *The Structure of Scientific Revolutions*, p86

Thomas Kuhn propounded a theory of scientific advance in terms of transitions between paradigms – the general conception of the nature of scientific endeavour within which a given enquiry is undertaken (Kuhn 1970). This philosophy may be adapted to plot the course of innovation, the paradigm being specified in terms of the technological framework in which the innovation has been created. In such a schema, advancement will be by gradual extrapolation of the parameters which define the paradigm. This progress will continue uninterrupted until it is perceived that a different set of parameters will yield a greater rent. At this stage, it is likely that a jump to a new paradigm will take place.

With an electric arc, it is necessary to position two carbon rods so that their tips are separated from one another by a closely defined amount. As the tips are consumed by the arc, their spacing must be corrected. Initially, this adjustment was by hand, but ever more elaborate clockwork mechanisms were substituted, with the further refinement that some variants, which followed the construction developed by Archerau, included a solenoid within a feedback loop to obviate the need for an external agency. Davy's charcoal was replaced by Foucault's retort carbon, which was harder, and hence more durable but, nevertheless, still represented a development of the existing train of thought (Jarvis 1955b, p152).

When Jablochkoff's Candle was introduced, however, it signalled a fundamental change of direction as it possessed no moving parts, thereby offering a fundamental economic advantage (Fürst 1926). The structure was basically simple, with the carbons mounted parallel to one another. It enjoyed immediate success, followed by a wave of popularity during which it was installed in public places in Paris, London and New York. At this stage its drawbacks became apparent – the arc was frequently blown out by the wind or extinguished by voltage fluctuations in the primitive electricity supply which was available at the time. Once broken, the arc could not be re-struck, since it was initiated by a priming bridge of conductive material, which was positioned at the tips of the virgin carbons and was consumed during the original establishment of the burning arc. A typical working lifetime of the carbons was twenty minutes, after which they had to be replaced by hand, although some lumieres did contain a number of sets of carbons which were energised successively.

The high cost of consumables was the death knell of the Jablochkoff Candle, which enjoyed, perhaps, a decade of popularity following its conception in the mid-1870s. Domestic users turned increasingly to the new carbon filament incandescent lamp, which had a much longer working life, (around 400 hours), whilst new variants, such as the enclosed arc and the flaming arc, continued the evolution of arc lighting along the previous line of development. Present-day technologies would overcome many of the nineteenth century disadvantages, but nowadays public lighting is provided by gas discharge lamps such as the sodium vapour lamp, which are much more efficient and have working lifetimes of many thousands of hours, so there is no demand for arc lamps for this task.

The example of the Jablochkoff Candle shows that it is the perceived advantage, rather than the actual advantage, which triggers a paradigm shift. The luminous flame gave way to the arc lamp, which was succeeded, in turn, by the incandescent lamp and then the ultra-violet-stimulated fluorescent tube. The thermionic valve was replaced by the transistor and then the silicon integrated circuit, whilst the horse-drawn carriage yielded to the motor car driven by an internal combustion engine. Each of these changes presented a financial advantage and was adopted with varying degrees of enthusiasm. On the other hand, Edison's proposals for a steam-powered incandescent lamp and an X-ray-stimulated fluorescent lamp were either not economically or physically viable and failed abjectly, thereby demonstrating that novelty alone is insufficient incentive for making a change.

The point-contact transistor was, in essence, a serendipitous discovery, albeit within the context of an investigation targeted at finding a suitable physical basis for a solid-state amplifier (Bardeen 1956). It was, by the same token, a false start because its fragility, inconsistency of characteristics and poor electrical performance would have ruled it out as a long-term solution to the problem. It was, however, hugely successful as many companies began working on its development (Cullis 2004, Appendix 7). They were driven by the prospect of the Philosopher's Stone of a viable solid-state amplifier. There was also an element of oligopolistic response, since, had they ignored a potentially successful development, it was virtually certain that they would lose market share.

As soon as the melt-doped, grown junction was established as a viable manufacturing process, Shockley's microwatt transistor superseded its pioneering point-contact predecessor. However, the reign of the grown-junction transistor was also short. High wastage of expensive single crystal, an essential component of the device, the inability to produce devices with a uniform specification, and undesirable electrical properties, such as high parasitic collector resistance, meant that, when Hall and Saby of General Electric (Hall, 1950, US Pat 2999195) and Pankove of RCA (US Pat 3005132) came along in 1952 with the alloyed-junction process, which was much more economic in its use of the germanium semiconductor source material and which permitted the manufacture of large batches of devices on a continuous production line, the earlier process was rapidly abandoned.

At the end of the decade, the twin processes of planar diffusion and epitaxial deposition offered a further quantum leap in manufacturing economics and thus displaced the alloyed-junction transistor (and its extrapolated developments, the drift transistor, the post-alloy diffused transistor and the alloyed-emitter, diffused-base mesa transistor) as the dominant manufacturing process.

On the other hand, the surface-barrier transistor (US Pat 2885571), although it was produced by sophisticated automatic machinery, did not offer an economic advance since the low punch-through voltage, which was a consequence of the device topography, meant that it was not sufficiently robust to withstand the operating conditions which would frequently be experienced in practice. It waned to insignificance, along with its derivatives, the micro-alloy transistor and the micro-alloy, diffused transistor.

Nernst, when working on the Welsbach gas mantle, produced an electric lamp which was its electrical analogue. Initially, it had a significant disadvantage because its luminous radiator rod needed to be primed by heating with a flame, but Nernst overcame this problem by using an electric heater and a control circuit which disconnected the heater when the rod had reached its working temperature. The structure he devised was more complex than that of the incandescent filament lamp. Although its lifetime was comparable, it had a greater luminous efficiency than that of the carbon filament lamp. This was, however, less than that of the metal filament lamps which came on the scene at about the same time. The Nernst lamp enjoyed a brief spell of popularity in its native Germany and was also manufactured in the USA (Bright 1949), but it rapidly faded into obscurity when the technology of tungsten became established. The fact that it was a recent introduction did not prevent its supersession as soon as a superior innovation appeared.

It might be expected that the pioneer in a new development would be the one who is the market leader in that field. Investigation shows that, paradoxically, the opposite takes place. The incandescent carbon filament lamp was invented by Swan and Edison, neither of whom carried out significant work on its forerunner, the arc. The principal developers of the arc, likewise, had no involvement with its predecessor, the luminous flame. Von Welsbach, von Bolton, Feuerlein and Just and Hanaman, the originators of the sintered, extruded-refractory-metal filament lamp, were not employed by the market leaders in the manufacture of carbon filament lamps. General Electric, which held around 80 per cent of the US domestic market, was, however, quick to purchase the US patent rights to Just and Hanaman's tungsten filament lamp, which offered a significant technical advantage over its [General Electric's] then current products and hence was the key to preserving its market power.

By the end of the nineteenth century, the undersea cable companies had settled down into a cosy cartel arrangement through which prices were maintained at a level which guaranteed them a handsome profit. In Britain, the Post Office had a statutory monopoly of telegraphic and telephonic communications (6 QBD 244). It fell to an outsider, Guglielmo Marconi, to see the potential of Maxwell's theory and Hertz's experiments and lay down the foundations of wireless telegraphy.

When the Bell System, which had been prevented by a consent decree under US anti-trust legislation from establishing its own manufacture of transistors for external sale, embarked on a programme of licensing the newly invented transistor, it offered established valve manufacturers the opportunity to take patent licences and receive know-how ([1965] RPC 335). This gave them an advantageous position in setting up the new industry. However, this situation was short-lived and newcomers were soon making the running with innovations.

Although the first paradigm shift in this industry was the introduction of the alloyed-junction transistor, which originated in the laboratories of General Electric and of Radio Corporation of America, both of which also manufactured valves, the move to silicon, which supplanted germanium as the preferred material for device fabrication, was led by Texas Instruments, a company which had no track record in the electronics industry (Manners 1996a). Fairchild Camera and Instrument Corporation, another start-up operation in semiconductor device fabrication, was the source of planar technology, whilst the microprocessor came from Intel, a breakaway company established by former employees of Fairchild. Each became established, in turn, as market leader.

Edison and Swan, who were responsible for the introduction of the carbon filament, came to dominate the new lighting market which they had established. Intel, which, in the early days of the microprocessor, was forced to concede second-sourcing arrangements to establish credibility with its customers, became the sole supplier of its proprietary product line by the time the product had reached the fourth and fifth generations. These examples demonstrate that, within a paradigm, development is progressive and orderly. It takes place without fundamental changes, each advance following logically from the current *status quo*.

Occasionally, the natural progression will be interrupted by a paradigm shift. This step is substantial and represents a quantum transition from the accepted way of thinking. Nernst's electric lamp based on Welsbach's gas mantle, Philco's electrolytic process for production of surface-barrier transistors, Fleming's thermionic diode detector and Fairchild's planar transistor are examples of such changes. Some were successful and some failed. However, an invention involving a paradigm shift will be universally adopted only when it increases the actual or perceived prospective economic returns.

Edison and Swan's carbon filament was replaced by Just and Hanaman's extruded metal one, but General Electric acquired the patents to preserve its market power. Intel created the microprocessor and uses its resulting cash mountain to buy up promising new technologies. Marconi became the dominant supplier in wireless communications by organising a patents pool which increased the cost of market entry for newcomers.

A paradigm shift involving a change in the nature of a product will not usually be initiated by a market leader. He may, however, use his market power to acquire control of, or otherwise neutralise, it. The advantages brought about by the change may be tangible, such as a reduction in production costs, or virtual, such as avoidance of intellectual property monopolies. These economic advantages will promote the likelihood of a change in the relative competitive power of the players. In consequence relative market position is most likely to alter at this stage.

6.4 THE 'RED QUEEN' COROLLARY

'Well in *our* country,' said Alice, still panting a little, 'you'd generally get to somewhere else – if you ran very fast for a long time, as we've been doing.'
'A slow sort of a country!' said the Queen. 'Now, *here*, you see, it takes all the running *you* can do, to keep in the same place. If you want to get somewhere else, you must run at least twice as fast as that!'
Lewis Carroll, *Alice Through the Looking Glass*

The Schumpeter A-phase of an innovation is a period of great change. Advances are rapid and the steps are large. During the 1950s, manufacturers in the semiconductor industry were jostling one another to introduce transistors produced by new processes. Over a period of ten years, devices such as the *pnp* alloyed-junction transistor, the silicon transistor, the *npn* bipolar transistor, the drift transistor, the surface-barrier transistor, the post-alloy-diffused transistor, the double-diffused mesa transistor, the planar diffused transistor and the epitaxial transistor were introduced by such companies as General Electric, Texas Instruments, Western Electric, Philips, Fairchild Camera and Instrument and Philco (Cullis 2004, Appendix 7). Each successive device introduced some improvement in technical and economic performance. Technological leadership of the industry changed hands several times. By the mid-1960s, in order to manufacture a small-signal, gold-doped, silicon planar epitaxial switching transistor, which was then the staple product of the industry, it was necessary to make use of the patents of fourteen different companies (Cullis 1966a).

The consequence of the propensity of the paradigm shift to promote change in the relative market positions of the players may, *pace* Carroll, be dubbed the 'Red Queen' Corollary – when the frequency of innovation is high, it is necessary for the participants to redouble their efforts to maintain market share.

6.5 THE DEVELOPMENT LOCUS

6.5.1 Timing and Critical Path

As a result of its simple structure, the Jablochkoff Candle had potential for success since the then current development path of arc lamps was to ever more complex, moving mechanical arrangements. However, it suffered from two significant failure mechanisms by which the arc was extinguished – the wind might blow it out or it could fall victim to voltage fluctuations in the notoriously unreliable power supplies which were the norm in the late nineteenth century. Both of these drawbacks could have been rectified by technology which was developed later. Transistorised power supplies, regulated by zener diodes, provide a reliable, high-impedance constant-current source, which is what is needed to drive an electric arc in a self-sustaining manner. The other fault could have been eliminated by placing the carbons at a slight angle to one another, instead of arranging them in parallel, and by substituting a modern positive-temperature-coefficient thermistor material for the kaolin separator, which would have ensured that the arc, if doused, would re-strike automatically.

These two technologies did not appear until around ninety years after the Jablochkoff Candle was first mooted. By this time, other, better, alternative sources of illumination were firmly established. The opportunity cost of developing a modern equivalent would have been prohibitive, so an idea which was potentially promising in 1875 would not even merit consideration at the beginning of the twenty-first century. Furthermore, the concept of the enclosed arc, which appeared only two decades later and which would have ameliorated the performance, did not cause the paradigm to be re-visited.

The Pointolite lamp, in which an arc was struck between two small tungsten spheres mounted in a sealed bulb, applied several of the principles on which the Jablochkoff Candle could have been redesigned successfully using later technological developments. When it was invented at the beginning of the twentieth century, however, this new lamp had to compete with incandescent lamp techniques which were, by then, fairly mature. It therefore could not offer the prospect of an increased innovation rent which would justify the paradigm transition.

As early as the nineteenth century, the view was held that an invention would only succeed when the time was right (Houston 1894, p8). Since innovation is driven by the prospect of reward, it follows that it will only be adopted when there is economic advantage to be gained by so doing. The technological environment is continually changing. In consequence, the input costs of an innovation and the opportunity cost of adopting alternatives may also be expected to be in a state of flux.

It follows that many innovations are ephemeral. The success of an invention depends on its felicitous temporal juxtaposition to suitable enabling technologies. Houston's conclusion is correct. Technological evolution is a time-critical, binary decision process. After an option has been rejected, the opportunity cost of returning to it will usually be greater than that of continuing along the established path. The opportunity cost itself will also vary with time, usually increasing, and thereby reinforcing, its negative influence.

6.5.2 False Starts

Edison commenced his work on the incandescent lamp by constructing the filaments of platinum. He attempted to overcome the problem of the filament fusing (which was a consequence of the proximity of the melting point of platinum to the temperature required for incandescence) by incorporating a current regulator in the supply circuit (US Pat 214637). This was not successful, so he turned his attention to the use of carbon for the light source, since this had a higher sublimation temperature. His first carbon filament lamps were constructed using a tar putty consisting of syrup and lamp black, which was kneaded between the thumb and forefinger to form a thin 'sausage'. The technique proved not to be viable for consistent production. He then tried carbonised cardboard. Again the structure was not robust and the lifetime of the lamps was short. Next he launched a comprehensive search for an alternative vegetable fibre. Empirical tests indicated that fibres of a particular variety of bamboo were suitable, so he organised a source of supply from Japan (Cullis 2004, Appendix 3).

Competitors, including Swan, also worked with carbonised cardboard but, instead of adopting bamboo fibre, progressed to filaments manufactured from extruded cellulose, which proved much more satisfactory since it gave a consistent, uniform product.

After a decade of steady production, the carbon filament was superseded by metal filaments, first osmium, followed in short order by tantalum and tungsten (Bright 1949). Initially these filaments were prepared from metal powder which was mixed with a hydrocarbon binder, extruded and fired to a high temperature, to drive off the binder and sinter the metal particles together. Later, in the case of tungsten, as understanding of the metallurgy improved, a malleable thin wire was produced by hot working.

General Electric tried a composite filament of metallised carbon during the 1890s, but this did not offer a significant advantage over plain carbon and was completely superseded as soon as solely metal filaments became available.

The first transistors, discovered serendipitously by Bardeen and Brattain, were made by pressing two metallic points in close proximity to one another on to a block of germanium. This was a method of construction which was easy to reproduce, but the resulting transistors were inconsistent, noisy, failed at relatively low voltages and were unreliable. They were replaced by the microwatt grown-junction transistor devised by Shockley, but this had a high parasitic collector resistance and usually exhibited a low gain with an accompanying poor high-frequency performance. Although it was more robust than the point-contact diode, it was wasteful of raw materials, fragile and costly to construct, so, early in the 1950s, the grown-junction transistor itself was superseded by the alloyed-junction transistor, which was much more economic in its use of raw materials and could readily be made in batches which were fed continuously through a belt furnace. In the mid-1950s, the double-diffused mesa transistor offered much improved high frequency performance, but this was, in turn, replaced at the end of the decade by the planar epitaxial structure, which has remained current up to the present day.

During the 1950s, Philco produced a series of transistor manufacturing technologies (the surface barrier transistor, the micro-alloy transistor, the micro-alloy, diffused transistor) based on electrochemical etching of germanium wafers. They used a highly sophisticated automated plant controlled by infra-red sensors. Although the transistors produced by this plant were ahead of their competitors in terms of high-frequency performance – at that time difficult to achieve – they suffered from other disadvantages, such as low punch-through voltage, which resulted in their failure in use. The technology was ring-fenced by patents and, for this reason, as well as the technological drawbacks, was never adopted by competing companies, although one or two plants were set up by companies which manufactured under licence.

After the initial success with the Apple II, Steve Jobs turned his attention to producing a computer with a user-friendly interface (Cringely 1996). He adopted the WIMPs (windows, icons, mice and pull-down menus) concepts originated by the Xerox Palo Alto Research Centre to produce, first the Lisa, then the Macintosh computers. The 'Mac' was extremely profitable and Apple guarded its proprietary position jealously. By contrast, the IBM PC, its main rival, had an open architecture and ran under the Microsoft MS-DOS operating system, which was available to any manufacturer that wished to adopt it. IBM clones, produced using 'clean room' techniques to avoid the threat of copyright litigation, proliferated. When Microsoft introduced its Windows graphical user interface, which had many of the features of the Mac operating system, the writing was on the wall for Apple, which experienced a relentless attrition of its market share. Although Apple pioneered the graphical user interface for consumer use, it failed in its attempt to control the market by refusing to license its operating system software. When, eventually, it did open its system to others, it was too late because, by then, its market share was small and dwindling. It no longer had a critical mass of users and all that was left was a 'vulture' market which destroyed Apple's last vestige of profitability.

The false start is the corollary of the paradigm shift. Although a company may not recover its investment, the initiation of the paradigm shift provides an opportunity to bid for market leadership. A strong proprietary position at the outset will provide protection for the necessary investment, but it may well inhibit adoption of the paradigm shift by competitors and thus contribute to its failure.

Since the decision to adopt an innovation is based on *perception* of the prospective innovation rent, it follows that, where the perception is not borne out in practice, the innovation may be abandoned because it does not yield the expected return.

The false start may be due to a mistaken perception of the economics of a paradigm shift or simply premature obsolescence of a shift that was undertaken because it was the best option available at the decision-making time.

6.5.3 Progression

Metallic incandescent lamps had their genesis with the sintered, extruded osmium filament invented by Auer von Welsbach ([1912] RPC 401). Osmium was displaced successively by tantalum and tungsten, metals which were less amenable to the fabrication process but which had higher melting points. Since they were thus capable of operating at higher temperatures, they formed more satisfactory lamp elements. In due course, the extrusion process was replaced by high-temperature working of the tungsten, which gave it a more robust and durable nature.

The tetrode thermionic valve superseded the triode as a high-frequency amplifier because the introduction of the screen grid reduced the parasitic capacitance between the anode and control grid, permitting higher gains to be achieved. The subsequent invention of the pentode valve, with its suppressor grid, eliminated the deleterious effect of the secondary-electron-emission characteristic of the tetrode and gave rise to a further improvement in performance ([1934] RPC 333). These developments attained economic viability whilst the thermionic valve was the principal means of electronic amplification.

The first alloyed-junction transistor had an emitter formed by alloying a pellet of ductile indium to a wafer of *n*-type germanium. An improvement in emitter efficiency (dependent on the ratio of holes to electrons in the forward current) was obtained by the incorporation of gallium, a *p*-type dopant with a high segregation coefficient, in the emitter pellet (US Pat 3078397).

The post-alloy-diffused transistor took this process a step further by including both *p*-type (gallium) and *n*-type (arsenic) dopants in an indium carrier pellet (Beale 1957). Due to its segregation coefficient being an order of magnitude lower than that of gallium, indium effectively behaved as an inert carrier, which was used because it had appropriate metallurgical characteristics to ensure a good mechanical and electrical connection to the lead-in wires. Substitutional *n*-type dopants have diffusion coefficients in germanium of at least an order of magnitude greater than substitutional *p*-type dopants. A high-temperature, post-alloying diffusion step therefore permitted the fabrication of a graded-impurity, drift-field region in the germanium wafer and this enhanced the high-frequency performance of the devices.

Arsenic and antimony, the customary *n*-type dopants for germanium, are hard and brittle materials. They also have different expansivities and are therefore unsuitable for applications which involve thermal cycling and for making mechanically strong alloyed connections to a germanium wafer. To overcome these problems, ohmic contacts to *n*-type germanium and rectifying contacts to *p*-type germanium were made by means of a pellet of lead, to which either arsenic or antimony had been added. The lead acts as an inert carrier which has appropriate metallurgical properties for the mechanical and electrical connection, whilst the arsenic or antimony modifies the conductivity of the germanium.

Like Newton, we all stand on the shoulders of giants. Within a paradigm, development *does* follow a steady and logical progression, but learning is an incremental process. Most innovation, therefore, will progress gradually, with advancement being achieved in small stages as existing knowledge and experience is extended. This will limit the speed of introduction of the innovation since the serial process will incorporate all of the delays inherent in its components.

6.5.4 The Learning Curve

A semiconductor device is fabricated by means of a large number of process steps which are performed sequentially. At each stage a proportion of the devices will fail to meet the desired specification. The overall manufacturing yield of good devices is the product of the yields for each of the individual process steps. Typically, there may be of the order of twenty of these steps. If, for example, the yield for each of them is 90 per cent, then the overall percentage of good devices would be $(0.9)^{20} = 12.1$ per cent. This means that approximately eight times as much starting material must be fed to the production line as would be needed if the yield of perfect devices at each stage were 100 per cent. Just a small improvement in efficiency at each stage, to 91 per cent, would increase the overall yield to 15.1 per cent, an improvement of 25 per cent in the numbers emerging from the production line. The overheads, in terms of starting materials and production costs, however, remain constant. Eventually, physical limitations are reached, preventing any further increases in efficiency (Cullis 1966b).

When a new device is first manufactured, yields are small, but they increase rapidly as efficiency at each process stage improves. This permits the manufacturer to lower his selling price whilst still retaining the same overall profitability, since the fixed overheads are distributed over a greater number of sales. After some time, the efficiency approaches an asymptotic value determined by physical constraints.

At the early stages of an innovation, there is uncertainty of the outcome of many of the contributory elements. Combined serially, they have a cumulative influence on the variability of the end-product. The effect of this is that, if high standards are set, yields will be low, but as experience increases, a greater proportion of devices will meet the specification.

6.5.5 The Pendulum Effect and Moore's Law

In 1964, some five years after the introduction of the planar integrated circuit, Gordon Moore made the empirical observation that the number of devices which could be fabricated on a given area of a silicon wafer doubled every year. He predicted that this effect would continue into the foreseeable future. This relationship became known as Moore's Law. It was subsequently modified to 'a doubling every eighteen months', but has prevailed for three decades.

This improvement in packing density was achieved by the sequential introduction of novel photolithographic processing techniques. The planar process for the manufacture of semiconductor devices depends on etching predefined apertures in a layer of silicon dioxide formed on the surface of a thin slice of silicon. The ability to make these etched features smaller permitted more devices to be fabricated on a given area. When an improved photolithographic process was introduced, the development path traced a new learning curve in which manufacturing volume approached a higher asymptote. Whilst this was taking place, further improvements in photolithography were being developed. These further improvements established another new learning curve with a still higher target volume for the semiconductor device manufacture. The procedure was iterative, with each new photolithographic process giving rise to an order of magnitude improvement in packing density of devices on each slice.

The cost of these improvements was substantial. Initially, each new generation of photolithographic equipment cost ten times as much as the previous one. During the 1990s, this increase fell to a factor of two. The cost of other equipment used in semiconductor device fabrication has risen commensurately.

The introduction of each new generation of photolithography offered an order of magnitude improvement in the number of devices produced per slice of silicon. This benefit was taken in the form of improved technical performance – partly as greater capacity, partly as greater speed of operation. There was also a reduction in price due to the increased packing density of devices per slice. All of these gains contributed to increased shipments and permitted the cost of the new equipment to be recovered over a larger sales volume, hence requiring a smaller unit contribution.

see   http://www.iiasa.ac.at/Research/TNT/WEB/Research/Understanding_ the_dynamics_of_/DRAM_1/dram_1.html

As an invention follows its learning curve, it produces an increasing rent. Quantum changes due to paradigm shifts in the manufacturing procedures are superimposed on the effect of improvements in efficiency. A primary innovation will also benefit from the supplier's improvements. Indeed, advances in the primary innovation may be triggered by supply-side changes.

The relationship epitomised by Moore's Law is the limiting case of a succession of paradigm shifts induced by seductive market economics. The graphical representation of Moore's Law is, in fact, the tangent to the learning curves of the individual paradigms. A plot of the computing power of the personal computer exhibits a similar characteristic.

Moore's Law is a special case of the temporal change in an innovation-sensitive variable. One may define a parameter (Moore's Parameter?) indicative of the rate of change. The limiting value of this parameter is determined by the sum of the response times of the technologies contributing to each successive paradigm shift. Technological advance exhibits a pendulum effect, swinging between advances in technology serving primary consumers and a learning phase in which the supplier enters a learning mode prior to the move to the next paradigm.

6.5.6 The 'Parkinson-Pareto' Phenomenon

The economist C. Northcote Parkinson (of eponymous Parkinson's Law fame) made the somewhat facetious observation that work expands to fill the time available for it. In general terms this may be stated as a premise that enhanced returns resulting from a change in an input factor will be negated by consumption. In other words, not all of the benefits of innovation will be manifest in increased rent.

The advance in capabilities of each successive generation of personal computer has been accompanied by a phenomenon akin to Parkinson's Law – *'The operating system expands to fill the available memory'* (Cullis 1985b, p69). Malfunctions are reported to the user by means of error messages. With the early computers, the message was terse, consisting of one or two words ('Syntax error', 'Disk error'). As capacity expanded, the messages simply became more verbose although their significance remained the same. Likewise, the actual programs were initially written in compact machine code, whereas later they were compiled from high-level languages, a practice which makes for less efficient use of the machines' resources. The change did, however, have a beneficial effect in that it was far less labour intensive. There was a net economic gain because expensive humans were supplanted by cheap hardware.

A microprocessor is capable of performing a disparate set of operations in response to instructions which are fed to it in the form of a binary sequence of electrical pulses. It is controlled by a clock circuit which regulates the speed at which the binary pulses are handled. Each successive generation of microprocessor was capable of executing more complex commands than its predecessor. Thus the original Intel 4004 worked with four-bit instructions and a 4-bit data word length. The 8008 moved to 8-bit operation and the 8080 had a 64-kilobyte address space. The 80286 was a 16-bit device with a 17-megabyte address space, whilst the Pentium heralded 32-bit and the Pentium Pro 64-bit operation. Not only was the capability of each device greater than its predecessor, it performed its functions at a faster rate.

During this process of evolution, a number of competing manufacturers commenced to adopt a different design philosophy. Instead of attempting to follow the established line of progress – which was highly constrained and involved the use of 'clean room' techniques to emulate the proprietary microcode which was a central feature of the chip design. They introduced the concept of the Reduced Instruction Set Computer (RISC) – a device which performed only simple functions, but did so very quickly. The complex operations of the mainstream processors were synthesised by a sequence of these simple operations. The advantage of this alternative approach was two-fold. Firstly, it avoided the intellectual property rights of Intel, which manufactured the original processors and, secondly, it transferred control of the operating system design from the processor manufacturer to the user, lowering the development overheads of the chip maker whilst creating greater freedom for his customer since he was not constrained to use the processor in a specific manner determined by the nature of its instruction set. This reversal of trends was triggered by a Pareto analysis (using the so-called '80-20 Rule') of the use of the microprocessor which demonstrated that the most complex functions were used only on rare occasions (Cullis 1986, p92).

Within a paradigm, as an innovation matures, less efficient use is made of the new resources. A compromise may be struck between these new resources and other input factors, for example to reduce the dependence on labour. If a paradigm becomes resource-limited, an enforced shift to a new one will take place.

6.6 THE 'SAILING SHIP' EFFECT

Swan and Edison invented the carbon filament incandescent lamp in 1879 and, by the middle of the next decade, it had become widespread. Arc lamps, however, continued to be used long after this time, major developments such as the enclosed arc and the flaming arc increasing the period of utility. Even after it fell into general disuse, the arc continued to be in demand for niche applications such as searchlights and cinema projectors. The Pointolite tungsten arc lamp was another late development which provided a useful point source for microscope illumination (Fleming 1921).

The invention of the Welsbach mantle extended the use of gas lighting well into the twentieth century ([1900] RPC 141). In this case, there was an additional incentive, since the conversion from gas lighting carried the overhead of installing an additional power supply to the premises. Thus there was a strong reason not to supply electricity for lighting where there was also a requirement for gas for heating and cooking.

The junction transistor was announced in 1948 and actually constructed in 1950. Semiconductor device manufacturers, however, continued to file patent applications on inventions concerned with point-contact transistors as late as 1955. The point-contact transistor had to all intents and purposes been replaced by the alloyed-junction transistor in mainstream production by 1962, but even as late as 1965, RCA, one of the originators of the alloyed junction, filed a patent application for a variant of the point-contact transistor (Cullis 2004, Appendix 7).

The obsolescence of an existing technology is apparent to an innovator as soon as he contemplates a paradigm shift. Since communication is imperfect, this intelligence will not immediately be apparent to his fellow market participants, who will continue development within the ambit of the original paradigm. This is the origin of the well-known 'sailing ship' effect, manifest as major improvements in a technology long after it is superseded. Inventions are frequently made long after a technology is superseded and may extend its viable lifetime.

6.7 REPEATED AND SIMULTANEOUS INVENTION

Edison and Swan independently produced carbon filament lamps using very similar processes; Shockley devised solid-state amplifying devices which had a great resemblance to those devised by Lilienfeld. The author patented a junction-gate field-effect transistor with a vertical channel produced by sub-epitaxial, planar diffusion (GB Pat 1010404). Yamaha subsequently manufactured a power field-effect transistor based on the same principle (Cullis 2004, Appendix 1). Another of the author's inventions was the etched-trough, metal-oxide-semiconductor field-effect transistor (MOSFET) which was devised as a means of incorporating short-channel field-effect transistors in a complementary-symmetry integrated circuit (GB Pat 1084937). Siliconix subsequently used an identical device topography to produce power field-effect transistors with a low 'on' resistance.

Ambrose Fleming carried out characterisation experiments on Edison Effect lamps during the 1880s (Fleming 1883). When faced with a need for a detector of radio waves a couple of decades later, he remembered his earlier investigations and put the invention to new use (Fleming 1924).

Invention is a cyclic event. If conditions are not apposite for success when an invention is first made, there is a finite probability that it will be re-invented, or that the original invention will be remembered, when the environment favours success. In some instances, an old invention may be presented as a solution to a new problem.

Given that, in general, inventors receive an education which includes many common elements – the fundamental laws of physics and the principles of mathematics are basic tenets – it is to be expected that, if they are presented with a particular problem, they will come up with similar solutions. Indeed, these inventions are likely to be simultaneous, if many people are working on a pressing need. On other occasions, they will be repeated at intervals, as a result of re-visiting an old problem.

6.8 MISSED OPPORTUNITIES

In 1883, first Upton, then Edison noticed a shadowing effect on the inner surface of the glass bulb of a carbon filament incandescent lamp (Jehl 1937). Edison performed some experiments which provided a preliminary characterisation of the phenomenon. He then gave up to concentrate his efforts on the electric light.

In 1875, with his Etheric Black Box, Edison achieved a tentative demonstration of a form of wireless transmission. In the late 1880s, this was repeated on a grander scale with the Grasshopper telegraph, which failed due to lack of reliability in its operation. His patents demonstrate that he was working on an incorrect theoretical basis (communication by electromagnetic induction rather than by radio). However, had he shown the same determination that he exhibited with the lamp, he could well have succeeded in taking wireless communication from these unpromising beginnings to the achievement of commercial success.

On other occasions, Edison persisted when others had clearly demonstrated that the path he was following was not the correct one. He continued to promote the cylindrical phonograph long after Berliner had proved that a commercially viable approach would require a flat disc recording. Obstinacy, tempered by the NIH syndrome (not-invented-here), kept him in the backwater of direct current power transmission long after Westinghouse had made a success of Tesla's alternating current system.

Julius Lilienfeld, as his patents indicate (Cullis 2004, Case Study 3), had a fair inkling of the properties of semiconductor devices. Unfortunately, his intuitive understanding was not backed up by viable materials technology and he was unable to construct working devices based on the principles he had set out. Within the existing state of the art, however, he was able to make good electrolytic capacitors and, therefore, went on to concentrate his efforts where they would meet success.

The converse of the repeated invention is the missed opportunity. This is not necessarily the consequence of an incorrect concept. It may be the result of failure to follow through with sufficient determination, occasioned by absence of early success resulting from lack of suitable materials for the execution of the idea, or simply because there are more pressing demands on the innovator and he can find success more easily along other avenues – the innovation analogue of the economist's opportunity cost.

Imperfect knowledge, inaccurate focus or misperception may cause an inventor to overlook a potential invention. Cognition is a necessary complement to physical attributes.

6.9 FAILURE

Although Edison achieved success with a number of his inventions, such as the quadruplex telegraph, the phonograph and the carbon filament lamp, he also experienced many failures. His first commercial enterprise, the vote recorder, failed because, although it achieved its technical objective of speeding up voting, the politicians for whom it was intended, used the delays created by the process of voting to filibuster; they did not want the operation made more efficient because it would have removed this weapon from their armoury.

Edison was an empiricist. After having developed the duplex and quadruplex telegraph, he extrapolated the idea and attempted to devise a sextuplex telegraph, which was not technically feasible. He used up all of the money he had earned from his earlier successes in this fruitless exercise.

An insufficient understanding of the background physics was the root of his failure with the steam-powered lamp, the X-radiation-excited fluorescent lamp and the incandescent analogue of the Jablochkoff Candle. None of these phenomena would have produced a sufficient technical effect to achieve an economic advantage. The aerophone, the phonomotor, the tasimeter and the odoroscope also fell into this category. His proposal for vacuum storage of meat and fresh vegetables was conceived in ignorance of anaerobic chemical and bacterial action. It was also not cost effective in comparison with alternative methods of food preservation.

The concept of the pyromagnetic motor and generator could possibly have been made to work, given appropriate materials and construction techniques, but Edison's designs, based on the construction used for the wood- or coal-burning stove of the late nineteenth century were doomed, *ab initio*, to failure.

The cylindrical phonogram and direct current power transmission were not economically viable in the face of competing products, but Edison would not accept this until long after it was apparent to everyone else.

The manufacture of iron briquettes was developed satisfactorily, but the venture failed when the discovery of new cheap sources of iron ore undermined the costing of Edison's process.

Unless an innovation exhibits an economic advantage, is physically feasible and receives a whole-hearted commitment from the innovator or his successor, it is likely that it will fail.

It is ingenuous to expect all innovations to be a success. Only in a world with perfect knowledge would this prospect be plausible. By its nature, innovation is undertaken in a climate of ignorance and may, therefore, be expected to fail more often than it succeeds.

6.9.1 The Consequence of Failure

There is no substitute for a wooden hull.
Report on Admiralty Trials, Woolwich 1830 (Airbus Industrie advertisement in *Scientific American*)

W.H. Preece, the 'Electrician to the Post Office', was questioned about interference on telephone lines caused by a.c. electric cables. Preece had conducted tests and found that interference was negligible if there was a separation of at least six feet. Asked to look ahead, Preece said he saw no reason to think that currents in electric cables would increase, nor did he think the telephone would be widely adopted by the public in Britain. It was being widely used in America, but things were different in Britain, said Preece, because 'we have a super-abundance of messenger boys'.
Evidence to the Playfair Committee, 1879

The physician can bury his mistakes, but the architect can only advise his client to plant vines.
Frank Lloyd Wright

Whilst it is human nature to boast about one's success, people tend to gloss over their deficiencies. Preece enjoyed a high reputation at the time when he made the above statements. He was a Fellow of the Royal Society and his opinions were reported widely in America. Although his prognostications were shown to be incorrect, his standing in society did not diminish.

Edison's concept of a steam-powered lamp using a rare-earth oxide light radiator, which was based on the principle of an element at one focus of an ellipsoidal reflector heated by a remote platinum resistance element positioned at the other focus, failed because the underlying physical basis was unsound. He is remembered for the telegraph and the incandescent lamp. No-one pays any attention to the fact that he was the inventor of the odoroscope or the aerophone.

Despite its retrospective importance, Lilienfeld's work on solid-state amplifying devices had disappeared into obscurity when, after his death, an American Physical Society prize was endowed through a bequest by his widow (Sweet 1988). Although there had been some assessment of the structures he had proposed, virtually the only information that was available was that which was published in his patent specifications.

Success prevails – error fails – failure fades. Like biological evolution, technological innovation is a process of survival of the fittest. Unsuccessful proposals or analyses fade into obscurity or are covered up. Technologists are like medical practitioners – they bury their mistakes.

6.10 CONCLUSION

Innovation tends to follow an orderly progression in which advancement takes place by a process of extrapolation or analogous substitution. Occasionally, a quantum shift to a new paradigm will take place. This occurs only when the actual or perceived economic returns will be increased thereby. These may take the form of a tangible improvement in a manufacturing process to increase yield, or they may make an operation less hazardous, for example by circumventing competitors' patents. Typically, such a shift will not be initiated by an existing market leader, although a consequence may well be that the relative competitive power of the participants will alter, which increases the chances of a change in market leadership. The corollary is that it is necessary for participants in a innovation-rich market to take continuous steps to maintain market share. This may include the use of market power to control or neutralise the effects of the paradigm shift.

The success of an invention depends on two criteria – it must be linked to suitable enabling technologies and there must be a potential need for it. The former is an absolute requirement and the latter a relative one. Both of these parameters will vary with time. Not only must demand be created, but the innovation must present a more attractive proposition than alternative offerings. The consequence is that innovation is a time-critical, binary decision process in which the opportunity cost of returning to a rejected option will usually exceed that of following the current line of development – once an innovation is passed over, the chances of returning to it are slight. The opportunity cost of changing paradigms is also time-dependent, with the result that some innovations will be ephemeral.

Since the criteria for success of an innovation are the existence of an economic advantage, physical feasibility and commitment from the inventor, it follows that innovation is a socio-deterministic process. This does not mean that heroic inventors are less likely to make inventions. Indeed, they will have a greater propensity to do so because of their enhanced faculties. Their inventions will, however, fail if they do not meet these requirements. Inventions which fail disappear into obscurity, whatever their origins.

Innovations follow a learning curve of increasing efficiency. This permits a manufacturer to maintain profitability whilst reducing his selling price, which asymptotically approaches a value determined by physical constraints. When this stage is reached, no further significant improvement can take place without a paradigm shift.

Occasionally, a paradigm shift may represent a false start. If the gains are marginal, a deterioration in operating economics will spell failure. The instigator of a shift may possess a strong proprietary position, either by knowledge of secret processes or possession of intellectual property rights. This increases the cost of market entry for competitors, who may thus either continue along an existing development path or adopt further alternatives. If a paradigm is not adopted universally it may fail for lack of critical mass.

The economic dividend created by innovation may not all be taken in the form of increased speed or efficiency of operation. As an alternative, the innovation rent may be captured from reduced cost of labour, raw materials or overhead contribution made possible by the enhanced performance.

Advance in technology serving primary consumers oscillates between a learning phase in which the supplier enters a new paradigm and a profit-earning phase in which the supplier operates the technology at maximum efficiency.

Moore's Law, which was expounded in the context of the semiconductor industry, stating that the density of components on a chip will double every eighteen months, is the limiting case of a series of paradigm shifts. The magnitude of the characteristic time interval is dependent on the response times and the learning curves for the manufacturer of semiconductor devices *per se* and of the suppliers of equipment used for their manufacture. The fact that the relationship has remained constant is due to the need to maximise returns from each successive paradigm before moving on to the next one. It is fortuitous that the response time of the equipment supply industry is sufficiently short to permit this. Each iteration is accompanied by a substantial increase in the cost of market entry.

The proposition may be generalised for other industries in which there is progression by means of a series of pendulum swings between successive advances in a primary industry and a secondary industry which supplies the means of production to the primary industry.

There is a tendency to re-invent. This may be the repetition of thought processes in response to similar stimuli such as reiteration of a need or the fresh statement of an old problem. The invention will succeed when physical constraints are removed, for example by the development of new materials, and the economic environment is right. Inauspicious phasing of these conditions will result in missed opportunities. Perception also plays a role – inventions may be conceived after they are obsolete. However, such inventions may have the effect of extending the viability of a mature technology.

Although an heroic model is appropriate for certain inventions such as Tesla's alternating current machines, evidence from the case studies supports a primarily socio-economic model for invention. Circumstances conducive to paradigm shifts in the course of innovation have been highlighted. This leads to the conclusion that the timing of the emergence of an innovation is crucial to its success. On the one hand, the opportunity cost of change means that paradigm shifts, once initiated, may be irreversible, whilst, on the other hand, the success of a paradigm shift may be dependent on achieving a critical mass.

The need to create an infrastructure will moderate the uptake of an innovation. It may also provide a Keynesian influence for suppliers. In such instances, bipedal advance can result in a generalised example of the Moore's Law phenomenon observed in the semiconductor industry.

For specific applications, an individually optimised approach will prevail over a general-purpose design – the complex-instruction set microprocessor overcame the challenge of the reduced-instruction set competition.

Innovations may reappear at intervals, but will only succeed if all of the ambient circumstances are right. This could include a requirement for an inventor with a receptive mind to take advantage of lateral thinking or serendipity.

Learning is an incremental process, but provides an opportunity to control markets by response-time monopolies.

7. 'All Change!' – Stimuli and Constraints

Technically the material was what the research program called for, a new polymer with adhesive properties. But in examining it, Silver noticed amongst its other curious properties that this material was not 'aggressively' adhesive. It would create what 3M scientists call 'tack' between two surfaces, but it would not bond tightly to them. Also – and this was a problem not solved for years – this material was more 'cohesive' than 'adhesive.' It clung to its own molecules better than it clung to any other molecules. So if you sprayed it on a surface (it was sprayable, another property that attracted Silver) and then slapped a piece of paper on the sprayed surface, you could remove all or none of the adhesive when you lifted the paper. It might 'prefer' one surface to another, but not stick well to either.

P.R. Nayak and J.P. Ketteringham, *Breakthroughs!*, p58

Once you've got a machine to function, it generally continues to do so and you forget the maddening struggle to reach that point. The users are a nerve-wrackingly different proposition.

Harold Jackson, *The Guardian*, 16 February 1989

Every time chip performance doubles, the number of electrons required for a gate is reduced by a factor of four. We will run out of electrons. The statistical effect of electrons will be lost. The CMOS end point will occur early next century.

Maurice Wilkes (inventor of microprogramming),
Electronics Weekly, 12 March 1997

Stroud, when asked which one ergonomic office flaw he would change, said it would be the workers.

Paul Bray, *Daily Telegraph*, 12 November 1991

7.1 INTRODUCTION

If it ain't broke, why attempt to fix it? Change is not initiated without motivation. In a capitalist society, this will usually be some form of economic influence. Examples presented in the previous chapter showed that change may take the form of a primary innovation creating intrinsic growth of a mainstream development which generates its own returns, or a secondary innovation which is a necessary ancillary to the progress of a generic invention. Rent may be real – either extant or latent – or perceived, giving rise to the phenomena of market pull and production push. Technological development provides a vehicle for innovation. A new material may provide a stimulus. Equally, the properties of that material might furnish constraints which control the way in which an innovation evolves.

Will disadvantageous properties constitute a threat or are there ways in which potential limitations could be turned to advantage? This chapter analyses the stimuli which give rise to new inventions and the constraints which determine the course of their development.

7.2 THE LAWS OF PHYSICS AND PROPERTIES OF MATERIALS

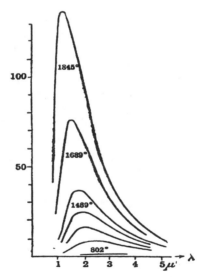

Source   Houston 1915

Figure 7.1 Radiation from heated platinum

The wavelength of radiation emitted by a heated body is governed by the Stefan-Boltzmann Law of Black Body Radiation, which determines the minimum temperature at which a useful proportion of the radiated energy will fall within the visible range (Houston 1915, p445). The relationship between radiation intensity and wavelength for a black body at different temperatures is shown in Figure 7.1. This indicates that, at lower temperatures, most of the energy is radiated in the form of heat, whilst, if the body is at a higher temperature, a greater proportion is emitted in the form of visible radiation. In consequence, if a body, such as the filament of a lamp, is raised to a particular temperature, it will act as a source of illumination, but the useful proportion of radiation which is in the visible range is not amenable to control. Some further physical mechanism, such as the incorporation of a fluorescent phosphor, is required to overcome this constraint.

Early experimental work on incandescent lamps was based on the noble metals, platinum and iridium, because they were not oxidised by heating to a high temperature and, as a result, the filaments would not suffer attrition as a result of exposure to atmospheric gases (Cullis 2004, Case Study 1). However, filaments made from these materials proved unreliable because, to achieve incandescence, it was necessary to heat them to a temperature too close to their melting point. At such elevated temperatures the metal softened and the filaments frequently fused.

Carbon exists in the solid phase at much higher temperatures, but initially could not be substituted for the noble metals because, even in the presence of minute quantities of oxygen, it is oxidised to form carbon dioxide. This problem was tackled by mounting the carbon 'burner' in an evacuated vessel. Early vacuum pumps were not adequate and left sufficient residual oxygen to react with the carbon. When Sprengel and Geissler devised better vacuum pumps, it was found that the carbon was still oxidised – this time by oxygen which had been adsorbed by the carbon and which was driven off when it was heated to an elevated temperature. Edison and Swan overcame this independently by the technique of 'running on the pumps' in which the filament was heated *in vacuo* to increasingly elevated temperatures.

When eventually a sufficiently good vacuum was obtained, despite the fact that the carbon filaments survived, the performance of the lamps still degraded slowly due to the sublimation of small amounts of carbon, which was deposited as an opaque film on the inner surface of the glass bulb, reducing the amount of light which was emitted.

Although carbon became the material of choice because it could be heated to a higher temperature, it was, in turn, superseded by the refractory metals osmium, tantalum and tungsten as metallurgists successively solved the problem of forming thin wires from these materials. At first, the lamp filaments were made by mixing metal powder with an organic binder to form a paste which was extruded and fired to drive off the binder and sinter the metal particles together. Subsequently a method of hot working was devised to form flexible wires of tungsten. Many years later, the operating temperature of the filament was raised through the agency of the incorporation of a small quantity of halogen in the atmosphere within the lamp envelope. This had the property of acting as a transport medium to re-deposit tungsten on the hot spots of the filament, thus making the filament less susceptible to fusing. Fused quartz was employed in the envelope in place of normal glass as it was able to withstand the higher temperature.

In this case, the innovation progressed by improvements until it was eventually limited by constraints resulting from the physical properties of materials. These constraints provided a stimulus to search for means by which they might be overcome, but these solutions were, in turn, subject to new and different physical barriers.

The mechanism underlying the triode valve was control of a current of electrons generated by thermionic emission from a heated cathode coated with barium oxide or thoria, materials selected for their low work function (the energy required to drive an electron from the surface of the material) (Cullis 2004, Case Study 2). The heater required to raise the cathode to its working temperature consumed around 2 watts of electrical power, whilst the high-tension circuit to control electron flow used a further 2.5 watts. A bipolar transistor performing the same amplification task as a thermionic valve requires no heater because it operates at room temperature. It does not require a high-voltage source and even early examples drew only two milliwatts from the power supply – a more than two thousand times improvement in energy efficiency. A further direct consequence of the lower power consumption, which results from the different physical principles governing its *modus operandi*, is that, as the transistor dissipates less energy, the associated electronic components, the performance of which is degraded by heat, will be much more reliable.

Three materials which could have formed the basis for the semiconductor industry were the elements germanium and silicon and the compound gallium arsenide. These materials form single crystals and are hence much more suitable for the fabrication of consistently reproducible devices than polycrystalline cuprous oxide, cuprous sulphide and selenium, which were the semiconductor materials commonly available in the first part of the twentieth century.

Quantum physics proposes that, in semiconductor materials, charge carriers may exist only in certain energy states. A semiconductor is characterised by a so-called band gap – a range of forbidden energy states and by the mobility of free charge carriers within its crystalline structure. A wide band gap makes the material suitable for the fabrication of electronic components with high breakdown voltages, whilst a high charge carrier mobility is desirable for a good high-frequency performance. Of the three materials, gallium arsenide has the widest band gap and highest carrier mobility, but its constituent elements, gallium and arsenic, have a high vapour pressure at elevated temperatures, which means that manufacturing processes would be difficult to control. Germanium has a higher carrier mobility than silicon, but the latter actually became the semiconductor of choice for the manufacture of integrated circuits because it possesses manageable physical and chemical properties. Of especial value was the stable, passivating glassy oxide which could readily be formed on the surface of a crystal, its amenability to epitaxial deposition in thin layers, straightforward incorporation of substitutional impurities within the crystal lattice and convenient chemistry in which dopants could be introduced by chemical vapour deposition of their halides and hydrides.

7.3 ENABLING INVENTIONS

Until the end of the eighteenth century, all knowledge of electrical phenomena was based on electrostatics. At this stage, Volta, developing Galvani's observations, constructed his *pile* and *couronne des tasses*, thereby making available a source of continuous current for the first time. Humphry Davy seized upon this and prevailed upon his patrons at the Royal Institution to provide him with a two-thousand-cell battery. His experiments with this laid the foundations of electrochemistry and enabled him to perform demonstrations of the electric arc, the incandescent filament and the luminous gaseous discharge which were the bases of three major techniques for converting electrical energy into light.

By first propounding a theory of the relationship between electricity and magnetism, and then constructing a machine which translated these principles into practice, Faraday made possible the generation of electricity using mechanical energy, which was freely available in the form of steam or water power. Gramme and Henry turned Faraday's experiments into practical generators, which permitted the substitution of cheap and plentiful coal for the expensive fuel (zinc) which was consumed in voltaic cells to provide a continuous source of current. This reduction in input costs made it possible for the electric arc and, later, the incandescent filament lamp, to compete successfully with gas.

Early carbon incandescent lamps suffered attrition of the burner due to 'air washing' and oxidation of the carbon. This gave rise to premature failure. The development of the mercury pump by Geissler and Sprengel was the keystone invention which permitted greatly improved vacua to be created. This, together with the technique of 'running on the pumps' to remove occluded gases, made lamps based on thin carbon filaments viable and hence it became possible to sub-divide the light.

Swan, Powell and others developed the process of extruding a continuous filament of cellulose material which was subsequently carbonised to provide a lamp filament. Auer von Welsbach adapted this technique by mixing refractory metals with a hydrocarbon binder and extruding the mixture to form filaments which were heat-treated to decompose the binder and sinter the metal particles to form the first metal wires which were capable of operating at a higher temperature than carbon.

Fleming's deafness stimulated him to adapt the Edison Effect lamp as a non-auditory detector of wireless signals. De Forest modified Fleming's resulting diode to make his, more sensitive, Audion detector. The properties of the Audion enabled weak signals to be amplified and thus formed the foundation for the growth of the electronics industry.

In each of the above examples, an enabling invention or the propounding of a new theory was required before development of a paradigm could take place.

7.4 THE ECONOMIC MOTIVATION

Although Tesla's alternating current machines were conceived theoretically, they solved the pressing practical problem of providing a system in which electrical power could be transmitted over long distances and thus yielded a significant economic gain.

The first primitive four-bit microprocessor, the Intel 4004, was created to meet a need for a simple controller. Its computing power was limited, but further development of the operating software made it able to perform more extensive functions than the one for which it was originally conceived. By a process of extrapolative development, the 4004 evolved into the 8008, the 8080, the 8086, the 80186, the 80286, the 80386, the 80486, the Pentium and the Pentium Pro. Each new processor was capable of running on the software designed for its predecessor, but at a much greater speed. This generated sales and created a market base which made viable the development of new software which would run only on the latest generation of the microprocessor. Each time, this new software was capable of performing both different and more elaborate tasks than its predecessors. The need for users continually to purchase upgrades provided a steady source of income to support the software developers.

Associated with each generation of processor was the ability to store data in a transient memory. The first general-purpose personal computers had four thousand (4K) bytes of data storage capacity. This capability grew exponentially – 16K, 64K, 512K, 1M – and, in a subsequent generation, a Pentium IV processor running several applications concurrently under Windows XP required at least 64 megabytes of random-access memory chips. As the microprocessor has developed, there has also been an explosive growth in peripheral hardware such as printers, scanners, disc drives, memory chips, visual display units (both flat-screen and cathode-ray-tube based) and software – word processors, spreadsheets, databases, image processing, optical character recognition and computer-aided design.

Edison, on occasion, was content simply to close the loop and allow the gains from one innovation to finance later ones, possibly unrelated, simply because he wished to invent for its own sake. For example, he used his profits from the quadruplex telegraph in an attempt to devise a sextuplex system, whilst his ore refining enterprise spawned a Portland cement plant for prefabricated building construction. Shockley, too, regarded his tally of inventions as an indicator of success in research.

7.5 COUPLED PARADIGMS

I remember arguments that 64K was about the right size for memory because that was as much as a human being could handle. But we've developed this marvellous spiral, where software people seem to write things that will barely run in this generation of machines, so we have to upgrade the hardware, and then they write software that needs even more powerful hardware. That works out very well for the hardware people, who would rather make more powerful processors and bigger memory chips. No one I know is predicting that's going to stop yet. In fact, it's going to continue for quite a while – I hope it does.
Gordon Moore, *The Guardian*, 27 March 1997

The more complex microprocessors and memory chips, made possible by the improvements in photolithography, found application in more powerful personal computers (PCs). The first generally used PCs, such as the Apple II, the Commodore Pet and the Tandy TRS-80, were those based on the Mostek 6502 and the Intel 8080 eight-bit microprocessors, which were capable of addressing 64 kilobytes of memory. A wide range of applications programs was written for these computers, but the most significant of these was VisiCalc, the first spreadsheet software, which permitted users to perform 'What if?' calculations and motivated users to purchase computers specifically to run the application.

This first generation of PCs was superseded some three years later by a range of machines based on sixteen-bit processors from Intel (the 8086) and Motorola (the 68000). The IBM PC and the Apple Macintosh established themselves as *de facto* standards. Every three years or so, a new, more powerful generation of PCs took the place of its predecessors. Software was developed to take advantage of the increased power of the new machines. Certain programs, particularly word processors, spreadsheets, relational database managers and computer-aided drafting, achieved widespread adoption. Some, such as Lotus 1-2-3, WordStar, dBase and AutoCAD gained high popularity. Improved versions, each with added features, were written to take advantage of the new properties of each successive microprocessor. Users, in turn, were persuaded to purchase this upgraded software and a new machine on which to run it, despite the fact that their existing machines were not worn out and that their existing software continued to perform to its original design specification. Suppliers who did not match the advances of their competitors disappeared whilst newcomers took their places. VisiCalc was replaced by Lotus 1-2-3, which was superseded by Excel; Electric Pencil gave way to WordStar, WordPerfect and ultimately Microsoft Word; dBase was supplanted as market leader by Paradox and then Access.

Expansion of broadcasting led to a demand for valves with improved operating characteristics. New valves with improved performance permitted users to advance the frontiers of radio transmission. Development of microprocessors of ever greater speed and capacity, driven by demand for ever more powerful computers and the relentless advance in size of dynamic random-access memory (DRAM) chips, following the pattern laid down by Moore's Law, spawned new silicon processing techniques.

7.6 THE 'AVIS' EFFECT

The market leader has a tendency to rest on his laurels. In the words of the advertising slogan of Avis, the challenger to Hertz in the US car rental market, 'When you're second, you try harder.' Number 2 has the advantage that hindsight is more effective than foresight and it can avoid some of the pitfalls met by a pioneer.

After the initial (Schumpeter A-) stages, the manufacturing process for the carbon filament lamp stabilised. In most of the markets where they both participated, Edison and Swan pooled their resources and united to suppress competitors. For the remainder of the lifetime of the patents, they enjoyed a relatively comfortable existence, milking the cash cow that their monopolies had created. The consequence was that there was no incentive to change the product (Cullis 2004, Case Study 1). The significant development which signalled the demise of the carbon filament, the extruded, sintered metal filament lamp, was devised by an outsider, Auer von Welsbach, who was able to use the patents associated with the new development to establish the Osram lamp business in Germany.

After initial sparring for position, the cable telegraph companies set up a cartel and made a price-fixing agreement which guaranteed them a handsome profit (Cullis 2004, Case Study 2). It was left to an outsider, Guglielmo Marconi, to conduct experiments with Hertzian waves and to lay the foundations of the wireless communications industry. Eventually cable and wireless were merged into a single commercial operation, but, by this stage, wireless had assumed a dominant role and the cable companies had to be content with the role of junior partner.

In the semiconductor industry, the two most significant innovations – the adoption of silicon as the basic material for device fabrication and the conception of the planar process for the manufacture of integrated circuits – came respectively from Texas Instruments and Fairchild Camera and Instrument Corporation, two companies which, when they initiated these changes, were only bit-part players on the transistor stage (Cullis 2004, Case Study 3).

7.7 CONCLUSION

The laws of physics constrain the freedom to innovate. Frequently, choice of material is a compromise between desirable physical properties and ease of processing. It may also be a compromise between opposing physical properties. During the course of development, new processes may evolve to overcome these difficulties, but will, in turn, be subject to fresh constraints.

The laws of physics and properties of materials will therefore make the progress of some inventions difficult, or simply impossible. They may equally open up fresh avenues or create a prejudice in favour of a particular line of development.

Many innovations cannot be realised until some enabling discovery is made or some basic theory is propounded. A major departure from existing practice may require the agency of an enabling invention to make it viable. This stimulus provides a keystone on which the paradigm shift will be supported. Such a fuse or trigger for innovation may be the application of a similar idea in the same field, an analogous development in another, possibly non-related, field, the development of an enabling technology or discovery of a new material with better properties than the one currently used.

Innovation will require some form of driver to supply the economic power to fuel its progress. The invention of the incandescent lamp met an inherent need by providing artificial light, thus extending the length of the natural day – financial gain arose from the ability to work longer hours. The need to communicate provided the motivation for the electric telegraph, whilst the reduction in the requirement for skilled operators stimulated the change from telegraphy to telephony.

In some instances a new technology will generate its own economic motivation. The ability to broadcast to many receivers from a single radio transmitter led to a new form of entertainment, demand for which created a derived need to innovate in ancillary technologies such as the thermionic valve. Occasionally, too, the innovation may be powered by factors other than the purely economic, for example when an inventor takes his pleasure simply from the successful realisation of his ideas.

When the adoption of a new paradigm offers a large increase in innovation rent, it will stimulate a transfer regardless of the fact that the previous paradigm continues to offer undiminished returns. Market participants will be forced to make the change since without it their operations would cease to be viable. This premature obsolescence, which gives rise to a concept of a life-cycle treadmill, is a special case of the 'Red Queen' syndrome.

A corollary to the revelation that an innovation may create its own economic motivation is the proposition that the new industries which result may interact with their progenitor in a synergistic manner. A coupled system, in which advances in one innovation create an order of magnitude improvement in innovation rent from another, behaves like a relaxation oscillator, flipping between alternate modes in which one innovation passes through a learning phase whilst the technology for a fresh paradigm shift develops in the other.

A follower in a developing market enjoys the benefit of hindsight. It is therefore more likely that a paradigm transition will originate from a player outside the current market leaders. The portents which favour a newcomer are two-fold – a head-to-head confrontation with the market leader is avoided and there is no NIH factor to be overcome.

8. Faith, Hope and Clarity – the Inventor's Role

When a distinguished but elderly scientist says that something is possible, he is almost certainly right. When he says it is impossible, he is very probably wrong.
Clarke's First Law, Arthur C. Clarke, *Profiles of the Future*, (1962)

If Newton could not predict the behaviour of three balls, could Marx predict the behaviour of three people? Any regularity in the behaviour of large assemblies of particles or people must be *statistical* and that has quite a different philosophical taste.
Tim Poston and Ian Stewart, quoted by Ian Stewart in *Does God Play Dice?*

He knows a lot but he doesn't stick to the job. I set him at work developing details of a plan. But when he happens to note some phenomenon new to him, though easily seen to be of no importance in this apparatus, he gets side-tracked, follows it up and loses time. *He can't be spending time that way!* ... We have got to keep working up things of commercial value – that is what this laboratory is for. We can't be like the old German professor who as long as he can get his black bread and beer is content to spend his whole life studying the fuzz on a bee!'
Thomas Edison, quoted by Francis Jehl in *Menlo Park Reminiscences*, p862

When heads were added, they were nearly always PhDs, and the problem with PhDs is that they are headstrong; they won't do what you tell them to.
Robert X. Cringely, *Accidental Empires*, p108

No inventor can be a man of business, you know.
Charles Dickens, *Little Dorrit*

8.1 INTRODUCTION

Potentially the least predictable aspect of innovation is that which involves the agency of human beings. For instance, polytechnic individuals will bring a broader range of skills to the task than the average man skilled in the art but, in order to succeed, will they need to possess greater facility than average when applying their knowledge? Must they think also laterally? It is possible that they will be exceptionally motivated but will this, in turn, engender the perseverance necessary to carry ideas to fruition? How will the propensity to invent vary throughout their lifetime? It may be postulated that, since other pursuits, such as business activities, will occupy the time of older men, inventors will be more prolific in their youth.

This chapter examines the contribution to innovation made by inventors, when they make it and what 'makes them tick'. It concludes by analysing the disparate characteristics of the behaviour of inventors, in order to identify those traits and circumstances which are more conducive to inventing.

8.2 THE INVENTIVE MIND

8.2.1 Breadth of Vision

Joseph Swan trained initially as a pharmacist. Whilst employed in this business, he made a number of chemical inventions, including the carbon photographic process, a method of tanning leather and a new technique for purifying opium (GB Pat 4745/1877). He diversified into the electric lamp and was a pioneering inventor of the incandescent carbon filament. Later, in an endeavour to improve the filament, he harked back to his chemical roots and developed a process for the extrusion of a structureless thread of carbon-based material (GB Pat 5978/1883). As well as making this material into lamp filaments by heat treatment, he realised that it also had application as a textile. The invention became the foundation of the artificial silk industry.

When he visited Paris he was given a demonstration of Planté's lead-acid storage battery. On his return to England he commenced work on these cells with a view to producing a portable miners' lamp, making several improvements to the method of construction (GB Pat 2272/1881). Even towards the end of his life, he continued with his scientific activities and when he died he was trying to find suitable materials for the construction of a fuel cell.

When Swan returned to the development of the incandescent lamp at the end of the 1870s, he formed an alliance with Charles Stearne (Swan 1929, p62), who had particular knowledge of high vacuum techniques and R.E. Crompton, who had already established himself as an expert manufacturer of electrical generation and distribution equipment (Crompton 1928, p93).

The range of Thomas Edison's inventions is legendary (Cullis 2004, Appendix 6). Starting with the vote recorder, he extrapolated the principles employed in its construction to devise improvements in the electric telegraph, the telephone and, finally, wireless communication by induction. Initial attempts to record telegraphic signals gave rise to the phonograph, which he continued to improve into his twilight years. The lamp and its infrastructure spawned a plethora of inventions, whilst early ideas for magnetic separation of ores were the foundation of large industrial ventures at the turn of the century. He worked for many years on electric batteries and electrochemical deposition. In addition, his creative mind indulged in flights of fancy with pyromagnetic motors and generators, the tasimeter, various acoustic devices, vacuum preservation of meat and fresh vegetables, flying machines, military projectiles and the production of rubber.

Edison reinforced his limited formal education by reading widely, a habit he acquired in his youth, when he spent the stopover between his morning and evening news-vending stints ensconced in the reading room of the Young Men's Association in Detroit. One of his initial acts, when he founded his laboratories at Menlo Park, was to set up a well-stocked library, and his first priority when embarking on a new development was to read the current literature on the subject.

8.2.2 Many Hands Make Light Work

When Edison was embarking on the development of the incandescent lamp, he set up the world's first industrial research laboratory at Menlo Park. He staffed it with craftsmen who possessed a wide range of skills, thereby supplementing his own practically acquired, empirical knowledge. At Bell Telephone Laboratories, Shockley was supported by an army of scientists and technicians with skills in subjects such as materials technology and electronics which would be useful in the quest for a solid-state amplifier. When developing high-temperature superconductors, Paul Chu called on the services of Robert Hazen for x-ray measurements and Arthur Freeman for theoretical calculations (Hazen 1988).

8.2.3 The 'Jesuit' Syndrome

Research for my Ph.D. at the Massachusetts Institute of Technology later contributed to my motivation toward solid-state electronics at Bell Laboratories. I was one of Professor Slater's students when his chief interest emphasized wave functions in crystals. My thesis involved sodium chloride. About fifteen years later, I saw that a feature of the band edges for my thesis calculations must represent a general situation and published a brief note applying it to electron and hole masses in connection with transistor-related semiconductor theory.
     William Shockley

Bardeen and Brattain's discovery was very exciting news, perhaps even more so for me than for many others because I had long nourished an interest in germanium that had started with my undertaking graduate study at Brown University under Prof. Charles A. Kraus, American Chemical Society president, and Willard Gibbs, Franklin and Priestley Medalist, who was one of the two outstanding US experts on germanium at that time. My master's and doctor's theses were on germanium. It was a material studied only for its scientific interest; its complete uselessness fascinated and challenged me. My concentration on this shiny metallic-appearing material during my graduate school days resulted in a continuing personal sentimental attachment for germanium, which, to me, at least was and is an exotic element. This deep but little personal attachment influenced me from time to time over an eighteen-year period after leaving Brown to seek some way of capitalizing on this and interest acquired years before.
     Gordon Teal

It was a fateful moment. Not only did strontium titanate help Müller to get his doctorate, it led him to study the crystallographic literature about the class of materials to which this compound belongs and set him on a road which would become apparent only years later.
     Gerald Holton *et al. How a Scientific Discovery is Made*

In his youth, Joseph Swan attended lectures on scientific subjects at the Sunderland Athenæum. In the *Repertory of Patent Inventions* he read an account of Starr's incandescent lamp. He attended a lecture by W.E. Staite and saw him demonstrate incandescent lighting using a platino-iridium wire. He later commented, 'It was like a seed sown in my mind.'

During the 1850s, Swan carried out extensive experiments on incandescent lighting by carbon filaments. He abandoned the work in 1860, but eventually returned to it and developed a successful lamp.

What part do an inventor's roots play in his later career? The above quotations indicate that the philosophy of St. Ignatius Loyola ('Give me a child until he is seven and I will show you the man.') applies also to inventors. Early exposure to a particular technology can create a latent bond which persists for the remainder of the lifetime.

8.3 ETHICS

Human nature has its less attractive side. Traits such as covetousness and dishonesty may be displayed in the context of inventions as well as in other aspects of an inventor's life. Such behavioural characteristics may be manifest in the exploitation of the weak and a lack of balance in treading the fine line between truth and falsehood.

8.3.1 *'Droit du Seigneur'*

Edison clearly exploited his employees, many of whom were recent immigrants and would have regarded themselves as beholden to him for having given them employment and dependent on him for future beneficence. He may even have selected them for their vulnerability, although this cannot be demonstrated. He did part company abruptly with those who, like Tesla, stood up to him or did not bend to his will. He looked upon their work as his own, taking credit for their achievements. There is strong evidence from correspondence between William Hammer and Francis Jehl, and from the similarity between the apparatus illustrated in Jehl's *Menlo Park Reminiscences* and the drawings of US Patent 251536, that Edison claimed inventorship which was properly due to Jehl. Nowadays, such an act would be deemed to be fraud on the US Patent Office. It has its counterpart in modern academe where it is the custom of some heads of department to take credit for papers written by their subordinates.

In Edison's case this behaviour was a sub-set of a wider trait – the vainglorious attempt to amass a large tally of patents. To this end he filed applications on trivial improvements, mere variants and non-workable ideas.

To a lesser extent, Shockley behaved in a similar manner and filed patent applications on inventions which were non-starters. Like Edison, he regarded the grant of patents *per se* as an indicator of prestige and achievement, although there is no indication that he appropriated the credit for inventions made by his co-workers.

8.3.2 Fraud and Economy with the Truth

Although Edison was not averse to lying, cheating and stealing if he thought it would help him to achieve his ends, engineers and scientists in general have a code of absolute honesty (Cringely 1992 p12, Grayson 1995). There is, however, a distinction between inventions, which are protected by patents, and intellectual creations protected by copyright. The person at the

Clapham workstation does not feel much inhibition when making a copy of somebody else's proprietary software – indeed, at one stage it was estimated that, for every legitimate copy of the WordStar word processor, there were five pirate ones – but the same person would think twice before stealing an invention. This may be due to the relative effort involved, since it is very easy and cheap to put a book on a photocopier, or slip a floppy disc into a computer, but it is usually a major effort to duplicate a hardware construction. The likelihood of detection is also smaller.

8.4 MOTIVATION

8.4.1 The 'Will to Think'

At the middle of the nineteenth century, there was a great movement to improve public sanitation and a consequential expansion of municipal water supplies. A need arose for a means of metering in order to prevent waste. William Siemens perceived this need and resolved to contrive a solution. He eventually devised an arrangement based on a screw thread or helical vanes. This proved to be very successful and earned a royalty income in excess of £1000 per annum for many years.

In 1940, Enrico Fermi, the atomic physicist, was designing experiments to study the retardation of high-energy neutrons when passing through graphite, a process which would be vital to the construction of a nuclear reactor. The prospect that these experiments would be performed was assured when the US government allocated funding to the project. This indication provided the motivation for Fermi to devote his mental resources to the solution of the problem.

William Shockley conceived the junction transistor on 23 January 1948. He prepared a detailed theoretical analysis of its *modus operandi* for a patent application which was filed on 26 June 1948. A subsequent review of his notebook entries showed that this analysis was sufficient only to show how experiment might be combined with theory of *pn* junctions. A detailed exposition did not follow until a later stage. What stimulated the thought process necessary to develop the mathematical relationship necessary for the invention of the junction transistor was Shockley's desire to make a personal contribution to what was clearly going to be a major commercial innovation and, secondly, a desire to resolve some of the unexplained questions concerning the operation of the point-contact transistor.

8.4.2 Determination and Persistence – the 'Grass Widow' Effect

Following our growth of the first germanium single crystals, John and I sought to improve the equipment, and on completion of the movable puller equipment we continued working with it at nights in Building I. It turned out impossible to get a separate small laboratory assigned to the equipment. The best bargain that I could make was permission to set the puller in the middle of a large metallurgical shop, on a lower floor, for use at night as long as I would promise to roll the puller equipment into a closet when we or I finished each night so it wouldn't be in the way of the metallurgists during the daytime.

This meant that frequently around 2 or 3 o'clock in the morning I had to disconnect from the wall approximately 30-ft hydrogen, nitrogen, and water-cooling lines leading to the puller as well as high-power electric lines to the high-frequency heater. Then the puller, which was about 2 square ft and 6 or 7 ft high, with the above line attachments, was rolled into the storage closet and the high-frequency heater moved some 25-30 ft into an unused shop corner. About 4.30 pm when the technicians started getting ready to go home, I could reverse the process and begin crystal-growing experiments again.

This became pretty much a way of life for me during almost all of 1949. Naturally, this led to unusually long work days and weeks in view of my carrying my regularly assigned project on silicon carbide during the days. My family, i.e. my wife and three small sons, of course, bore the burden of my long hours at work away from home. Though I am sure they were lonely at times because of the little time I had to participate in their activities, they were interested and excited by their thoughts that the research I spent so much time on seemed that important.

    Gordon Teal

The Lab phone rang as I was about to leave. It was Margee. 'Hey, remember me? It's after eight o'clock and I'm sort of hungry. Are you by any chance playing with hydrogen again?'

I sighed. 'No, it's not hydrogen this time. I'll tell you all about it when I get home. I'm on my way, I promise.'

I kept my word and left a few minutes later. But I'd be breaking a lot of other promises in the next four weeks.

The sky was still dark at 6:30 a.m. It was too early to get up on a Saturday, but I had slept well and felt driven to get back to work. Quietly slipping out of bed so as not to disturb Margee, I threw on an old pair of jeans and a sweater and headed downstairs for a hasty breakfast. I was back at the Lab by 7:30.

I responded sympathetically and Margee soon calmed down. With the kids safely deposited at school, she suggested we relax and share a big breakfast. 'I want to hear all about your trip,' she added.

'I don't have that much time.' I must have sounded remote because her tone of voice changed suddenly.

'What do you mean? You've been working for two days straight.'

'I know, but I have to get to the Lab. I picked up some useful information in Chicago and have to get to work on it.' By this time I was in the shower and had to talk loudly to make myself heard over the water. 'I'll just grab a quick bowl of cereal on my way out.'

There was no response for a minute or so. Then she drew back the shower curtain and stared at me. Her voice was hard. 'OK, I understand. But I hope you have your goals in life in the proper balance.' And then she turned abruptly and walked away.

I didn't know what to say. I wanted to be with her, but for the moment nothing was more important than this experiment.

Like video game addicts we kept trying models and making maps. I processed the new data every hour now, only twelve or fifteen new reflections at a time. We were sure that the solution would soon be ours.

I had promised Margee that I would meet her and the kids for a pizza dinner out. My mid-afternoon estimate was to meet at 5:00 p.m., but at 4:30, with several different models yet to try, I knew I'd never make it. I called home briefly to adjust the schedule to 5:30 and went back to the computer.

We shuffled oxygens in the remaining possible sites, at the barium levels and at the copper level between the two barium atoms. All of the possible structures gave similar residuals of about 8 percent, and all had flaws. It was 5:00 p.m. and we still had more to do.

My second call home was not unexpected. 'How about six?' I asked, without explanation.

'Fine, no problem. See you then.' It may have been our shortest phone conversation on record.

The family's volatile eating schedule was thrown off once again by a particularly knotty problem in describing one of the low-symmetry variants of the perovskite structure. The lower the symmetry, the greater the number of different atoms that must be described separately to build the unit cell. It was almost 6:00 p.m. when we got it right.

One more time. 'Hi! Guess what? It'll be six-thirty for sure. I promise.'

I actually made it to the eating place by 6:50, where the large pizza with extra cheese and sausage was just being sliced. Other than her lightly mocking 'Nice timing, Bob,' Margee seemed unperturbed by my erratic schedule. Perhaps she sensed that we had almost solved the problem and that things would soon be back to normal.

At last, forty-five minutes late, we boarded the plane, taking off just in time to reach Washington within the legal limit. I was exhausted, but home was not my first destination. Art Freeman's exhortations about the green phase had done their damage; I knew I wouldn't be able to sleep until I had mounted the largest available crystal and begun the x-ray process anew. If I followed the right route, the Lab was on the way home from the airport anyway.

It was just after midnight when I phoned home to assure Margee that I was safe and at work. She was not exactly happy at the decision, but she wasn't surprised either. By this time my nocturnal habits were all too familiar. After a few sympathetic questions about the lecture and flight home she left me alone to the quiet confines of the x-ray lab. The diffractometer with the black crystal was grinding away, but I did no more than glance at the output to make sure things were in order. For the time being the perovskite-like black compound was forgotten. I was after the green phase this time.

Robert Hazen

These extracts from autobiographical writings of two inventors show that the driving force of discovery is subservient to the social demands of family life. Edison, too, was a compulsive worker, who regularly toiled into the small hours, fostering the legend that he needed no sleep. In fact, he would bed down in a corner of the laboratory, not wishing to spend the time returning home, which was only a few steps from his Menlo Park laboratory.

In the pioneering days of the personal computer, the 'nerds' lost all sense of time. Development of their programs became an obsession. They worked round the clock for days on end, cat-napping in the lab, and surviving on a diet of Coke and pizza. The night before the launch of the IBM PC, Bill Gates worked through, checking his software. He appeared for the launch, unkempt and without even having taken time out for a shower, when, in the words of a colleague, 'He *needed* a shower' (Cringely 1996).

8.4.3 The Product Champion

Nernst, when working on the gas mantle devised by Auer von Welsbach conceived a source of illumination using the same physical principles – radiation of light by an incandescent mixture of refractory oxides – but replacing the gas flame by an electric current flowing through a resistive load as the energy source to heat the oxides to a temperature at which they emit visible rays. This development was away from the main-stream of electric lighting which, at the time, was based on the incandescent carbon filament. Nernst developed his lamp from an impractical prototype in which the initial heating of the refractory rod required the agency of an external flame, to a viable product in which the priming was performed by the passage of an electric current through a pre-heater element which was automatically disconnected when the lamp reached operating temperature. The actual lamp was a plug-in replacement for the commercially available incandescent lamps. Nernst assigned his rights to AEG, which manufactured and sold them for a brief period. Production was abandoned when metal filament lamps, notably using tungsten, became widely available.

Post-war work on the solid-state amplifier at Bell Telephone Laboratories was based largely on the materials developed by Lark-Horowitz at Purdue University for the manufacture of diodes for use as high-frequency detectors in wartime radar receivers. These devices used polycrystalline ingots of germanium or silicon as the starting material. Gordon Teal, however, was convinced that single crystals would be more suitable as a source material for the transistor. He worked at night, in the face of great difficulty, and successfully developed apparatus for growing single crystals of germanium.

Whilst mainstream development of the junction transistor was concerned with bipolar devices, Tezner, in France, worked on the junction-gate, field-effect transistor (JUGFET). Many of his designs required physical processing of individual devices rather than batch processing of ever larger groups, which was the trend elsewhere. He did manage to produce and sell small numbers of JUGFETs, but they satisfied only a niche market and, even for this, were eventually supplanted by metal-oxide-semiconductor field-effect transistors produced by a variant of the planar process.

Companies, also, may fulfil the role of product champion. Philco installed a highly sophisticated plant to produce transistors by a method in which an electrochemical etching process was controlled by a beam of infra-red radiation which was directed through a germanium wafer. Transistors produced by this method had excellent power gains and a high-frequency performance exceeding that of contemporary transistors fabricated by other processes. They were, however, fragile and vulnerable to a phenomenon known as low-voltage punch-through, which frequently resulted in catastrophic failure. After unsuccessfully attempting to establish the process, Philco returned to the use of methods used by other manufacturers in the industry.

Early transistors did not perform well at high frequencies and were not suitable for use in the signal-frequency amplifiers of radio and television receivers, which was a major potential application. Philips addressed this problem by devising the post-alloy diffused transistor (PADT). Two tiny pellets, one of indium and gallium and the other of indium or lead alloyed with a small quantity of arsenic or antimony, were alloyed to a wafer of germanium which had been pre-diffused with an *n*-type impurity. Although it did produce transistors with the desired characteristics, Philips was the only significant manufacturer to adopt this technology, which was superseded after a few years by the planar manufacturing technique which gave transistors with as good, or better, performance but with much less operator involvement in their fabrication.

8.4.4 Cognitive Dissonance

The birth of the point-contact transistor was a magnificent Christmas present for the group as a whole. I shared in the rejoicing. But my emotions were somewhat conflicted. My elation with the group's success was tempered by not being one of the inventors. I experienced some frustration that my personal efforts, started more than eight years before, had not resulted in a significant inventive contribution of my own. In response to this frustration, for the next five years, I did my best to put the Labs – and myself – in the lead for transistor

patents. (I had some success; most of my 90-odd issued US patents relate to the transistor.) The efforts that I made with this motivation account for much of the peak of notebook entries for the month from 24 December 1947 to 24 January 1948. This peak includes the four or five pages that cover the disclosure of the concept of the junction transistor.
    William Shockley

I was told by a well-known expert that mass-produced transistors would never use single-crystal material – the costs of single crystals, according to him, would be much too great in comparison with ingots and, besides, the metallurgically prepared ingots were very good material. Bill Shockley was opposed to work on germanium single crystals when I suggested it, because, as he has publicly stated on several important occasions, he thought that transistor science could be elicited from small specimens cut from polycrystalline masses of material.
    Gordon Teal

The CuCl controversy raged, as scientists at Bell Laboratories convincingly demonstrated that *pure* CuCl was not superconducting. Paul Chu countered with an alternative theory: perhaps superconductivity only occurred in impure CuCl as a result of unusual electronic behavior at the boundaries between CuCl and impurities. Chu's concept of 'interface superconductivity' has never been proved, though it is still a favorite theory of his.
    Robert Hazen, *Superconductors: the Breakthrough*, p33

The above three quotations give, in the inventors' own words, typical attitudes to the relationship between their own achievements and those of others. Rivalry is, in general, a powerful stimulus to greater achievement in many activities. Inventors are likely to be jealous of their reputations, particularly in the modern academic world where to be first past the post brings fame and recognition, whereas coming second is to be consigned to oblivion.

8.4.5   Recognition

When Bell Telephone Laboratories started the research project which ultimately led to the transistor, they assembled a multi-disciplinary team. Materials scientists were key members. They developed the Czochralski method of crystal growth and zone refining and levelling, which made possible the production of high-purity, single-crystal germanium. The preparation of this high-quality material was the fundamental step which led to the fabrication of the junction transistor.
    The materials scientists' research was painstaking and their success gradual. On the other hand, Bardeen and Brattain's discovery of the point-contact transistor effect was serendipitous, whilst Shockley's theoretical conception of the junction transistor was a development of ideas which had first been presented in the previous decade. However, it was Shockley,

Bardeen and Brattain, not Pfann, Theurer and Teal (the materials scientists), who were recipients of the Nobel prize for the work. Similarly, it was Chu who gained the same accolade, not Hazen or Freemen, whose crystallographic measurements and theoretical calculations made a major contribution to the determination of the structure of perovskite high-T_c superconductors.

8.4.6 Financial Incentives

Although Edison regarded invention as his *raison d'être*, he did not pursue activities for which he would not expect a commercial return. His objective was to earn a fast buck which he could plough back into his research laboratory. He dedicated the tasimeter to the public because it had no prospect of generating a profit and abandoned his work on the phonograph when the initial tin-foil version remained merely a scientific curiosity. He did not return to it until a decade later, and then only when Bell successfully marketed a better machine.

Tesla struck a deal with George Westinghouse, who offered him a million dollars and a royalty of $1 per horse power for his patents on alternating current machines (O'Neill 1944, pp75-82). However, when Westinghouse sought his financial backers' approval of the deal, he was told that it was not financially viable. He was forced to go back to Tesla to re-negotiate. Tesla accepted a revised arrangement, by which he received merely the lump sum, saying, with good grace, it was more important that his ideas were accepted. When the payment was made, Tesla devoted it all to further research. Westinghouse, on the other hand, had a steady output of practical inventions until his death. These inventions were intended to make money which could further his business plans.

8.5 THE PROFILE OF INVENTIVE ACTIVITY

8.5.1 The Creative Crescendo

William Shockley, when analysing activity associated with the invention of the transistor, noted that the period immediately before the breakthrough was associated with an increased number of entries in the laboratory notebooks of the members of his team and attributed this to the heightened mental activity stimulated by a mutual feeling of impending success and a desire to contribute to it.

The classic view of invention is that it arrives by *Geistesblitz* or a flash of inspiration. Does such activity occur uniformly over an inventor's career, or are there some times at which his output is more prolific? It will be difficult to form a positive opinion on this point, since most inventors produce only a small number of significant inventions. Better data can be gathered for heroic inventors, since the number of their inventions is greater and their careers are usually reasonably well documented.

Using empirical data derived from patent statistics, histograms were plotted to show the profile of invention over the lifetimes of prolific inventors who engaged in this activity up to their death. These graphs (Figure 8.1) all displayed similar characteristics. The overall pattern during an heroic inventor's career falls broadly within a gaussian envelope, with the peak occurring during the thirties. The propensity to invent exhibits distinct maxima, coinciding with new technological interests. A further common characteristic is a lull in middle age, followed by a further spurt of activity when the inventor makes a fresh start, possibly after a spell concerned with commercial activities. Such conclusions must, of necessity, be purely indicators and a pointer to a need for further study.

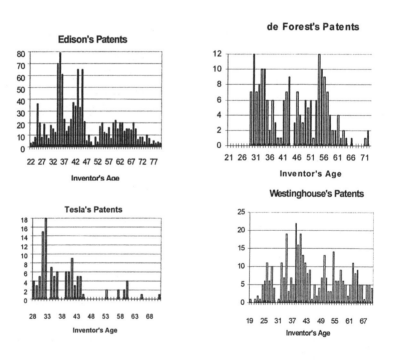

Figure 8.1   Variation of heroic inventor's propensity to invent with age

8.5.2 The Hokey-Kokey or Butterfly Inventor – the 'Dilettante' Approach

Edison commenced his long career as an inventor by working on the electric telegraph. In 1869, he formed a partnership with Pope and Ashley to produce stock ticker and private telegraph equipment. He developed the duplex and quadruplex telegraphs for Western Union and then moved on to the acoustic telegraph, which led to the telephone and phonograph.

In 1876, he set up the world's first industrial research laboratory at Menlo Park, where he brought the phonograph to fruition. In 1878, he turned his attention to the incandescent lamp, losing interest in the phonograph and telephone. He formed the Edison Ore Milling Company in 1879, but did not devote sufficient time to the project to make it viable. A similar fate befell the electric railway, which attracted Edison's interest a year or two later. The 1880s were a period of frenetic development of the electric light and the necessary infrastructure, but Edison sold out, with a sigh of relief, in the next decade.

In 1894 he commenced work on movies and in 1899 he started development of an alkaline storage battery for electric cars. The next year he finally abandoned his ore milling project. In 1902 he set up a Portland cement plant with a view to producing low-cost buildings. None of these ventures enjoyed the success of the electric lamp and some were complete failures.

A century or so after Edison had commenced his trail, Clive Sinclair left school at seventeen and, after four years in technical journalism, formed a company in 1962 to sell electronic kits by mail order. He was an innovative circuit designer, creating a match-box-sized radio receiver, a 'class D' amplifier based on reject transistors from the Philco-Plessey plant at Swindon and a hi-fi amplifier using the newly released power transistors.

In 1967, he launched his first pocket calculator and rapidly became the leader in the British market. When the large American and Japanese corporations began to compete, he turned his attention to digital watches (the infamous Black Watch with short battery life and poor reliability) and a pocket television with a one-inch screen.

In 1979, with the advent of the personal computer, he set up Sinclair Research to manufacture the ZX80, the first PC to retail for less than £100. Over 100,000 were sold in six months and its successor, the ZX81, broke the million barrier. These computers, and their successor, the Spectrum used audio cassettes to store programs and data, but Sinclair's first sixteen-bit machine, the QL (quantum leap), which was based on the Motorola 68008 microprocessor, used a proprietary tape-based, micro-cassette storage system when rival machines had adopted the floppy disc. The QL was also beset with reliability problems due to poor quality control. Sinclair Research lost market share and sold out to Amstrad, which produced machines which were less exciting technically, but could be expected to perform to specification.

A brief flirtation with battery-powered transport then followed with the ill-conceived and notorious C5 electric tricycle. This suffered from inadequate range and speed and needed to sport a flag on a pole in order to bring it within the line of vision of lorry drivers who might otherwise run over the vehicle. At a later stage, Sinclair attempted to launch a bicycle with an electric motor. Subsequently, during the 1990s, he started ventures in integrated circuit and satellite television receiver manufacture (Elliott 1993, p69).

8.5.3 Dilution of Effort

During the early part of the 1880s, with development of the central generating stations for the supply of current for the electric lamp, an interest arose in the use of electricity for power for railways. Edison commenced work on this concept, laying down an experimental track at Menlo Park. He adapted the 'long-legged Mary-Ann' dynamo for operation as a motor and mounted it horizontally on a wheeled chassis for use as a locomotive. The development showed signs of success and Edison was responsible for a demonstration railway which operated for 118 hours and carried 26,805 passengers at the Chicago Railway Exposition in June 1883. However, the period of this development coincided with the installation of the infrastructure for the incandescent lamp. Edison was therefore unable to devote enough effort to the railway and fell behind other developers. Eventually he ceded control of the activities to S.D. Field and concentrated his attention on the lamp (Josephson 1961, p242).

8.6 THE ABILITY TO COMMUNICATE

Heinrich Göbel trained as a scientist in Germany and, as a young man, was introduced by his tutor, Professor Mönighausen, to the mysteries of the incandescent filament. He emigrated to New York in 1848 and established a small store. He resumed his scientific experiments and, after an unfortunate experience with the arc lamp, in which he was prosecuted as an arsonist, he turned his attention to the incandescent filament. In 1854, some fifteen years ahead of Edison, he constructed a practical lamp using a carbon filament operating *in vacuo* in a glass bulb.

Unfortunately, Göbel had a poor command of English and failed to exploit his ideas commercially. He did not patent his inventions and his only claim to fame was when samples of his lamps were produced as evidence of prior art in litigation of Edison's patents. Again as a result of Göbel's lack of eloquence, counsel had little difficulty in casting doubt on the relevance of this work, which was dismissed by the Boston Circuit Court when holding Edison's patents valid.

8.7 CONCLUSION

A substantial house requires a strong foundation. By the same token, an inventor with sufficient breadth of vision to make great inventions must have a catholic education to provide him with sufficient tools with which to work. Inventions are solutions to problems. The inventor will also need an enquiring mind, firstly to identify, and secondly, to solve the conundrums he encounters. In consequence, many successful inventors are polytechnic and will think laterally to solve current problems.

Since the process of invention demands an ability to extend thought beyond its normal boundaries and to apply widely disparate skills, an alternative to the quest for an heroic inventor might be the provision of plural capability through the agency of more than one person. However, where the manifold inventive qualities are provided by means of a multi-disciplinary group, it will be necessary for interpersonal relationships to be good to achieve the rapport and communication necessary for success.

Some inventors acquire a strong attachment to a subject on which they work early in their career. In such cases they may subsequently return to this subject and make significant inventions in the field.

Some principals exercise the *droit du seigneur* and take credit for inventions made by their employees or subordinates. The propensity to steal an idea varies inversely to the effort involved and the likelihood of retribution.

Clearly, an inventor will not invent unless he has a reason to do so. This act needs a stimulus – categorised by Shockley as the 'will to think' – to serve as a starting gun, as a result of which the inventor sets out on the trail of discovery. The stimulus to work on a new idea may be necessity, the apocryphal mother of invention, the provision of funds or other facilitators which make a project feasible, or the cognition engendered by exposure to a parallel or analogous development.

Having embarked on the process of invention, the motivation must persist so that it is followed through. Often the degree of persistence will be high. Inventors will need extreme devotion to their task – if necessary to the exclusion of all other interests, including their families. Obsession is a principal ingredient of success. The wives and families of inventors can provide a testimony to the determination and persistence needed.

Not only must an inventor have sufficient determination to carry his baby to full term, he must also act as midwife at the birth and then as nanny to take his mewling infant through to maturity. He must not lose heart when others tell him his offspring is ugly. If *he* does not have faith, then he cannot expect others to act as surrogate. They will often waver when an alternative comes along, rather than sticking with their original concept and improving it to meet the challenge.

Companies, as well as individuals, may serve as a promoter but, whilst an innovation may survive as the result of the efforts of a product champion, it will not do so in the face of significantly adverse economics.

Cognitive dissonance engenders a determination to succeed – some inventors are stimulated into greater efforts by the success of their rivals. They wish to surpass the achievements of others in an endeavour to make their own individual mark.

Although all men may be created equal, experience shows that some are blessed with a 'silver spoon' whilst others are pre-ordained merely to serve. The choice of scientific discipline will be crucial to the potential rewards to be gained. The intellectual effort of an astronomer working, for example, on the nature of particle interactions in stellar nuclei, will be as great as that of the engineer who designs a nuclear fusion generator based on the same particle interactions, but his material rewards will certainly not be commensurate. Certain aspects of a subject have greater 'sex appeal' and will accordingly be given more approbation.

Financial reward must be adequate but studies have shown that it is not a motivator. Employees often rate job satisfaction and approbation as much more important factors in spurring them onward. The fact that inventors are prepared to work under conditions of great hardship (Teal 1976, O'Neill 1944) suggests that the quest for money is not a reason that they invent. Although, as with creative artists, success can bring great financial rewards to a few, financial gain is not necessarily a motivating factor for inventors. They may frequently be more interested in inventing for invention's sake and, like a compulsive gambler, plough back their returns into fresh inventive activity until, finally, the gains are dissipated.

An heroic inventor's propensity to invent falls broadly within a gaussian envelope, with the peak occurring during the thirties. It exhibits distinct maxima, coinciding with new technological interests. Typically, there is a lull in middle age, followed by a further spurt of activity when the inventor makes a fresh start, possibly after a spell concerned with commercial activities. Due to the small sample on which these conclusions are based, they must, of necessity, be purely indicators and a pointer to a need for further study.

Another aspect of invention for which, again, it is only easily possible to find data for heroic inventors, is the constancy of subject matter of their interests. Lateral thinking is an essential component of many inventions but, if not focused, mental activity of this nature is likely to give rise to spurious inventions – those in an unrelated field. Such inventions, although meeting many of the accepted criteria for inventiveness, may prove to be irrelevant to the advancement of the primary innovation. If inventors are attracted by invention for invention's sake, it is likely that they will shower attention on all of their inventions or flit from invention to invention according to their interest of the moment.

Pioneering inventors do not necessarily carry innovation through to maturity. Instead they develop a product to their own satisfaction and then leave others to reap the benefits whilst they move on to pastures new. Hindsight is better than foresight and ground breakers do not make the best profits. It is the successors rather than the instigators who enjoy the fruits of invention. The role of the pathfinder is to establish credibility, to breach the 'fear, uncertainty and doubt' threshold. Successful inventors do not necessarily make great entrepreneurs.

Lack of follow-through is one cause of an inventor's lack of success. Another possibility, also the consequence of a prolific mind, is dilution of effort. Single-mindedness is an essential component for the success of an invention, so, if the efforts of an inventor are spread too thinly, failure will be the inevitable consequence.

Whilst there was synergistic gain to be had from the adaptation of the technology developed for electricity generation to its converse, the provision of traction using electrical motive power, Edison would have been more successful had he concentrated his efforts on fewer inventions.

A light hidden under a bushel will never illuminate the world. Inventors are, by definition, concerned with new and unfamiliar concepts, ones which are not understood and, possibly, not easy to understand. In such circumstances, above-average communications skills will be necessary to inform the aides and entrepreneurs who will be necessary for the development and exploitation of the innovation. It is of no value to produce good ideas if they are not communicated and the know-how transferred successfully into commerce.

9. Carrot and Stick – the Influence of Official Policy

We say 'disastrous' advisedly because few circumstances could be more prejudicial to the welfare of the industry as a whole than that entire branches should fall into the hands of monopolists who use their position to crush out all progress in hands other than their own.

The Electrician, 20 June 1890

Indeed, the public interest may itself require that the number of licensees shall be limited, because it may well be that the public interest is best served by ensuring a steady supply of the patented article by preventing the flooding of the market, and a drastic reduction of the price by wholesale competition.

Extract from the judgement of Luxmoore J,.*Applications by Brownie Wireless Co. Ld., for the Grant of Compulsory Licences* [1929] RPC 457 at 474

International competition is intense. It is said that by mid-January 1988, Japanese companies had filed more than 2000 patents and had spent more than $30 million on studying the new superconductors. As the 1-2-3 story shifts from scientific research to commercial development it is clear that a small army of patent lawyers will be among the chief beneficiaries.

Robert Hazen, *Superconductors: the Breakthrough,* p255

This was the first of an endless series of patent litigation waged against me and my company, and by us in turn against infringers of my patents, litigation which until recent years has harassed and held back development of the art throughout its long history, which resulted chiefly in the enrichment of a host of able patent attorneys, and which eventually might have ended in absolute and unconscionable monopoly – not by the original inventors and pioneers – but by those mercenary interests who had amassed and could command the most gigantic aggregations of capital.

Lee de Forest, *Father of Radio,* p159

9.1 INTRODUCTION

The previous two chapters have presented examples which showed that intrinsic factors, including the laws of physics and the psychology of inventors, have a direct influence on the course of innovation. However, second-order vectors, such as statutory intellectual property monopolies, government policy and international treaty obligations and political considerations reflected in public attitudes, may also be expected to be determinants of market structure. Military procurement resulting from war or the threat of war would provide an impetus, whilst physical regulation, competition law and industry regulation may act as operating constraints.

This chapter considers the influence of these determinants of change. It is, furthermore, possible that their impact will vary with the temporal phasing. Will factors such as patent monopolies exert major control early in the innovation cycle, when competition is mounting, but be relegated to a subsidiary role at a later stage, when market positions have stabilised? If so, it will be important to take timing into account when making prognostications about the development of an innovation. Examples are selected from the case studies and the last half-century of the electronics industry to highlight dynamical effects of these imposed influences.

9.2 INTELLECTUAL PROPERTY MONOPOLIES

Creative activities like writing and drawing and economic activities such as investment in commerce and industry have for long been considered meritorious. States have, by the grant of monopolies, fostered the proprietary rights of those who make such contributions to the national wealth. Copyright protected the early printers and patents nurtured new inventions. Trade mark registration was introduced towards the end of the nineteenth century to assist with the development of commerce in the products of the Industrial Revolution. In recent years, *sui generis* rights, including semiconductor mask protection and database rights, have been created to meet the special needs of the electronic component and information technology industries.

9.2.1 Patents

I myself remember being concerned as a judge with a dyestuff patent of very great complexity. I think that the plaintiffs were an English company controlled by the great German fabric industry which was known all over the world. In connection with that case, I was told that there were about 2,000 people employed by the German parent company, simply for the purposes of investigating different combinations of materials which would enable them to produce new dyestuffs. They had had to work day after day with slight alterations of the quantities of material – and sometimes of the material itself – put into dyestuffs. The Germans, with a pertinacity worthy of a better cause, patented in this country thousands of these materials in the hope that, after the patents were obtained, at least one of the thousands, or a much greater number, would be discovered to be a really useful article which would repay them for all the huge sums expended and for all the great trouble they had taken in connection with this kind of research.

Lord Maugham during the debate on the second reading of the 1949 Patents and Designs Bill, *Hansard (H.L.)*, 29 March 1949

A patent is intended to be a bargain between an inventor, or his successor-in-title, and the state. He makes his invention public and, in return, the state grants him a monopoly of exploitation for a limited period. This permits the patentee to prevent others 'making, using, exercising or vending' the invention covered by the patent. Thus it may either deny a potential competitor the opportunity to participate in a market or it may put up his cost of market entry by forcing him either to use methods or processes which avoid the patent or to pay a premium, such as a royalty or lump sum, for a licence to use an invention.

9.2.1.1 Renewal fees

A patent is not an untrammelled right. Patent laws normally include provisions to restrict the undue exercise of the monopoly. One such measure is renewal fees, which are levied annually to create an incentive to relinquish the monopoly after its utility is exhausted. In most territories, these fees are on an increasing scale to induce the patentee to allow the patent to lapse before the full statutory term expires.

Lee de Forest ran out of funds shortly after his overseas patents on the Audion were granted. He was unable to pay the renewal fees and the patents were abandoned. When, in due course, he came into collision with the Marconi Company, which possessed the rights to Fleming's diode detector and needed to be able to make triodes to construct electronic amplifiers, a stand-off was reached in the USA, where the Audion patents had remained in force because, at the time, renewal fees were not levied in that territory, but elsewhere he had no negotiating position.

This stalemate was a major factor in shaping attitudes in the developing electronics industry. It provided a cautionary example and helped to create a culture of cross-licensing or simply ignoring the existence of patents, which persisted throughout the remainder of the twentieth century.

9.2.1.2 Compulsory licences and licences of right

During the course of the second decade of the twentieth century, the use of ductile filaments of hot-drawn tungsten became the preferred method for the manufacture of incandescent lamps, replacing the extruded metal filaments which had been pioneered by Auer von Welsbach in Germany, some fifteen years previously. By 1915, around 90 per cent of lamps were made by the new method, which gave a considerable improvement in durability as the filaments were much more resistant to shock. The luminous efficiency, however, was not significantly better than that of the lamps produced by earlier techniques.

To produce drawn-tungsten filament lamps legally required a licence under nine separate patents owned by several different companies which had acquired them from the original inventors ([1915] RPC 202). These companies and their licensees, a group which included all manufacturers of substance in the United Kingdom, had formed a cartel known as the Tungsten Lamp Association. This group controlled over 100 patents on inventions which contributed to the evolution of the incandescent filament lamp and was prepared to grant licences to all comers, subject to their agreement not to sell lamps at below a specified price.

The Robin Electric Lamp Company had devised and patented a dual-filament construction which effectively doubled the life of an incandescent lamp, since, when the first filament failed, a second one could be brought into operation. Robin sought a licence from the cartel or, in the alternative, a supply of drawn-tungsten wire with permission to use it in the manufacture of tungsten lamps. One member of the cartel had offered to manufacture lamps to Robin's design but insisted that the double-filament lamps be sold at a price which would remove the economic incentive for the public to purchase them. Robin then threatened the Association with an action for a compulsory licence. This was met with an offer to supply tungsten wire, which Robin could have obtained from a Swiss manufacturer for ½d per metre, at a price of 5d per metre. This imposition would have added 10d, for the wire alone, to the manufacturing costs of a lamp which otherwise would have cost about 4d.

The prices set by the Association were based on the manufacturing costs of a carbon filament lamp of equivalent luminous efficiency and bore no direct relationship to the cost of manufacture of a tungsten filament lamp. They were clearly designed to shield existing manufacturers from competition. The thrust of the licensing policy was to force new manufacturers to join the cartel.

The licensors charged royalties of 10 per cent on lamps produced for the UK market and 5 per cent on lamps produced for export. The effect of these royalties was that in the UK, a lamp would be sold for between 2s 6d and 2s 9d, in Germany for 1s 9d and in the Netherlands, where there were no patents, for 10d. Over a period of seven years the cartel sold some 30 million lamps.

At that stage markets were organised on a national basis. There was some exporting, but this was to traditional overseas markets (such as the British Empire). There was no general agreement on tariffs and trade (GATT), and governments tended to protect their domestic markets by high import duties.

Pursuing its attempt to obtain a supply of drawn-tungsten wire, Robin Electric made an application, under Section 24 of the Patents and Designs Act 1907, to the Board of Trade for a compulsory licence under the relevant patents. They argued that, by the practice of selling to the public complete lamps and not making the wire available separately, the Patentees compelled the public to pay exorbitant prices for the wire made under the Association patents. The members of the Association also reaped large profits from the manufacture of lamps and so maintained a practical monopoly in tungsten drawn wire lamps. Robin argued that, if there were an industry in the manufacture of the wire, there would be many other uses for the wire since it was stated in the Association's advertisements to have a tensile strength equal to that of the best steel, and not to corrode. For example, the wire could be used for making electrically powered heating apparatus.

This was the first petition under the compulsory licensing provisions to come before the Court. It thus presented the judge with an opportunity to create a fundamental precedent, since he was bound to consider the interests of the public as well as those of the petitioners. On the facts, he could have made a decision which would have severely curtailed the monopoly power on the basis that, by lowering prices, electric lighting would be made available much more widely. (This would not necessarily have been contrary to the interests of the manufacturers, since overall sales volume would have been thereby increased.) However, at the time, the climate of public opinion was not antipathetic to cartels. Mr. Justice Warrington therefore passed over the opportunity to start the pendulum swinging in a contrary direction – he gave judicial approval to the concepts of retail price maintenance, pooling of patents and control of an industry by a few dominant suppliers.

> The two respondent companies, together with the *General Electric Company*, are the owners of a large number of patents, including the nine, the subject of this petition, relating to incandescent lamps with drawn tungsten wire filaments. These three companies have pooled their patents ... and thus control to a large extent the industry concerned with the manufacture of drawn tungsten filament lamps. To prevent the cutting of prices and thus to ensure their profits they require from dealers who take their wares an undertaking not to sell below certain list prices. The result is that the price of lamps with a drawn tungsten filament is considerably higher in this country than it is abroad. There is however, no evidence that the price is so high as to be a serious burden to the consumer and, in fact, it has in the last two or three years been

considerably reduced. The supply of lamps is adequate to meet the demands of the public.

In my opinion, the trade or industry to be considered is that of the making of tungsten filament electric lamps and the starting by the Petitioners of a trade in their particular lamps would not be the establishment of a new trade or industry. It would be nothing more than the entry of a fresh trader into an existing trade or industry. There is no ground for the suggestion that the trade or industry has been unfairly prejudiced by any act or omission of the Respondents.

Warrington J. *In the matter of a petition of the Robin Electric Lamp Company Ld.*, [1915] RPC 202

The issue was re-visited a decade and a half later when another small manufacturer, the Brownie Company, was trying to break into a market dominated by a cartel led by Marconi, which controlled the patents relating to wireless broadcasting. Again the judge came down in favour of a cartel, strengthening the hand of the major players and reducing the prospects of competition.

First, is it in the public interest that a licence should be granted? I put this consideration first because each of the parties who have argued the matter before me have put this forward as the first and paramount consideration. The learned *Comptroller* has answered this question in the affirmative on this narrow ground: The *Marconi Company* has secured what he calls a super-monopoly by aggregating in its hands all the vital patents controlling the manufacture of broadcast loud speaker receiving sets, that is, valve receiving sets, and has licensed a large number (over 2,300) of manufacturers who are engaged in the vast trade of manufacturing such valve receiving sets, and has therefore precluded itself from refusing arbitrarily to grant any licence to a particular manufacturer, while (as the *Comptroller* puts it) granting licences freely to his competitors. The learned *Comptroller* goes on to state that 'Such an arbitrary exercise of monopoly rights seems to be contrary to every principle of public policy.' I cannot agree with this view. In the first place the *Marconi Company* is entitled to such monopoly rights as flow from the ownership of the Patents it has acquired. Such rights are no greater and no less by reason of the fact that the Patents were acquired by assignment or purchase rather than by original application or by reason of the fact that the Patents are contained in a number of grants instead of a single grant. It is admitted that a patentee is entitled to work his invention either by himself or his licensees; he may limit the number of his licensees, and he may select such licensee at his own free will and pleasure, subject only to this, that he must not abuse his monopoly rights. If the patent is in fact being worked in such a way that public demand is being supplied to an adequate extent and on reasonable terms, no one can complain, and public interest does not in such circumstances require that a particular manufacturer who desires to manufacture and sell the patented article should be granted a licence to do so. Indeed, the public interest may itself require that the number of licensees shall be limited, because it may well be that the public interest is best served by ensuring a steady supply of the patented article by preventing the flooding of the market, and a drastic reduction of the price by wholesale competition.

The question to be determined in the present case is not whether any licence should be granted, but whether a licence should be granted to a particular person. In

my view there is nothing in the evidence to establish that it is in the public interest that a licence should be granted to the Applicant the *Brownie Company*.
Luxmoore J. *Applications by Brownie Wireless Co. Ld., for the Grant of Compulsory Licences* [1929] RPC 457 at 474

9.2.1.3 Use by the state – Crown user provisions

A third way in which a patent monopoly may be curtailed is the reservation, by the Crown or state, of the right to use a patented invention for its own purposes (in practice, for defence or in connection with its other obligations, such as the National Health Service).

Guglielmo Marconi was keenly aware of the potential military advantages of radio and, in 1899, demonstrated his system to the French and British navies (Goodwin 1995, p4). The Admiralty's communications expert was convinced and recommended that the Royal Navy be equipped with wireless. Marconi, Lodge and Muirhead, and the Germans, Slaby and Braun, were invited to tender. Marconi's proposals proved technically superior, but concerns were expressed about potential interactions with shipboard ordnance and navigation equipment. Tests allayed these fears, but the Admiralty was not disposed to accept Marconi's commercial terms. They therefore invoked the provisions of the 1883 Patents, Designs and Trade Marks Act, which permitted the Crown to manufacture a patented invention if it were urgently needed for defence purposes. The Admiralty-made equipment was inferior to that of Marconi, so eventually the Navy conceded and agreed to purchase on Marconi's terms.

As the state's user right was not a provision which exerted a major influence on the development of the electrical industry, except during times of war, the next significant event did not arise until there was an explosive growth of wireless communications and its accompanying requirement for large numbers of thermionic valves (electron tubes) during World War I. Before the war, the De Forest Co. and the Western Electric Co. had met all demands in the USA. However, although De Forest's High Bridge factory supplied many thousands of tubes to the US government during the war, its production facilities were inadequate to supply all of America's wartime needs. Western Electric's plant was engaged solely on the production of telephone repeater tubes which could not be used for military applications and, furthermore, its factory techniques could not be adapted to large-scale production (Stokes 1982, p12). In consequence, the lamp manufacturers General Electric and Westinghouse, both of which had the necessary facilities and were the only companies with sufficient expertise in mass production techniques, were drafted in.

In 1916, the US Supreme Court granted immunity from patent infringement to manufacturers of munitions, thereby permitting any company capable of doing so, to manufacture thermionic valves for military use. In order to provide flexibility for users, standards were established for electrical characteristics and the mechanical arrangement of the bases and pins which provided the electrical connections.

Apart from GE and Westinghouse, the only other American wartime tube manufacturers were De Forest and Moorhead. Moorhead had, by then, become the subject of patent infringement proceedings, but he was saved by the moratorium declared by the Supreme Court. He secured contracts to supply both the American and British governments. For the British orders the tubes supplied were based on the standard French and British wartime designs, a consequence of the requirement for interchangeability.

By the end of hostilities, the new structure of the manufacturing industry was firmly established along different lines from those which would have resulted had the effect of the patent monopolies not been affected by the special wartime arrangements.

9.2.1.4 Patent litigation – the influence of the nature of the legal system

That Fessenden infringement suit dragged on for three years. A federal judge in Vermont could see no difference between the patented fine wire dipping into an electrolyte and a fine end of one sealed into a glass insulator, *although the latter long preceded the Wollaston device,* and *was not patented,* but free to be used by all and sundry! Such are the quirks of an astute 'legal mind.' So we were all found guilty of 'infringement,' and fined.

Lee de Forest, *Father of Radio*, p162

The recent *Baywatch* case highlights the unacceptable risks of litigation of which the courts should not be proud. In an era of increasing specialisation amongst legal practitioners, litigants are perhaps entitled to a similar level of specialisation from the judges who hear their cases. ... in *Baywatch,* whilst the defendant to the action may have been satisfied with the result, justice was not done and the English court system failed to give to both parties the fairest day in court. The allocation, in particular, of a deputy judge having no background in the practice of intellectual property law made the litigation of this dispute in this country not much safer than a game of dice, and litigants deserve more. They surely pay for more.

Ray Black, *Baywatch: Sour Grapes or Justice,* [1997] 2 *EIPR* 39

The legal system is one which has evolved by custom and use. Although, in recent years, there have been international moves towards harmonisation and, indeed, intellectual property has been in the vanguard of this movement, administration of the law is a conservative process and many idiosyncrasies resulting from differences of national approach still remain. During most of the period covered by the case studies, intellectual property rights were protected by national laws and the resulting divergences may be expected to have an observable effect.

Edison's invention of the carbon filament lamp was a technical advance of a relatively minor nature. All of the integers of the construction were available separately before the date on which the patent application was filed. The only difference between Edison's lamp, devised in 1879, and that of Heinrich Göbel, which was produced in the 1860s, was that Edison's vacuum was produced by successive use of Geissler and Sprengel pumps, whereas Göbel created a Torricellian vacuum by filling the glass bulb with mercury and then inverting it, which would have achieved the same effect. A critical additional step was the use of the technique of 'running on the pumps', to eliminate the deleterious effect of emanation of gases occluded in the filament material. However, this development was contributed by Swan and, indeed, did not feature in Edison's patent claim.

In Germany, where litigation on patent infringement is of an inquisitorial nature, the ambit of the invention was judged to be narrow and Rathenau's (AEG's) carbon filament lamp was held not to infringe. The courts thus left AEG free to develop an industry unencumbered by the burden of paying royalties to Edison. A contributory factor in this decision was the fact that Edison and Swan pursued separate commercial interests and did not unite against the opposition. Their contributions to the art were thus considered individually and deemed to be less meritorious.

England and the USA, on the other hand, have a common law system, in which an initial judgement acts as a precedent by which later proceedings are bound. Edison started an action in England against Swan, but they quickly settled and joined forces under the banner of the Edison and Swan *United* Electric Light Company – a tactic which Edison had learned earlier during his battle with Bell when developing the telephone (6 QBD 244).

Proceedings were commenced against a weak opponent (Woodhouse and Rawson). The contribution made by Swan was suppressed in order to bolster the strength of Edison's patent. Multiple actions were pressed. False evidence led to obfuscation. Eminent scientists were retained as expert witnesses, not because they had specialist knowledge of the art – which they did not – but rather because their reputations would be likely to impress the judge. The weak opponent collapsed. Judgement was given in favour of Edison and a very broad interpretation placed on the ambit of his patent claim. Despite the dubious circumstances, a later court held that it was bound by this decision, which had been handed down by a substitute judge, who was not accustomed to hearing patent actions.

In subsequent proceedings ([1889] RPC 243) the judge in the court of first instance became impatient at the plaintiff's conduct of the action. He roundly criticised counsel and curtailed his arguments. Thus prejudiced, he gave judgement against Edison, holding that the basic carbon filament lamp patent was invalid. The Court of Appeal provided a backstop and overturned the decision, but they could well have allowed it to stand, with the consequence that there would have been much more open competition during the development phase of the lamp industry in the United Kingdom.

9.2.1.5 The extraneous influence of patents – the roar of the paper tiger

The grant of a patent is a tortuous process. It involves the submission of a specification – a detailed document which sets out the nature of the invention – to an official organisation which carries out an inquisitorial examination to determine the novelty of the invention and whether it merits the grant of a patent. Knowledge of the state of the art is, at this stage, frequently imperfect and, in many cases, patents are granted for inventions which subsequently prove not to have satisfied the requirements for patentability. Such patents are invalid, but, nevertheless, stand alongside valid ones and may have equal effect on the play and counter-play of potential competitors.

On 23 June 1943, the US Supreme Court handed down an historic decision (de Forest 1950, p456) that Marconi's four-tuned-circuit patent, which had formed the basis for all successful development in wireless communication, was invalid. Referring to earlier work of Stone and Tesla (US Pat 714756), the court held that this had disclosed the principle of adjustable tuning applied to the circuits of the transmitter and receiver, which was the basis of Marconi's invention. Marconi's patent had been granted in 1903, and thus the question of its validity was not finally resolved until twenty-three years after its expiry.

In the same proceedings, the Supreme Court also held that Fleming's patent on the diode detector was also invalid as its claims were broader than the actual invention. (Fleming claimed a diode detector *simpliciter*, whereas his actual invention was the application of an Edison Effect lamp (a thermionic diode) to the demodulation of a high-frequency alternating current signal.) Again, the decision of invalidity was taken many years after the expiry date of the patent, which had been the basis of infringement proceedings and had been licensed widely. Both of these patents had played a major part in shaping the development of the wireless equipment and electronic component industries.

Litigation places extreme demands on the resources of the litigants. During the infringement actions between Edison and Swan and Woodhouse and Rawson ([1886] RPC 167 [1887] RPC 99) the resources of the Edison Ponders End factory were diverted to producing specimens for use in evidence. Owing to the contradictory nature of the counter-evidence given in the witness-box, the judge then decided he needed the instructions set out in the Edison patent specification to be tested by carrying them out in the presence of an independent expert. He appointed Sir George G. Stokes, then President of the Royal Society, to be the assessor. All the legal counsel, witnesses and experts then adjourned to the Ponders End Lamp Factory, and ordinary workmen were told what to do and left to do it, fabricating carbon filament lamps with tar-putty and then operating them with an electric current. The lamps were duly made and operated for a dozen hours, demonstrating, for the court, the sufficiency of the description in the patent specification (Fleming 1934, p104).

Whilst the plaintiffs' production was being disrupted in this way, other effects were exerting an influence on the defendants' operations. This was a rapidly developing art and they were concerned that their trade secrets would become public during the course of the legal proceedings. The senior partner (Woodhouse) was occupied almost completely with the litigation (*Electrician*, 4 November 1887, p548) and this placed such a strain on him that he became ill and died (*Electrician*, 30 September, 1887 p435).

9.2.1.6 The patents paradox – patents as innovation inhibitors

> I am very much preoccupied with devices for the improvement of the electric lamp. For 18 years there has been no radical change in it, only such changes as arise from practice in manufacture. Now there are signs of radical and far-reaching changes, and I am naturally anxious that those changes, if they do come, as I expect they will, may not find us unprepared for them, nor wholly unconnected with them. I am busy considering a patent specification.
> Letter of 31 July 1898 from Sir Joseph Wilson Swan, *Sir Joseph Wilson Swan F.R.S.*, p124

The inventions which laid the foundation for the manufacture of the carbon filament lamp were conceived around 1880. The Edison and Swan United Electric Lamp Company used its patents to establish an effective monopoly, behind which it sheltered for the next decade and a half. During this time the company effected no radical innovation, contenting itself with making improvements such as the extruded cellulose filament, which enhanced its manufacturing efficiency and profitability. Meanwhile, overseas inventors, such as von Welsbach, von Bolton and Feuerlein in Germany and Just and Hanaman in Austria, were prevented by the Edison and Swan patents from exploiting the carbon filament. They turned their attention to alternative materials and developed lamps with filaments of refractory metals which eventually superseded those made of carbon.

Towards the end of the nineteenth century, Edison and Swan had established a dominant position in the manufacture of carbon filament incandescent lamps. By a succession of patent infringement actions they had forced most of their competitors out of business. The Netherlands and

Switzerland, at this time, had no patent laws and thus became havens for refugee lamp producers. Absence of patents permitted economic migrants, such as Pope and Robertson, to set up and become skilled in manufacturing techniques. Swan's former associate, Charles Stearn, plied his trade from Zurich and Frits Philips, in Eindhoven, established the Philips Gloeilampenfabriek, which later became the basis of one of the world's major multinational electrical manufacturers.

In due course, the international community coerced the Dutch into reinstating its patent laws, but, by this time, most of the minor manufacturers who had set up in the Netherlands had either returned to their native lands (Robertson and Garcke) or been taken over by Philips.

In the USA, the suspension of patent laws during the first world war favoured established manufacturers rather than the innovating newcomers. De Forest was squeezed out by General Electric and Western Electric. The patterns of trade were thus distorted by change in the statutory regime.

9.2.2 Trade Marks

Commerce and industry are continually changing and extending their boundaries. Laws which may be adequate for their needs at a particular time will not meet the changed circumstances some years later. Patents were an appropriate way of protecting the advances made in the industrial revolution, but ceased to be suitable for the age of market power at the end of the nineteenth century. Trade mark registration, which was introduced at this time, was then a major protector of business interests. Indeed, the desire of their margarine manufacturers to avail themselves of the trade mark provisions of the Paris Convention was a major factor in the Dutch acquiescence to international pressure to reintroduce a patent system in 1912. Initially trade marks protected products. Then they were extended to services. Now we are experiencing a further extension with domain names, which are used to identify users of the Internet.

Communication between human beings may be visual, aural or, less commonly, tactile or olfactory. An undesired characteristic of all communication is noise, which is interference generated within the communications system that serves to mask the desired message. Noise may take many forms, such as other people's conversations at a cocktail party, ink blots or smudges on a child's exercise book, or reception of spurious 'atmospherics' at the same time as a radio or television programme. Particularly when communication is undertaken for purposes of entertainment, noise can seriously mar the performance and enjoyment will be greatly reduced.

Since tolerance of noise in entertainment applications is so low, inventors have striven since the early days of recording and broadcasting to find ways of reducing the background noise of these media. The long-playing record introduced during the 1950s did much to improve the reproduction of sound. Although clicks and pops were still present, the mean background noise was actually quieter than many master tape recordings from which the discs had been produced. Many listeners noticed this when one band on an LP record ended and there was a pause before the next one began. It was apparent that records could be improved in noise level if the master tapes could be made less noisy. Dr. Ray Dolby, an American physicist who had studied and settled in England, devised a solution which was adopted by virtually every recording company and important independent studio in the world (Cullis 1973).

The approach adopted by Dolby was to divide the audible spectrum into four bands of frequencies, processing each band in a separate circuit to reduce the effect of noise present in that range of frequencies. In this way, when the music became loud because a bass drum was struck, there was no effect on noise reduction at high frequencies. The exact process of noise reduction consisted of applying one step during recording which was then cancelled by an exactly symmetrical step, in reverse, during playback. The significant point of the Dolby system was that an increase in level during recording was introduced only at low levels when the music was not loud enough to drown the noise.

The original Dolby system, known as the Dolby A system, found widespread acceptance in recording studios. Although not expensive by studio standards, the equipment cost about £200 per channel, partly because of the complexity and partly because it had to be built to a degree of reliability as high as could be reached. It was therefore not a commercially viable proposition to use the Dolby A system in domestic consumer equipment.

Tape recording first came to prominence during the 1950s. In early machines the magnetic recording tape was mounted on reels which commonly held 366m of tape. At the usual recording speed of 190mm/sec these played for about half an hour. The original machines recorded a single track on 6.25mm wide tape. In an endeavour to record more material on a given tape, twin and multiple track recording and slower tape speeds were introduced. Open reel tapes were inconvenient to use due to the problems of threading the tape on to the machine, but this difficulty was overcome by the use of cassettes which could simply be dropped into place. Through a vigorous licensing campaign and rigid enforcement of standards, the Dutch Philips group achieved world-wide acceptance of the system they had developed. (A contributory factor was the grant of royalty-free licences.) In the Philips' system, four tracks were recorded at a speed of 47.5mm/sec on a tape 4mm wide.

As the area of tape employed per unit time falls (i.e. number of tracks increases or tape speed is reduced), so the signal-to-noise ratio of a recording is degraded, whatever the quality of the apparatus used to generate or play back the recording. Noise is, in consequence, a major problem for users of tape recorders operating at slow speeds with narrow track-widths, and this served to inhibit rapid acceptance of the cassette tape recorder.

Subjective tests in connection with the development of the Dolby A noise reduction system established that high-frequency hiss was the most troublesome component of noise present in tape recordings. A simplified version of the Dolby A noise reduction system which operated only on the high frequencies was devised. Designated Dolby B, the system gave a worthwhile improvement in performance at a price which could be borne by the domestic market.

From his youth, Dolby had possessed a strong interest in tape recording. At the age of sixteen he joined Ampex Corporation, which was to become the world's principal manufacturer of video tape recorders, to work on various aspects of sound reproduction, instrumentation and video recording. Moving to the Cavendish Laboratory in Cambridge in 1957, he studied the properties of long wavelength X-rays until 1963, when he undertook a two-year appointment as a member of a United Nations' advisory team to the Central Scientific Instruments Organisation in India. During this period Dolby conceived the principles of his noise reduction system. Returning to the United Kingdom in 1965, he set up Dolby Laboratories Inc. to translate his ideas into hardware, and constructed the prototype of his type A noise reduction apparatus. He approached Arthur Haddy of the Decca Record Company who was, at that time, investigating a number of noise reduction systems. Decca displayed immediate interest, and in 1966 purchased from Dolby a number of A301 studio noise reduction units. At this time the resources of Dolby Laboratories were fully occupied on the production and further development of studio equipment, so it was not until they were prompted by an approach from Henry Kloss of KLH, a successful and rapidly growing American hi-fi company, that a consumer equipment noise reduction system was seriously considered. As a result of this approach the B system was developed, and in return for a lump sum payment, KLH was granted exclusive rights for a period of two years. The payment enabled Dolby to increase his development and production facilities, thus boosting his capabilities.

The advantages of the Dolby noise reduction systems were clearly demonstrable, and one by one manufacturers of tape equipment approached

Dolby for a licence to use them. Impetus to the movement was given by the sale, at first by Decca and then by the other record manufacturers, of prerecorded, Dolby B-encoded tapes. In 1971 the nature of royalty payments was changed from a percentage of the ex-factory price to a small fixed sum for each unit. The fixed sum was set on a reducing scale, the first 10,000 sets per quarter being at a relatively high rate, the next 40,000 being at a reduced rate and all in excess of 50,000 being at a relatively low rate. This rate structure fitted in well with the practical breakdown of the market since small producers catered for relatively small and specialised market segments which could bear the increased cost, whereas the large producers served the extremely price-sensitive mass markets where small cost changes have a significant effect on volume of sales.

From its small beginnings, the turnover of Dolby Laboratories had by 1972 grown to around £1m per annum. The main source of income was the manufacture of A system apparatus for professional markets, but B system licences were already making a significant contribution.

Future expansion came from the incorporation of B system facilities in a greater proportion of tape recorders as its incremental cost was reduced and from the use of the B system in FM stereo broadcasting, as it permitted reception under the adverse conditions at large distances from the transmitter, thus effectively increasing the service area. Another development which achieved widespread acceptance was a cinema noise reduction unit for improving the sound track of films.

Both the Dolby A system and the Dolby B system were protected by patents in the major countries of the world. The trade marks used by Dolby and its licensees were also comprehensively protected.

In 1972 there were some forty licensees throughout the world and, with numbers of this order, a standard licence agreement was necessary. Although there was some scope for negotiation at the commencement of the licensing programme, this rapidly disappeared as the numbers increased.

Dolby Laboratories provided thorough technical support through their expertise in noise reduction techniques and a condition of their licence was that all designs of apparatus incorporating Dolby noise reduction facilities should be submitted for a stringent technical evaluation. The test report concluded with a list of changes to be made in the manufactured apparatus, some mandatory to comply with the standards laid down, the others recommended for improved performance.

Trade mark rights were carefully preserved by detailed specification of the manner and nature of permitted use. A pooling arrangement was created to permit any licensee to take advantage of any improvements to the system devised by Dolby or another licensee.

When Intel was attempting to consolidate its dominant position in the manufacture of microprocessors, it changed its practice of allocating a sequential number to the next generation of devices. Instead, it coined the name Pentium and mounted a huge public awareness campaign to induce the end-user to ask for a machine based on an Intel device. Intel also offered financial incentives to personal computer manufacturers who would place the 'Intel inside' label on their products. The ploy was a development of the ancient 'knocking copy' practice, since the inference was that a non-Pentium processor was, in some way, an inferior product. The strategy was extended in 1997 with the introduction of multi-media capabilities. This was accompanied by the branding of products with the acronym MMX – multi-media extension (*Electronic News*, 27 March 1997).

In the case of Dolby, an innovation protected by patents permitted the creation of a company solely for its exploitation; this company grew steadily under the protection of a patent umbrella, whilst developing a trade mark for post-patent-expiry continuation of licence income. Manufacturing activities provided the initial major contribution to revenue, but licensing permitted the company to exploit markets which were beyond its capacity to satisfy.

9.2.3 Copyright and Design Registration

The Xerox Palo Alto Research Center (PARC) carried out an investigation of the man machine interface with the objective of making computers more user-friendly. They devised a graphical display in which functions were selected by moving an on-screen pointer to a symbol (an Icon) and then pressing a switch on a flying lead (a Mouse). The screen could be made to show different aspects (Windows) of a program which was currently running. Commands were selected from 'Pull-down' menus. These features (WIMPs) were incorporated in a computer (the Star) but Xerox management did not put the machine into production.

In December 1989, Steve Jobs of Apple Computers visited the Xerox PARC (Cringely 1996, p189). He immediately appreciated the commercial significance of the graphics-based user interface (GUI) and instigated a programme at Apple to develop a new computer incorporating these concepts. This computer was the Lisa, a machine which was expensive to make but which was, in due course, followed by the ground-breaking Macintosh.

Eventually, Microsoft also developed a GUI-based operating system (Windows) for the IBM PC. Apple then sued Microsoft for stealing what, it alleged, was the 'look and feel' of Apple's software. This action failed.

Lotus, a software manufacturer, in a follow-up to a successful action against Paperback Software, Inc., sued Borland, the producer of the Quattro Pro spreadsheet which used a similar menu and command structure to the Lotus 1-2-3 spreadsheet. This action was unsuccessful, but it forced Borland to redesign its program.

9.2.4 Semiconductor Mask Design and Database *Sui Generis* Rights

When the planar process was introduced in 1959 for the fabrication of transistors and, in due course, for integrated circuits, regions of a silicon wafer were selected for modification by means of photolithography, an adaptation of a process used in printing. Pre-defined areas were etched through a protective layer of silica which had been formed on the surface of the wafer. Impurities, which altered the conductivity characteristics of the silicon, were then introduced by a process of high-temperature diffusion. The geometry of these diffused regions determined the unique electrical properties of the device formed from them.

Following an inspection of a completed planar semiconductor device, it was a relatively simple process to reverse engineer it by making a photolithographic masks with identical topography. Particularly with

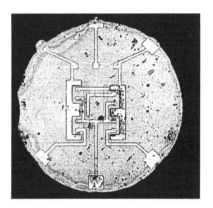

Source   Weber 1981

Figure 9.1 The first planar monolithic integrated circuit

integrated circuits, it was therefore possible to avoid a lengthy and costly development process by the simple expedient of a two- or three-hour microscopic examination.

It was accepted that the design of the masks, being functional, would not enjoy the protection of artistic copyright; neither would they satisfy the requirement of inventive step necessary to qualify for patent protection. After a number of abortive attempts, the US government created a *sui generis* intellectual property right, passing the 1984 Semiconductor Chip Protection Act, for this purpose. Although not obliged to extend this protection to semiconductor devices originating abroad, America granted reciprocal rights to other countries possessing similar legislation. Japan enacted its statute in 1985, the EC adopted a Directive on the Legal Protection of Topographies of Semiconductor Products in 1986, the UK implemented the directive by secondary legislation (Design Right (Semiconductor Topographies) Regulations 1989) and other countries including Australia, Sweden and Switzerland had created similar laws by the end of the decade (Christie 1995, p5).

With the advent of the information society, collocations of information have assumed considerable economic importance. The European Community, after due deliberation, promulgated its Database Directive in March 1996. This was a basis for legislation to be introduced in member states to protect the investment in the creation of electronic and other databases. It, too, was a *sui generis* right and was intended to coexist with, and supplement, other intellectual property, such as copyright or trade mark registration, which might already protect the information.

9.3 REGULATORY CONTROL AND STANDARDS

Public opinion in Britain in the third quarter of the nineteenth century was strongly against private monopoly. When the electricity industry was being established around 1880, it was still necessary to obtain a private act of Parliament to build a power station and dig up the streets to lay supply cables. Many of the provisions of the Electricity Supply Act (1882), the purpose of which was to reduce this bureaucracy, were modelled on the Tramways Act (1870), which was intended to regulate the horse-drawn tram. One such provision was the transfer of the generating plant and distribution mains to the local authority at break-up value after twenty-one years. This limited window for the recovery of the considerable capital investment involved in the construction of a power station severely inhibited development and no new electricity supply companies were established until the measure was repealed in 1888.

When Marconi commenced his experiments with wireless in the 1890s, control of wired telephony and telegraphy in Britain was firmly in the hands of the Post Office as a consequence of the 1869 Telegraph Act and the decision of the court in the case of *Attorney-General v. The Edison Telephone Company of London Limited* (6 QBD 244). Similar provisions restricted access to the telegraph market in other countries (Goodwin 1995, p10). Marconi perceived a potential niche market for his new technology and set out to establish a chain of coastal stations for the purpose.

Whilst the government was not concerned about the operations whilst they were at the embryonic stage, when they showed signs of commercial success, the General Post Office acted to protect its monopoly control of communications. A Wireless Telegraphy Act was passed in 1904, requiring all UK wireless stations, both fixed and mobile, to be licensed by the GPO. It also laid down regulations regarding the certification of operators and the avoidance of interference with other commercial and naval stations. The Marconi coastal stations were licensed for a period of eight years. In 1909, the GPO indicated that it wished to take over the operation of the coastal stations, for which a cash offer was made. As part of the deal, the GPO would have access to all current and future Marconi patents relating to ship-to-shore operation. The Company was informed that its licence to operate would not be renewed at the end of the eight year period in 1912, leaving Marconi with little option but to accept (Goodwin 1995, p23). In September 1909, nine Marconi shore stations were transferred to GPO ownership. Other countries, with the exception of the United States, followed suit and coastal stations became the responsibility of governments.

9.4 PUBLIC POLICY

At the end of the eighteenth century, France was in a state of turmoil and feared invasion from neighbouring powers. In 1792 Claude Chappe introduced in France a semaphore which consisted of a system of arms pivoted to wooden pillars that were mounted on towers spaced up to ten miles apart. Successful trials were carried out in 1794 over a chain of towers erected between Paris and Lille, a distance of some 148 miles. In response, the British Admiralty adopted a shutter-telegraph proposed by Lord George Murray. This was in operation between London and Dover from 1795 to 1816, when it was superseded by a semaphore invented by Admiral Sir H.R. Popham. Neither of these mechanical devices could operate during fog. They had therefore to be supplemented by post horses (Jarvis 1955).

Between 1806 and 1814 Ralph Wedgwood, a member of the famous pottery family, developed an electric telegraph. In 1814 he submitted his plans to Lord Castlereagh at the Admiralty, only to be informed that 'the war being at an end, and money scarce, the old system [of shutter-semaphores] was sufficient for the country.'

Sir Francis Ronalds, a Fellow of the Royal Society and, later, Honorary Director of the Kew Observatory, had a similar experience. He constructed a large-scale experimental telegraph system at his house in Hammersmith.. This employed an air electrical influence machine as a source of static electricity and a pith-ball electrometer as an indicator. Two dials, which were rotated in synchronism, were placed at the transmitting and receiving ends of a line which passed to and fro between two wooden frames positioned at opposite ends of his lawn. The cumulative length of the path was eight miles. Characters were marked on the dials and a trigger signal sent by discharging the line when the desired character reached an index position.

When his experiments had reached a satisfactory conclusion, Ronalds wrote to the First Lord of the Admiralty.

Upper Mall, Hammersmith.

Mr. Ronalds presents his respectful compliments to Lord Melville, and takes the liberty of soliciting his lordship's attention to a mode of conveying telegraphic intelligence with great rapidity, accuracy and certainty in all states of the atmosphere, either at night or in the day, and at small expense, which has occurred to him whilst pursuing some electrical experiments. Having been at some pains to ascertain the *practicability* of the scheme, it appears to Mr. Ronalds, and to a few gentlemen by whom it has been examined, to possess several important advantages over any species of telegraphic hitherto invented, and he would be much gratified by an opportunity of demonstrating those advantages to Lord Melville by an experiment which he has no doubt would be deemed decisive, if it should be perfectly agreeable and consistent with his lordship's engagements to honour Mr. Ronalds with a call; or he would be very happy to explain more particularly the nature of the contrivance if Lord Melville could conveniently oblige him by appointing an interview.

Shortly afterwards he received the following reply:

Admiralty, July 29th 1816.

Sir,

I am desired by Lord Melville to acknowledge the receipt of your letter of the 11th instant. His Lordship has left town for some weeks, but he has requested me to see you on the subject of your discovery if you desire it.

I am, Sir,

Your most obedient, humble servant,

R. N. Hay.

Before he had a chance to respond in the affirmative he received a further communication from Mr. Barrow (afterwards Sir John Barrow), the Secretary of the Admiralty.

Admiralty Office, 5th August, 1816.

Mr. Barrow presents his compliments to Mr. Ronalds, and acquaints him with reference to his note of the 3rd instant, that telegraphs of any kind are now wholly unnecessary; and that no other than the one now in use will be adopted.

Stanley Mullard was born in 1883 just as Edison and Swan were beginning to make a success of the carbon filament lamp. At the age of fourteen he started work in a small electric-lamp company managed by his father. In 1910, after a brief spell at a large well-run lamp factory in France, he joined Ediswan, where he made his mark by improving quality control on the production line. In 1913 he was put in charge of the clamp laboratory, where he encountered the soft triode valves which were being made for Marconi (Geddes 1991, p48). Whilst working in the laboratory, he developed the Pointolite, a high-intensity, sealed tungsten-arc lamp. Through this, he established an all-important contact with the Royal Naval Signal School at Portsmouth.

In 1916, Mullard was invited to accept a commission in the Royal Naval Volunteer Reserve force and set up a large laboratory and valve-testing station in London to monitor the production of 'R' valves for the armed services. During his service career he forged strong contacts with officers from the Signal School, and was instrumental in realising a proposal for the use of fused silica instead of glass for the envelopes of high-power transmitter valves. This was attractive because it offered the prospect of greater reliability as it had a higher melting point and lower expansivity than glass, but it was extremely difficult to work. Following demobilisation, Mullard continued to work on the idea with ex-colleagues still at the Signal School. By mid-1920, he had established the silica valve as of great potential importance to the Royal Navy and was asked if he could produce the valves in quantity. The Mullard Radio Valve Co. Ltd was registered on 17 September 1920, with the Radio Communication Company, a competitor of Marconi in marine radio, as a major shareholder.

Sustained by the silica valve, Mullard diversified into the manufacture of the industry-standard 'R' valve by producing a variant of the basic design which was better engineered but cheaper. His improved quality control meant that he could profitably sell at 15s (75p), half what his competitors were charging. They were forced to come down to his price, suffering a substantial reduction in profitability.

In 1923 Marconi decided to enforce its position and picked on Mullard's start-up company as a potentially soft target. They commenced proceedings for infringement of two key patents, allegedly relating to the 'R' valve. Mullard defended the action vigorously, calling on his links with the

Admiralty for support. As a company founded to supply the Royal Navy with silica valves vital to its communications, Mullard had received an assurance of Admiralty support in its defence (Sturmey 1958, p43). Unusually for proceedings involving an ostensibly private organisation, his defence was prepared by the Treasury Solicitor. The verdict, when eventually the case reached the House of Lords, was a typical 'whitewash' decision – that the patents were valid, but not infringed ([1923] RPC 159, [1924] RPC 323).

The practical realisation of the integrated circuit was conceived at the end of the 1950s. It was apparent that this new device would have a major impact on the future development of electronics. The first applications were limited to such programmes as Army battlefield missiles, the antiballistic-missile effort, some secret cryptographic gear at the National Security Agency, the X-20 Dyna-Soar military manned space programme and the Saint, Surveyor and Syncom spacecraft, where the technical advantages of small size, low power dissipation and increased reliability transcended the disadvantage of astronomical cost. Of particular significance was the Minuteman missile programme. The United States had fallen behind the USSR in rocket engine power and was seeking an alternative way to achieve strategic parity. The decision was made to increase the effectiveness of its intercontinental ballistic missiles by upgrading the Minuteman with weight-saving microcircuits. This required what was then, an unprecedented production rate of 4000 integrated circuits a month and was the key to taking Texas Instruments to world leadership in the semiconductor industry (Weber 1981, p121).

9.5 THE EFFECTS OF MILITARY ACTIVITY

Ordnance procurement is likely to have a major influence on innovation. Military strategists are always seeking bigger bangs and more effective weapons and delivery systems, coupled with an element of surprise – their success depends on out-manoeuvring their opponents. In consequence, they are prepared to spend large sums on research and development to achieve these ends. Although there may be no commercial application from the resulting core technologies, it is inevitable that there will be useful spin-off from these research programmes, simply because of the scale of operations.

Military expenditure springs principally from a desire for defence against potential aggressors. There may also be an offensive component for international policing operations and, in rare instances, from bare aggression where a government has territorial aspirations. Whilst the latter will result in a largely planned level of expenditure, the defence budget will depend on the nature and magnitude of a perceived threat. As such it will be subject to unforeseen, and possibly large, fluctuations as external circumstances change.

9.6 DIRECT INTERVENTION

During the 1950s, the Japanese government, through its Ministry of International Trade and Industry (MITI) made a policy decision to develop its electronics industry (Manners 1995, p43). It set out to achieve this by putting steep tariffs and restrictive quotas on the import of advanced semiconductor devices (silicon chips), by requiring American companies wanting to sell chips into the Japanese market to license their technology to local companies and by requiring Japanese companies which obtained such licences to sub-license the technology to other local companies to spread technological understanding as widely as possible.

Initially, the major companies were reluctant to invest in microelectronics. However, towards the end of the 1960s MITI opened up the semiconductor industry to inward investment, although it restricted the percentage of a Japanese company's capital that could be foreign-owned. Amongst the first to take advantage of this relaxation was Texas Instruments, which built a factory in Japan in 1968. This policy change laid the basis for future competition with America by transferring US technology to Japanese workers.

In 1976, despite protests from the manufacturers, who did not want to share their technology secrets with their rivals, MITI set up the so-called VLSI (very large scale integration) programme. This was led by the VLSI Technology Research Association, which drew together top technologists from all the major companies. Two groupings were formed. Hitachi joined with Fujitsu and Mitsubishi, whilst Toshiba worked with NEC. The project cost ¥70 billion, ¥30 billion from MITI and ¥40 billion from the companies involved.

A measure of the success of this venture is that, in 1983, NEC and Hitachi commenced production of the most advanced version of the then most widely used memory chip – a 256-kbit dynamic random-access memory (DRAM) – a full year before any American company. Two years later, when the semiconductor industry entered one of its cyclic recessions, all US companies ceased selling DRAMs, whereas the Japanese companies all stayed in. Between 1978 and 1988 six American producers dropped out of the ranks of the world top ten – RCA, Fairchild, General Instrument, AMI, Rockwell and National Semiconductor – and were replaced by six

Japanese companies – NEC, Toshiba, Hitachi, Fujitsu, Mitsubishi and Matsushita.

In Europe, even after four decades of governmental support in the forms of financial assistance and protective tariffs, semiconductor manufacturers produce less than 10 per cent of the world's output of chips.

In Germany the major player, Siemens, spent $200 million in the 1970s to boost its microelectronics capability. Of this sum, $40 million came from the German government. In the 1980s it met the increasing costs of microelectronics research and development by working with other companies in a series of co-operations to make advanced memory chips. First it combined with Philips in a billion dollar programme. They were subsequently joined by SGS-Thomson in the $4 billion Joint European Submicron Silicon Initiative (JESSI). In the early 1990s Siemens continued the process of collaboration, with a billion dollar joint research and development effort on 256-megabit memory chips with IBM and Toshiba. The partnerships have been subsidised by the German, Dutch, French and Italian governments and the European Commission.

After Philips, the second biggest European microelectronics company in the mid-1990s was the Franco-Italian company SGS-Thomson. Throughout its life, the company has received generous support from the French and Italian governments and its specialities – such as EPROM chips – received Eurofunding for R&D and a protected trading environment through EU political moves.

In Britain, the government has steadily primed the semiconductor pump. In the 1960s, it supported Marconi-Elliott Microelectronics, Plessey and Ferranti. In 1967 it gave Elliott Automation a contract to install a metal-oxide semiconductor (MOS) plant. Government finance for research in semiconductors was $8 million in 1968, about a third of what America was spending. In 1978 the UK-government-backed National Enterprise Board funded a new chip company called Inmos to the tune of $176 million. Its lead product was the transputer, a microprocessor intended for parallel-processing computing. This was technically brilliant, but well ahead of its time. Eventually Inmos and its transputer were sold off to Thorn, which subsequently passed it on to SGS-Thomson. Also in 1978, the UK government instituted a $200 million five-year collaborative research programme, the 'Alvey' project. This also failed. A decade later the chip-making operations of GEC, Plessey and Ferranti had all been folded into one medium-sized chip company.

Taiwan also had aspirations to establish a microelectronics industry. In 1976, its government research body, the Industrial Technology Research Institute (ITRI) purchased from the Radio Corporation of America, state-of-the-art complementary metal-oxide-semiconductor (CMOS) technology to set up a microelectronics laboratory. ITRI refined the RCA process year by year, its electronics arm setting itself to build factories which were capable of reproducing the laboratory process in a manufacturing environment. As each new level of process technology was developed and the factory constructed, the team of technologists which had developed the process in ITRI's lab would move over to the factory to transfer the technology to the new plant.

On three occasions the factory has been handed over to a new company to be its first manufacturing facility. The first was United Microelectronics Corporation (UMC), Taiwan's largest chip-maker; the second time was with the Taiwan Semiconductor Manufacturing Company (TSMC), and the third time with Winhond Electronics Corporation.

The ITRI arrangement was complemented by a policy of sending its brightest engineering students to American universities, many of whom subsequently worked for US chip companies before returning to Taiwan to join local companies. By the mid-1990s, Taiwan had six microelectronics companies in the $100 million-plus league, which was more than any country in the world apart from America and Japan.

The South Korean government provided support for a developing semiconductor industry in two ways. In 1979 it set up the South Korean Institute for Electronics Technology (KIET) with $60 million in backing to develop technology and transfer it to the industrial companies, and in 1982 it announced the 'Semiconductor Industry Promotion Plan' aimed first at import substitution, then at exports. In the 1980s, when massive factories were built in South Korea, they set up companies in America to recruit clever technologists to pick their brains, they bought Silicon Valley companies to acquire their technologies, they licensed technology and products from the Americans and Japanese, and they manufactured products for other companies.

Between 1983 and 1989 the South Korean output of chips went up from $500 000 worth a year to $1.5 billion. Now three South Korean companies, Samsung, Goldstar and Hyundai, are amongst the world leaders.

9.7 COMPETITION LAW

By 1911, General Electric (GE) had built up a dominant position in the US market. It had eliminated most of its smaller competitors by aggressive patent litigation; it held a majority interest in National and it had a market-sharing and price-fixing agreement with Westinghouse Electric, the only other manufacturer of significance. By gaining patents on machinery and improvements in production processes and lamp design features, it maintained an effective monopoly in manufacture of the carbon filament lamp long after the main patents had expired (Bright 1949, p156).

On 3 March 1911, the Department of Justice brought anti-trust proceedings against GE and its associates under the Sherman Act. GE prepared to fight the charges, but reconsidered and accepted a consent decree, which was handed down on 12 October 1912. In the interim, the cross-licensing agreement with Westinghouse expired and GE purchased the 25 per cent of United shares which it did not already own. The agreement with Westinghouse was not renewed, although its arrangements continued to be observed.

The consent decree required GE to take over and operate National's business in its own name; price-fixing and market-sharing agreements were to be discontinued and restrictions on the freedom of lamp-making machinery and glass manufacturers to supply third parties were no longer to be exercised.

Of major significance were the matters on which the consent decree was silent. No restriction was placed upon a manufacturer's right to build up a dominant patent position. The decree expressly stated that patent licences could specify any prices, terms and conditions of sale desired, although they could not fix resale prices. The timing of the proceedings was particularly fortuitous for GE, since the new metal filaments were rapidly replacing the ordinary carbon lamp and an open market for the latter was not of much importance. General Electric's control over prices charged by its licensees was not seriously affected. It retained its patent monopoly over the new types of lamps and it circumvented the prohibition against resale price fixing by developing a new method of distribution. The anti-trust action therefore did not significantly change the situation in the American lamp industry.

At the time of the invention of the transistor, the Bell Telephone System was precluded by anti-trust proceedings from setting up electronic component manufacture. It decided therefore to exploit the invention by licensing its patents. In September 1951, it held a symposium, which was attended by some 300 delegates, to disseminate to industry information concerning transistor manufacture and the applications of transistors to electronic equipment. A second symposium was held in 1952 and a third, which was primarily devoted to the technology of silicon, in 1956. A fee of $25,000, which was treated as an advance payment of potential royalties, was charged for attendance. The licence on offer extended only to the right to manufacture transistors and contained no grant in relation to specialised circuits. (This was significant because the master patents on the transistor also contained claims to its use in a circuit.) The licensor also expressly disclaimed any obligation to transmit information and know-how.

The first major application for transistors was in the manufacture of radio receivers, which was an activity not covered by the initial Bell licences. This production attracted the attention of the patentees, who proceeded in the years 1960 to 1962 to license most United Kingdom producers of broadcast sound receivers to utilise transistors. In all, a sum of the order of £1,500,000 sterling was paid to the Bell System by United Kingdom manufacturers, who also were obliged to cross-license their own patent holdings in the USA.

Under a further consent decree made in 1956, the patentees accepted the onus of granting, to all comers, royalty-free licences under all its United States patents dated from before 24 January of that year ([1965] RPC 335), a factor which subsequently proved significant in negotiations with Intel.

9.8 INTERNATIONAL TREATIES AND HARMONISATION OF LAWS

The first international treaty to have an effect on innovation was the Paris Convention on Intellectual Property, which was signed in 1883. This provided for equal treatment of all subjects of the signatory states. Specifically, it provided for right of priority for patent applications, so that a patent application filed in any one territory could be followed by an application in another Convention territory within a year and the later application would take as its filing date the date of the initial application. This, and other streamlining of procedures, greatly enhanced the power and value of intellectual property rights.

Almost a century later, an explosion in international trade threatened to create a log-jam in the national patent offices of the world when the rate of filing new applications began to exceed the rate at which the offices could examine them. Initially, the Dutch and German patent offices coped with the problem by introducing a system of deferred examination. Under this, patent applications were filed in the customary way, but were not examined for novelty and patentability until a separate request for examination was made. The examination request could be delayed for up to seven years. As the potential commercial viability of most inventions becomes apparent within a few years of their conception, this meant that many patent applications were abandoned before it was necessary to have them examined.

Shortly after the introduction of deferred examination in the Netherlands and Germany, a group of European nations negotiated the European Patent Convention, agreeing to set up a common patent office, which would carry out the examination procedures on behalf of the national patent offices. At around the same time, the Patent Co-operation Treaty performed the same function on a global scale, in this case, using the US, European and Japanese Patent Offices as the examining authorities. These treaties greatly reduced the duplication of effort which had previously characterised the granting of patents.

As with intellectual property, other areas developed a need for international regulation. With wireless communications, Marconi set out from the outset to establish a dominant position. He sought an exclusive licence from the British government to communicate with ships and also with Empire and foreign land-stations. The Marconi wireless system was superior to those of his competitors, but he also bolstered his position by adopting a policy of not accepting messages from vessels equipped by rival companies. These competitors, and in particular the German ones, were intent on preventing the establishment of a Marconi monopoly. With this objective, Germany called a preliminary international wireless conference in Berlin on 4 August 1903, which was attended by representatives from Germany, Great Britain, Austria, Hungary, Spain, Italy, Russia, France and the USA. Each country promoted its national interest. Germany suggested that all shore stations should accept messages from any ship, whilst Britain and Italy suggested that all countries should adopt the most efficient system, that of the Marconi Company. Six Powers signed the Final Protocol, which was based on the German proposals (Goodwin 1995, p18).

A full international conference on wireless telegraphy was held in Berlin in 1906 and was attended by twenty-nine nations. The main business was to ratify the Protocol of the preliminary 1903 conference, which incorporated mandatory intercommunication between stations using different manufacturers' equipment.

The delegates adopted a Convention drawn up by the German government and modelled on the successful International Telegraph Convention of 1875. It included measures for universal communication and laid down operating procedures which eliminated the jamming techniques to which rival companies resorted to further their commercial interests. The conference established the Bureau of the International Telegraph Union at Berne as the central administrative organ of the Wireless Telegraph Conference. The Convention came into effect on 1 July 1908 for an 'indefinite period'.

The proposals were considered by a House of Commons Select Committee, which approved ratification by a single vote. For the Marconi Company this represented a final defeat in its quest for a complete monopoly of marine wireless communication. Large sums of money had been invested in building many more coastal stations than its rivals, but their revenue-earning capacity was to be severely limited by the agreed maximum rates. Furthermore, there was no guarantee that Marconi-equipped ships would communicate with Marconi coastal stations. For the German company Telefunken, however, which had the full backing of the German government, the conference was a triumph because it completely negated the effects of Marconi's technological superiority.

Patent law has had an equivocal approach to computer programs, which, under UK and European but not US law, were a statutory exception to inventive acts capable of being protected by patents (largely due to a perceived difficulty in classifying and searching prior art in this field). This exclusion was circumvented by decisions of the court that a standard computer programmed by a novel program was patentable, but more recent decisions, notably *Raytheon Co.'s Application* ([1993] RPC 427), set the legal pendulum swinging in a contra direction. At a conference held at the British Patent Office in 1994, a clear message was given by representatives of the computer industry that, in their view, computer software should be protectable by patents in the same way as any other industrially applicable inventions.

When the development of the planar process for the manufacture of semiconductor devices made it possible to circumvent the long and expensive research and development path and make devices similar to those of other manufacturers through the simple expedient of visual examination of their products, the United States enacted the Semiconductor Chip Protection Act of 1984 (Christie 1995, p5). As this was a *sui generis* right, it was not obligatory for the USA to extend reciprocal rights to foreign nationals. Other nations followed suit, however, with their own version of this law and in 1989 a diplomatic conference in Washington concluded a treaty on the protection of intellectual property in respect of integrated circuits. Similarly, when information technology became commercially important, the European Community promulgated a Database Directive which provided for a uniform law protecting databases in countries of the European Union.

9.9 CONCLUSION

The underlying philosophy behind the grant of letters patent is that the associated monopoly will act as an incentive to the creation of new inventions. However, the 1623 Statute of King James, which is the precursor of modern patent law, was originally drawn up as an act of political expediency. It was intended to curtail the right of the monarch to grant monopolies for the supply of the everyday necessities of life, whilst at the same time not inhibiting the trade activities of the merchant adventurers who established trade with remote parts of the world. The path between this Scylla and Charybdis was the act of introducing new manufactures to the realm and, if a person performed this act, the state would grant him a monopoly for the term of two apprenticeships (fourteen years). Although patent law has evolved over the years (most recently as a result of international harmonisation), it is questionable whether such a crudely fashioned statute is an appropriate instrument to encourage innovation.

If an invention is successful, fees for the renewal of patent rights will not act as an inhibition, but, on rare occasions such as that which obtained in the early days of the electronics industry when de Forest's impecuniousness denied him overseas protection, their influence will be significant and achieve an effect which is counter to that desired by public policy.

As the original intention behind the grant of letters patent was to encourage the introduction of new methods of manufacture into the realm, it would have been contrary to this philosophy to permit the patent to be used in a wholly negative manner, to prevent working of an invention by third parties, when it was not being exploited by the patentee himself. Until the middle of the nineteenth century, patents could be revoked if the inventions were not put into practice within a specified time (Davenport 1979, p79). The concern persisted and the 1883 Patents Act introduced a provision that the Board of Trade could compulsorily grant a licence if the needs of the public were not being met or the exercise of another patented invention was being blocked by the patent. The 1883 Paris Convention on the Protection of Intellectual Property acknowledged the right of signatory states to make such provisions in their national laws. The 1902 Patents Act reintroduced the power to revoke a patent if the monopoly was being abused in this way and the 1907 Act transferred these matters from ministerial prerogative to judicial decision.

Whilst the public policy implications of compulsory licensing provisions were, no doubt, well intentioned, their ultimate effect depends on how they are administered. Judicial attitude can tip the balance in either direction. The final arbiters are the courts and, if the judges are not minded to apply sanctions, then the legislation will be without teeth. When it favours established companies against newcomers who offer innovatory products and marketing techniques, the judiciary strengthens the dead hand of oligopoly.

Intervention by the state, particularly if it occurs with embryonic innovations, may often be prolonged. It will therefore distort patterns of trade and thus fundamentally alter the dynamic balance.

Strength of patent protection may be influenced by the nature of the legal system under which it is obtained. An adversarial legal system leads to more extreme decisions which will thus have a greater influence on the progress of innovation. In individual cases, an inexperienced or irascible judge may have a significant bearing on the development of an industry. The performance of counsel may have a similar result.

At the microeconomic level, the fact that the law is administered by human beings may have an effect. Judges are required to adjudicate arguments advanced by counsel, some of whom will be more proficient than others. In some legal circuits in the USA, patent cases are decided by jury, an even more unpredictable process. Courts obtain guidance from expert witnesses, who frequently will present differing views since they are paid by opposing litigants to support their cases. Under such varying conditions, it is unreasonable to expect consistency between judgements and the maintenance of clear objective standards over intervals of many years.

Litigation is expensive. It has been said that recourse to the law is open only to the very rich and the very poor. This adage will also apply to businesses, with the further proviso that litigation will distract key employees from their mainstream occupations. Legal battles are therefore to be avoided.   By corollary, intellectual property rights will have a penumbra of influence which extends beyond the literal monopoly because the mere prospect of legal proceedings will carry with it the impending risk of incurring these huge costs.

The grant of a patent, with its *prima facie* presumption of validity, provides a tool which can dominate the evolution of an industry. Because technological development is a binary decision process, it is not possible to reinstate the initial *status quo* if the patent is subsequently found to be invalid. The roar of (even) a paper tiger may justifiably cause a potential victim to quake.

In practice, it is questionable whether the offer of a monopoly creates an increase in the desire to innovate. Certainly, in recent years decision makers in the engineering industries have suggested that the prospect of a patent monopoly has not influenced their intention to invest in new innovations (Taylor 1973). On the other hand, without some temporary shelter from competition, it is unlikely that the huge R&D expenditure of the pharmaceutical companies would have been forthcoming. What is likely to hold universally is that the temporary monopoly afforded by a patent will permit the establishment of patterns of trade which will persist after the expiry of the statutory monopoly (Cullis 1973).

The justification for the grant of patent monopolies is that they are assumed to act as a stimulus for innovation. A question posed by this proposition is 'What kind of innovation?' The main concern of providers of capital is uncertainty and risk. The knowledge that an innovation will be accompanied by a monopoly mitigates the initial risk and financiers will thus be more prepared to support the research which leads to the initial invention. However, both they and the inventors will not wish to hazard the gains to be achieved from an advance, so there is a disincentive to engage in activities which will supplant an innovation.

The patent system stifles pioneering innovation, as the grant of a basic patent frequently coincides with the transition from the Schumpeter A- to the Schumpeter B-stage of development. It permits the establishment of strong, viable organisations by putting up the price of market entry to subsequent participants.

Other forms of intellectual property right can be complementary to patents. They may be used to extend the monopoly enjoyed by an enterprise. Trade marks are a means of protecting market power, which may be used to cement the patterns of trade established by letters patent. In a consumer market, promotion is a significant part of the package offered; in countries where patent protection is not available, trade mark registration may provide an adequate substitute. Once the well-known trade mark is applied, no major additional effort is necessary to coerce potential licensees since the innovation itself offers the real consumer benefit.

When computer software became commercially important, there was no obvious intellectual property right by means of which it could be protected. Lawyers cast around and concluded that the intellectual creation most similar to a computer program was a literary work. They therefore adapted the provisions of literary copyright for the protection of software. This has given rise to various anomalous situations. For example, it is entirely permissible to reverse-engineer a computer operating system by so-called 'clean room' techniques in which a team which has made a minute examination of the original program draws up a specification for a team of 'virgin' software writers, who have had no exposure to the original software, to simulate it by designing an operating system which performs identical functions. Since they have not seen the original software, and since copyright protects simply against the act of copying, the second team cannot be guilty of copyright infringement. Literary and artistic copyright is intended to protect an author's original work. It therefore subsists for the duration of his lifetime and for seventy years after his death. Such a term is entirely inappropriate for computer software, the utility of which may well be exhausted after an interval of eight years.

New technological developments occasionally fall outside the scope of existing intellectual property protection. In such cases, either the law evolves by adapting existing measures or, if the development is of sufficient significance, new *sui generis* rights are introduced.

Regulation exists to promulgate the will of the government. Where indirect influences, such as intellectual property laws, are ineffective, or too slow, to give effect to public policy, governments may act directly to achieve their will. This can be by way of investment from the national purse or by way of ordinances which specify how things are to be done.

Regulatory control can suffocate a new development at birth. Certainly, in the initial stages, it will exert a dominant influence. The modelling of new legislation on non-pertinent precedents may not achieve the desired result as in the case of the nineteenth century Electricity Supply Acts, which were based on the Tramways Act.

Public policy may favour a particular course of action which proves impossible to carry out in the light of prevailing circumstances. Successive governments have promulgated the myth that they control the national economy but, in the modern world, they are entirely at the mercy of international events. As a result of this blinkered perception, the measures that they take to introduce changes will be impotent in the face of countervailing measures adopted by those whom they wish to control.

Competition policy frequently ignores the realities of market economics and merely results in the destruction of competitive strength of a domestic supplier which cannot rely on a substantial home base. Control of world markets simply passes to a dominant foreign supplier who is not subject to the restrictions. Regulatory control will suffocate the mewling infant of innovation. Britain does not succeed at innovation because of the harsh regulatory regimes with which it surrounds inventions. To nurture seedlings requires a hot-house environment.

The effect of military procurement is to distort the patterns of trade which would otherwise develop. This may favour an industry, as in the case of the Minuteman intercontinental ballistic missile, which was the source of strength of US integrated circuit manufacture, or slow its progress, as with the electric telegraph at the end of the Napoleonic wars, when fast communication between the Admiralty in London and the navy ceased to be of paramount importance.

As part of a national economic strategy, a government may decide to invest in a specific industry which it perceives as likely to be of increasing importance in the future. Although there will, initially, be a large element of 'me-too-ism', since this practice is often used to nurture 'sunrise' industries, such intervention could initiate a wave of innovation if the local industries become established.

A focused approach, backed by firm government direction, can form the foundation for a strong industry. However, if the operation goes off at half-cock, it is doomed to failure.

Intellectual property rights are an element of social engineering and sound engineering practice requires the provision of a safety valve to relieve an excessive build-up of pressure. Competition laws were enacted to provide a countervailing effect to the excessive exercise of monopoly, either *de facto* or statutory. However, since these statutes are applied only when a situation gets out of hand, it is questionable whether they have the power to exercise control *at that stage* – large and resourceful companies can, by dint of throwing money at the problem, outwit the regulatory authorities. However, the strain on the companies' resources may attenuate their mainstream operations. Particularly deleterious are the demands placed on the time of senior management, who will be diverted from their mainstream activities.

Trade has become a global affair and, due to their nature, some activities, such as communications, cannot be contained within national boundaries. In the interests of order, it is therefore necessary to have agreement on regulation of those activities which affect relationships with foreign countries. This may require treaties to regulate the conduct of the signatories in a uniform way. Laws may also need to be harmonised to give effect to these agreements. This trend towards equalisation and harmonisation will, however, have an effect of levelling down. It inhibits the high fliers and curtails any early dominance which they might otherwise have been able to establish. On the other hand, a so-called level playing field in areas such as intellectual property will favour those who are able to command the support of natural advantages such as a strong domestic market.

The law is resourceful. It will adapt and supplement existing processes to take account of new economic and technological development. However, this takes time and the result is frequently less than perfect. International agreement harmonises procedures and, by streamlining them, eases the path of innovation in general, although it may inhibit individuals and companies who are in the vanguard.

10. Chicken and Egg – Do Existing Markets Control Inventions...

You will be able to give the working classes a light cheaper than gas that does not produce heat, does not vitiate the air, and which will enable them to do twice as much work.
Sir William Preece, *Report to Cheltenham Town Council*, 1893

There are countless inventions every year, but not one in a thousand ever gets beyond being an invention and becomes something of practical use to humanity. It is therefore as much a question of the commercial man's ability as of the inventors as to whether or not any developments shall become useful to the public.
Morning Post, 19 November 1909

... innovation itself is being reduced to routine. Technological progress is increasingly becoming the business of teams of trained specialists who turn out what is required and make it work in predictable ways. The romance of earlier commercial adventure is rapidly wearing away, because so many more things can be strictly calculated that had of old to be visualized in a flash of genius. On the other hand, personality and will power must count for less in environments which have become accustomed to economic change best instanced by an incessant stream of new consumers' and producers' goods – and which, instead of resisting, accept it as a matter of course. The resistance which comes from interests threatened by innovation in the productive process is not likely to die out as long as the capitalist order persists. It is, for instance, the great obstacle on the road toward mass production of cheap housing which presupposes radical mechanization and wholesale elimination of inefficient methods of work on the plot. But every other kind of resistance – the resistance, in particular, of consumers and producers to a new kind of thing because it is new – has well-nigh vanished already.
Joseph Schumpeter, *Capitalism, Socialism and Democracy*, 1950

British Telecom said any move which consolidated the market was welcome. A spokesman said: 'We have about 150 licensed competitors. We have seen the arrival this year of AT&T as a big competitor. The joining together of Mercury and others creates a more definable opposition.'
'We would like to see good solid competition with whom we can slug it out with fair, competitive and commercial terms and say goodbye to the industry regulator whose hand increasingly slips in to control what we do.'
The Guardian, 23 October 1996

10.1 INTRODUCTION

Interaction between an innovation and the economic environment may occur on many fronts, some active and some passive. The innovation will be subject to various influences, of which some may have a positive and some a negative, effect – they may open up fresh avenues or create a prejudice in favour of a particular line of development. For example, marketing may be expected to be a stimulator of demand, whilst the needs to raise finance and create an infrastructure will be inhibiting factors.

It is likely that the need for cash will exhibit a threshold – an innovation will not get off the ground without sufficient finance. However, provided the provision is adequate, increasing the level beyond that threshold will not bring about an increase in the level of innovation as the law of diminishing returns comes into play. Is the solution to a problem therefore more likely to be found by thinking more smartly, rather than by throwing money at it?

Continuing the analysis of examples, extracted from the case studies in particular, this chapter adopts a bottom-up approach to view multifaceted socio-economic factors which contribute to or inhibit the progress of innovation. It examines the disparate elements in isolation to establish a foundation for the proposition that their cumulative influence serves as a determinant of innovation.

10.2 FINANCE

10.2.1 Bank-Rolling the Heroic Inventor

The progress of the incipient heroic inventor is illustrated in the following three extracts from the biography of S.Z. de Ferranti. He wrote to his father in June 1881:

> On Monday last I went to, the offices of the British Electric Light Co. (having heard that they were taking on electricians) and applied for a place as such. Mr Ward (their engineer) asked me a good many questions about myself and other things and finally said he would write to you about it. So I think that I stand a good chance of getting a place provided they pay me well enough. He also said that he would let me know by the end of this week.

In the same letter he tells of his first commercial success: the sale of the small dynamo he had made:

> While in the Euston Road I went in to Caplatzi and found that my machine was sold and also got the £5.10.0. If I get employment next week I shall put £7.0.0 or so in the Post Office...

On 12 July in the same year, he wrote to his mother from Siemens' works at Charlton:

The only thing which I should like would be to be a bit better paid; which I hope will be the case later on.

But I must say that I have got a most fortunate place, that is I am alone with a very nice gentleman in the Experimental Department which is as good for me as if I was spending piles of money weekly on experiments. Our work is to try all the experiments for the Electric Light Department; also all the new machines and different combinations of different lamps; to measure the strengths of currents given out and Horse-power absorbed by the same, etc. etc. Three workmen do all that we require or tell them to do, so that there is no hard work and we can keep fairly clean and are supposed to look and act as gentlemen only...

When Ferranti returned to London, Mr. Alfred Thompson took him to St. Benet Chambers, Fenchurch Street – the offices of Messrs. Ingledew, Ince & Colt, and introduced him to Francis Ince. They talked; Alfred Thompson left and Mr. Ince took young Ferranti to lunch.

From that first eventful meeting Sebastian de Ferranti came away somewhat dazed. He was only eighteen, the City was a place hitherto unknown to him. He had never before lunched with a lawyer, and this one fascinated him, for he had the technicalities of electrical science at his finger-tips. Mr. Francis Ince was an enthusiast who pursued law for his livelihood and science for his diversion. He had a large and rapidly-growing practice in Fenchurch Street; his brother, Edward Brett Ince, was at the Bar and soon to become one of the leading Q.C.s. Unlike many enthusiasts, Mr. Francis Ince was, before all things, a practical man who believed and succeeded in getting things done.

In 1881 London was still lighted mainly by gas, oil-lamps, and candles. Electricity was beginning slowly to make its way. In Ferranti this enterprising lawyer saw a young genius and a genius after his own heart.

'And you mean to tell me you're content to be at Siemens,' he said, 'earning £1 a week! Good God!'

Lawyers see life on the seamy side; small wonder, then, that they become suspicious of all men.

'Ferranti,' he said, 'if you continue at a job like that I'll tell you what will happen. As soon as they discover you've got inventive ability they'll offer you £5 a week and proceed to rob your brains. You'll do the inventing and they'll collect the cash.'

This was rather bewildering, but it chimed in with certain thoughts that had arisen in Ferranti's own mind.

'Perhaps I'd better ask for a rise,' he suggested.

'For God's sake don't do anything of the sort,' Francis Ince advised. 'Just clear out. That's no place for you. Then there's only one thing for you to do.

You must start right away on your own. You might stay there till your teeth fall out and never get a dog's chance of doing anything.'
Ferranti objected that he had no capital.
'Leave that to me,' said his new friend.
As a result of this meeting, Ferranti's invention of the zigzag armature for dynamos was taken in hand by Mr. Alfred Thompson and Mr. Francis Ince. The first company (Ferranti, Thompson and Ince, Ltd.) in which Ferranti was interested was formed in 1882; he being given the post of engineer to the company though only eighteen years of age.

William Siemens came to England in March 1843 as an economic migrant. He brought with him a process for electro-gilding developed by his brother Werner. He made contact with the Birmingham firm of Elkingtons whose business was electroplating. They evaluated his technique and, having decided that it was commercially viable, paid him a lump sum for his rights. They sent him to their patent agents to have the invention protected, but deducted the costs of patenting from their payment to him. They were also sufficiently hard-headed to insist that he worked at their plant until they were satisfied that his know-how had been transferred satisfactorily.

Edison established his reputation with a series of inventions relating to telegraphy and the phonograph. Whilst working for Western Union, he attracted the attention of Grosvenor Lowry, their attorney. When Edison began work on the electric light, Lowry saw his opportunity for a successful speculation. He put together a consortium of financiers to bank-roll the Edison Electric Light Company.

Although Heinrich Göbel was a much more modest inventor, he did not hide his light under a bushel. Instead, he wheeled it round the streets of New York on a trolley and exhibited it in his shop. Despite the fact that his ability to communicate was limited by his poor command of English he, nevertheless, eventually attracted commercial sponsors who wished to exploit his invention. However, this source of sponsorship did not survive the failure of Göbel to press a claim against his successful commercial rivals.

When Tesla had developed his theory of alternating current machines, he presented a paper to the American Institute of Electrical Engineers. Amongst his audience was George Westinghouse, who immediately perceived the huge commercial prospects for these inventions. He made an offer of a million dollars for the patents and was sufficiently canny to appoint Tesla to a technical post in the Westinghouse Company, to get the new manufacturing operation up and running.

Steve Wozniak was a techno-freak who cobbled together the Apple I computer to impress his acquaintances at the Homebrew Computer Club.

His friend Steve Jobs realised that there were many people who were interested in programming and making computers do things, but who did not have the technical ability to assemble the hardware for themselves, which was, at that time, the only way to obtain a working machine. He persuaded Wozniak to develop his machine into one which was suitable for production. Finance was arranged by Mike Markkula, a veteran from Intel. Aided by VisiCalc, the first spreadsheet, the Apple II became an overnight success (Cringely 1992, p64).

10.2.2 Raising Capital in Victorian Times

I never mean to have anything to do with industrial undertakings in the sense of lending our name
> Everard Hambro, 1881

Company accoucheuring is not particularly popular in the House, and the best firms are chary of meddling with it. They prefer good steady everyday work which involves no special responsibility and only a reasonable amount of brain labour. To turn over familiar stocks like Trunks or Eries by the thousand day by day and week by week is the ideal existence of a prosperous broker. His morning letters and his afternoon cables are quite excitement enough for him. Surrounded by a circle of well-to-do clients, who can be trusted to take up their stocks or meet their differences without a murmur on pay-day, he is happy in his small world. From his office to the House, and from the House back to his office, is an ample round of existence for him. When he feels seedy or wants diversion he can have his Saturday to Monday at Brighton or the Isle of Wight. What could a well-endowed citizen wish for more? Such a man has no inherent love of novelty, and his predisposition is to suspect everything in the way of originality. Whatever might throw the big machine out of gear finds in him an avowedly prejudiced critic.
> *The Statist*, 1886

The initial interaction between the young electrical industry and the City of London can only be described as an unmitigated disaster (Kynaston 1994, p340). Companies such as Brush endeavoured to milk the financiers by franchising their patents whilst retaining an equity interest in the franchised operation. Many other enterprises were set up on an inadequate technological platform. Their subsequent failure destroyed confidence – the prime requirement for a satisfactory relationship with providers of capital. The regulatory environment exacerbated this situation as the 1882 Electricity Supply Act required private electrical undertakings to transfer their assets to the local authority at a knock-down price after twenty-one years, a period which was insufficient to ensure an adequate return on the investment. In May 1882, the *Electrician* summed matters up in the following manner.

The existing state of things with regard to electric light companies is deplorable. Company after company is promoted and floated with a huge capital when it is absolutely certain that for years to come there will not be legitimate business enough to any per centage on a large part of the capital subscribed ... This speculative gambling is a curse to true enterprise. Rotten companies, not worth the paper their prospectuses are printed on, are always started when the public lose their heads, as they seem to have done now, to the loss of the ultimate holders of shares. Companies may be and are brought out legitimately, and are worked by honest men. Unfortunately the public will not discriminate ...

The consequence was that very few undertakings were set up until the 1888 Electricity Supply Act increased the pay-back period to forty-two years. Those public companies which survived were, for most of the remainder of the century, short of capital and had to pay out unrealistically high dividends in order to prevent a complete collapse of confidence (Kennedy 1990, p31).

Commenting on the breakdown of confidence and its effects, David Kynaston (1994, p243) observed:

Ultimately it was a failure of quality control, a failure to distinguish between the bad and the good and then discourage the bad, keep faith with the good. No one can blame the public for succumbing to a mania – but the job of the professional intermediary, whether company promoter or stockbroker, is to apply objective analysis precisely at the times when it is not only reason that is at a premium.

It was a catastrophic start for the industry, as those public companies (including Brush, but not Hammond) that had survived the roller coaster of 1882 found themselves for most of the rest of the century hobbled for capital and having to pay out unrealistically high dividends in order to prevent a complete collapse of confidence on the part of an already deeply sceptical stock market. This was disastrous, for by this stage in its economic development, starting to be caught up by Germany and the United States in terms of its mature industries, Britain should have been looking to the new industries – above all, electrical engineering, chemicals and in due course motor cars – in order to regain its unquestioned industrial ascendancy. All three of these new industries were high-tech and capital-intensive, so there could be no question of relying on traditional forms of self-finance and local finance. In other words, the role of the London capital market was pivotal. The point, however, was not so much the *total* supply of funds that it did or did not channel into these new industries, but rather whether it was capable of effectively applying the element of long-term, disinterested discrimination. The experience of the 'Brush boom' suggested that, in terms of the crucial latter service, there was ample room for improvement.

10.2.3 The Creation of Infrastructure – Its Cost and Delays

Before Edison and Swan could establish the manufacture of the incandescent lamp, a whole new infrastructure had to be created. Central stations needed to be developed and either cables laid in the streets to carry electricity to the customers' houses or individual generating plant installed on the clients' premises. Even a means of measuring the quantity of electricity which had been supplied was not available – the first installations relied on counting the number of lamps and, later, on weighing a metal plate which had been subjected to electrolytic deposition of silver by the supply of current to the user.

Edison relied on a vertically integrated organisation in which he developed everything himself. Swan, on the other hand, used the services of independent suppliers, such as Crompton and Siemens. Both systems, however, created a huge demand for capital which could not be met from internal sources.

In the modern semiconductor industry, although in the early days plant such as alloying furnaces, epitaxial reactors and photolithographic machinery was developed and constructed by the device manufacturer, a network of independent suppliers quickly grew up. Cash to pay for this was generated by huge sales to eager end users who were prepared to pay what appeared to be extortionate sums for the new devices. The industry has been characterised by a cyclic succession of fat years followed by lean years as the participants mount the new learning curve.

Each successive generation of device has, however, required ever more sophisticated and expensive machinery for its construction. Capital costs have risen steadily with each new introduction until, currently, the device manufacturers are reaching the stage that they can no longer afford to finance the infrastructure from their individual resources. The 64Mbit chips which shepherded in the millennium, required factories costing $1.6bn each for equipment to process the 7,500 wafers a week in the 0.3µm line-width lithographic technology which became the norm (Manners 1996a).

10.3 MARKETING

But Mr Alan Sugar, Amstrad chairman, denies this. The machines had been fully tested and the decision to include a fan was simply to reassure people, he said.

'I'm a realistic person and we are a marketing organisation, so if it's the difference between people buying the machine or not, I'll stick a bloody fan on it,' he added.

'And if they say they want bright pink spots on it, I'll do that, too.'

'What is the use of me banging my head against a brick wall and saying, "You don't need the damn fan, sunshine." ?' Mr Sugar asked.

Another reason is its image, according to Quinn. 'DBS (Direct Broadcasting by Satellite) is glossy. You get a glossy dish with a go-faster stripe on it. With cable they come and dig up your roses.'

'ASO [active sideband optimisation] is a single circuit. There will be no Skoda version' says Nokia.
Reports in *Electronics Weekly*

A self-evident fact is that no-one will buy a product unless he is aware of its existence so, clearly, it was necessary for publicity methods to evolve concurrently with innovations. At the present time, marketing is a highly developed art. Could early inventors rely on similar assistance? In the nineteenth century, in fact, many present-day marketing techniques were already firmly established. Swan was a firm believer in the influence of opinion formers and many of his initial lighting installations were in the homes of the great and good, such as the Marquess of Salisbury and Lord Bute (Cullis 2004, Appendix 5). Edison was of a similar view, although the opinion formers he chose were the financier J.P. Morgan and the actress Sarah Bernhardt. The Victorian public flocked to exhibitions, the award of gold medals being an accolade which received wide publicity. In his memoirs, Ambrose Fleming, the inventor of the thermionic diode detector, recalled having been inspired by an exhibit of Edison lamps at the Crystal Palace Electricity Exhibition in 1883 (Fleming 1921, p159). William Siemens puffed his inventions at meetings of learned societies, as did many of his contemporaries (Pole 1888, p188).

10.4 STRATEGIC UTILISATION OF PATENTS

10.4.1 Patents as a Mainstream Source of Income

At a time when the cost of manufacture of a carbon filament lamp was about 9d, Edison and Swan were able to command a retail price of 3s 9d in those territories where there was strong patent cover, but only 1s 0d in those countries where patents were weak or non-existent.

At the end of the 1950s, Texas Instruments made a major breakthrough with the invention of the integrated circuit by Jack Kilby. At Fairchild Camera and Instrument Corporation, Noyce and Hoerni's development of the planar diffused silicon transistor also heralded a new advance for semiconductor device manufacture. During the 1960s, these two companies cross-licensed one another, their relative patent strengths being such that neither could exert a dominant influence over its rival. Other companies in the industry, however, were required to make substantial payments to both companies for the right to manufacture silicon planar integrated circuits. Fairchild derived a considerable income in lump-sum payments for the right to use the technology, whilst Texas Instruments preferred to settle on a royalty basis, thus establishing a long-term income stream. TI's strategy was aided by a delay in the grant of the Kilby Japanese patent, although payments ended abruptly with a strange decision of the Japanese court that the patent did not cover *modern* large-scale integrated circuits. During the early 1990s, a quarter of TI's profits came from patent royalties (Zipper 1990).

10.4.2   The Comfort Blanket – Patents as Security in a Start-Up Market

The Edison and Swan United Electric Light Company was set up to exploit the monopoly on the carbon filament lamp established by Edison's and Swan's patents. The success of the company turned on demonstrating the validity of those patents and, in consequence, of being able to use them to defend a dominant position in the market place. The associated costs had a highly cash-negative effect on the company's accounts in the early days of the market development. The position is highlighted in the following statement by the company chairman.

> You know that we are possessors of patents, and I suppose a large measure of our prosperity will depend on the validity of those patents. This is the second concern in which I have been concerned in which the investments have turned largely on the possession of patents – the telephone and the business of electric lighting – and I have arrived at one conclusion, that anyone who stakes his money on a patent is a fool. That is a general proposition which I shall be prepared successfully to defend, if it needed defence, with the experience that we have before us – I mean until the validity of the patent has been established. We are fortunate in our concern in one respect, that the cost of our patents for a large part has taken the form of a contingent payment to Mr. Edison. The other portion took the form of an actual payment to an illustrious inventor. If that gentleman and his friends had been in the position that Mr. Edison is in, and had only claim on the concern for contingent value after the people who had put their money into it had received a reasonable interest, the position of this company would have been very different to what it is, and we should have been paying a very large dividend.
>
> The Chairman, in reply, said it would be observed that they spoke of the cost of patents &c. &c. and further expenditure thereon £4,467, which included the legal expenses incurred by the Company in upholding their patents, and they had from time to time, dealt with that matter in a similar way, debiting capital with the legal expenses. They were capital charges. What was the cost of patents? Some people who do not think it out would consider it would be the amount paid to the patentee. But then if when the patentee was paid the patent was assailed, and they had to fight in order to establish its validity, the expenses so incurred had to be added to the costs of the patent. That was the view which the Directors took of the matter, and the view of the auditors – that the cost of protecting the patent was part of the cost of the patent itself. Thus it was made a capital charge. They did not know what was going to arise hereafter, and some day there might be amalgamations, and so on, and obviously to charge revenue a very heavy expense incurred solely for building up the

patents would be taking money out of their pockets to-day to put it into somebody else's pocket in the future. He had known companies which were very prosperous that paid capital charges out of revenue, but that was because they did not wish to excite avaricious competitors into too ready action by paying too large dividends. Poor companies could not do that. In the previous year they debited in the same way £8,104 to capital, the bulk of which also represented legal expenses a year ago. He thought they had every reason to be satisfied with the economical nature of the legal expenses considering the 'lights' whom they had to employ. [A reference to the Attorney General and other silks retained in litigation.] With regard to the application of profit he had properly proposed the report and accounts because they had to adopt the report and accounts to confirm that there was a profit. They thought that they were bound by justice and prudence also, to apply that profit to writing down the losses of previous years, rather than to distribute it by way of dividends. When they took the business over, it was a putting together of two concerns which had not been over wisely administered, though he would not say they were unwisely conceived. They had had in the working of the concern great losses. Three years ago they lost £28,000 on the working account. The following year, as a result of re-arrangement that £28,000 was turned into a profit of £12,000, which they wrote down; the profit of £24 made last year was an amount dealing with which did not give them much trouble. But now they had a substantial sum and the question was should they pay it out? They thought it was no good starting a legal hare, and that therefore they had better using the amount in writing down instead of paying it away in dividends. That was a proceeding which came to this, that instead of taking it now they applied the money to the improvement of the property. The key of the patents had six years to run from November next. That might not be considered a long time, but with the reputation which they had built up, and which they were building up, a great deal might be done in that time.

    Chairman's address to the Fourth Annual General Meeting,
Edison and Swan United Electric Light Company Limited,
9 August 1887
The Electrician, 12 Aug 1887, pp302-303

10.4.3   Patents as a Means of Retaining Control in a Mature Market

In the USA, General Electric and its predecessor company Edison General Electric used Edison's patents to control the carbon filament lamp market during the last two decades of the 1800s. Towards the turn of the century, the development, in Germany, of the osmium filament by Auer von Welsbach and the tantalum filament by Feuerlein and von Bolton and the development in Austria of the tungsten filament by Just and Hanaman, threatened this dominance. GE responded by purchasing the US rights to their patents, perpetuating its monopoly, which it subsequently further reinforced with its own development of the ductile tungsten filament lamp by Coolidge and Langmuir. The cost to GE for the purchase of these patents was some $760,000, but this investment was recovered in a mere couple of years, due to the premium it was able to charge the consumer by virtue of its dominant market position.

After its early patents on the telephone had expired, Bell Telephones set out to achieve patent protection for all improvements in its techniques, however minor they might be, and for all possible alternatives as a means of preventing its competitors entering its technological field.

10.4.4 Hanging Together Rather than Being Hanged Separately

When the telephone was being established in London, intense rivalry existed between the Bell and Edison companies which were competing for the business. Neither company had a dominant technical lead over the other since Bell's company possessed a good receiver and an inferior transmitter, whilst Edison had a good transmitter and a poor receiver (Clark 1977, p62).

Commercial success turned on maintenance of the equipment and lines which supplied the customer. The tale of rival gangs of workmen engaged in almost open warfare was recounted in a contemporary account by George Bernard Shaw:

> These deluded and romantic men gave a glimpse of the skilled proletariat of the United States. They sang obsolete sentimental songs with genuine emotions and their language was frightful even to an Irishman. They worked with a ferocious energy which was out of all proportion to the actual result achieved. Indomitably resolved to assert their Republican manhood by taking no orders from a tall-hatted Englishman whose still politeness covered his conviction that they were relatively to himself inferior and common persons, they insisted on being slave-driven with genuine American oaths by a genuine free and equal American foreman. They utterly despised the artfully slow British workman, who did as little for his wages as he possibly could, never hurried himself; and had a deep reverence for one whose pocket could be tapped by respectful behaviour. Need I add that they were contemptuously wondered at by this same British workman as a parcel of outlandish adult boys who sweated themselves for their employer's benefit instead of looking after their own interest. They adored Mr. Edison as the greatest man of all time in every possible department of science, art and philosophy, and execrated Mr. Graham Bell, the inventor of the rival phone, as his Satanic adversary, but each of them had (or intended to have) on the brink of completion an improvement on the telephone, usually a new transmitter. They were free-souled creatures, excellent company, sensitive, cheerful, and profane; liars, braggarts, and hustlers, with an air of making slow old England hum, which never left them even when, as often happened, they were wrestling with difficulties of their own making, or struggling in no-thoroughfares, from which they had to be retrieved like stray sheep by Englishmen without imagination enough to go wrong.

The battle between workmen was accompanied by a massive marketing campaign. According to the Edison company, the Bell system included a magnet and a coil and the sound transmitted along the wire lost much of its force on the way, whereas in the Edison instrument, the sound was unattenuated.   On the other hand, according to Bell, the Edison electrochemical telephone could scarcely be considered a practical instrument, the use of which had been completely abandoned in the United States and on the Continent – a statement which did not accord with the facts.

In September 1879, the telephone was beginning to enjoy commercial success and attracted the attention of the Post Office, which had a monopoly of telegraphic communications as a result of the 1868 and 1869 Telegraph Acts. The Postmaster-General, Lord John Manners, announced that the telephone was a telegraph within the meaning of the (Telegraph) Acts of 1868 and 1869, and that private companies would only be allowed to operate under licence. Edison and Bell both refused to apply for licences and, as a result, in 1880, the government took action against Edison (6 QBD 244). Edison retained, as expert witnesses, a glittering galaxy of scientists that included Lord Rayleigh, Sir William Thomson (later Lord Kelvin) and Professor John Tyndall, but still lost the action. As a consequence of this defeat, on 8 June 1880 the two companies amalgamated to form the United Telephone Company and took, from the Post Office, a thirty-year licence for which it paid 10 per cent of its profits.

With the carbon filament lamp, Edison and Swan were adversarially involved in patent infringement proceedings which did not, however, come to court. During the preliminaries, it rapidly became clear that the issue of inventorship was not clear cut. Whilst Edison had an earlier filing date for some features, Swan was clearly the first on others. The two companies therefore decided to pool their resources and present a united front to litigate against third parties. This tactic met with considerable success, since what would have been a weak and fragmented patent position became one of strength, with the upholding of broad claims which permitted all opposition to be eliminated.

10.4.5 Cross-licences – Patents as a Source of Hidden Income

The Bell Telephone System was prevented by a 'consent decree' under US anti-trust law from exploiting the invention of the transistor by direct manufacture and sale ([1965] RPC 335). The only viable course open to it was therefore to undertake an extensive licensing programme. Bell embarked on a major educational exercise, firstly to inform the industry of the potential of its new development and, secondly, to realise a share of the income that this innovation would generate.

Bell held seminars to which any company prepared to pay earnest money of $25,000 was invited. Attendees were taught how to make transistors. In return, as well as the lump-sum payment for transfer of know-how, Bell received a running royalty. Rates were not tied to actual products, but were based on field of use and global turnover in that field, a policy which made for simple accounting procedures..

The magnitude of the payment was negotiated on a company-by-company basis and took account of the value of the intellectual property rights which the licensee could offer by way of cross-licence, but invariably resulted in a net payment. This arrangement was of immeasurable value to Bell, because it meant that no account need be taken of competitors' patents when planning future business ventures. It also provided commercial intelligence as the annual returns furnished details of competitors' turnover in each technical field.

10.4.6 The Pool – Patents as Currency

During the middle part of the twentieth century, British radio and television manufacturers pooled their patents. With the UK Radio and Television Patents Pool, each patent submitted by a member was allocated one point in a system designed to evaluate the contribution of inventions to the progress of the industry. A few patents of exceptional merit were assessed individually and further points allocated according to the degree of commercial use of the invention. Manufacturers paid a levy, based on their volume of production, into the pool. These proceeds were then paid out to patentees in proportion to their aggregate points score. Some companies, such as EMI, which, by the late 1950s, was no longer a manufacturer but by virtue of agreements with foreign companies such as Telefunken, had rights to important patents (including the PAL system colour television patents) were a net grantor and derived considerable income from the licensing arrangements. Others, such as Thorn, contributed little by way of R&D and were content to pay for freedom to use. (Geddes 1991)

10.5 STIMULANTS

10.5.1 Hams and Hackers – Amateur Activity

The Marconi Company, which dominated the British radio industry, was steeped in a tradition of point-to-point communication for utilitarian purposes, so the concept of broadcasting for entertainment came more easily to amateur radio enthusiasts. When war time restrictions were relaxed following cessation of hostilities in 1918, pre-war 'hams' were joined by men who had encountered radio in the services and now took it up as a hobby; radio telephony began to take over from wireless telegraphy as the main interest. Amateurs had to be licensed by the Post Office, which had absolute control over radio communication. Licences to operate receivers were granted fairly freely but transmitters, restricted to a power of ten watts, could be operated only by those who could 'satisfy the Post Office that their qualifications, apparatus, knowledge of the subject and objects, are sufficiently good to satisfy the grant.' Those objects, the Post Office told them, 'should be scientific research or ... general public utility' and music should be transmitted only for test purposes. But it was only natural for the more extrovert to enliven their transmissions by reading out amusing newspaper cuttings and playing gramophone records or even musical instruments, to the delight of their listeners (Geddes 1991, p9).

The first significant personal computer was the Apple II, the successor to the Apple I, a machine designed by Steve Wozniak, a technological wizard with applications of digital electronics (Cringely 1992, p62). The Apple II had a floppy disk drive for data storage, did not require a separate Teletype printer or video terminal, and offered colour graphics in addition to a text display. It employed clever hardware tricks to get good performance at an affordable price. Wozniak found a way to allow the microprocessor and the video display to share the same memory; his floppy disk controller, developed during a two-week period in December 1977, used less than a quarter of the number of integrated circuits required by other controllers at the time. He made the Apple II a colour machine both to prove that he could do it and so he could use the computer to play a colour version of Breakout, a video game that he and Steve Jobs, who later became the commercial driving force of the company, had designed for Atari. He even wrote Apple's original BASIC interpreter to convert programs written in high-level language into commands which controlled the machine's operation, which was installed in read-only memory and constantly available, rather than needing to be loaded each time the machine was switched on, which was the case with earlier computers.

A chance consequence of the *ad hoc* construction of the Apple II was that it was built around the Mostek 6502 microprocessor, rather than the Intel 8080, which was to become the progenitor of the IBM PC and its clones. The reason for this was that Wozniak chose the one which was available at his local store when he went shopping for the components to construct his computer. This decision set Apple on the path to using Motorola processors, which had a similar architecture to the 6502, rather than the Intel processors which would be used by the rest of the industry.

Serendipity and amateur status were equally prominent in the authorship of the first significant software application program written for personal computers. Dan Bricklin was a business school student when he learned the technique of making 'What if?' calculations on a matrix layout on the blackboard (Cringely 1992, p65). He conceived the idea of performing the calculations electronically, with a computer screen serving as a window on to a much larger virtual display. He wrote a routine in BASIC and used this to demonstrate the feasibility of his concept. This was the forerunner of the spreadsheet, now used universally as a business tool.

Bricklin and his partner Robert Frankston developed the program for the Apple II simply because that was the computer loaned to them by their publisher, not because the machine had any particular advantage over others which were currently available. VisiCalc, as the program was subsequently called, became the first 'killer' application – software which was so valuable that users would go out and buy a computer simply to run it. They failed to patent the concept (although this would have been possible under US law) and so, in due course, when new machines and more powerful spreadsheets (notably Lotus 1-2-3) came along, VisiCalc was superseded.

10.5.2 The Influence of War and Military Procurement

In March 1910, having successfully set up a link across the Atlantic, the Marconi Company submitted to the government a proposal for a chain of wireless stations to link up the British Empire (Sturmey 1958, p84). It sought permission to erect a transmitter at eighteen places on British territories. At this time, the Post Office was not prepared to commit itself because Treasury funding was not available.

Protracted discussions took place and eventually the Imperial Wireless Telegraphy Committee, representing the British and Dominion governments, was appointed by the Postmaster-General to consider the Imperial Chain. The Committee recommended at a meeting on 9 August 1911 that the Post Office should draw up a scheme of terms to be offered to the Marconi Company. Proposals for a scheme based on Marconi's plans were agreed in 1912. Implementation was delayed for a further review by a Select Committee, which finally reported on 14 January 1913 that the Imperial Chain was urgent and that the first six stations should follow the 1912 agreement. A contract for the stations was signed with the Marconi Company on 30 July 1913.

Construction of the first station at Leafield was begun early in 1914, there having been some delay due to technical improvements made by Marconi's which had to be approved by the Post Office. When war broke out, the government decided not to proceed with the chain.

Despite this setback, the 1914-18 war gave an enormous impetus to the development of radio due to its use by the fighting services. Radio was adopted widely for point-to-point communications and whilst people in England had been reluctant to see radio services established, other countries had adopted a different attitude.

One reason for this difference in outlook was that, whereas it had been widely supposed that the German cables would be cut by the British fleet, it was deemed inconceivable that the British cables could ever be cut, due to the invincibility of the Royal Navy. In fact, the Pacific cable was cut, on 7 September 1914, at Fanning Island, and although temporary repairs were made in September it was not until 30 October that full working was restored. Not only, therefore, was the development of radio communication stimulated by international jealousy of the British cable position, but also by exposure of the inadequacies of the world cable system in an emergency (Sturmey 1958, p126).

The German position, on the other hand, was completely different. Since 1906, a combination of cable and wireless telegraphy had been employed to maintain communications between Berlin and the German colonies and garrisons overseas. Initially, the power of the radio transmitters was insufficient to span the distances to the receiving stations in the Far East. The German High Command was apprehensive about the vulnerability of the cable links and worked at improving both transmitter and antenna technology to increase the range of the radio communications. The concern was justified since, on the outbreak of World War I, the British immediately cut the German cables. The Germans also used the Lieben-Reiß relay valve to amplify received signals. Further improvement in radio receiver performance resulted from adapting techniques employed in captured French 'R' valves and, by the end of the war, full communications with the outposts of the German Empire were provided by radio alone (Pickworth 1993).

When the USA entered the war in 1917, the government suspended patent law, which had the effect of unblocking the stalemate with the Marconi Company which prevented De Forest's manufacture of the Audion valve. Western Electric, the only other valve manufacturer of substance, and De Forest did not, however, have sufficient manufacturing capacity to satisfy military needs, so General Electric's and Westinghouse's lamp-making plants were commissioned for this purpose.

A major decision at this time was that production would be to standard designs, with common electrical characteristics. This meant that a valve produced by one manufacturer could be used as a plug-in replacement for one produced by another.

Large numbers of valves were produced to these common standards, so that, by the end of the war, GE and Westinghouse, which initially had no valve-making capability, were strong suppliers in the market. De Forest, which initially had had the potential to establish a dominant position by virtue of its possession of the Audion patents, was reduced to the role of a minor player in the market and was eventually taken over by the Radio Corporation of America.

'An industry with a wartime record such as yours should turn to the tasks of peace with confidence,' said the President of the Board of Trade to representatives of the radio industry in August 1945 (Geddes 1991, p285). After the end of the fighting, the USA abruptly cut off lendlease, and the British nation's survival depended on selling consumer goods to overseas buyers. Because the industry had produced vital military equipment, its factories were in good order and setmakers could quickly switch back to products for which there was a large latent demand. The only problem was a shortage of components, which was met, to a certain extent, by cannibalising surplus military equipment. Very quickly, the industry built up production and achieved export sales of 390,000 units a year.

Valve-makers were faced with overcapacity as in 1946 the post-war demand for valves was only 45 per cent of that for 1944 and there were huge numbers of valves in the government's stockpile. This problem was overcome by selling the valves back to the manufacturers at a price of £5000 per million; those considered saleable were re-sold as new at their normal trading prices, most of the profits going to the government. By 1954 some 27 million valves had been sold in this way, many of them being installed in domestic receivers. Two types of particular note were the EF50 and the SP61, television receiver valves which had been 'called up' at the outbreak of war for use in radar and communications receivers and now, when 'de-mobbed', were used in televisions once again.

The end of the second world war was marked by a build-up of military posturing between the east and west. For logistical reasons, the US Air Force, in 1952, was extremely concerned with reducing the weight and size of electronic equipment. It estimated that 40 per cent of its electronics could be handled by transistors saving 20 per cent in size, 25 per cent in weight, and with 40 per cent fewer failures. With the advent of the silicon transistor it set up a $15 million transistor development project, which commenced in 1956 (Manners 1995, p22).

The chief beneficiaries were the established electron tube manufacturers, but these companies were not necessarily the ones which subsequently contributed most to the development of the industry. However, in the late 1950s, military procurement represented over half the American market for transistors. The space race between America and the USSR became the motivation for huge government investment which underpinned the US semiconductor industry.

10.5.3 The Move to Multinational Operation

Until relatively recently, the electrical industry was organised for national markets. Although Edison created a number of overseas companies to manufacture and sell incandescent lamps, these were invariably set up on a territory-by-territory basis to take account of local differences. Thus in England, where Swan had made inventions which potentially could have destroyed his patents, Edison formed a joint company. In Germany, he established a local company, which, however, broke away and changed its name to Allgemeine Elektrizitäts Gesellschaft (AEG) when he failed to establish a strong patent position. The English company developed its own technology, but AEG continued to use Edison's bamboo filament for many years. Meanwhile, in the USA, Swan sold his know-how to Edison's rival, Brush, despatching his engineer, James Swinburne, to provide the necessary instruction.

During the 1960s there was a move towards globalisation of the electronic component and communications industries. This started with US companies, such as International Telephone and Telegraph Corporation, which already had operations in many countries and needed only to apply common standards and management (Flaschen 1966).

Since many of the physical problems were universal in nature, a world-wide solution yielded economies of scale. Exceptions were where parochial decisions, such as the setting of national standards for broadcast television transmission, or even the plugs and sockets used to connect power cables to the electrical mains, prevailed long after international standards were considered to be desirable.

10.6 COMMUNICATION

10.6.1 Publication

There is strong circumstantial evidence that Göbel invented the carbon filament lamp ahead of Edison but, due to poor command of English, failed to publicise his achievement, which withered away. Viewed from a twentieth century perspective, the physical specimens produced during litigation demonstrate Göbel's case convincingly but, in the emotional atmosphere of the time, the weight of the evidence was insufficient to convince the US Circuit Court. It is probable that that august body was swayed by the reputations of expert witnesses such as Elihu Thomson in the same way that the English courts were influenced by famous names in corresponding British litigation. Edison and Swan, on the other hand, were each aware of what the other was doing – there was tremendous publicity in the daily papers and financial markets, and a vigorous technical press was supplemented by meetings of learned societies at which current technological issues were discussed openly. James Swinburne, for example, published a series of tutorial articles in the *Electrician*, describing the techniques for manufacturing carbon filament lamps. (This was mirrored during the gestation of the transistor industry by papers published in journals such as *Proceedings of the Institute of Radio Engineers* and the *Bell System Technical Journal*.)

Once Edison and Swan had shown the critical steps of using the combination of thin carbon filaments and high vacuum to make lamps which would survive for a reasonable length of time and could be connected in parallel (or 'multiple arc' as it was then known), many others, including Lane Fox, Maxim, Farmer, Sawyer and Man, possessed the necessary skills to put the invention into practice. An explosive expansion took place. A similar phenomenon was observed when Bell announced details of the invention of the point-contact transistor. Many companies which had been engaged in the manufacture of germanium and silicon diodes for radar receiver detectors had the appropriate skills and immediately were able to make transistors.

10.6.2   'Fairchildren' – a Phenomenon of Silicon Valley

William Shockley was a native of California and, when he quit Bell Labs to set up the Shockley Transistor Corporation with the backing of Beckman Instruments, he established his operations in Mountain View, in former apricot drying sheds (Cringely 1996, p36). He was a good scientist, but a poor manager of people. Relationships deteriorated and, in 1957, Robert Noyce and eight other engineers left to set up Fairchild Semiconductor Corporation with finance from Sherman Fairchild, arranged by an investment banker, Arthur Rock. Shockley's company gradually went downhill and was sold off to Clevite, which, in turn, sold it to International Telephone and Telegraph Corporation.

Fairchild had a very flat organisational structure. It grew rapidly and by 1960 was the eighth largest transistor company in the world. Five years later it was world No. 3, and by 1968 it was the world's largest transistor manufacturer, riding high as a result of the invention of the planar manufacturing process by Noyce and Jean Hoerni.

During the 1950s there was a huge expansion in the transistor industry. The success of companies was based on the ideas of their engineers and it became apparent that, as the established companies had no technical advantage, a group of transistor engineers with a new development could compete with the best companies in the industry and beat them.

For Fairchild, the first defection of engineers to start a new company came in 1959, only two years after starting up. This was followed by two more in 1961 and another in 1963. Then there were breakaways from the defectors. A chart of the Silicon Valley chip companies looked like a family tree springing from one ancestor – Fairchild. In due course, these companies became known as the 'Fairchildren'.

Besides Intel, which was also formed by Noyce, two of the other companies founded by technologists leaving Fairchild became billion dollar companies – Advanced Micro Devices and National Semiconductor. A company could prosper only by gaining a technical lead on the competition. Since established companies are usually slow to back new ideas, the Fairchildren had the opportunity to succeed. In 1955 the top ten makers of transistors in America (and also in the world) were Hughes, Transitron, Philco, Sylvania, General Electric of the US, Clevite, Westinghouse, Motorola, RCA and Texas Instruments. Twenty years later, in 1975, all except the last three had been replaced by Fairchild, National, Intel, Signetics, General Instrument, American Microsystems Inc. (AMI) and Rockwell (of which five were Fairchildren founded in the 1960s). Constant innovation was the basic ingredient for success.

10.6.3 Know-how Trading

I was sent by my company to visit our representative in Sunnyvale, in order to get help with a technical problem that they were having. Our guy had part of the answer, and he knew where to find the rest of the information. After work, he took me to a bar in Silicon Valley. Then he called over engineers from adjoining tables, who were acquaintances of his. They really enjoyed telling us what to do. By 9pm, I had the solution to our company's problems. The next morning I flew back to Stuttgart. I was really amazed at how freely people communicate in California.

Hans Reiner, *Silicon Valley Fever*, p84

Fairchild Semiconductor Corporation was the initiator of the planar process for fabrication of transistors and integrated circuits from wafers of silicon. It was, however, quite willing to educate its rivals in its proprietary techniques. The contribution to the 'bottom line' from these activities was significant – a payment of $7m from one company alone. (This was a substantial sum in the early 1960s, when the payment was made). Fairchild probably held the view that it was smart enough to stay ahead of the opposition but eventually, emaciated by defections of key personnel, the company ceased to be a force in the market place.

When the Osram Company in Germany developed the metal filament lamp, British and American rights were sold to the English General Electric Company and the American General Electric (which, although they had similar names, were completely independent).

10.6.4 Delphic Forecasting

> In a lot of respects, it's become a self-fulfilling prophecy in that the industry uses that exponential change to decide how rapidly they have to develop new technology. It's recognised that if you don't get to a certain point at a particular time, you fall behind.
> Gordon Moore, interviewed by Jack Schofield,
> *The Guardian*, 27 March 1997

The management of innovation is concerned with controlling the dynamics of change in an uncertain environment. The task would be simplified if it were possible to make predictions about the future with a reasonable prospect of success. One possible tool by which this could be accomplished is the technique of Delphic forecasting. To perform this, experts in a particular field are asked individually or collectively to make prognostications. The underlying assumption is that, being experts, they are likely to be more accurate in their forecasts. Usually such prophecies cannot be verified, so the value of the technique, other than as a comfort factor, cannot be assessed. However, for a landmark issue, in which it traced the history of the electronics industry in the twentieth century, *Electronics* magazine gathered together a panel of industry gurus to canvass their views on likely developments which would have taken place by the end of the millennium, a time frame of twenty years (Weber 1981, p254). The experts chosen were managers and entrepreneurs who had shaped the electronics industry over the previous twenty years.

Typical predictions made by this panel were that communication would be based on 'a three-legged stool of fiber optics, large adaptive antennas in space and – a new development – non-military spread-spectrum communications', that 'Electronic technology will diffuse as lesser developed countries pick up the technology and run. Eventually it will be diffused out to where it can be produced least expensively' and that there will be 'more mixed material chips, for example, made of silicon and gallium arsenide, [there will be] more knowledge about defects, increased use of energy beams in fabrication [of semiconductor devices], a true non-volatile random-access memory, and solid state technology applied to solar energy. And ... a book-sized solid state TV.'

standing – Paul Richman, President of Standard Microsystems, Gordon
   B. Thompson, Manager of Communications Studies at Bell
   Northern and Gordon Moore, Chairman of Intel
seated – Ralph E. Gomory, responsible for IBM Research Division,
   Simon Ramo, Vice-Chairman of TRW Inc, Carl Carman,
   Engineering Vice-President of Data General and George
   Heilmeier, Engineering Vice-President of Texas Instruments

Source   Weber 1981

Figure 10.1   The Delphic panel

At the turn of the century it is now possible to assess with certainty the
accuracy of their predictions.   Collectively, the panel made some one
hundred and thirty forecasts.   Of these, 69 per cent were accurate, 28 per
cent were wrong and 3 per cent were indeterminate.

10.7 DIRTY TRICKS

10.7.1 Fighting Companies

In 1897, General Electric dominated the US lamp industry.   It had a cross-
licensing and pricing agreement with Westinghouse, its only competitor
with a significant market share.   It had also formed an association with six
other manufacturers, with the object of fixing prices and market share.
During the next four years, a further ten companies joined this organisation.
At this time, GE produced about 50 per cent and Westinghouse about 12 per
cent of the lamps which were sold in the USA (Bright 1949, p144).

Although GE held numerous improvement patents, it was no longer in a position to shelter behind the master patents, which had, by then, expired. GE and Westinghouse were, however, able to produce better lamps due to their greater production volumes, so the opportunity to participate in a price maintenance and market-sharing arrangement was a powerful inducement to small companies to join the scheme. Management of the pool replaced use of patents as the mechanism by which GE controlled the industry.

Arrangements were crystallised on 3 May 1901, when most of the small companies amalgamated to form the National Electric Lamp Company. GE purchased around three-quarters of the common stock of the new company.

National was nominally run by its own officers and it was publicly represented to be a competing association of lamp producers, GE taking no open part in the management. However, the price and market-sharing agreements which General Electric had signed with the members of the 1896 association were continued. General Electric and National acted in harmony on the pricing and marketing of lamps, and continued the agreements with Westinghouse and made new ones with five small lamp-making firms which did not become part of National.

GE and other lamp producers also signed patent licensing agreements. These became the vehicle for price fixing and market sharing. Later, when National had established a central engineering department for its subsidiary companies, a cross-licence was established. Nevertheless, despite provisions for the mutual interchange of patent licences and technical information, the flow of technical information continued to be preponderantly from GE to National.

The net effect of all of these changes was that General Electric acquired about two-fifths of the industry for an initial cash outlay of $120,000. Sales competition was restricted, and General Electric received about three-quarters of the cash dividends of more than $600,000 paid by National between 1904 and 1910. There was also an enormous appreciation in the capital value of the shareholding. General Electric and National, together with Westinghouse, controlled more than 90 per cent of the domestic market for incandescent lamps. The price and licence agreements with other domestic producers not part of National left only 3 per cent of United States lamp production outside General Electric control.

Thomas Watson Sr. was, in 1913, a leading salesman for National Cash Register (NCR). In this capacity, he ran a covert company which resolutely eliminated all competition in the second-hand cash register market, with the objective of supporting NCR's sales of new machines (Heller 1994, p90).

In due course, Watson was among thirty co-conspirators who were indicted for this campaign. He was found guilty and sentenced to a $5000 fine plus a year in the Miami County jail. The sentence was never actually carried out, but, a few months later, he was fired by John Patterson, the founder of NCR. Watson subsequently went to work for the Computer-Tabulating-Recording Company, the precursor of IBM, which he developed into a thrusting sales-led organisation on the strength of Herman Hollerith's punched-card system. His ruthless philosophy was to avoid conflict if possible, but under no circumstances to relinquish a dominant position. He would take any necessary action to eliminate the competition and, if this policy involved confrontation, would devote as much resource as would overwhelm the opposition.

The concepts carried over in a very attenuated form as a marketing ploy in the UK brown goods industry. The oligopoly of radio and television manufacturers produced what was essentially the same model under a variety of brand names, which were presented to the buying public as completely independent companies, with the objective of increasing the price of market entry to new competitors (Geddes 1991). For example, the Rank Organisation sold under the names Bush, Murphy, Top Rank, Dansette, Rank Arena, Leak and Wharfedale; Pye used Pye, Pam, Ekco, Dynatron and Invicta; ITT used Kolster-Brandes and RGD, whilst Thorn sold Ferguson, HMV and Marconi. Mostly, these were names of predecessor companies which had ceased to exist as independent manufacturers as a result of mergers and take-overs.

10.7.2 Bulls, Bears, Stags and Brush Babies

During the 1870s, Brush Electrical developed a system of arc lighting, together with the ancillary electricity generators. These were much in demand for public lighting schemes. Brush chose to exploit this development by a form of franchising in which small, local operations were set up with a licence under the Brush patents. These companies – the so-called Brush Babies – were then floated, with Brush retaining an equity interest. With the advent of the incandescent filament lamp and central power stations, many of these companies failed, taking with them the confidence of the providers of capital (Kynaston 1994).

10.7.3 Knocking Copy

Knocking copy – the denigration of competing products – was evident in a particularly aggressive form when the electrical industry was becoming established at the end of the nineteenth century. Edison developed it almost to an art form, targeting first the suppliers of gas lighting and then electricity generators who used the alternating current system for electricity distribution. In the latter instance, Edison was firmly wedded to the outmoded direct current system and steadfastly refused to go over to the superior alternating current. He embarked on a campaign to convince the public that the rival system was dangerous. He staged a succession of demonstrations in which ever larger animals were electrocuted. The final act was the covert purchase of a Westinghouse alternating current generator which he then sold to the state penitentiary to power the first electric chair.

10.7.4 Fear, Uncertainty and Doubt – the 'FUD' Factor

'Nobody ever got fired for buying IBM' was the received wisdom in the computer industry. The company dominated the market and thus the safe choice was to buy IBM computers. IBM played on this, creating an atmosphere of 'fear, uncertainty and doubt' to induce customers not to defect to its competitors. An example of how this tactic operated is exemplified by its conflict with Control Data Corporation which led to an anti-trust action against IBM.

CDC had a mere $60m sales at the time, but was skilful at producing very large, very powerful computers, a province that IBM regarded as its own. In 1961, IBM introduced a new computer designed to compete in this area, but it was late to the market place and 40 per cent under specification. To compensate, IBM cut the price from $13.5m to $8m, but, in the meantime, CDC launched its model 6600, which had three times the power and a price of $7m.

The entire IBM organisation felt the backlash of this humiliation and its response was to attack CDC's customers with a move which, even in IBM, was regarded as sailing extremely close to the wind. In April 1964, the company announced plans for a new supercomputer with a performance way ahead of Control Data's 6600. This computer existed only on paper, but the announcement had the desired effect – the 6600 order book dried right up because the customers did not want to invest large sums in obsolescent equipment (Heller 1994, p19).

10.7.5 Personnel Poaching – Hogan's Heroes

Bolstered by the invention of the planar transistor and integrated circuit, and its income from know-how and patent licensing deals, Fairchild Semiconductor grew steadily during the 1960s. However, there was conflict between the owner and the operating managers. In 1968, Bob Noyce, Gordon Moore and Andy Grove quit to set up a new venture at Intel. Sherman Fairchild responded by hiring the entire management team, led by Les Hogan, from Motorola's semiconductor division. For his services, Hogan received a salary of $120,000 and stock options which were worth what was, in those days, the astonishing sum of $2.5m (Manners 1995, p130).

Although Hogan's Heroes, as they were dubbed, had taken the turnover of Motorola's semiconductor operations from $5 million to $230 million, they were not successful at Fairchild. Almost immediately, one of them – Jerry Sanders III, quit, taking some of the company's top talent to set up Advanced Micro Devices, which quickly became an industry leader and has survived to the present day as a junior partner in the microprocessor oligopoly.

10.7.6 'Corner on Counsel!'

Lamps which allegedly were infringements of Edison's carbon filament lamp patents were installed at the Albert Palace, Battersea. Edison and Swan did not take action against Brush Electric, the manufacturers of the lamps. Instead they sued the manager, Holland, who was responsible for the installation, and the Jablochkoff and General Electricity Co., Limited, the distributors. The reason for this tactic was that Brush had paid retainers to the leading counsel at the Patents Bar, so that it could avail itself of their services in the event of litigation. Had Edison and Swan taken direct action against Brush, they would have had to have been represented by less eminent lawyers as Brush would have exercised its retainer. As it happened, when, in due course, Brush was joined as third party to the action, the company found that Edison and Swan had already hired the senior barristers, pre-empting the advantage Brush sought to obtain by paying in advance for an option on their services (Swinburne 1886).

10.7.7 Bearing False Witness

> It is now admitted that the carbon burner of Swan's lamp was formed into its shape before it was carbonised, and this removes one of the points much relied on by the Plaintiffs in the former action.
> Cotton LJ, *Edison and Swan v. Holland* [1889] RPC 243)

Edison, as a young man, when he was developing the telegraph, acted as if he had no conscience. He made agreements and broke them when it suited him, taking advantage of the delays in the legal process to order his business affairs in a way which was advantageous to himself (Conot 1979, p279). He stole his employees' inventions, but was not averse to falsely including another inventor on his own patents, for purely commercial reasons.

During infringement proceedings against Woodhouse and Rawson ([1886] RPC 167, [1886] RPC 183, [1887] RPC 99), a favourable judgement was obtained on the basis of evidence which subsequently proved to be false. The obfuscation was admitted in later proceedings ([1889] RPC 243) but, nevertheless, the court held that it was bound by the earlier decision.

In the USA, Edison adopted a similar unethical approach. In litigation, his opponents submitted that Heinrich Göbel had invented the carbon filament lamp more than a decade before the date of Edison's patent. There was strong circumstantial evidence to support this contention, but Göbel was a weak witness with a poor command of the English language. Experts of great reputation and charisma were called to cast aspersions on Göbel's achievements.   In consequence, Edison gained a highly favourable judgement which left him with broad patent protection.   Adoption of unethical tactics led, therefore, to strengthening of an otherwise weak position.

10.7.8 Using the System, the Triple 'D' – Delay, Domino and Double Whammy

When Edison and Swan were establishing the carbon filament lamp operation in the United Kingdom, they used their patents as a major weapon in their battle against their competitors.   Proceedings were started against the firm of Woodhouse and Rawson, a small company with few resources at its command.   Separate actions for infringement of different patents were set in motion simultaneously ([1886] RPC 167, [1886] RPC 183) to increase the chances of success and tie up the resources of the opponent.   When this action was successful, proceedings were commenced against a stronger adversary, the Brush Electrical company, but with the precedent of the earlier decision to bind the court.   In this latter case, however, the competitor was not attacked directly, but through the medium of its customers and distributors ([1888] RPC 459).   With these two dominoes knocked down, the rest of the industry fell into line and the Edison-Swan Company enjoyed a monopoly for the remainder of the life of the master patents.

Fleming's diode detector patent contained claims which were clearly invalid as they covered inventions which had been published by Edison some twenty years earlier.   The Marconi Company, which had acquired the ownership of the patent, sued de Forest for infringement.   During the proceedings, counsel for Marconi attempted to pre-empt an attack on the validity of the patent by disclaiming the illegal claims.   He obtained a favourable judgement in the court of first instance and it was not until 1942, some thirty years later, that the issue was finally decided by the Supreme Court.   By then, the patent was long past its expiry date and, although it was eventually held to be invalid, during the period of its normal lifetime all parties had treated it as if it were valid and had conducted their business accordingly (de Forest 1950, p321).

10.8 CONCLUSION

This chapter has presented examples which illustrate the socio-economic factors that lead to the making of inventions.

At the base of the pyramid of innovation is the inventor. If he does not have resources, or, in the limit, the necessities of life to enable him to survive, then it might be expected that inventions will not be forthcoming. Invention is, as has already been shown, a creative activity, stated by many inventors to bring its own rewards. Other creative beings, such as artists, musicians and authors, have been known to exist on meagre incomes. Many do not achieve recognition until after their death and, indeed, the value of their works often increases dramatically when the supply is thus curtailed. If inventors are like other artists, they will not need an economic motivation to invent. Nevertheless, although the inventors may derive sufficient reward from the act of conceiving new ideas, there is the prospect that they will attract support from others who seek to gain from the resulting innovations – either a form of 'gravy-train' effect or simply the analogue of the patron of the arts.

Heroic inventors may, like Edison or Tesla, find patrons or sponsors. Even if the world does not beat a path to the door of the inventor of the better mousetrap, he will usually manage to beat a path to the door of a sympathetic financier. There is, however, no way of telling how many great inventions have passed into oblivion because the inventor has not made contact with a source of continuing finance. If Göbel had been the sole inventor of the light bulb, this might well have been the case.

Finance is usually forthcoming for inventions of merit. However, providers of capital will expect a commercial return on their investment with, probably, a substantial premium to compensate for the high risk involved with innovation. Sources of finance are rarely altruistic. They have high expectation of dividends and a need for constant reassurance. Confidence is an extremely important factor and, if it is not fostered by good communications, capital will no longer be forthcoming. This is particularly important when an industry is changing rapidly during the initial stages of its development.

As the case studies have shown, public attitudes to private monopoly have altered over the years. Public attitudes to financing innovation have also changed. The 1880s, for example, were not a propitious time for UK companies with a voracious demand for capital. Until the turn of the century there had been a legal restriction on underwriting industrial shares. As a result very few industrial securities were quoted on the Stock Exchange. This constraint on marketability was made worse by the Stock Exchange's determination to preserve the monopoly rights of jobbers. Furthermore, the leading merchant banks were reluctant to sponsor domestic industrial issues, partly due to their risky reputation and partly due to the small and therefore unprofitable size of most of the issues. A century later, Jobs and Wozniak found ready support from Mark Markkula and Silicon Valley became a seedbed for the venture capitalists.

At one moment, 'dot-com' companies are flavour of the month – a short while later they are beyond the pale. Such fluctuations are unpredictable and thus can only be determined by empirical observation.

Innovation exhibits a great diversity of financial needs, ranging from the minimalist demands of the point-contact transistor or the spark transmitter to the major social investment required to set up the infrastructure of the incandescent lamp.

An invention is, by definition, a novelty. It therefore follows that, the greater the change which is brought about by the invention, the lower will be the probability that the wherewithal to bring it into effect will be in existence. Some inventions will require little change, but others, which result in major paradigm shifts, may need new manufacturing methods and materials, with all the attendant problems that they will bring. The requirements may be met by means of a network of suppliers – the Japanese *keiretsu* approach which was favoured by Swan – or a fully vertically integrated organisation, such as that developed by Edison. The vertically integrated approach will exacerbate the risk, but, by the same token, will also ensure that all of the rewards collect in a single basket. The risk may be further increased, since it is less likely that one organisation will possess the polytechnic skills necessary to service all aspects of an innovation.

The magnitude of investment in infrastructure may affect its rate of growth. However, one man's cost-of-sales is another man's innovation rent. If the investment requirement is met by suppliers who have a product to sell, they will view the prospect as an opportunity rather than as a cost. The net result is that innovation exerts a Keynesian influence on the economy, with a major development, such as the microprocessor, leading to a massive expansion. In some instances, the sheer magnitude of investment in infrastructure required to support an innovation may serve as a moderating influence on its rate of growth.

Marketing acts a stimulus since sales are boosted by its application. The basic tools, such as exhibitions of new products and publication of papers by learned societies, have been used, virtually unchanged, since the nineteenth century.

The grant of a patent is a right to make, use, exercise and vend the subject invention to the exclusion of all others. A patent is a monopoly and, as such, it permits its proprietor to distort the market. Although this right may be invoked in the obvious manner, simply by charging higher prices because there is no competition, it could also be used to advantage in other ways – by licensing in order to exploit markets which may not be so accessible and by combination with other monopolies, either with third parties or as a solo enterprise, to enhance market power. Positions can be strengthened by synergistic combination with others – either overtly by cross-licensing or covertly by the creation of cartels. Since patents represent value, they can also be treated as a form of currency in deals between organisations. The incremental income which patents represent might be used as security in the same way as any other asset of a business.

The success of start-up operations is critically dependent on confidence. In a developing market, a company needs some form of security. This can be provided by intellectual property rights, of which, at that stage, patents are usually the most significant. By putting up the cost of market entry for competitors, patents can provide confidence for financiers. They can boost direct income by permitting a premium price to be charged or by exacting a levy or royalty on sales made by licensees, and indirect income by mitigating actual or potential liability through cross-licensing agreements. Often, in the latter case, the mere removal of the need to consider third parties' intellectual property rights is of significant financial value. This contribution to profits is submerged and does not appear in company accounts, thereby reducing liability to taxation. As well as these hidden returns in the form of freedom of future action, cross-licensing also has the advantage that it may give access to intelligence about the magnitude and nature of competitors' sales. This may, in practice, be of greater value than the direct or notional income obtained from royalties.

How is it possible to assess the relative merits of, on the one hand, Kilby's and, on the other hand, Noyce and Hoerni's contribution to the development of the integrated circuit? All that can be said is that they were both fundamental to the success of the new industry. The valuation of patents in licensing deals is usually a rough and ready process which depends more on the patentee's ability to exact a royalty than on the merits of an individual invention. (Why, other than for reasons of custom and use in a particular industry, should a royalty rate be 5 per cent rather than 4.5 per cent or 5.5 per cent?) The abacus rather than the analyst is often the key to relative power. In a patent portfolio, numbers bring strength because the cost of litigation is high, both in immediate financial outgoings and in the indirect cost of its disruptive effect on the mainstream business operations. Proliferation of intellectual property rights equates to a greater threat perceived by competitors.

In patents pools and cross-licensing agreements, it is frequently the practice to apportion contribution on the basis of numbers, with little attempt at a qualitative evaluation of the merit of the licensed inventions. This engenders blanket filing of patent applications, regardless of value or, even, possible validity. There is some logic in this approach, because the nuisance value of a patent as a potential basis for litigation is independent of its strength.

'United we stand, divided we fall.' By combining, two companies can turn a weak position into one of invincibility. The synergistic effects enable them to overcome potentially strong opposition. In the initial phase of an innovation, two companies with relatively weak intellectual property holdings will achieve a disproportionate gain in strength by combining their holdings. Later, a dominant position may be preserved by use of market power to acquire successor rights, either by direct purchase of the master patents which cover a major paradigm shift or a group of patents which collectively preserve the proprietorship of the current technology. A related practice which preserves market power is the take-over of companies with promising, and possibly competing, innovations.

Whilst the main engine which drives innovation will be the prospect of return on the investment, a variety of extraneous factors may be expected to provide a stimulus. Inventors, it has been seen, are frequently motivated by the intrinsic interest of the process of invention. By the same token, the excitement of technological change will attract many who do not seek to gain directly from furthering the cause of an innovation.

Amateur enthusiasts often play a major part in the development of new industries. Some go on to become a dominant force, whilst others lack the necessary motivation and entrepreneurial instinct and fade into obscurity. In the obituary of Donald Davies, the inventor of packet switching, a technique which made the internet possible, Brian Oakley, who ran Britain's strategic computer research initiative, is quoted as saying: 'He was an ideas man, and didn't follow through. It wasn't that he couldn't have, it was just that he chose to move on to the next idea. But one of his key features was that he would pick things up well before other people realised they were going to be important' (*The Guardian*, 26 June 2000).

The effect of military procurement is to create a major perturbation in normal market forces. This may upset the natural balance between participants and enable some to gain a dominant position they would not otherwise have achieved. It tends to favour established players who have the resources which permit them to respond to the new demands.

'Necessity is the mother of invention,' and there is no greater necessity than the threat of war. Preparation for hostilities will encourage governments to provide resources for ventures which would not be justifiable on normal commercial criteria. Although, ultimately, such standards will be applied to the commercial ventures which follow, much riskier projects will see the light of day when military criteria are used to justify them. Some of these will be pursued to a successful conclusion and will form the foundation for economic growth. The US space programme was the single major factor in establishing the strength of the American semiconductor industry, whilst government directives in Japan, Korea and Taiwan, at a later stage, took large sections of that industry to the Far East.

The size of return is dependent on the size of a market. The input costs, on the other hand, will be determined by the nature of a development, with, possibly, only a small component of the infrastructure costs being incremental. A move to global operation dramatically reduces the proportional allocation of the fixed cost of amortising the development expenditure and thus changes the economics of introducing new inventions. It will therefore serve as a stimulus to innovation.

De facto local standards (such as the Edison-screw lamp connector, which was based on the cap for a kerosene can, an artefact which was readily available and to hand when the demountable light bulb was invented) persist because the cost of changing them far exceeds the advantage to be gained by global standards. By corollary, good solutions to a problem are frequently rejected because of incompatibility with the current *modus operandi*.

Diffusion of information is an important factor in the success of innovation. Surprisingly, much valuable know-how is simply given away. Learned societies, descendants of the mediaeval trade guilds, are a major influence. The technical press and learned societies have always been a rich means of diffusion of know-how. Possibly, the need for peer approval feeds this source of dissemination. Personnel migration is another significant vehicle. Maintenance of secrecy has not usually been a viable option in the engineering industry because many people possessed the skills necessary to effect an innovation, once its feasibility had been canvassed. Proliferation of numbers of people privy to information increases the risk that it will be leaked.

The law has always held an equivocal attitude to secrecy and employment. On the one hand, an employee may not take his employer's secrets if he leaves but, on the other hand, in his new post, he is permitted to continue to exercise the skills he acquired previously. Straddling this fine line is an opportunity for a small leak to become a raging torrent. In an environment where intellectual property monopolies either *are* not or *can* not be rigorously enforced, personnel movement is a potent vehicle for diffusion of knowledge. Nowhere more than in the electrical industry were people more aware of the marketability of their personal services and, for the modern sunrise industries, a major means of disseminating know-how was the exodus of technical experts.

It is, of course, not necessary for employees to change their allegiance to act as a vehicle for diffusion of knowledge. Their employers, too, may recognise that their know-how is a marketable asset which may be realised. This is obviously a two-edged sword, since know-how, once transferred cannot be retrieved. If this high-risk strategy is to be followed, then the compensation in the form of benefit received must be commensurate or there must, in the alternative, be some countervailing effect which will neutralise the danger. An example of this somewhat curious method of technology diffusion is the transfer of know-how between competing enterprises (von Hippel 1988, p91).

Even more surprising than the sale of know-how, which does at least yield a contribution to revenue and may be partially neutralised by response-time effects, is the free disclosure of information by way of seminars and technical journals. Certainly, this was common practice in the semiconductor industry – any company with a sufficient knowledge base could immediately take advantage of new information gleaned in this way. Significant information was sold or given to competitors. Frequently in such instances, no overt attempt was made to preserve a potentially dominant position.

Diffusion of the knowledge gained is an important adjunct to innovation – it is of no value if the innovator does not pass on to others what he has added to the general body of knowledge. US patent law is quite specific on this point, enjoining the applicant for a monopoly to describe the best method known to him of putting the invention into practice. The new development must be described in terms which are intelligible to the man skilled in the art and in such a way as to enable him to put the idea into practice.

In forecasting future developments, there is some evidence that Delphic methods achieve a better success rate than random selection.

An unethical attitude to business will often lead to an advantage. Particularly in the early stages of development of an industry, a punch below the belt will achieve a disproportionate effect. Techniques which have been used with success include fighting companies, multiple patent infringement actions to tie up senior personnel, poaching key employees and fighting the weak rather than the strong. In a dominant position, an empty threat, made by someone who is in a position to carry it out, can achieve as much as the full-blown action.

The key to success is to stay one jump ahead of the competition. In modern society the accepted mores are based on conventions of telling the truth rather than lying, and abiding by the law, rather than by endeavouring to circumvent it. Advantage may therefore be gained by contravening these customs, thereby injecting an element of surprise into the business strategy. Such activities are, however, likely to be contrary to the law and therefore will not be practised overtly.

Public policy usually favours markets where there is open competition, since it is presumed that this will result in the lowest prices to the consumer and that low prices are in the consumer's best interest. Low prices are, however, not usually in the *supplier's* best interest. He, therefore, may wish to create an illusion of a competitive market but, in reality, manipulate prices to maximise his return. One way of achieving this is by means of fighting companies, which are companies over which he exerts a covert control whilst, to the outsider, he appears to be in competition with them. He can then exploit the elements of imperfect competition in the market to his advantage. For example, he might operate the fighting company at a loss, charging low prices to starve other competitors of cash, and thereby emaciating them, or he might operate a purchasing ring in order to extract more favourable deals from his suppliers. By creating apparent competition, companies can frequently create or strengthen a monopoly position.

Capital is an essential requirement of innovation. Provision of capital is based on imperfect knowledge. Hence there is an uncertainty factor in making an investment decision. Whilst providers of capital endeavour to discount risk, they also seek to maximise the knowledge base for their decision-making process. The early stage of innovation is that at which the uncertainty is greatest. It is at this stage, therefore, that the investor is most vulnerable to false intelligence. The relationship between the providers and users of capital is one of trust, and betrayal of that trust will result in loss of confidence and reduce the future supply of capital.

One way that risk can be reduced is by increasing sales relative to those of competitors. This may be achieved by the normal practice of trumpeting the virtues of a product, but a similar result can also be achieved by casting doubt on the performance of rivals.

In the early stages of development of an industry, no holds are barred and underhand tactics may eliminate opponents. Later, when the industry has matured, action which affects competitors will be more circumspect, for fear of retaliation.

Actual exercise of power is not necessary to achieve a strong strategic advantage. Mere possession of such power is sufficient. The latent threat that the power will be exercised can achieve a commensurate effect.

Where all else fails, character assassination and a few lies may lead to success.

A company which can obtain a disproportionate supply of a scarce resource will have a great advantage over its competitors. These resources may not be obvious targets and a double advantage will be gained since there will also be an element of surprise in the action of acquiring them.

Know-how is an essential component in the development of innovative products. Know-how resides in the minds of those who put innovation into practice, so, if these people can be persuaded to change their allegiance, that know-how could be transferred at less than fair market value. Personnel are a mobile resource. An organisation can quickly decay if it does not look after its employees.

Tactics will be a major factor in the conduct of litigation. The law moves slowly and thus the period of uncertainty before a formal verdict is handed down will be long. This may be exploited to tie up key personnel of competitors. It may also be used to shelter behind an invalid patent since, by the time a decision is made, a fast-moving industry will have moved on to the next development.

In a common law system, where precedent reigns supreme, an impregnable position may be built up by stages. Weak opponents are tackled first and the outcome can be made more certain by hitting them with multiple suits.

11. ... or Do Inventions Make Markets?

The total world market for computers is five, or at the most, six machines.
Thomas Watson Sr., Chairman of IBM in the 1940s

It was our job to make sure that for well-placed rivals like GE and RCA, the computer marketplace seemed too risky a bet.
Thomas Watson Jr., quoted by Robert Heller in *The Fate of IBM*

There are, of course, many companies who have no reason to consider anything except IBM, ICL, etc., which they buy on religious grounds. Indeed it may be worth their paying twice the price for half the performance just to avoid the cost overhead of researching the topic and then dealing with a separate supplier. The IBM PC is a standard, and buying it saves worrying about anything else, including such tricky considerations as software.
Jack Schofield, *The Guardian*

Don Estridge, the man responsible for the IBM PC, really defined compatibility for us. Before that compatibility pretty much meant recompiling software. The Intel architecture carries some warts, some wrinkles that we'd rather not have. It would be nice to throw it away and start with a clean sheet of paper. But with all that installed software, that's not something we can do.
Gordon Moore, *The Guardian*, 27 March 1997

Most people didn't want DEC – or even worse, the dreaded IBM – to set a standard. Interested parties therefore gathered to agree on their own.
Jack Schofield, *The Guardian*

At IBM they're celebrating. IBM invented the IBM PC which briefly gave it 100 percent of the market, but it's been losing market share virtually ever since, culminating in losing its first place to Compaq in 1994. Until the end of '95, IBM's PC business remained in revenue decline – not a healthy situation in a market growing as fast as the PC industry. This year, however, IBM reversed the trend..
Ben Tisdall, *Personal Computer World*, October 1996, p40

11.1 INTRODUCTION

At any given time, the structure of a market is the culmination of historic, current and anticipated economic forces. Innovation may change this situation by the introduction of a substitute for one of the products or processes which contribute to the market. On rare occasions, an entirely new product or process emerges and completely alters the dynamic balance of the economy. The incandescent lamp and the transistor are examples of substitutes. The thermionic valve, on the other hand, was a pioneering product, making possible techniques such as radio broadcasting, which had not been feasible previously.

The decision to introduce an innovative substitute will be based on felicitous economics. It will be taken up if it offers the prospect of a greater rent than the existing product or process (bearing in mind that the cost of change will include that of creation of the necessary infrastructure and *may* need to take into account unamortised investment in the precursor). For a pioneering innovation, however, no current market will exist. There may be *latent* demand – applications of coherent radiation had been widely canvassed in theoretical papers and were immediately realisable when the laser was invented – but for other novel inventions, there will be no immediate market. Buckminster-fullerenes, a new form of carbon based on molecules containing sixty or more atoms, had to undergo protracted evaluation to determine their properties and, subsequently, potential applications, whilst with high-temperature superconductors, applications were tantalisingly apparent, if only the properties of the materials could be realised and, if they were, a suitable method could be devised for their fabrication.

A new product will have assured sales provided it achieves the perceived returns. However, the progress of an innovation will depend on the characteristics of the market which it is entering. The nature of the reaction to the threatened competition will vary, both with the market and the situation of the innovator. This chapter examines the influence of product and process innovation on market structure to test the proposition that markets are created by new inventions.

11.2 THE INITIAL MONOPOLY

11.2.1 Response Time – *Après Moi le Deluge*

When the Bell System announced the discovery of the point-contact transistor effect, many other companies applied the skills they had acquired in the manufacture of semiconductor diodes for radar receivers and immediately produced a transistor. When Edison and Swan publicised the carbon filament lamp, Lane Fox and others instantly made copies. With successive generations of microprocessor, however, Intel was able to enjoy a period of several months before AMD and Cyrix introduced their equivalent to the market.

11.2.2 *De Facto* Standards

When Edison was looking for a way of making his light bulb demountable, the screw cap of a kerosene can was readily to hand. This was adapted to provide the means of retaining a lamp in a holder whilst, at the same time, permitting it to be removed when the lamp needed to be replaced. Edison's company eventually acquired control of 80 per cent of the US market with the consequence that the 'Edison Screw' became the accepted way of fixing a lamp in place. Its use also extended to other countries, such as Germany, where the local industry was set up with Edison know-how. In England, however, a bayonet cap arrangement, devised by Swan, was adopted to solve the same problem, with the result that a non-tariff barrier to import and export of lamps was created. The cost of replacing many millions of installed lamp holders created a considerable obstacle to the establishment of a universal standard.

A similar situation arose with standards for television transmission. When high-definition television was introduced, each nation set up its own system. Britain adopted a 405-line and France, initially a 441-line and subsequently an 819-line picture. There was no international exchange of programmes, so compatibility was not important. Cessation of transmissions during the second world war provided an opportunity for a fresh start, but this did not materialise. When, eventually, with the advent of Eurovision, cross-border exchange of programmes commenced, it was necessary to devise special conversion techniques to overcome the difference in standards. With colour television, a pan-European standard of 625-lines with PAL encoding became the norm (following a rear-guard action by France), but there were still some national differences. It was not until many years later when digital techniques were introduced and the Motion Pictures Experts Group (MPEG) standards were promulgated that the problem was satisfactorily overcome.

The USA was the first to introduce colour television and set up the National Television System Committee (NTSC), which agreed a system which was compatible with existing monochrome apparatus. Information about the colour content of the picture was provided by a separate signal, which was transmitted on a sub-carrier. This was susceptible to phase changes during propagation, giving rise to distortion in the colour rendering of the picture. (The NTSC system was jokingly dubbed 'Never Twice the Same Colour'.) When European nations considered setting up a standard, they modified the NTSC system to overcome this problem by the trick of inverting the phase of the colour signal with each successive line of the picture. This was the so-called PAL (phase alternate line) system devised by Dr. Walter Bruch of Telefunken. Phase errors, which were responsible for colour distortion, were averaged out by this technique. Although PAL was superior to NTSC, the cost and logistics of replacing the installed transmitters, receivers and studio equipment meant that it was not possible for the USA to go over to the newer system (Geddes 1991, p375).

A consequence of the adoption of the PAL system was that Telefunken, its originator, and EMI, Telefunken's exclusive UK licensee, derived an assured income from licences under the Bruch patents, infringement of which was inevitable. Although licences were granted freely to European television manufacturers, Japanese manufacturers were restricted to selling sets with screen sizes of less than twenty-one inches diagonal dimension, in an attempt to reduce the strength of the competition (Geddes 1991, p389). (Such an arrangement would not be permissible under current European competition law.)

France, in an attempt to protect its domestic industry from European as well as Japanese competition, adopted yet another non-compatible system (SECAM). The communist bloc made a similar decision but the reason for this was to retain control of its economy and to prevent its population from receiving Western television programmes from neighbouring states which transmitted using the PAL system.

When the semiconductor industry began to expand with the introduction of the silicon planar and epitaxial manufacturing processes, Fairchild Semiconductor Corporation devised general purpose amplifying and switching transistors (the 2N709 and 2N914). The electrical characteristics of these devices satisfied the somewhat non-exacting requirements for construction of amplifiers and switching circuits then in common use and so this design of transistor was adopted by most of the companies in the industry.

When domestic video recording was introduced, one of the earliest systems was produced by Philips. Rival systems were introduced by Sony (Betamax) and the Japanese Victor Company (VHS). Due to the wider sales territories served by the Japanese companies, a battle for dominance developed between Betamax and VHS. Eventually, despite the technical superiority of the Betamax system, the greater marketing effort of JVC and the companies which it had licensed prevailed. The Philips and Sony systems faded into obscurity whilst the VHS system became an industry standard. This mirrored the situation which obtained when the Philips Compact Audio Cassette system, rather than the Grundig DC cassette, replaced the unwieldy reel-to-reel magnetic recording tape.

11.2.3 Inherited Market Power

Britain was a maritime nation and possessed a strong rope-making industry. Rope-making techniques were adapted to manufacture the cables used for telegraphs. In the mid-nineteenth century, as a result of its Imperial sources of raw materials, the British had an effective monopoly of world trade in gutta-percha, which was used in the manufacture of shoes and medical instruments. When the material was found to have ideal insulating properties for electrical conductors, it was pressed into service in the construction of undersea cables. Britain rapidly became world leader in the cable industry.

Edison used his patents on the carbon filament lamp to drive out his competitors. His successors, first Edison General Electric and then, after the merger with Thomson-Houston, General Electric (GE), used the combined strength of a multiplicity of minor patents to consolidate their position. The companies utilised the patent monopoly to regulate the supply of components to competing manufacturers and to control resale prices, thereby generating large profits and an extremely positive cash flow. When new technologies, in the form of metal filaments, threatened the dominant position, GE used its war chest to purchase the patent rights to *all* potentially competing technologies.

The prototype of the thermionic valve was a carbon filament lamp to which an extra electrode was added. Valves were made in the same factories and using the same plant and manufacturing techniques. During the first world war, even lamp factories which had no prior history of valve construction were pressed into service to meet the military demands for valves for wireless communications.

When the Bell System was seeking licensees to manufacture the transistor, the existing manufacturers of thermionic valves were invited to an initial seminar. They were the first to set up production plant and rapidly established themselves as major players in the new industry. The initial developments were made by Bell, which, of course, had a head start, but the first paradigm shift in the fabrication of junction transistors – the alloyed junction – came from General Electric and the Radio Corporation of America. Philco, another valve producer, subsequently attempted to make a major change with the introduction of an automatic plant which produced Schottky barrier transistors by an electrolytic etching and plating technique.

By 1955, newcomers to the industry – Hughes, Transitron, Germanium Products, Texas Instruments, Motorola and Clevite – were setting the pace and, by 1957, the recent entrants had taken over 60 per cent of the market from the established companies. The first fifteen years of the transistor was a period of rapid change (Cullis 2004, Case Study 3) and, with each paradigm shift in the manufacturing technology, a new set of companies came to the fore.

Although the microprocessor had its origin at Intel, several manufacturers produced eight-bit devices with broadly comparable performance characteristics. The most significant were the Mostek 6502, the Intel 8080 and its 'second cousin' the Zilog Z80. The 6502 was used in the Apple II and the Commodore Pet microcomputer and the 8080 and Z80 formed the heart of the Sinclair ZX80 and S100-bus machines, such as the North Star Horizon.

Because it ran VisiCalc, the first spreadsheet program, the Apple II achieved great popularity, but no one machine attained a dominant position. The turning point did not come until 1981, with the introduction of the IBM personal computer. Big Blue, as IBM was known in the trade, was the dominant player in the computer industry and the supplier of choice for computer professionals. There was a saying that 'No-one ever got fired for buying IBM [computers]' and, certainly, IBM used the marketing ploy of FUD (fear, uncertainty and doubt), playing on the suggestion that, if users departed from IBM machines, they would meet serious problems. IBM had a near monopoly in the supply of main-frame computers and a dominant position in the supply of minicomputers. It had become complacent and did not notice the threat posed by the microcomputer until the revolution was well under way.

When IBM realised that its future markets were under attack, it quickly cobbled together its own machine from standard building blocks. The processor was the 8088, a cut-down version of Intel's 8086 sixteen-bit processor, with an eight-bit external data bus and an operating system, MS-DOS, purchased from Microsoft, the company which had written the Basic interpreter for the first PCs. (The MS-DOS operating system was actually bought in by Microsoft in order to meet the timescales set by IBM.) The IBM PC became a *de facto* standard overnight, not because its performance was good – others were better – but because its case carried the IBM logo (Cringely 1992).

Although the IBM personal computer was an immediate success, that very fact immediately attracted the attention of other manufacturers. The computer was constructed from standard components, but fear of anti-trust proceedings had prevented IBM from placing on its suppliers any restriction against selling these components to third parties. Thus other would-be imitators could go to Intel and purchase a set of chips, to Microsoft for operating system software and to Shugart for floppy disc drives. Designing a case to hold the components was within the capabilities of the least accomplished 'metal basher' so the only thing they lacked was a read-only memory, basic input/output system (ROM BIOS) – a chip containing the instructions and routines which controlled the flow of data within the computer and between the computer and the outside world.

The personal computer was a piece of equipment which sold for a much lower price than the main-frame and mini computers which had previously been the norm. What is more important, the price was *so* low that many company employees could purchase one without going through the trauma of obtaining the approval which is customary in business prior to the acquisition of major items of capital equipment. This had two significant consequences. Firstly, large numbers of personal computers found their way into companies under the guise of purchase of 'calculators', often for petty cash, and, secondly, because the purchases were made directly by the users, the management information and data processing departments of large companies lost control of what was to become the mainstream of computing.

As a result of the cut-throat competition in the new market, margins on personal computers were pared to 20-30 per cent rather than the 60-80 per cent which was customary in the main-frame market. This severely restricted IBM's cash flow and led to a squeeze on profit margins. When IBM responded by introducing a new proprietary micro-channel architecture and new operating systems (PCDOS 4.0 and OS/2) which contained serious flaws and did not offer any advantage over their predecessors, the migration to competing products accelerated.

11.2.4 Statutory Monopolies

Although, initially, Edison resolved not to use his incandescent lamp patents aggressively, his successor company, General Electric, was unable to defeat competition by commercial means and, in the mid-1890s, set in hand a war of attrition to establish a dominant position. By a series of predatory actions, GE gradually eliminated the small companies which had been making inroads into the lighting business until the industry consisted only of GE, Westinghouse and United States Electric, which was effectively controlled by GE.

Having driven out small competitors, General Electric turned its attention to its only significant rival, Westinghouse. The new adversary was able to compete on more equal terms. Not only did it hold patents relating to the manufacture of electric lamps, but the deal which George Westinghouse had made with Nikola Tesla meant that he held a significant patent position in the generation, transmission and use of alternating current. GE and Westinghouse concluded a patent cross-licensing agreement and, although lamp patents were not included in this deal, a large number of patent infringement suits on lighting technology between the companies were suspended.

When the need arose for a more reliable detector of radio waves than that offered by the coherer, J. Ambrose Fleming remembered his research on 'Edison Effect' lamps and adapted these devices to create the diode detector. He assigned the patents on it to the Marconi Company, which had retained him as a consultant.

Working independently, but with knowledge of Fleming's results, Lee de Forest invented the Audion three-electrode valve. This was initially used as a sensitive detector, but was later developed into a general-purpose amplifier of weak electrical signals. He patented his invention but, due to financial difficulties, was unable to pay the annual renewal fees on his overseas patents. In consequence, they lapsed, leaving him with protection only in the USA.

When the Marconi Company attempted to develop wireless communications in America, it clashed with the De Forest Company, which was attempting to do the same thing. The result was stalemate. Marconi needed an amplifier for weak signals to make radio viable over long distances. De Forest had an amplifier – the Audion valve – but its manner of construction was covered by the claims of the Fleming diode patent, which was owned by Marconi. Neither could make progress without a licence from the other, and these licences were not forthcoming, as the following extract from de Forest's autobiography makes clear.

And now [towards the end of 1914] L.F.H. Betts, of the firm of patent attorneys who had from the beginning represented the American Marconi Company, the same firm whom I had good reason to know and respect for the long, tough battles they had given me twelve years before on the vertical antenna patent of Marconi, notified us that their clients regarded the Audion as an infringement of the Fleming valve patent. Betts requested a conference with Captain Darby as our attorney before filing suit.

At this conference Darby informed them that our information was to the effect that the Marconi Company was even then infringing the Audion tube patent. The De Forest Company would be compelled to file countersuit under our own patent claims. Betts suggested the wisdom of an interchange of licenses on the patents in suit. I was agreeable to accepting such a proposition until Betts stated that such an agreement must stipulate that the De Forest Company would not enter the wireless telegraph field – in short, must confine itself to the radiotelephone.

This limitation we could not accept. We were already building some direct-current radiotelegraph transmitters designed for marine telegraph, and installing them under contract aboard two coastwise vessels. It was in fact this very activity in the marine field, now to be their own exclusive bailiwick, which had determined the Marconi Company to bring new patent suits, if necessary, to stop our competition.

It might have been part of the wisdom to have accepted Betts's proposal and ended then and forever the subsequent litigation.

Darby and I decided not to compromise but to fight. One weighty factor in this decision was the fact that the Fleming valve patent contained several obviously invalid claims, claims broad enough actually to cover the ancient 'Edison effect.' Farnsworth, who was called in to lead our attack, as having had valuable early experience in battling with Betts and Marconi, argued that the Marconi Company, now admittedly using the grid Audion, had absolutely no defense. We could at once obtain an injunction against their continued use of the Audion, which they now found so essential in the conduct of their long-distance transmissions. Meanwhile, their suit must fail from patent invalidity, and we could enter into the more equitable type of contract to which we felt we were entitled.

At the trial's opening Betts did two amazing things: he filed a disclaimer of the broad invalid Fleming claims and admitted the validity of my grid Audion patents and the infringement thereof.

Farnsworth at once moved for a permanent injunction against the Marconi Company, this procedure seeming to us incontestable. But we had 'reasoned without our host.'

'Oh no,' quoth the Honorable Judge Julius Mayer, 'these parties came into court and in forthright and manly fashion admitted their sins. They should not be punished for so doing. Injunction is denied!'

Outraged by this miscarriage of justice, we immediately appealed the decision to a higher court. Nearly two years elapsed, however, before our appeal came to a hearing. During this time the Marconi Company continued manufacturing Audions pending final decision ... The lower court's injunction against us was sustained and we were ordered to render an accounting to the Marconi Company for all the Audions which we had made and sold from the beginning. But to add to the general confusion, Judge Hough held that the Marconi Company, having admitted infringement of our patents, were likewise accountable to us for the Audions that they had manufactured. A Master was appointed to supervise the mutual accounting required. Henceforth, both companies were enjoined from making and selling tubes without the other's consent.

As a result of this decision, the radio-tube industry remained in a hopelessly tangled mess until the Fleming patent expired in 1922.

The climax came many years later (1943) when the U.S. Supreme Court found the Fleming valve patent to have been invalid all the time.

Before then my own patents had long expired and the opportunity of profiting from my invention was lost forever. (de Forest 1950, pp321-6)

In the early days of its existence, Intel had few financial resources and lived a hand-to-mouth existence. It failed to patent both the memory chip and the microprocessor. However, by the time that it had manufactured several generations of these devices, Intel had become cash-rich because its microprocessors had become *de facto* industry standards as a result of the success of the IBM personal computer and it was able to exploit the copyright protection for micro-code embedded within the microprocessors.

11.3 FREE COMPETITION

Free competition is a market structure beloved of policy makers. Possibly this is because low retail prices and freedom of choice are valued more highly than strong suppliers and certainty of returns for manufacturers. In a market which is a net importer of innovation, patents will assist the export of revenue. For this reason, the Dutch experience of patents at the middle of the nineteenth century was highly skewed in favour of foreign patentees. The local perception, therefore, was that patents were not in the national interest and, after vigorous lobbying by industrial associations, the patent system was abolished in 1869.

Lack of patent law meant that there was no hindrance to the introduction of new technology. Day-to-day life in the Netherlands was not affected, except that retail prices of new introductions, such as the light bulb, were substantially lower than in countries where patents existed. Electrical articles equal in quality to their foreign counterparts could be produced for two-thirds of the cost since there were no royalties to pay (Heerding 1986, p249).

The Netherlands had no native electrical industry. Absence of patent legislation gave small companies, and those which were just starting up, freedom from litigation and thus improved their chances of survival. As a result, several entrepreneurs, including a number of fugitives from the United Kingdom, set up factories to manufacture electric lamps and export them elsewhere in Europe. Amongst these was Gerard Philips, who had worked in England and was familiar with the problems involved in establishing an electrical enterprise. Another was Robertson, who decided to set up manufacture in Holland when Edison's and Swan's patent monopoly prevented him from doing so in the United Kingdom.

Another industry which was strong in the Netherlands was the manufacture of margarine. Theodorus Mouton, who owned margarine and pharmaceutical factories, argued that in the space of fifteen years, a larger number of margarine factories had been set up in the Netherlands than would have been the case under a patent system (Mouton 1890).

11.4 OLIGOPOLY

By the early 1890s, the Edison and Swan United Electric Light Company (Ediswan) had used its patents to establish a monopoly in the market for incandescent lamps. In other countries, notably Germany and the USA, either the patent position was weak, or ownership of the rights was in different hands, and other companies acquired the necessary skills to set up viable manufacture. When the Edison and Swan UK patents expired, these overseas companies entered the British market. During the first decade of the twentieth century, the British General Electric company, which had its origins in the Dutch free-for-all and subsequently acquired know-how from Auer Gesellschaft in Germany, British Thomson-Houston, which was a subsidiary of the American General Electric, and Siemens, which had a sister company in Germany, became major players with Ediswan.

In Germany, Edison failed to establish a master patent and, as a result, the native companies, Auer (Osram), Allgemeine Elektrizitäts Gesellschaft (AEG) and Siemens all became major suppliers. In the USA, the market became a duopoly as only Westinghouse, with the benefit of Tesla's patents on alternating current machines, had a sufficiently strong counter-position to resist the lighting patents held by GE. (There was a third company, US Electric, but this may be discounted since it was controlled by GE and, following the anti-trust case in 1911, was absorbed into GE's operation.)

During the 1930s manufacture of wireless receivers was a cottage industry. Components could be readily purchased and anyone with a modicum of skill and a soldering iron could assemble a set on his kitchen table. It was a small step from this to a rudimentary factory and a production line. Enthusiasts such as Eric Cole (Ekco), Frank Murphy (Murphy) and Harry Roberts (Roberts Radio) were able to establish themselves alongside the established electrical manufacturers such as Philips, Marconi and GEC (Geddes 1991, p103). After the second world war, this fragmentation could no longer be supported and the industry became consolidated by a series of take-overs and mergers. Initially at least, the individual names were preserved, usually as a means of brand differentiation. Thus the Rank Organisation controlled Bush, Murphy, Dansette and Arena; GEC owned GEC, Sobell and McMichael; ITT sold RGD, Regentone and Kolster-Brandes; Thorn had Ferguson, Marconiphone, Ultra, Pilot and HMV, whilst Pye sets were to be found under the guise of Pye, Pam, Invicta, Ekco, Dynatron and Pamphonic. There was the occasional start-up, such as Perdio, which arrived with the transistor radio, but these companies either failed to meet the competition from the major players in the oligopoly or were restricted to niche markets.

With the advent, in the 1970s, of very large scale integration (VLSI) which followed the invention of the planar process for the manufacture of integrated circuits, two significant products emerged to take advantage of the ability to place large numbers of devices on a single chip. These were the microprocessor and the memory circuit. Of these, the memory device, the principal application of which was temporary storage of data in computers, consisted of a matrix of identical cells each capable of storing one bit (binary digit) of information. Early memory chips contained one thousand such cells. As techniques improved, 4 kilobit (4K), 16 kilobit and 64 kilobit devices were introduced. By the early 1980s, 256K chips were being produced. By 1995, the norm was 16-megabit, with 64M and 256M in the pipeline and techniques for one gigabit (10^9) being contemplated (Manners 1995, p90).

Initially, memory chips were produced solely by US companies such as Texas Instruments and Intel but, in 1983, stimulated by the Japanese Ministry of International Trade and Industry, Nippon Electric (NEC) and Hitachi commenced production of 256K dynamic random access memory (DRAM) chips, a full year before the American companies.

The memory chip is essentially a black box. It is accessed by way of an address bus and a data bus, the electronic architecture of which follows *de facto* industry standards. Provided these interfacing standards are complied with, it does not matter what internal construction is adopted by the device manufacturer. There was no master patent covering the concept of a memory chip and, within the constraint of the need for compliance with the common access protocols, there were many ways of making them. It was therefore open to any manufacturer with the resources to set up a factory and commence production.

In the subsequent years, other companies, including Fujitsu, Toshiba, Siemens, the Korean *chaebols* – Samsung, Hyundai and Lucky Goldstar – and a clutch of Taiwanese companies entered the market. Due to the lack of product differentiation, sales were based purely on price. The industry was of a cyclic nature and the companies either moved in synchronism, matching prices and the introduction of the next generation of chips, or they left the market.

11.5 THE EMERGENCE OF THE CARTEL – CROSS-LICENCES, TRUSTS, POOLS AND COMBINATIONS

Patents are of little use in the semiconductor industry. There are so many innovations taking place that you are bound to infringe somebody else's patent. If everybody in the industry decided to defend their patents, the only guys who would make money are lawyers. So instead it's more customary to grant an agreement that I won't bother you if you won't bother me. When the agreement is set up, if I have more patents in my file than you do, maybe you should pay me a small fee.

Marcian E. (Ted) Hoff

This statement by the inventor of the microprocessor encapsulates the philosophy which has permeated the electrical industry since the nineteenth century.

When Edison's and Swan's patents on the carbon filament lamp expired in 1893-4 other manufacturers set up factories in Britain. Competition from continental, particularly German lamps was fierce and, in 1905, in an attempt to counter this threat, the British Carbon Lamp Association was formed by the major British producers. The agreement provided for maintenance of minimum prices to the wholesaler, but not beyond (MRPC 1951, p10). In Germany and the USA also, major manufacturers had come to a price-fixing agreement to alleviate the effects of competition.

Between 1906 and 1909 metal filaments were developed in Europe and in the United States and the tungsten filament lamp soon replaced the carbon filament lamp. British manufacturers were not responsible for any significant technological development from 1878 until 1935, when they introduced the fluorescent tube. However, they aggressively acquired the United Kingdom patent rights under a series of comprehensive agreements with the principal American and German companies. These agreements provide for a cross-licensing or assignment of patents and for the exchange of technical and manufacturing experience on payment of a royalty by the British parties. They also provided for territorial restrictions on manufacture and sale. A point of significance is that two British manufacturers were originally subsidiaries of an American and a German company, a third was, before 1914, closely associated with a leading German lamp-maker in the production of lamps in this country and acquired its principal trade mark (Osram) through that association, and a fourth was the subsidiary of a Dutch company.

In 1912, British Thomson-Houston, the General Electric Company and Siemens entered into an agreement to pool their metal filament lamp patents and grant licences to other British lamp manufacturers. The same year these three companies, with Ediswan (all of which were already members of the British Carbon Lamp Association), formed the Tungsten Lamp Association, an association based on patent pooling, the objective of which was to promote and protect the interests of manufacturers of and dealers in electric lamps in the United Kingdom.

The members of the two associations subsequently merged to form the Electric Lamp Manufacturers' Association of Great Britain Ltd (ELMA). The Association fixed common retail prices and trade terms based on the annual quantities purchased, and maintained a system of exclusive agreements, exclusivity and price maintenance being supported by a register (known in the trade as the 'Black List') of persons who were only to be supplied at full retail prices.

In 1920, a government Sub-Committee on Trusts found that the Association controlled between 90 per cent and 95 per cent of the output of the industry and that whilst the Association might not necessarily pursue a policy of inflated prices and inordinate profits as a result of its position, there would be no effective check in the shape of competition should it decide to do so. The Sub-Committee found also that 'immoderate profits' were being made on the manufacture of lamps before 1914 and the discounts allowed to distributors ought to be reduced. It drew the inference that non-association manufacturers, whilst still making a satisfactory profit and despite their smaller output, were able to sell at a lower price than Association members. Since, however, Association retail prices were universally adopted, the effect of these lower prices was reflected in terms to the re-seller rather than in any benefit to the public. The Sub-Committee further drew attention to the close connections between patent rights and the formation of ELMA, to the grant of licences by the patent-owning members of the Association to other members against payment of royalty, to the continued acceptance by members so licensed of patents held invalid in the High Court and to restriction (normally to a 10 per cent per annum increase) imposed on the output of lamps manufactured for the home market under licence. The Sub-Committee regarded this method of limiting expansion as more harmful than a simple percentage quota would have been, though they were aware that there would have been objections to such a system. The Sub-Committee also drew attention to the danger that the interests of the British industry would be subordinated to American interests, and that an international combination might 'control supplies and dominate prices over a considerable part of the world', and it recommended that 'the operations of an Association which so effectively controls an important industry should be subjected to public supervision and control'. *The recommendations of the Sub-Committee were largely ignored.*

During the first world war, lamp-manufacturing plants were set up in many countries to replace the foreign sources of supply which were no longer available. This meant that, after cessation of hostilities, there was a vast excess of capacity, leading to large-scale dumping of product on the market. Such a situation could not be sustained and, in 1925, the leading lamp manufacturers of the world, under the initiative of General Electric of the USA, negotiated the General Patent and Business Development Agreement (the so-called 'Phoebus Agreement') which was named after its administrative office in Geneva. The members of ELMA formed a British chapter.

Phoebus divided world markets, except for the United States and Canada, into territorial zones and set market shares for each territory at the same level as in 1924. It prescribed a common policy on sales and established a basis for cross-licensing of inventions and standardisation. The agreement did not apply in the United States or Canada because the parties, by a series of complementary agreements, recognised the exclusive interests of the US General Electric Company (GE) and its licensees in those territories. GE's interests in territories outside the United States and Canada were governed by the same complementary agreements and also by equity interests in companies which were party to Phoebus. The agreement prevailed until the second world war. It was then replaced by a series of less far-reaching agreements. Eventually the arrangements were swept aside by the globalisation of trade and the rise of the influence of competition law.

As well as setting market quotas, Phoebus proscribed the independent acquisition of outside lamp-manufacturing businesses. These could only be purchased and run collectively. Businesses which were so acquired were used to produce low-cost lamps which were sold as non-premium brands to meet the competition of manufacturers who were outside the agreement.

When public service broadcasting was set up in the United Kingdom through the establishment of the British Broadcasting Corporation, the passing of its predecessor, the British Broadcasting Company, did not leave the radio industry unstructured. In 1923, receiver makers had formed the National Association of Radio Manufacturers of Great Britain (NARM), to fight price-cutting by retailers and to promote exhibitions (Geddes 1991, p62). This was succeeded in 1926 by the Radio Manufacturers' Association (RMA), whose first major act was to organise opposition to the patent royalty, of 12s 6d per valve-holder, levied by the Marconi Company if a receiver used any of thirteen Marconi-controlled patents. Following an application by the Brownie Wireless Co. of Great Britain Ltd. for a compulsory licence under the Marconi patents, the Comptroller-General of Patents found that Marconi was abusing its position and granted a licence at a lower royalty than the then going rate of 12s 6d per valve-holder ([1929] RPC 457). Although this decision was subsequently overturned on appeal, the members of the RMA used it as a lever to negotiate a new royalty of 5s 0d per valve-holder.

Valve-makers combined much more aggressively. By the beginning of 1924, ELMA had a valve manufacturers' committee meeting under its auspices. In June 1924 this became the Valve Manufacturers' Association and in July 1926 the British Radio Valve Manufacturers' Association (BVA). The BVA was a restrictive organisation. No-one who handled

BVA members' valves was allowed to handle anyone else's, and, when Metropolitan-Vickers joined the Association in 1926, it had to raise its prices considerably to conform to the tariff.

Valves were relatively short-lived components and the replacement market was important. Since a valve was almost always replaced with an identical new one, the valve-maker was prepared to supply the set-maker at little more than cost price in order to obtain the profitable replacement sales, at prices several times higher.

In the 1930s, over-production and high productivity of radio receivers in America led to prices well below those prevailing in Britain. American receivers began to find their way on to the British market. This created a conflict of interest between set-makers and valve-makers. The imported sets used valves quite different from British ones, so the BVA members proposed to make the relevant American types. This evinced a vehement protest from the RMA on the grounds that it would encourage the import of American receivers by making replacements available from BVA retailers, who were barred from selling foreign-made valves. The BVA retreated, and by the end of the year all of its members except Mullard had signed an agreement not to make valves specially suitable for imported receivers, or for receivers assembled in the UK from foreign components.

From 1930, a radio receiver patent pool, administered by Marconi, had operated in Britain. Such pools, operated by the holders of relevant patents, licensed manufacturers to use all the patents in the pool in return for a royalty shared out amongst its members. To be viable, a pool had to be comprehensive enough to enable a manufacturer to make good receivers using only circuit arrangements covered by its patents. In 1933, a potential rival appeared when the Hazeltine Corporation of America, which held a powerful group of patents, including one for automatic volume control, joined Philco and Majestic in forming a British company, Hazelpat, to exploit their combined patent resources. Several of the key patents in the British pool expired at about this time, and the British industry decided to admit Hazelpat to the pool rather than engage in a trial of strength. By doing so they admitted Majestic and Philco to the fold, but gained protection against other American manufacturers.

11.6 THE 'OCEAN ROLLER' MARKET – SURFERS AND SINKERS

When Bell Laboratories launched the transistor, they invited the world's leading electronic component manufacturers to participate in the new venture. The potential rewards were apparent and the cost of market entry was low. The solid-state amplifier had been a Holy Grail for many years and the new device had the right characteristics. The currently used universal amplifier was the thermionic valve, which was unreliable, consumed a lot of power and generated heat which caused components mounted in close proximity in the same apparatus to deteriorate. The transistor, on the other hand, required one-thousandth of the power, operated at much lower temperatures and had a virtually endless life.

The stage was set and eager would-be manufacturers were clamouring at the door. Numbers of transistor producers grew rapidly. In 1951 there were only 4. By 1952, this had risen to 8, to 15 in 1953 and to 26 by 1956 (Manners 1995, p21). The initial contingent was drawn mainly from the ranks of valve manufacturers, including Western Electric, General Electric, RCA, Raytheon, Sylvania, Philco, CBS (Columbia Broadcasting System), Tung-Sol and Westinghouse. Newcomers without prior experience of valve manufacture were Hughes, Transitron, Germanium Products, Texas Instruments, Clevite and Motorola. In 1955, the top ten manufacturers were Hughes, Transitron, Philco, Sylvania, Texas, General Electric, RCA, Westinghouse, Motorola and Clevite, but, by 1957, new companies had seized over 60 per cent of the market.

Due to the rapid changes in technology as the grown-junction transistor replaced the point-contact transistor and this, in turn, was superseded by the alloyed junction, the post-alloy diffused transistor, the diffused mesa transistor and then the planar epitaxial device, which were all introduced by different companies, there was a rapid turn-over in market leaders. By 1975 all except three of the 1955 top ten had dropped out. The survivors were Texas Instruments, Motorola and RCA. The pay-off for staying the course was great. In 1959, the seven-year-old company Transitron was valued at $285 million, whilst Texas Instruments' shares had risen to $191 from $5, the level at which they had stood seven years earlier, when it commenced transistor manufacture.

Driven by increasing economies of scale, new products and new markets, improved yields due to technological advancement, with consequent lower prices and higher sales, the semiconductor industry has experienced a relentless growth. However, although the general trend has been one of expansion – in the 1960s at around 30 per cent per annum and, by 1995, at around 16 per cent per annum – the overall pattern has been cyclic, with periods of massive growth and profitability followed by lean periods of retrenchment, (Figure 11.1) corresponding with the introduction of new technology. These times of low returns have traditionally been periods of shake-out when companies have disappeared, either through mergers or take-overs or simply because their sponsors have decided to cut their losses and withdraw. Thus only three of the top ten valve-makers, General

Electric, Sylvania and RCA, occupied similar positions in the top ten transistor-makers in 1955. Only six top transistor manufacturers survived to be in the top ten microelectronics manufacturers of 1965, when the integrated circuit market was emerging. The six were Texas Instruments, Motorola, General Electric, RCA, Transitron and Philco, who were joined by Fairchild, General Instruments, Sprague and Raytheon. By 1975, Sprague, General Electric, Transitron, Raytheon and Philco had been replaced by National Semiconductor, Intel, Rockwell, Signetics and AMI and, ten years later, AMI, General Instruments and Rockwell had been replaced by Harris, Mostek and Advanced Micro Devices (AMD).

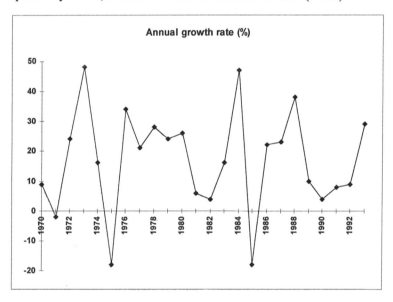

Figure 11.1 Annual fluctuations in US semiconductor production 1970-93

11.7 THE 'VULTURE' MARKET

After the initial success with the Apple II, Steve Jobs turned his attention to producing a computer with a user-friendly interface (Cringely 1996). He adopted the WIMPs (windows, icons, mice and pull-down menus) concepts originated by the Xerox Palo Alto Research Centre (PARC) to produce, firstly the Lisa, then the Macintosh computers. The 'Mac' was, initially, extremely profitable and Apple guarded its proprietary position jealously. Noone was permitted to license its operating system software. By contrast, the IBM PC, its main rival, had an open architecture and ran under the Microsoft MS-DOS operating system, which was available to any manufacturer that wished to adopt it. IBM clones, produced using 'clean room' techniques to avoid the threat of copyright litigation, proliferated. When Microsoft introduced its Windows graphical user interface, which had many of the features of the Mac operating system, the writing was on the wall for Apple, which experienced a relentless attrition of its market share.

11.8 THE 'PHOENIX' MARKET

Steve Jobs, one of the three men who set up Apple, left to establish a new company. After some time, when Apple was in the doldrums, Jobs was persuaded to return. He managed to rejuvenate the company, which then enjoyed a measure of success attributable, in part, to a cult following and, in part, to an 'anti-Bill Gates' reaction to Microsoft's domination of the personal computer market.

AMD, a start-up company which followed in the steps of Intel, existed for a number of years on the pickings of the vulture market left when Intel launched successively more powerful microprocessors. Eventually, Intel made a number of mistakes. It was forced to recall chips containing a bug in the numeric processor; it ignored certain key markets and it was slow to develop new product lines, with the result that it did not gain a sufficient response-time lead. At this stage AMD was there to take advantage of these lapses and achieved an improvement in its operating economics which put it in a position to mount a challenge rather than always following Intel's path.

11.9 THE BIPEDAL MARKET – THE FLIP-FLOPOLY

Sometimes complementary markets develop together. One example is the electric telegraph and the railways, where improvements in the telegraph permitted faster and closer running of trains, whilst increased traffic created a need for improved signalling.

The invention of the triode valve gave rise to radio telephony and, in due course, television, which generated a market for broadcast entertainment. The need for improved transmission and reception led first to the tetrode and then to the pentode valve. Improved valves gave rise to advances in communications technology, which, in turn, generated a need for further enhancement of the valves.

The invention of the transistor expanded the market for computers by significantly increasing the mean time between failures, which was a factor limiting the size of machines based on the thermionic valve. More powerful computers required more reliable transistors, fuelling successive changes in the fabrication technology and ultimately spawning the integrated circuit.

Photolithography was the foundation of the planar process for making semiconductor devices and was the enabling invention in the development of Very Large Scale Integration (VLSI). Moore's Law was the dramatic encapsulation of the advance of the bipedal VLSI-photolithography market. VLSI, itself, was the basis of improvements in the microprocessor and the memory circuit which made possible enhancement of the personal computer, which was further coupled to a market for ever more powerful software.

11.10 QUASI-STABLE MONOPOLY – THE 'THIRD LITTLE PIG' SYNDROME

'Little pig,' said the Wolf, 'if you will be ready at six o'clock in the morning, I will take you to Farmer Smith's field where there are fine turnips to be had.
'Very well,' replied the little pig, who was very fond of turnips.
But the Third Little Pig knew that the wolf just wanted to eat him, so the next morning he set off for Farmer Smith's field at *five* o'clock. He filled his basket with turnips. Then he hurried home.
At six o'clock the wolf knocked on the door.
'Little pig,' he asked, 'are you ready?'
'Oh,' said the little pig, 'I have already been to Farmer Smith's field and filled my basket with turnips.'
The Wolf and the Three Little Pigs

Although Intel invented the microprocessor when Ted Hoff designed the four-bit 4004, by the time the industry had moved on to eight-bit operation, several manufacturers were competing on more or less equal terms. Mostek's 6502 had a similar performance and operating characteristics to Intel's 8080, whilst Zilog's Z80 actually had a similar, but more comprehensive, instruction set. When IBM drew up designs for its original personal computer, however, it settled on Intel's 8088 processor to drive it. The reason for this choice was entirely rational. Internally, the 8088 was a sixteen-bit device and this was the next standard towards which the industry was moving. On the other hand, the external data bus, by means of which the processor communicated with the outside world, was eight bits wide. Eight-bit peripheral chips which controlled such operations were freely available, whereas corresponding sixteen-bit devices were still under development.

IBM made a firm commitment to the Intel processor, but it had a strong in-house semiconductor plant which was able to fabricate processors should Intel fail. This facility was not available to other manufacturers who wanted to make clones of the IBM PC. In order to provide confidence for them by ensuring continuity of supply, Intel entered into a number of second-sourcing agreements permitting others to make processors to Intel's designs.

IBM had an arrangement under which it could make Intel chips for its in-house requirements. It also purchased a 12 per cent interest in Intel for $250 million in 1982, because of Intel's lead in a technology vital to the development of IBM and the whole computer industry (Heller 1994, p123). This funding played a crucial part in enabling Intel to survive until it was able to dictate the running of the market. Intel needed further injections of capital from IBM to meet mounting development and capital costs. IBM's stake was increased piecemeal to 20 per cent in 1983-84. Intel had lost money for five consecutive quarters before the IBM investment. However, it used the IBM link astutely, ensuring that it was not dependent only on IBM business, which never rose above 20 per cent of Intel's sales and was only 15 per cent in 1986. Intel had an agreement with IBM which mirrored Microsoft's contract for the supply of software for the IBM personal computer, *viz.* there were no restrictions on sales to manufacturers of clones of the machine. (This highlighted, more than anything else, IBM's fear of possible anti-trust action. If it were shown to be using its market power overtly to force through one-sided deals, it had much to lose.) At this stage, in terms of cumulative sales, Intel took 80 per cent of the world's fastest-growing electronics market. By 1991, Intel's annual sales were $4.8 billion and it earned profits of $819 million.

It is interesting to track Intel's strategy during the transition from breakaway start-up company to industry behemoth (Heller 1994, p123). The company was formed when Gordon Moore, Robert Noyce and Andrew Grove obtained $30,000 from venture capitalist Arthur Rock to set up a company to make memory chips. This product, however, was destined to become a commodity, consisting as it did of, initially, thousands, and, subsequently, millions, of substantially identical devices, arranged in a matrix for ease of access. There was little to differentiate one chip from another and hence the opportunity to create a barrier to market entry was minimal – any company with sufficient capital to erect a suitable factory could participate.

With the invention of the microprocessor in 1971, the picture changed dramatically. The microprocessor itself performed various functions. It had registers to store data, counters to chart the progress of operations, an arithmetic logic unit to perform logical and numeric functions, and interfaces to communicate with external devices. Patent protection could be obtained for the functional aspects of the device, whilst the code for the built-in programs which controlled its functions was protected by copyright. (There was also *sui generis* protection for the masks used in its fabrication, but this afforded only a barrier to mechanical copying, not against cloning.)

Intel developed successive generations of microprocessor of ever-increasing complexity. Each was upwards-compatible with its predecessor. This meant that it would operate with software designed to run on the earlier device and so it was not dependent on, nor subject to the time delay associated with, a requirement to write new applications programs, a drawback faced by the disparate early microprocessors. The penalty was that it was not possible to make a fresh start when new design techniques became available. Effectively, each processor had to be built around the kernel of the previous generation.

In the early days, to instil confidence in its customers by convincing them that they could purchase without risk of failure of their supplier, Intel was forced to make 'second sourcing' agreements, which allowed competitors to manufacture its products. This also gave the competitors access to Intel's know-how and set them on the same learning curve of product development. Although these second-sourcing agreements were for specific products – the 80286 and 80386 microprocessors – since each processor served as the basis for the next generation, Intel had great difficulty in preventing the rival manufacturers from progressing along the same development path. The company was forced to litigate to stop them.

The identification code for each processor followed a set formula (80186, 80286, 80386, 80486) which possessed no proprietor-specific distinction. With what would have been the 80586, however, Intel broke the mould and decided to give it a distinctive name, the 'Pentium' processor. It registered this name as a trade mark and mounted a vigorous advertising campaign to increase public awareness, an action virtually unprecedented for a product of this nature. The publicity for 'Intel inside' the computer, accompanied by a four-note jingle, was aimed at establishing a reputation akin to the one which Dolby created for his noise reduction systems for sound reproducing equipment.

By this stage, Intel's competitors were reduced to cloning the products by utilising 'clean room' and other reverse-engineering techniques. This gave Intel a significant response-time monopoly, which it exploited by predatory pricing policies – as soon as the competing products came on stream, Intel lowered its prices, thereby starving the opposition of cash flow and profitability.

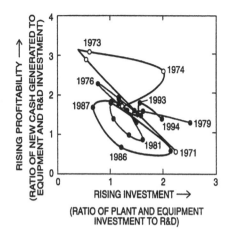

Source   Hutcheson 1996

Figure 11.2 Intel's profit v. investment in technology (1971-1994)

A phase chart (Figure 11.2) showing the relation between Intel's profits and capital investments in technology throughout the company's history traces loops that each correspond approximately to a six-year cycle. During each of them, Intel moves from a period of unprofitable operations caused by heavy investment to an interval of very good cash flow resulting from much lighter investment.

Intel had fought several battles along the way to its dominant position. IBM, in 1986, introduced the reduced instruction set or RISC processor. This was a device with a relatively simple architecture and the theory was that it could perform many simple operations extremely quickly, building up a simulation of the complex instructions of the complex instruction set (CISC) processor under the control of external software. Several companies introduced RISC processors, but none of them had any impact on Intel's market share. Processors such as the Acorn RISC Machine (ARM) found only niche markets, whilst Intel retained 80 per cent of the overall market.

In 1990, Motorola, IBM and Apple formed an alliance to manufacture the Power PC. This machine, based on a new Motorola processor and intended to run Apple Mac software, would also emulate the IBM PC. Nevertheless, its performance did not match that of an Intel-based machine and it was not a success.

Although Intel and Motorola followed separate paths in processor development, each working on its own proprietary designs, they both introduced devices of similar degrees of complexity and operating power at around the same time (Hutcheson 1996). Both manufacturers (and also the manufacturers of memory chips) have been constrained in their rate of advancement by the rate at which the makers of photolithographic apparatus have been able to develop new equipment capable of resolving ever greater detail, thus permitting more devices to be packed into a given area of silicon.

11.11 GLOBAL RATHER THAN NATIONAL MARKETS

For the first six-and-a-half decades of the twentieth century, the electrical and electronic industries were organised on a national basis. Indeed, in an economic climate which permitted price-fixing and market-sharing cartels to flourish, albeit possibly covertly, it was not in the interests of the major players to attempt anything contrary. By 1966, however, the multinational corporations were beginning to change their thinking (Flaschen 1966). Competition and the prospect of economies of scale which would result from not having to produce separately for markets which had the same fundamental requirements urged them to re-organise their businesses on a global basis.

With the advent of very large scale integration (VLSI), the Japanese Ministry for International Trade and Industry (MITI) saw the opportunity of achieving its declared objective of making Japan a major force in the world electronics industry. It set up industry groupings – Hitachi with Fujitsu and Mitsubishi and Toshiba with Nippon Electric (NEC) – to pursue research funded by ¥30 billion from MITI and ¥40 billion from the companies. The result of this enterprise was that, between 1978 and 1988, six American producers – RCA, Fairchild, General Instrument, AMI, Rockwell and National Semiconductor – in the world top ten were displaced by six Japanese companies – NEC, Toshiba, Hitachi, Fujitsu, Mitsubishi and Matsushita.

In the 1980s, South Korea decided to become a major player in the microelectronics industry and built massive factories in South Korea. It set up and purchased companies in Silicon Valley to acquire their technologies. These companies licensed technology and products from the Americans and Japanese and manufactured products for other companies. Between 1983 and 1989 the South Korean output of chips went up from $500,000 worth a year to $1.5 billion and three South Korean companies, Samsung, Goldstar and Hyundai, established themselves as world-class players (Manners 1995, p50).

Taiwan had its own variant of the use of government policy to establish a national influence on world markets, but the technology was acquired in a different manner. In 1976 the government research body, the Industrial Technology Research Institute (ITRI), took a licence and set up a laboratory to develop integrated circuits based on RCA's CMOS technology. Whilst the laboratory refined the process, its electronics affiliate, ERSO (Electronics Research and Services Organisation), commenced a programme of building factories to transfer the laboratory techniques to a manufacturing environment. At five-year intervals, when a factory was completed and a new level of process technology had been achieved, a team of technologists that had developed the process in ITRI's lab would move over to ERSO's factory. The factory would be handed over to a company which was to be established as a chip manufacturer. The first was United Microelectronics Corporation (UMC), the second was the Taiwan Semiconductor Manufacturing Company (TSMC), and the third was Winbond Electronics Corporation. As a result, by the mid-1990s, Taiwan had six microelectronics companies in the $100 million-plus league, more than any country in the world apart from the USA and Japan.

European companies have only a mediocre track record as world competitors in the semiconductor industry. British companies were among the attendees at the original Bell symposia which introduced the transistor to potential manufacturers and, during the 1960s, there was a thriving semiconductor industry in the UK. Gradually, however, during the cyclic shake-outs, these companies disappeared through take-overs and mergers (Manners 1995, p48).

In 1978, the UK government through the medium of the National Enterprise Board, a holding organisation for state-owned companies, backed the establishment of Inmos, a chip company set up to manufacture the transputer, a new form of microprocessor intended for parallel computing, a form of computer architecture intended for sophisticated 'number-crunching' applications. The transputer was difficult to use and not oriented to the mass computer market. It remained a niche market chip. Eventually Inmos and its transputer were sold off to Thorn, which sold it on (at a profit) to SGS-Thomson.

The French, also, were unsuccessful at sustaining a national semiconductor industry. During the 1970s a series of enterprises was set up to manufacture semiconductor devices but they all failed or were taken over except SGS-Thomson, which was sustained by subsidies and survived as a medium-sized company. Philips in the Netherlands and Siemens in Germany have also survived as second-division players, but they have also received substantial subsidies from European funds and the protection of European tariffs.

11.12 THE EVOLUTION OF MARKET STRUCTURE IN A TECHNOLOGY-BASED INDUSTRY

New products follow a standard learning curve. Initially they are cash-negative whilst new plant is set up; then production yields increase and sales expand in response to falling prices; finally, there is a period of high profitability and cash inflow as the makers produce efficiently in a mature market. The consequence of the highly geared nature of the economics of production is that the introducer of a new generation of device has an opportunity to control the cash flow of his competitors by means of a predatory pricing policy. By timing his price reductions to take account of their being at an earlier position on the learning curve, he can reduce their profitability and cash inflow so that they have fewer funds to invest in the capital equipment for the next generation of product. Furthermore, they have to finance the amortisation of the current capital equipment over the shorter interval to the introduction of the next generation.

The market power resulting from GE's equity holdings in overseas companies, together with its patent strength derived from Edison's original work, enabled it to exert a controlling influence on the world cartel which was set up in the lamp industry.

Market power in a parent industry is likely initially to carry over into a daughter industry. For companies with an effective monopoly, or for the major participants in an oligopoly, the premium, which their dominant position permits them to charge, makes it feasible to maintain their dominance by acquiring patents from potentially competing new entrants to the market, with the prospect of very short payback times on the investment. However, whilst large organisations may possess the resources and the market power to control a developing market, they may not be lean and hungry enough to respond to innovation by newcomers.

Following the exhaustion of an initial monopoly, either through expiry of patents or other reduction of entry barriers, newcomers will be free to enter a market. Attempts to do this may evince countervailing response by an incumbent monopolist. If they have sufficient power the newcomers will, nevertheless, enter the market and a duopoly or oligopoly will be created (Cullis 1973). In the absence of an external constraint, such as patent or trade mark protection, markets for innovations will evolve into an oligopoly.

In markets where there is an overlap of technological capability on the part of the suppliers, it is probable that there will also be overlap of intellectual property monopolies. Such overlap is customarily resolved by cross-licensing. It is a very small step from cross-licensing to sharing markets on a territorial basis, which, in many circumstances is quite legitimate because it means that a patentee can derive a return from a market which he does not have the resources to serve. From there, the next step on the slippery slope is collusion on prices and then the creation of a cartel. In an oligopolistic market, the participants frequently make anti-competitive agreements. If the regulatory regime permits, the arrangements will be overt. In situations where there is strong competition law, such agreements will be under cover.

Although Apple pioneered the graphical user interface for consumer use, it failed in its attempt to control the market by refusing to license its operating system software. When, eventually, it did open its system to others, it was too late because, by then, its market share was small and dwindling. It no longer had a critical mass of users and all that was left was a 'vulture' market which destroyed Apple's last vestige of profitability. By the very fact of being in the right place at the right time, the supplier of a vulture market may become a phoenix and acquire the advantages of response-time monopolies which inure to an innovator.

On occasion, markets develop in an inter-related manner. Examples presented above demonstrate the existence and mechanics of 'anti-duopolies', where two components interact symbiotically to extract greater rents from a market than either one would on its own. In a conventional duopoly or oligopoly, action by one of the market participants evinces countervailing action by the others. Such counteraction has a stabilising effect and tends to maintain the *status quo*. If, instead of a countervailing effect, the other market participants exert a reinforcing influence, the result will be akin to positive feedback and the market will have a propensity to expand.

Profitability in a new market follows the well-defined learning curve. There is an initial period of negative cash flow, followed by a spell of increasing income. If market entry is associated with a significant response time and is also one where further innovation can create product obsolescence, an innovator will have the means of controlling the cash flow of his competitors by introducing innovations before they have been able to reach the stage of positive cash flow. The opportunity to introduce such a regime is most likely to occur on the supply side of a bipedal market.

In any industry, when the factor cost of innovation is allocated on a per-unit basis, the larger the total number of sales, the smaller will be the innovation costs and thus the greater will be the innovation rent. This creates a prejudice favouring larger markets and, hence, increases the pressure to globalise. Even if, for reasons of transport and other costs, it is desirable to manufacture locally, there are always likely to be common costs which can be shared.

Multinational companies adopted a global marketing strategy in the light of the need for economies of scale to meet the perceived threat of international competition. It also gave them accounting flexibility through transfer pricing of services, such as research and development, which could be carried out in advantageous locations. Achievement of success did, however, require a single-minded approach analogous to that of a product champion of an innovation.

Market power shifted from IBM to Intel and Microsoft, which set the hardware and software standards, and to clone manufacturers such as Compaq and Dell which not only offered either a superior product at an equivalent price or an equivalent product at a lower price, but established their own brand reputation (Martin 1996). Partly this was the result of IBM's complacency, but, even if the company had decided to take pre-emptive action, its internal bureaucracy was so great that it would never have got a product to market in time. Its inertia would have prevented its responding quickly enough to counter the effects of innovation by others.

Once they had created a new market (noise reduction systems and the microprocessor, respectively) both Dolby and Intel set out to differentiate their products using trade marks. By this means, they would still enjoy an effective monopoly after their patents had expired.

By the end of the first decade of the twentieth century, manufacturers had already developed a mechanism for the resolution of patent conflicts. Between companies this was the cross-licence; on an industry-wide scale, it was the cartel or patents pool. The die had been cast with agreements between the cable companies at the end of the nineteenth century and the market-sharing arrangements in the incandescent lamp industry. What really established the pattern of compromise and the emaciation of patents was the dispute between the Marconi and De Forest Companies. In this particular case, settlement in the customary manner was blocked by a maverick inventor (de Forest) who was not prepared to compromise. The net result was the creation of paranoia in the electronics industry about the preservation of freedom to use innovations. This was intensified by the intersecting nature of patent monopolies for inventions in this field.

Following an initial period of competition or monopoly (either response-time or intellectual-property-based) the market for each new semiconductor product has evolved into an oligopoly. The overall pattern of the industry has been one of a rolling wave of success, with certain companies riding the crest for a period before, eventually they sink into oblivion. At any given instant, the market structure exhibits the normal characteristics of the monopoly, oligopoly or imperfect competition of which it is composed, but, in the longer term, the market participants change.

11.13 CONCLUSION

All subsequent market structures involving an innovation evolve from a monopoly since, at the outset, an innovator, by definition, possesses a monopoly. The simplest monopoly is the one which results from the inability of potential competitors to respond instantaneously to an initiative (von Hippel 1988, p59). During this period of delay, the instigator of an innovation enjoys freedom from competition whilst others make their preparation to enter the market. Even if there is no other advantage to be derived from being first, the response-time monopoly which it creates provides a short period to initiate patterns of trade which can be the basis for subsequent control of an industry.

Another non-statutory monopoly, complementary to the response-time monopoly, is one created by setting a standard which others are effectively compelled to follow through economic pressures. If the pioneer in a market does something in a particular way, then there is likely to be a cost penalty in creating an alternative approach. Being first to market gives the innovator an opportunity to establish *de facto* standards which determine the subsequent patterns of trade. More effective marketing often can enable a technologically weaker innovation to succeed.

The statutory monopoly provided by intellectual property rights, and patents in particular, enables an organisation to take control of the conditions at the outset of an innovation. It may then use this control to establish a position of strength from which it can dominate the mature market. Once this position is reached, there is little incentive to innovate further. However, the development of the market is significantly influenced by initial conditions. Once it has established market power by means of patents, an organisation will often use other forms of intellectual property such as trade-marks or copyright to entrench its position rather than to provide resource for further innovation. Paradigm shifts are therefore more likely to originate from organisations which wish to displace the monopolist. With computer software, although the protection afforded by copyright subsists for seventy years from the death of the author, the term of protection is, in effect, much shorter because 'clean room' techniques enable competitors to produce clones which have substantially the same performance.

Innovation creates new markets, which, from the perspective of the innovator, reduces competition. In Holland, the absence of a patent system affected only the start up of operations. There were no fundamental inventions from Dutch inventors. Within fifty years, the small competitive companies had fallen prey to normal commercial pressures and had either become or were subsumed into much larger organisations. This leads to the conclusion that patents control only initial conditions – in the long term, other factors will determine the structure of a market.

Unless there is demand, an innovation will not succeed. In an oligopoly which has evolved from an innovation, there will *ipso facto* be demand which will be satisfied by the oligopolists collectively. By suppressing competitive response, the suppliers will therefore be in a position to increase their return at the expense of the consumers.

At a given instant in time, a snapshot of a technology-based market may reveal the characteristics of an oligopoly. A later snapshot will give the same result, but it is probable that the suppliers will be different. This is because, in a rapidly changing technological environment, major innovation comes from non-established suppliers. If the innovations are successful, the newcomers will join the establishment. In the short term, however, the day-to-day behaviour of the market will remain that of an oligopoly. Such changes will occur more rapidly in a market where there is rapid technological change and, in particular, if this is accompanied by significant growth.

A characteristic of systems with positive feedback is that they are potentially unstable. Damping is introduced by factors which exert a restraining influence – a resistor in an electronic circuit, friction in mechanical motion, or viscosity in a fluid system. An electronic circuit, the so-called flip-flop, which has two driven components with positive coupling between them, alternates between two states in response to a trigger pulse. The economic analogue of such an arrangement would, to coin a phrase, be a 'flip-flopoly'. Bipedal markets of this nature advance with a marching gait, with one component changing paradigms as the other generates rent. If then, an external influence is applied, the system switches to the complementary state.

Although Intel used the intellectual property inherent in the microprocessor and followed a clear strategy to develop and maintain its monopoly, there were also several elements of luck along the way. During the short time interval in which IBM was making its choice of processor for its first personal computer, Intel had available an eight-bit data bus version of a sixteen-bit processor, which offered a well-defined upgrade path. IBM was cash-rich when Intel needed capital investment. IBM needed Intel to survive and was prepared to take an equity stake. Because IBM was big, it provided confidence for the prospective purchasers of the new personal computers. Furthermore, IBM's dominant position in the industry meant that it was apprehensive of anti-trust action and therefore was constrained to make a no-strings-attached deal with Microsoft and Intel for supply of the software and processors for the PC. This left Intel and Microsoft free to sell to third parties and hence boost the market. Once the paradigm was established, the user base resisted change and the choice of Intel processor and Microsoft software became self-perpetuating. The down-side of this regime is that it is akin to pyramid selling. Future investment in R&D is dependent on revenues from existing users upgrading their systems. Eventually, a stage will be reached at which the users decide that what they have is adequate for their needs and they don't need to upgrade any further. At that stage, Humpty Dumpty will fall off the wall.

The ROM BIOS chip-controlling software was the one contribution to the PC design which was made by IBM and, so IBM thought, was fully protected by copyright. However, copyright law protects only against the act of copying. It does not prevent someone starting from scratch and designing a chip which performs an identical function. This is just what companies such as Phoenix did. They produced a ROM BIOS chip which emulated IBM's, thus providing the last piece in the jigsaw puzzle. Any manufacturer could therefore purchase all of the components and assemble a clone of the IBM PC. These producers did not have the overhead of IBM's huge operation and could sell profitably at a much lower price, which they then proceeded to do.

When the IBM personal computer was introduced, a new generation of users was not influenced by the 'FUD' factor which induced company management information service departments to buy IBM products rather than those of untried start-up companies, thus reducing the effect of market power and creating an environment which would be more receptive to innovation. Free choice amongst *purchasers* replaced the concerted attitudes of corporate policy makers.

Another way of being there first is to be there already. Possession of a suitable manufacturing infrastructure and control of the supply of the raw material for a key component were major factors in the British achieving world dominance in the manufacture and operation of undersea cables. Market power in an earlier technology may create favourable factors for a new development. In some instances, there will be a common precursor or manufacturing technique. In others, a government placing a military contract will patronise established companies rather than newcomers.

The stand-off between de Forest and Marconi was a result of intersecting patent monopolies. De Forest's Audion could not be made without infringing the claims of the thermionic diode patent owned by Marconi, whilst Marconi could not make an electronic amplifier without infringing de Forest's Audion patents. Fleming, during the period around the turn of the century, had worked as a consultant, first for Edison and latterly for Marconi. In the former position he acquired background knowledge when he performed experiments on the Edison Effect. He later made use of this knowledge when faced with the problem of designing a sensitive detector for radio waves. His choice of a solution was influenced by progressive deafness, which guided him towards a visual display rather than the audible output devices which had characterised telegraphic communications hitherto. The English common law environment, and its approach to the association between master and servant, created a relationship which required the assignment of the fruits of an employee's labour to the employer. As a result of this, the Marconi Company received the patent rights to the diode detector. De Forest, on the other hand, was working as a private individual when he invented the triode valve. His limited resources meant that he was unable to pay the renewal fees on his patent. Foreign patents therefore lapsed, but the US ones which, at that time, were not subject to the payment of maintenance fees, survived, leaving him with a weak patent portfolio to support his negotiating position.

Technological change was the key to market entry. A group of engineers with a good idea could easily get finance to set up a new company. If the new idea was bad, the company failed, but if the new idea offered significant advantages, the start-up could quickly dominate the industry – Fairchild Semiconductor had been founded in 1957; in 1960 it was the eighth largest transistor company in the world. In 1965, it was No. 3 and by 1968 it had become the world leader. One engineer, Jean Hoerni, was involved in four break-aways in ten years: Fairchild, Amelco, Intersil and Union Carbide, all of which achieved a measure of success.

A difference between the operations of Intel and Motorola as producers of microprocessors is that, although Motorola was able to take advantage of the same advances in infrastructure as Intel, it had no competition in its (smaller) market for the Apple Macintosh. It was therefore able to set its pricing policy to optimise its cash flow. Intel, on the other hand, was under constant threat from AMD and others, and had to use its response-time advantage to control its competitors' cash flows. It therefore needed to innovate to maintain its response-time monopoly.

12. Many a Mickle Makes a Model

Sticking to it is the genius! Any other bright-minded fellow can accomplish just as much, if he will stick like hell and remember nothing that's any good works by itself. You got to *make* the damn thing work.
Thomas Edison (Conot 1979, p 468)

Inventors must not bruise easy.
Charles Kettering, Head of General Motors

There are major funding problems in lithography forcing reduction of the number of choices. We no longer have the luxury of spending major R&D money on a large number of lithographic technologies. We need to work a little more smartly than in the past.
John R. Carruthers, Report of the March 1996 SPIE International Symposium

'Toshiba was the master of manufacturing CMOS. We spent half a billion deutschmarks bringing up the Regensburg wafer fab and Toshiba taught us how to manufacture in it. But it didn't ramp up as fast as expected. We couldn't understand why a process that was doing so well in Japan wasn't working in Germany.
We asked Toshiba to send over their best engineers. We still couldn't get the yields. We concluded that the trouble was the hydrogen peroxide used for cleaning,' remembers Knorr, 'so this was sent from Japan. Because it is explosive, the airlines told us they would carry only one litre bottles. Hundreds of bottles were sent over. Still it didn't work. We still had low yields.'
'We had one chemist. A really crazy chemist,' recalls Knorr with a smile, 'he suggested that the stabilising solution put into the hydrogen peroxide in Japan – in quantities of a few parts in a billion – to stabilise the peroxide did something to the process. We found out that this was the cause of the problem.'
Jurgen Knorr, president of Siemens Semiconductor Division interviewed by David Manners, *Electronics Weekly*, 19 March 1997

Aux nouvelles que j'apporte, vos beaux yeux vont pleurer.
George du Maurier, *Trilby*

12.1 INTRODUCTION

A prerequisite to predicting the course of future events is the creation of a model which leads to an understanding of the interrelationship of the factors which moulded the shape of the past and present. Thus armed, one can approach the task of developing a strategy for the future which is based on the knowledge of those factors most amenable to control and, equally importantly, the most propitious time to exert an influence.

The concept of modelling of dynamically changing systems is based on the premise that certain mathematical relationships provide appropriate descriptions of observed characteristics. Manipulation of those relationships will then lead to an understanding of how those systems develop under different conditions and this will provide tools for adapting those systems to meet pre-defined criteria.

The initial chapters set out the context and highlighted factors which could change the evolution of technological paradigms. Then case studies showed how inventions formed the foundation for growth of the economy. Subsequent chapters took illustrations from the case studies to draw out the characteristics of individual factors of invention. This chapter considers how these building blocks interact to create a model of the process of innovation.

12.2 INTERACTION BETWEEN SYSTEMS

As a first approach, an innovation may be viewed as a black box (Figure 12.1). Borrowing from accounting practice, this is treated as having a capital flow and a revenue stream. To maintain dimensional integrity, the capital account is separated into an information flow, which has an input of raw know-how and output of refined know-how, and a cash flow, which is fed by the capital provision and generates the innovation rent. The revenue account comprises a materials-and-goods flow consisting of a finished goods output derived from raw material input and a cash flow comprising the customary sales revenue and cost of sales input.

The black box model of innovation does not exist in isolation. A significant component of its structure is the communication of the capital and revenue flows with the external world. This outside environment comprises suppliers of goods and services, other innovations and the markets for which they are jointly competing. The success criterion is maximisation of the innovation rent and this is fed from its revenue flows.

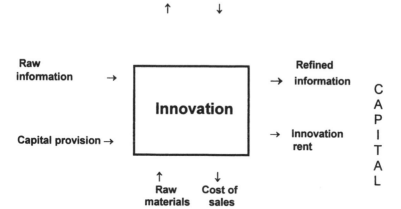

Figure 12.1   Black box model of innovation

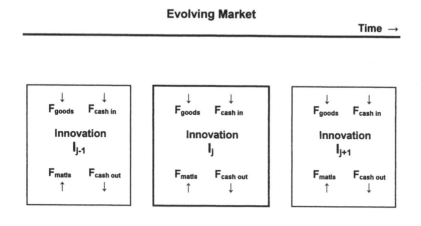

Figure 12.2   Innovation model interacting with the environment

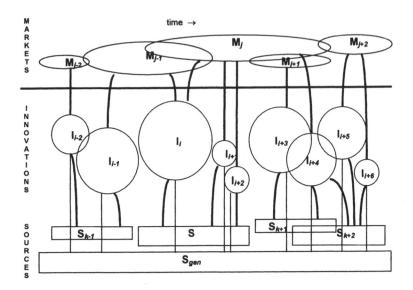

Figure 12.3   Schematic model of interactions between innovations and the environment

Successive innovations ...I_{i-2}, I_{i-1}, I_i, I_{i+1}, I_{i+2}... interact with a continuously evolving market and with a correspondingly evolving supply of infrastructure and sources of raw materials. Each innovation has its revenue flows of finished goods, raw materials, sales and cost-of-sales (Figure 12.2). For each flow, there is a complementary demand or offer to supply in the external environment (Figure 12.3). For instance, the finished goods flow is complemented by market demand. These two flows are in balance if there is no substitute product from another innovation system. On the other hand, the satisfaction of the market demand will be shared if a substitute innovation (say, I_{j+1}) appears. The requirement for artificial lighting was initially met by sources based on the luminous flame. When the electric lamp was introduced, first the arc, then the incandescent filament took a share of an expanding market. By corollary, an earlier innovation can establish a latent demand for a subsequent innovation. In practice, innovations will merge into one another and markets (...M_j...) and sources of supply (...S_k...) may be shared. Typically, there will be items of infrastructure (S_{gen}), such as utilities, which will be common to all innovations.

12.3 MATHEMATICAL MODELLING OF ALGORITHMS

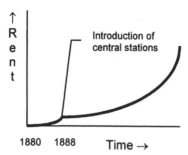

Figure 12.4   Variation of innovation rent with changing regulatory environment

Each innovation will have a unique logistic equation for innovation rent. An example of how an individual factor can influence the overall relationship is illustrated in Figure 12.4.   Edison and Swan introduced the incandescent filament lamp around 1880.   Initially, each installation was a stand-alone operation with its own electricity generating plant.   A few central power stations were constructed, but the enactment of the 1882 Electric Lighting Act caused a hiatus in further investment.   Growth of electric lighting therefore followed a learning curve based on the economics of individual installations.   In 1888, the penal provisions on reversion to local authority control were repealed and, once again, entrepreneurs began to construct central power stations.   The logistic curve of electric lighting then changed to one based on the economics of central power stations and distribution.

Other factors will influence the logistic curve in different ways.   For example, the laws of physics may create absolute limits to extrapolation of an inventive concept.   These limits will not, however, be reached instantaneously, but will be approached in an asymptotic manner as know-how is accumulated.   When the planar process for the manufacture of transistors was first developed, the line width of the metallisation which constituted the means of interconnection of components was around 100μm – the present generation of integrated circuit is based on a line width of around 0.2μm.   Whereas in 1960 a silicon chip contained just one device, nowadays there are many millions of transistors on each one.   A doubling of the achieved density of devices takes place every eighteen months. However, this increase cannot carry on indefinitely due to the Fresnel limit which optical diffraction places on the minimum size of features which can be resolved and due to the quantum nature of conduction imposed by the electrical charge of an electron, which becomes apparent at very low current levels.

Since each innovation will have a unique set of factors, determined initially by physical parameters, the status of the socio-economic environment and the psychology of the associated facilitators, it will not be possible to generalise the relationships which characterise its logistics. The development of these relationships for specific paradigms has already been set out in qualitative terms in previous chapters, but a further insight may be obtained by performing an initial audit of the factors to ascertain which parameters and variables are likely to have the major influence in each individual case. Observation, possibly supplemented by intuition, will lead to a series of statements concerning their interdependence. Curve fitting methods could then permit these relationships to be set out as mathematical equations, subject to a caveat concerning the limits within which such equations are applicable.

12.4 THE PROCESS OF MODEL BUILDING

Innovation exhibits many characteristics of biological systems (Mokyr 1990). For example, inventions, like species, emerge, wax, wane and die out. Progress is a binary decision process – once a decision is taken, the opportunity cost of reworking that decision may be prohibitive. Innovations follow technological paradigms which undergo transitions analogous to genetic mutations. Success is a process of survival of the fittest; provision of capital is analogous to supply of food or nutrients. Techniques for modelling biological systems may therefore be appropriate for modelling the dynamics of innovation.

According to Gold (1977), a model exhibits two specific properties. It is made up from a number of elements each of which corresponds to a component of the original system. For at least some of those elements, there exists a relationship which is analogous to that of the corresponding components of the original system. This is not a requirement that *every* element in the system should have its corresponding component in the model, nor that all relationships should exhibit exact correspondence. It is sufficient that the correlation meets the purposes of the model.

If the model is correlative, its purpose is to summarise and describe this relationship in a manner that may be used for prediction and control. The model-building process comprises gathering data which are considered to be relevant, postulating a relationship or relationships between variables and then testing to see how well these relationships predict observed data. If the correlation is not good, a different relationship is postulated and a further iteration performed.

One technique is to plot the relationships graphically and to make a qualitative assessment. For interpolation between data points, the most appropriate representation will probably be some form of curve, but it may be sufficient to adopt a straight line. Alternative descriptions may serve equally well, the selection being made according to the circumstances of the case. Extrapolation poses great problems, particularly with exponentially varying data. If the wrong assumptions are made, the results may be wildly inaccurate.

As well as indicating the relationship between variables, an explanatory model must throw light on the system's underlying causal mechanism. Predictions from the ensuing mathematical relationship are tested against observed data. Resolution of any disagreement between the model and the measurements requires an analysis of the physical basis of the discrepancy. Again the model building is an iterative process. When there is sufficient confidence, the model may be used extrapolatively.

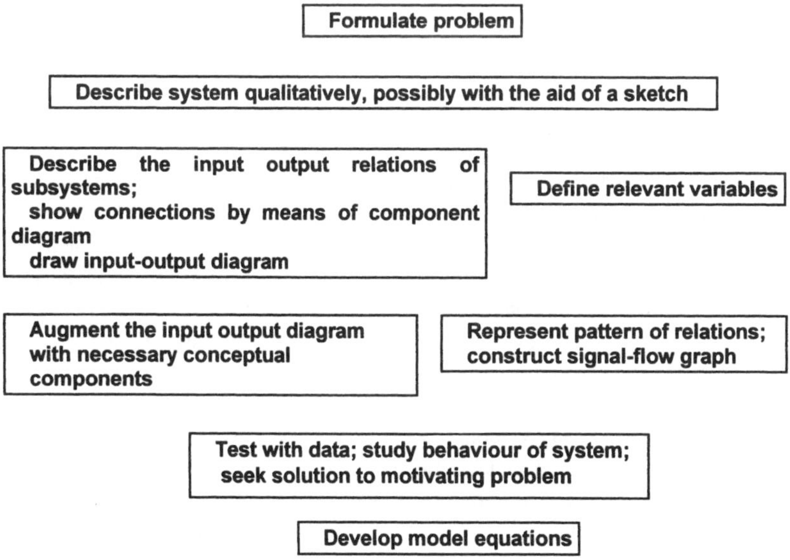

| Formulate problem |

| Describe system qualitatively, possibly with the aid of a sketch |

| Describe the input output relations of subsystems; show connections by means of component diagram draw input-output diagram | | Define relevant variables |

| Augment the input output diagram with necessary conceptual components | | Represent pattern of relations; construct signal-flow graph |

| Test with data; study behaviour of system; seek solution to motivating problem |

| Develop model equations |

Source   Gold 1977, p26

Figure 12.5   Outline of the process of building a mathematical model

With a mathematical model, each stage must follow logically from its predecessor. The end result is then a direct consequence of the starting assumptions. The model which is selected to represent a system may only be applicable under a particular set of circumstances.

If the mathematical analysis is used to test the validity of the starting assumptions, each stage within the analysis must be tested. A discrepancy leads to one of the following conclusions (Gold 1977, p15). Either a mistake has been made in the formal mathematical development, the starting assumptions are incorrect and/or constitute a too drastic oversimplification, intuition about the field is inadequately developed, or a penetrating new principle has been discovered.

A model does not necessarily exhibit all of the properties of its parent system, partly due to the idealisations and approximations which were made during its construction. In order to rationalise the model-building process, some interactions may be neglected or simplifying assumptions made about interactions between its components (*quaere* – the economists' *ceteris paribus* presumptions which were rejected by the initial hypothesis?). Such simplified models still serve a useful purpose provided the distortion they introduce is either discounted or eliminated. Models may also be rationalised by substitution of working approximations for the underlying mathematical relationships.

The procedure for constructing an explanatory model is to separate the system into its components, analyse the behaviour of those individual elements and then to study their interaction. After the initial formulation of the problem and the qualitative description of the system, the relevant components and variables are defined, broken down into subsystems and their interactions identified. The variables will be the inputs and outputs of the individual components. Their dimensions and relationships form the basis for construction of the model. This may be summarised in a flow diagram, which is represented by dependency statements of the form $X = X(A, B, C, ...)$. Analysis of the subsystems will lead to a series of equations setting out the relationships of the variables and thus give rise to the first model of the complete system.

Decomposition of a system is a process of compromise. A finer level gives simpler components, but more complex interactions. Subsystems do not have to correspond to physically identifiable elements of the overall system. They may thus be chosen to facilitate construction of the model.

It is convenient to represent the model diagrammatically as a series of interconnected boxes. Interconnections represent inputs and outputs. Any system having a given form of input–output relations and a common connection topography will have the same mathematical description. This may be expressed as a flow diagram and converted to a computer simulation.

A model may be regarded as having been conceived to explain the relation between the overall input from, and output to, the environment. It can be modified to obtain a different output or to increase its sensitivity to a particular type of input.

Parameters are the part of the structure of a system which determine relationships between the inputs and outputs. They may change with time as, for example, has the attitude of public policy to the private exercise of monopoly power. The values of parameters (and their changes) must be specified separately in order to determine uniquely the output that results from a given input. The estimation of the values of the parameters is an important part of the investigation of a natural system. The distinction between parameters and overall inputs is not always clear. In such cases, a pragmatic solution is to treat quantities that vary greatly as inputs and those which remain more nearly constant as parameters. Alternatively, the distinction between microeconomic and macroeconomic changes may be used for guidance.

Variables, which are not always observable or measurable, define the instantaneous condition or state of a system. The overall output depends on the instantaneous values of the variables.

A distinction between inputs, outputs, parameters and state variables may be made on the basis of the mutual dependencies which are specified by the equations of the model. Inputs and parameters depend upon none of the other quantities, outputs depend upon inputs, parameters and state variables, whilst state variables depend upon inputs, parameters and each other.

A signal flow graph represents pictorially the causal relationships between state variables. It aids visualisation of how the effect of changing a particular variable propagates. If the path contains a closed loop, then the feedback will have the effect of stabilising the system, if it exerts a negative influence, or of causing it to become unstable, if it exerts a positive influence.

Finally, an important part of the definition of any variable is the determination of its dimensions. The equations that epitomise relations between physical entities must be dimensionally consistent. By corollary, the requirement of dimensional correctness will often serve as a guide to the choice of the structure of an equation.

12.5 ALGORITHMS UNDERLYING THE MODEL

Tables 12.1 and 12.2 set out the elements of a model of innovation, showing the factors of the capital and revenue flows which, for reasons of dimensional integrity, have been separated as cash flows, goods and materials flows and knowledge flows.

Table 12.1   The components of a model of the dynamics of innovation

Element	Symbol	Interactions
Flows		
Capital provision	F_{Cin}	
Innovation rent, dividend	F_{Cout}	F_{Rin} F_{Rout} V_{MS}
Knowledge input	F_{Kin}	F_{Cin} P_{Fac}
Know-how out	F_{Kout}	V_{KH} V_{InD} P_{InS}
Cost of sales	F_{Rout}	F_{GMin} (V_{MS})
Sales	F_{Rin}	F_{GMout} V_{MS} P_{IP} P_{DM} P_{RM} P_{Reg}
		P_{Fac} P_{Mil} P_{Gov}
Raw materials	F_{GMin}	V_{Inf} P_{Phy} P_{InS}
Finished goods	F_{GMout}	V_{KH} V_{WC} V_{Inf} V_{WiP} V_{InD} V_{MS}
		P_{Phy} P_{DM}
Variables		
Know-how	V_{KH}	F_{Kin} P_{Fac} (P_{Mil})
Working capital	V_{WC}	F_{Cin} F_{Cout} F_{Rin} F_{Rout} F_{GMin}
Infrastructure	V_{Inf}	V_{InD} F_{Cin} F_{Kin} F_{Kout} F_{Rin} F_{Rout}
		P_{InS}
Work-in-progress	V_{WiP}	F_{Cin} F_{Kin} F_{Rin} F_{Rout} F_{GMin} F_{GMout}
Derived inventions	V_{InD}	P_{InS} P_{Phy} P_{Fac} P_{Mil} P_{Gov}
Market structure	V_{MS}	V_{InD} P_{IP} P_{DM} P_{RM} P_{CL} P_{Reg}
		P_{Mil} P_{Gov}

The innovation rent is the net capital cash flow

$$F_{Cout} = F_{Cin} + F_{Rin} - F_{Rout} \qquad (12.1)$$

$$= F_{Cin}(P_{InS}, P_{Fac})$$
$$+ F_{Rin}(V_{KH}, V_{WC}, V_{Inf}, V_{WiP}, V_{InD}, V_{MS}, P_{Phy},$$
$$P_{DM}, P_{IP}, P_{DM}, P_{RM}, P_{Reg}, P_{Fac}, P_{Mil}, P_{Gov})$$
$$- F_{Rout}(V_{Inf}, P_{Phy}, P_{InS}, V_{MS})$$

For a successful innovation, $F_{Cout} \gg F_{Cin}$, i.e. the initial capital input may be ignored and Equation 12.1 reduces to

$$F_{Cout} = F_{Rin} - F_{Rout} \qquad (12.2)$$
$$= F_{Rin}(V_{KH}, V_{WC}, V_{Inf}, V_{WiP}, V_{InD}, V_{MS}, P_{Phy},$$
$$P_{DM}, P_{IP}, P_{DM}, P_{RM} P_{Reg}, P_{Fac}, P_{Mil}, P_{Gov})$$
$$- F_{Rout}(V_{Inf}, V_{MS}, P_{Phy}, P_{InS})$$

Table 12.2   Temporal dependency of model parameters

Parameters	Symbol	Time dependency	
Seminal inventions	P_{InS}	Yes	Serendipitous, environment-sensitive, may be dependent on inventors
Properties of materials and the laws of physics	P_{Phy}	No	
Statutory monopolies	P_{IP}	Yes	Microeconomic (renewal fees, statutory term), Macroeconomic (new laws)
De facto monopolies	P_{DM}	Yes	Microeconomic
Response time monopolies	P_{RM}	Yes	Microeconomic
Competition law	P_{CL}	Yes	Microeconomic, Macroeconomic (new laws, public attitudes)
Physical regulation	P_{Reg}	Yes	Microeconomic, Macroeconomic (new laws, public attitudes)
Facilitators	P_{Fac}	Yes	Discrete steps (hiring and departure of facilitators)
Military procurement	P_{Mil}	Yes	Oligocratic
Government intervention	P_{Gov}	Yes	May be oligocratic

This gives an indication of the interaction between the innovation rent and the various state variables and control parameters. The actual factors, and the manner in which they play a part, will vary from innovation to innovation. However, some general statements can be made concerning the relationships. For instance, the efficiency of converting input raw materials to finished goods will improve with increasing know-how. This dependency will have some components which, to a first order, will vary linearly, but there could also be step changes if new materials, or possibly a different method of processing, were introduced. At low levels of efficiency, that is, at the initial stages of an innovation, mathematical methods used for evaluation of properties of dilute solutions, in other words, treating the variables as independent, might be appropriate, but, as the efficiency becomes greater, relationships will be more complex. At the latter stage, ignoring the effect of certain variables and their interactions would produce an inaccurate conclusion.

12.6 THE COMPONENTS OF A MODEL OF THE DYNAMICS OF INNOVATION

Modelling the dynamics of innovation is ultimately a Gestalt problem, that is, one which involves a perceptual pattern or structure possessing qualities as a whole and which cannot be presented merely as a sum of its parts. However, creating a model requires first that the system be analysed and the critical components identified. Their interrelationships are then explored, at least on a qualitative level, to provide intuitive criteria by means of which the model may be assessed.

Variables include knowledge and experience (know-how), working capital, infrastructure, work-in-progress and market structure. Control parameters will vary from innovation to innovation, but may include properties of materials, the laws of physics, inventions, statutory, *de facto* and response-time monopolies, competition law and physical regulation, facilitators (inventors, entrepreneurs and product champions), military procurement and government intervention.

In general form, the logistic equation of flows associated with innovation is given by

$$\frac{dF_i}{dt} = F_i(V_1, \ldots, V_n; P_1, \ldots, P_m) \tag{12.3}$$

where V_i are the system variables and $P_1, \ldots, P_m$ are control parameters which are imposed by the external world. Both the system variables and the control parameters are complex non-linear functions. Table 12.1 summarises the interactions between the components of the rudimentary model illustrated in Figure 12.1

A variety of methodologies is available for the construction of models. In practice, a combination of approaches may be adopted, different techniques being apposite for particular subsystems. One way is to construct a correlative model of the relation between two (or more) variables, that is, of the behaviour of the individual component of the system. This correlative model of the individual subsystem then becomes a part of the structure of the explanatory model of the entire system. It is useful only in explaining how individual components interact to produce the behaviour of the system. Correlative models in this context do not explain how the behaviour of the components – and, therefore, of the system – changes when conditions are varied.

Mechanistic and theoretical arguments are based on a knowledge of a causative relation between the variables. Initially, the relationship may be postulated. If the hypothetical model survives the test of agreement between the observed behaviour of the system and the behaviour of the model, it can be adopted with confidence. If there is insufficient information to hypothesise a fixed relation between two variables, it may be possible to build a model on the basis of average or expected relationships. Although the former is usually much easier, often sufficiently accurate and by far the most used, a general understanding of the underlying probability structure will allow a deeper insight into the mechanics of the system.

Even if there are insufficient data to construct a correlative or theoretical model, there is often enough information of a broad nature to be able to make confident statements about the relation between two variables. For example, it may be said that, at the outset of an innovation, patents will play a significant part in determining selling price, whereas, in a mature or dying market, their influence is played out. This may be represented in a three-dimensional graph relating incremental selling price to age of a patent and product life cycle. At the outset the ordinate is high, whilst after expiry of the patent or the end of the product life, it is zero.

In drawing the graph, very general knowledge is used to deduce the nature of the relation at the extremes. Assuming that the relation is unlikely to change in an abrupt way, a smooth curve is drawn to connect the behaviour at the two extremes. The precise shape of the intermediate region may rest on observation or be largely a matter of intuition. Qualitatively rationalised mathematical relations are especially important in the early stages of a study, in order to build a basis for further investigation. An attempt is made to match the shape to a mathematical equation, the curve of which has the same qualitative behaviour, so that the relation may be considered in the mathematical framework of the model for the whole system.

The following sections consider the contribution of the factors of innovation and their mutual interactions to the logistical equation.

12.6.1 Flows

The genesis of innovation is a germ of an idea which triggers the seminal invention. Usually this will set off a chain reaction in which the mind of an inventor collates the latent knowledge which has accumulated, possibly over many years. Once the cognition threshold is reached, the flash of inspiration will be released.

During the evolution of an innovation, know-how will continue to be acquired. It will be concerned with methods of enhancing the revenue stream – improving the processing of raw materials to give higher yields of finished goods, reducing manufacturing costs to give increased profit.

Refined information is an additional reward of an innovation. Instead of being retained within the enterprise, it may be transferred as an input to a further innovation or sold to other businesses wishing to participate in the current innovation. Export of know-how in this way is a form of capital transfer since, by its nature, know-how, once passed on, cannot be recovered.

The repository of know-how is the minds of inventors and other technical personnel. Such people come and go, carrying with them their accumulated knowledge. The flow of people is therefore a component of the information stream. On occasion, this may be of major significance, as it was in the case of the Fairchildren of Silicon Valley.

Leakage of information plays an important part in many innovations. Communication takes place on an informal basis and through the medium of publication in books and journals and papers read before learned societies. The effect is not entirely negative, since this communication is two-way. What it does mean, however, is that a company cannot rely on retaining the commercial advantage of keeping know-how secret, since employees will come and go.

Capital is an essential component of any new operation. With an innovation, it is required to set up the means of production, to finance the purchase of raw materials until a cash flow from sales revenue is established, and to create the infrastructure. In the latter case, direct finance is not always necessary. If, as with the Japanese *keiretsu* or the organisation of the motor industry, an operation is not vertically integrated, the prospect of a return on investment will encourage the suppliers either to raise capital themselves or to generate their own finance organically.

Once an operation is up and running, cash will be generated from sales. Some will be allocated to increase working capital, whilst the remainder will either be transferred to reserves or distributed as dividend or innovation rent.

As well as the customary cash transfers, revenue flows are represented by a product stream in which the value added by the enterprise is responsible for the excess of sales revenue over cost of sales. In knowledge-based industries, such as computer software, the added value may be in the form of a know-how element which, strictly speaking, should be regarded as a capital disposal. However, due to intellectual property rights (principally copyright) a licence to use the same item of knowledge may be sold to many people, thereby converting a capital sale into a revenue transaction.

12.6.2 Variables

12.6.2.1 Know-how

Knowledge and experience are clearly primary variables in the evolution of an innovation. At the outset, knowledge is small. As the technology matures, its magnitude and effectiveness increase. Experience is gained by a gradual process of accretion. This means that efficiency of manufacture will advance by small incremental stages. Synergism, relevance to an organisation's core activities and critical mass are important factors in deciding whether information will be utilised.

Know-how without communication is of no value. Lilienfeld devised methods of making solid-state amplifier devices. He did not succeed in manufacturing them and went on to pastures new. When Bell Laboratories set out on their quest for what was to become the transistor, they did not follow Lilienfeld's path as his ideas had already faded into obscurity. Instead, Shockley and his co-workers blazed their own trail. It was not until many years later, when litigation arose ([1965] RPC 335), that they considered the impact of Lilienfeld's work. Similarly, at the time that they were actively developing the carbon filament lamp, neither Swan nor Edison was aware of Göbel's earlier work.

Knowledge is a capital asset. Retained within the business as a trade secret, it will inhibit the uptake of an innovation by competitors. Alternatively it may be exploited by transfer to others, either as a direct sale for cash or kind, or the value may be realised gradually through licensing and a royalty on sales. On the revenue account, greater experience, for example, of handling of raw materials, will lead to higher yields and, thereby, gross profits. Maintaining a lead over competitors increases relative profitability and, through response-time delays, offers a market leader a degree of extra control. Knowledge also becomes stale. Unless continually replenished through R&D or hiring of personnel, it is therefore a wasting asset.

The utility of knowledge does not always increase monotonously with its acquisition. It may be accumulated gradually and then recognised suddenly through the phenomenon of *Geistesblitz* (flash of inspiration). Edison discovered a range of potential precursors of radio – the Edison Effect, the Grasshopper telegraph and the Black Box – but failed to convert these elements into a working communications system, probably because he was concentrating on the development of the electric lamp.   Wireless was developed by Marconi, who made it his primary focus of attention.

Latent knowledge may also become accessible as a result of a trigger event.   During the second world war many companies gained experience of techniques, such as metal whisker fabrication, electrode formation and device encapsulation, for the manufacture of germanium and silicon diodes which were used as detectors in radar receivers.   As soon as Bell Laboratories announced the point-contact transistor, these other manufacturers were able to redirect this know-how and make transistors themselves.   Immediately after Edison and Swan publicised their pioneering work, Lane-Fox, Sawyer and Man, Maxim and others all had the ability to exploit the embryonic invention.

Edison and Upton could see no useful application for the Edison Effect lamp, but Fleming, who was afflicted with progressive deafness and needed a non-auditory detector for wireless signals, could.   He recalled his experiments on the Edison Effect some twenty years earlier and realised that it would solve both of his problems (Fleming 1934).   Fortuitously, the thermionic diode was more efficient than alternative devices which were currently available and so it became widely adopted – serendipity may also play a part in the acquisition of knowledge.

A perspicacious agent who will recognise and develop the idea is a necessary factor in the exploitation of theoretically derived inventions, the emergence of which is contingent on the existence of correspondingly heroic inventors – every Trilby needs a Svengali.   This agent may be the inventor himself, who performs the role of product champion.   A routine invention, which requires only the extrapolation of existing thought processes, is relatively common, whilst the lateral transition or topological manipulation falls between these extremes.

Innovators' attitude to information is paradoxical.   Although technical knowledge is a valuable strategic tool, they frequently give it away to competitors through the medium of learned societies, conferences and publication in technical journals.   This diffusion may be the legacy of the mediaeval scholars, but its advantages are not immediately apparent. Perhaps it serves just as a taster, because the practice of selling know-how is also widespread.   Perhaps it is an acceptance of the inevitable, because secrecy is difficult to maintain due to free movement of technical personnel. Perhaps also, it is because information rapidly becomes stale and response-time delay is perceived as providing an adequate safeguard when know-how is passed on.

12.6.2.2 Derived inventions

Following the seminal invention, ideas arise for improvements, different applications of the original idea, use of alternative materials and improved manufacturing processes and machinery. All of these innovations will have the effect of increasing incoming revenue flow. Particularly in the Schumpeter B-stage, inventions will be concerned with improving such

Table 12.3   Characteristics of inventions

Type	Inventor	Rent magnitude	Risk	Examples
Serendipitous	Any	any level	High	Point-contact transistor, Edison's improved light bulb diode detector High T_c superconductors Buckminster-fullerenes
Theoretical	Usually higher intellect	Any magnitude, potentially large	Low	AC machines junction transistor Atomic bomb Laser
Extrapolation	Familiar with technology	Any magnitude usually small	Low	Tetrode, pentode, hexode and heptode valves High-efficiency alloyed emitter 8086, 80286, 80386, 80486 and Pentium microprocessors Higher fullerenes SiGe mixed crystal transistors
Product extension	Familiar with technology	Incremental	Low	Transistors used for space programme
Topological manipulation	Lateral thinker	Any magnitude	Low	'Low-energy' light bulbs Flip-chip transistor
Analogue	Familiar with other technology	Any level	Low	Nernst lamp Silicon transistor Gallium arsenide Integrated circuit
Emulation	Lateral thinker	Any level	Low	Incandescent filament lamp
Non-working, 'half-baked'	Acquisitive of patents	Nil or latent	High	Edison's fluorescent lamp 'Edison Effect'

factors as yields, process control and use of materials, all of which lead to higher profitability.

Derived inventions fall into a wide variety of categories, the characteristics of which are set out in Table 12.3. By definition, an extrapolation invention will effect a marginal improvement over its parent. Similarly, the magnitude of markets for inventions by topological manipulation, product extension, analogy and emulation will, at least initially, also be set by the market for the seminal development.

12.6.2.3 Working capital

Although innovation cannot survive without working capital, inventions do not usually founder for lack of financial backing. There may be an initial period of delay and uncertainty but, if an idea has sufficient potential, cash will usually be forthcoming. There is often a threshold effect as an innovation has to achieve a critical mass before it can survive. The level of investment required will vary with the technology – new software requires relatively little; a microprocessor plant may cost billions of dollars; in its day, the incandescent lamp required capital on a social scale to provide power stations, means of distribution, a system of metering and education of consumers.

An innovation which needs an extensive infrastructure acquires it by creating the prospect of innovation rent for its providers. Due to supply logistics, a demand for large amounts of capital may, however, exert a moderating influence on the rate of progress of the innovation – successive generations of silicon chip were contingent on the development of corresponding advances in photolithographic technology.

Good communications between innovators and their financiers are essential to preserve the confidence which is a dominant component in the provision of capital. Confidence is also enhanced by intellectual property rights, which serve to increase competitors' costs of market entry because the resulting monopoly makes it possible to charge a premium price to consumers or enables the proprietor to exact a royalty for the right to use the invention or simply block the path for would-be competitors.

12.6.2.4 Infrastructure

Infrastructure is closely linked with working capital, since one of the barriers to progress of an innovation is the cost of developing the associated infrastructure. This is particularly the case with pioneer inventions, which frequently have to begin all associated developments from scratch. To exploit the incandescent filament lamp, it was necessary to install power stations and distribution cables, to create a standard system of plugs and sockets for mounting the lamps and even to devise a method of measuring the quantity of electricity supplied to consumers.

The negative effect of the capital demands for the infrastructure provision will not be linear, since the costs for a mainstream development will generate innovation rents for the providers, thus serving to accelerate the investment. This Keynesian influence is partly responsible for the success of coupled paradigms since, so far as at least one component of the pair is concerned, the cost of infrastructure is discounted.

12.6.2.5 Work-in-progress

In the initial stages of its development, an end-product tends to be of variable quality and it is necessary to carry out a screening process to achieve a desired performance specification. As production matures, the certainty of meeting target characteristics increases. This is of particular importance when the product has to meet an externally imposed standard – for instance, light bulbs have to operate on the public electricity supply at 110 or 240 volts; integrated circuits are connected to power supplies of 3.3 or 5 volts – but, in any event, increased certainty of outcome (yield of product capable of the desired performance) will make a positive contribution to profitability.

An asymptotic limit to the learning curve will be set by external constraints such as the laws of physics and properties of materials. A shift in technological paradigm may ultimately be required to remove this block. The transition could, however, be precipitated earlier by felicitous economics. As efficiency of production increases with time, the phasing of the introduction of improvements will vary from manufacturer to manufacturer. If one can gain a lead over his competitors, he will achieve profitable operation at an earlier time. This will create an opportunity to adopt a predatory pricing policy which will, in turn, have a bearing on the profitability of the competitors.

12.6.2.6 Market structure

Market structure provides the environment within which innovations succeed or fail. It is moulded by factors such as finance, intellectual property monopolies and effectiveness of communications but, most importantly, by past history. It evolves gradually as an integrated response to all of these disparate influences.

Developing the biological analogy, innovation markets have a 'lion' phase when the initial patentee makes a killing and enjoys the exclusive fruits of a monopoly. Then there is a 'hyena' phase, when a pack of predators, often led by one who is bolder than the rest, circle round and eventually share the market which has been developed, possibly even driving off the original innovator. Finally, there is a 'vulture' phase, where the market has decayed and only the bones remain to be picked over by those who are content to take a profit where they find it. Occasionally, there may even be a 'phoenix' stage where an innovation, such as the gas mantle, rises from the ashes of a decaying technology. Such an innovation may serve as a springboard for expansion or it may simply delay the introduction of an alternative paradigm.

Innovation is associated with a temporary monopoly, which may result from the delay whilst competitors react, or from *de facto* standards which are created by being first in a field. This effect may be enhanced by the statutory grant of intellectual property rights. These temporary periods of exclusive control provide an opportunity for the innovator to initiate changes in the market structure. If he rapidly establishes a dominant position, he may exploit the characteristics of the learning curve to control competitors' income. By utilising the weapon of premature obsolescence, the market leader will have an opportunity to limit the cash flow of the followers. If this can be achieved, he will establish an indefinite monopoly. It will, however, be quasi-stable and will persist only so long as repeated innovation keeps his operations profitable whilst those of his competitors are starved of cash.

Like eddies and vortices in a river, patterns of trade persist long after the perturbing factors which created them have ceased to exist. The makers of a product which is superseded will usually be among the initial participants in the successor market, although some years later their relative status is likely to have waned. In general, however, the eventual steady state will be an oligopoly, which will emerge gradually when short-term influences, such as patents, have died away.

A quasi-steady state will develop in some markets. An apt example is the manufacture of transistors during the Schumpeter A-stage of development, before silicon planar technology was introduced. After the initial invention of the point-contact transistor, and partly due to the influence of US anti-trust laws which encouraged many early-day entrants to the market, a succession of different technologies became *de facto* standards for fabrication of semiconductor devices – first the grown-junction, then the alloyed-junction, then the drift-field transistor, followed by the post-alloy-diffused and the double-diffused mesa transistors. At any one time, the industry was an oligopoly, but as new lead technologies evolved, different manufacturers came to the fore and others fell by the wayside. During this period, the industry was growing at a rate of

30 per cent per annum and the innovations came from start-up or break-away companies. (It is a characteristic of oligopolies that mould-breaking innovations frequently come from without.) The market may be categorised as an 'ocean-roller' market – the wave continues to move forward, but its physical constituents appear, rise to the peak and then fall away.

Some markets have a bipedal structure and are based on linked innovations (as, for example, railways and the telegraph, the hardware and software of personal computers, or silicon chips and the photolithographic apparatus used in their manufacture). Progress in one component facilitates advances in the other, the net overall effect being that of a positive feedback loop. Systems of this nature resemble, and may indeed be simulated by, an electronic relaxation oscillator. They will tend to expand rapidly unless there is some dissipative influence which serves to dampen the response. Software writers created increasingly complex programs as the power of personal computers increased. Consumers eagerly purchased successive generations of computers to run the ever more sophisticated software. When eventually they decided that current performance was adequate for their needs (usually in the absence of a new 'killer application') the cash flow to the suppliers dried up, creating a recession in the industry. In such a bistable regime, where progress is by way of paradigm shifts undertaken alternately by a primary innovator and his supplier, the two markets may develop into quasi-stable monopolies of increasing strength.

Both bipedal-market and premature-obsolescence, quasi-stable monopolies will ultimately be curtailed by external limitations, such as optical limits in photolithography or charge-carrier drift velocities in semiconductors.

The actions of an innovator are constrained by a desire to maximise returns. If he has an effective monopoly, there will be little incentive for him to innovate. New paradigms are therefore more likely to originate with competitors wishing to create a substitute market. Once market power has been acquired, however, it may be used to purchase later inventions, thereby perpetuating and strengthening a position of dominance. Lewis Carroll's Red Queen would empathise with the market leader – it *is* possible to keep ahead of the pack and earn a 25 per cent return on turnover, but an ever-increasing investment is required to achieve this.

The 1960s saw the start of a move to global markets. The emergence of new industries such as the manufacture of semiconductor devices and their derivatives, computers and consumer electronics, accompanied by political initiatives, including the 1962 US Trade Expansion Act and the Kennedy Round of the General Agreement on Tariffs and Trade which reduced import duties by around 40 per cent, underpinned this expansion. One can discern a political parallel to market evolution economics, in which international treaties and bilateral agreements take the part of intellectual property monopolies. For instance, the USA enacted semiconductor mask protection laws and, in effect, imposed them on its trading partners to protect its integrated circuit industry – harmonisation of laws, particularly in the field of intellectual property, dragged the developing nations into the twentieth century. A consequence of the success of these sunrise industries was that Pacific Rim countries decided that it would be in their national interests to be active players in the industries which would form the foundation for the information economy which is about to succeed the manufacturing and agricultural economies which have been the basis for trade in the past. In contrast to corresponding initiatives in Europe, this intervention was successful. This may be attributed to the fact that a hungry man has a greater motivation than one who is comfortably off and that motivation is an essential element for success.

By analogy with the oligopoly of economics, the term oligocracy may be coined to describe the political interactions which are currently shaping the global economy.

12.6.3 Parameters

12.6.3.1 Seminal inventions

Seminal inventions are unpredictable. Tesla's alternating current machines generated innovation rents immediately and they grew to be of huge magnitude. Superconductivity was discovered by Kamerling-Onnes in 1911. It received a boost in 1986, with Bednorz and Müller's development of the so-called high-temperature superconductors. A report of the first truly commercial sale appeared in 1997, but this related only to a niche market but a 'killer application' which will provide the impetus to carry it forward as a self-sustaining success has still not emerged. Buckminster-fullerenes offer a similar potential, but are, currently, still a solution in search of a problem. The potential success of the microprocessor and the memory chip was apparent from the beginning as their fabrication was based on extrapolation of current technology and their markets were expandable if development of the fabrication technology fulfilled its promise.

There is no apparent relationship between the magnitude of the innovation rent and the likelihood of its receipt – the fortuitous combination of a stable, glassy oxide, a diamond crystal structure which would accommodate donor and acceptor impurities to release charge carriers having viable mobilities and a forbidden band-gap of the right magnitude to fabricate stable inverse-biased diodes, which made silicon such a suitable material for semiconductor device fabrication, yielded returns which transformed the global economy over a period of several decades. The point-contact transistor, which was the first tentative step along the road to the integrated circuit, was also the result of a chance observation, although, in this instance, the lifetime of the resulting product was only a few years as it was rapidly superseded by the junction transistor.

Inventions which are derived as a result of theoretical deliberations tend to be blockbusters – literally, in the case of the atomic bomb. An explanation for this is that such inventions are a self-selecting set – minor, theoretically derived inventions would not be reported and, possibly, would not even be identified as falling into that particular category.

12.6.3.2 Properties of materials and the laws of physics

> Human judges can show mercy. But against the laws of nature, there is no
> appeal.
> Arthur C. Clarke, *Maelstrom II* (1965)

Development of an innovation is constrained by the laws of nature. A simple example is that riding a bicycle requires more effort when pedalling uphill and will be easier if the route lies downhill, but, no matter how hard the rider pedals, he is unlikely to take off and fly (or at least, not very far) because the energy required is beyond the limits of the human body, whilst the aerodynamic shape of the rider and bicycle is inappropriate for the purpose.

An enabling discovery may act as a trigger for a new line of development. In particular, new materials may possess properties which make improvements feasible, create a viable solution to a previously insurmountable problem or simply change the economics in a favourable manner.

Silicon forms substantially perfect single crystals which can be doped with donor and acceptor impurities by diffusion, ion implantation or epitaxial deposition, to form localised regions with different conductivity characteristics. It also has a stable, glassy oxide which serves as a passivating layer to stabilise surface characteristics of the crystals. As a result of these physical and chemical properties, a wide variety of electronic devices can be formed in a silicon wafer. These can, in turn, be interconnected to act as building blocks for complex circuits, to perform highly sophisticated signal processing functions.

On the debit side, the properties of matter and the laws of physics also set limits to what can be achieved, so the solution which is adopted will frequently be a compromise between two differing physical constraints.

An inversely biased *pn* junction in a semiconductor device has a depletion layer the thickness of which depends on the potential difference applied across the junction. Thermal motion of the crystal lattice causes the generation of free pairs of electrical charge carriers. These are accelerated by the field across the depletion layer and, if they come into collision with semiconductor atoms, may cause ionisation and the creation of more hole-electron charge-carrier pairs. At a critical value of potential difference, this process will set off an avalanche effect and cause catastrophic breakdown of the junction. The initial generation of charge carriers depends on the width of the forbidden band gap of the semiconductor material and the temperature. Thus the properties of the semiconductor material act as a constraint on the maximum voltage which can be applied to a rectifier without its failure.

The distance between the emitter and collector junctions of a bipolar transistor (the width of the base region), together with the minority carrier mobility, determine the maximum frequency at which it will exhibit useful gain. The greater the gain desired, the narrower will be the corresponding base width. On the other hand, if a high operating collector-base (V_{CB}) voltage is desired, the base width must also be large to obviate the occurrence of the phenomenon of punch-through – the extension of the collector-base depletion layer completely through the base region. In this case a compromise must be chosen, since the properties of the semiconductor material produce conflicting results.

These two examples indicate the effect of limiting physical constraints resulting from the intrinsic properties of the materials. Sometimes the constraints arise simply because of the state of the art. When Julius Lilienfeld made his proposals for the construction of solid-state amplifiers, the only semiconductor materials commonly in use were cuprous oxide, cuprous sulphide and polycrystalline selenium. None of these materials would sustain minority charge carriers for a sufficient length of time for them to have a diffusion length large enough to permit the construction of a bipolar transistor. Thus it was not feasible, in the 1920s, to make a bipolar transistor. It was not until materials technology had greatly improved during the second world war, that the serendipitous discovery of the point-contact transistor effect became a possibility Positive-temperature-coefficient materials, which were developed in the twentieth century for fabrication of thermistors, would have made the nineteenth century Jablochkoff Candle more reliable and a more lasting success.

The way that this control parameter impinges on the innovation model will depend on the circumstances, even to the extent that the timing itself may be critical.

12.6.3.3 Statutory, *de facto* and response-time monopolies

Temporary monopolies put up the cost of market entry to competitors. In the case of intellectual property rights, this is in accordance with public policy as they are intended to encourage invention. However, the influence is equivocal. The monopolies provide comfort for their proprietor by protecting his position and lay the basis for strong companies by reducing competition but, at the same time, they remove the incentive to innovate. Competitors, on the other hand, need to circumvent the monopolies and, hence, are more likely to adopt innovative solutions, even if the economic returns are marginal. So, whilst patents offer the inventor a significant advantage in the early stages of an innovation, the lethargy they induce has the effect that paradigm shifts will usually need outsiders with appropriate resources to introduce them.

After the initial developments were complete, Swan waited until his patents expired before he turned his attention to improvements in the carbon filament lamp. By this time, von Welsbach, Feuerlein and von Bolton in Germany and Just and Hanaman in Austria had made great strides with the refractory metal alternatives which eventually would replace carbon.

Although a patent monopoly is of limited duration, it provides a respite from competition within which new patterns of trade may be established. The monopoly may, however, be curtailed abruptly as a result of procedural errors, vagaries of the judicial system, hostilities, or even such mundane matters as failure to pay the statutory annual fees for maintenance of the patent, a factor which weakened de Forest's bargaining position with Marconi.

The phasing of the impact of patents on innovation is unpredictable. Fleming's US patent on the diode valve detector inhibited the launch of the triode, which was blocked by an injunction until the patent expired. However, as a result of litigation which commenced while it was still in force, the patent was ultimately declared invalid. By this time, the industry was firmly established and its structure could not be changed, due to the binary-decision-tree nature of the evolution of innovation.

Further uncertainty and delay is introduced by the legal process. Will there be an appeal and, if so, to what level of court? What will be the idiosyncratic influence of judges and counsel? Is the mere cost of litigation an inhibiting factor, particularly for impecunious organisations or individuals?

Law making is an iterative process in which legislatures adapt existing laws or create new ones to meet the changing needs of commerce. There is inevitably a time lag and, furthermore, the new laws do not always, from the outset, contain all of the necessary or desirable provisions. For example, when computer programs began to be significant commercially, the law of literary copyright was used to protect the proprietary interests. Although this was unsatisfactory in many respects, in the absence of a better alternative, it has continued to be used. There has, however, been a recent move to allow patents to be granted for computer programs.

In the global economy, harmonisation of laws is subject to diplomatic agreement, an even more tortuous and drawn-out process than national law making.

The consequence for innovation is that governing laws will usually be an imperfect match for the needs of industry. Although there may be some improvement in this situation as laws are amended, there will always be a time delay before imperfections are corrected.

12.6.3.4 Competition law and physical regulation

A countervailing force, opposing the undue exercise of market power, is provided by competition law and by direct regulation. During the early stages of innovation, such control can exert a dominant influence on the development of the market structure of a new industry. Subsequently, it tends to cause merely a brief hiatus before the industry resumes its former road map. Intervention, either directly, in furtherance of government policy, or indirectly, as a result of military procurement, has a major effect on start-up companies. At a later stage, it serves to reinforce the industry *status quo* as supply contracts will usually go to established suppliers.

In the nineteenth century, as a result of strong public feeling against private monopolies, Parliament introduced the 1882 Electric Lighting Act, to regulate the installation of power stations which were needed for public electricity supply. Based on the 1870 Tramways Act, which transferred the assets of the horse tramway operators to local authority control after twenty-one years, the 1882 Act did the same thing with the capital assets of the electricity supply companies. Even ignoring the fact that, at this time, electricity supply was a far riskier venture than tramway installation, the pay-back period chosen was totally inadequate for the financiers to recover their investment. The net result was that the regulation hobbled the development of the UK electricity industry. It was not until the window was increased to forty-two years by the 1888 Electric Lighting Act, that capital investment in the industry resumed.

The British government attempted to introduce competition into the UK telecommunications market by licensing Cable and Wireless' subsidiary, Mercury, to set up as an alternative supplier. Mercury had no infrastructure, whereas British Telecommunications' (BT's) greatest asset was probably the holes in the ground through which passed cables connecting every consumer to its network. Mercury was therefore forced to piggy-back on BT's connections, adding a cost penalty to a service which would compete, at least initially, on price. BT also had a huge cash flow, from its existing customers, and a reservoir of workers who would be made redundant, reducing input costs as new technology took over. BT therefore had the financial muscle to match any pricing strategy which Mercury might adopt, thereby preventing Mercury from penetrating the market.

By the time the cable television companies came along to challenge BT's monopoly of connections to the consumer, BT was operating in a different market. It had metamorphosed into a global player with international alliances.

When creating the duopoly by enfranchising Mercury, no proper assessment was made of the value of BT's holes in the ground or latent reserves of discardable workers who would be released by change in technology from electro-mechanical to electronic switching techniques. Furthermore, no account was taken of the move towards globalisation in the telecommunications industry. Had government policy achieved what it purported to do, the UK would now have two emaciated domestic suppliers instead of one feeble niche supplier and one major multinational. Without inside information, it is not possible to determine whether the political decision was ingenuous or Machiavellian.

12.6.3.5 Facilitators (inventors, entrepreneurs and product champions)

The human factor is the wild card in the process of innovation. Inventors have extraordinary minds and hence do not conform to conventional norms. A number of ground rules may be applied to reduce the uncertainty associated with their contribution. Certain traits are desirable. An inventor should be polytechnic and a lateral thinker. He needs to be motivated, persevering and have a supportive family who will tolerate a single-minded devotion to technological pursuits. Whilst these wide-ranging characteristics were to be found in the heroic inventor, nowadays the disparate skills may alternatively be provided, in the aggregate, by a team of people. However, ability to communicate is *sine qua non*, particularly since, due to its novelty, many of the concepts associated with an invention may be unfamiliar even to the man skilled in the art, let alone to a layman.

The propensity to invent is age-dependent. It reaches a peak between the ages of thirty and forty-five – when the inventor has acquired sufficient knowledge and experience, but is not yet distracted by other calls on his time. There will be bursts of activity stimulated by fresh ideas. An inventor will often form an attachment to a technological specialism early in his career. He may subsequently abandon it, but then return to it at a later date.

Financial reward provides less motivation than the intrinsic satisfaction of inventing. Indeed, some inventors derive such gratification that they lay claim to the inventions of others. Another aspect of the link to the actual process of invention is that some inventors subsequently lose interest and leave others to carry out the exploitation and reap the rewards. Yet other inventors, who would wish to carry an invention forward to fruition, do not have the necessary ancillary attributes.

An important component in the successful implementation of innovation is the product champion. His single-minded persistence is frequently the deciding factor on whether or not an idea is abandoned. At an early stage, this may be crucial, since decisions will be based on value judgements and marginal consideration.

12.6.3.6 Military procurement and government intervention

To underscore my point, let me walk through a case study with you: that of relationship between the Pentagon and semiconductor industry. The invention of transistors from semiconducting silicon made possible the information age. Semiconductors and related solid state technology are already ubiquitous in both military and civilian applications and are produced by a vast international manufacturing network. In 1965, the DoD [Department of Defense] purchased more than 50 percent of the semiconductors manufactured in the U.S. Today DoD purchases less than one percent of a much larger market. In 1995, the U.S. electronics and semiconductor industry generated $457 billion dollars, while the world market was estimated to be almost $976 billion dollars.

The United States dominated the semiconductor industry until the mid 1980's when focused investment by the Japanese industry and government, as well as complacency in the U.S. resulted in Japanese companies taking over market share in several critical equipment and material technologies.

Goaded into action by almost the entire loss of an industry and the prospect of the Pentagon having to buy critical technology from overseas suppliers, the federal government, undertook some initiatives. In some instances, the technology that made the recovery possible was the result of investments made by the Defense Advanced Research Projects Agency or DARPA, which basically acted as a source of venture capital to leverage high risk, long term defense research projects. Another successful initiative was a partnership between the semiconductor industry and government known as Sematech which sponsored pre-competitive research and development. The aim of Sematech was to ensure U.S. leadership in semiconductor manufacturing processes, materials and equipment. Later this year, the Federal Government's direct funding of Sematech will end and industry will assume full responsibility.

Over the past six years U.S. companies, helped by the Federal Government initiatives, fought back. Today U.S. companies share worldwide leadership in many semiconductor equipment and material technologies with their Japanese competitors. A critical component in the recent ability of U.S. firms to compete is their reliance on advanced technology for manufacturing processes. The semiconductor industry has benefited from the existence of a technological base, largely generated by patient federal investments in science over the past thirty years.

The technology equation for national defense is now more complex. Let's go back to our case study. A critical industry like semiconductor equipment and manufacturing is no longer exclusively the domain of the Defense Department. Declining procurement budgets mean that the ability of the government to maintain defense sensitive technologies is limited. Product lifetimes are becoming ever shorter which means that companies are forced to reduce their long term research and development.

At the same time, our foreign competitors are making massive coordinated investment to capture the next round of computer chips and communication technologies. For example, Japan recently announced the creation of a private sector semiconductor industry/government partnership to build the next generation of computer chips with an annual budget of $190 million dollars. The semiconductor manufacturing industry is not at all sure it will win the next round of competition that will evolve over the next five to seven years.

Senator Joseph I. Lieberman, reported in *Electronic News*, 12 May 1997

This speech by a US senator highlights the complex relationship between innovation and military procurement and government intervention. In the initial stages of the semiconductor industry, R&D was supported almost entirely by military expenditure. Later, commercial development took over and the market became driven by the normal economic laws of supply and demand. Then various national governments, notably those of Japan, South Korea and Taiwan, decided that it would be in their interests to nurture indigenous manufacturers. They poured large amounts of cash into the establishment of local factories. They also concentrated on the manufacture of products such as memory chips which would be produced and sold in large volumes. They were successful and captured a major proportion of the world market for these devices. US companies fought back by invoking anti-dumping rules and by introducing greater technological sophistication.

At the same time, several European governments also perceived the importance of the new industry, but they made only a half-hearted attempt at investment, which, by and large, failed in its objective due partly to lack of follow-through and partly to lack of focus.

The pointer to success in government intervention is underlying need. US military procurement was motivated by the cold-war threat of annihilation; the tiger economies' growth was driven by the prospect of changing from a subsistence to a consumer economy; the European initiatives were merely glints in the eyes of committees, civil servants and politicians.

12.7 TIMING AND LOGISTICS OF CHANGE

Much innovation is the result of the recognition that there is a problem to be solved. Inventions that are initially conceived theoretically fall into this category, although the exposition of the theory may not necessarily coincide with the revelation that a problem exists. The essence of a serendipitous invention, at the other extreme, is that it is a random event, that is, provided the socio-economic environment does not change substantially, the invention has an equal probability of occurrence in a given time interval δt, regardless of when the sampling takes place, whereas the emergence of other categories of invention is dependent on the presence of either precursors or market demand.

It is an essential feature for survival of an invention, that the source technology is adequately developed. During the 1920s, Lilienfeld conceived a solid-state amplifier device with a structure similar to that subsequently devised for the transistor. At the time, materials technology was not sufficiently advanced for the proposal to work, because the lifetime of minority charge carriers in polycrystalline semiconductors, which were all that Lilienfeld had available to him, is negligible – techniques had to be developed for creating monocrystalline ingots of high-purity germanium before the physical requirements could be met.

An innovation is not a system which will thrive in isolation – it must interact with its environment. Not only must the invention appear at a propitious moment for viable exploitation – when there is, at least, a latent demand – the idea must emerge when the technology is ripe for its implementation. The Jablochkoff Candle is an apt example. It was developed in the mid-1870s, when generation of electricity by mechanical means using either steam or water power had just become feasible. Its precursor arc lamps required moving parts to maintain correct spacing of the carbon electrodes. The incandescent filament lamp was not yet a working proposition, but a demand for artificial light had been created by gas and oil lamps, which gave a feeble illumination. At the time, there were no alternative sources of light which would function as efficiently as the Jablochkoff Candle, which became widely adopted both for public lighting and for use within buildings. It enjoyed a decade or so of popularity before it was superseded by various forms of incandescent filament lamp (which were more reliable and had a longer life).

Table 12.4 summarises the temporal characteristics of different types of invention. Innovation normally follows a series of ordered steps which are extrapolations of, or substitutions for, the current technology. From time to time there is a lateral shift to a new path. Incentive for adoption of an invention arises from the anticipation of rent, or the reduction of levies

Table 12.4   The timing of inventions

Type	Stimulus	Frequency	Predictability	Timing
Serendipitous	Revelation of problem Chance observation	Sporadic	Statistical	At any time; May follow directed effort
Theoretical	Inventor-dependent	Inversely dependent on height of inventive step	Inventor-dependent	At any time after identifying a problem
Extrapolation	Deficiency in precursor	Dependent on precursors	Relatively high probability	Schumpeter B-stage; Increases with knowledge of invention
Product extension	Identification of applications	Invention dependent	Depends on nature of invention	Follows seminal invention
Topological manipulation	Fresh problem which can be solved by manipulation of previous innovation	Invention dependent	Apparent from nature of invention	Follows seminal invention
Analogue	Need for improvement of precursor	Dependent on existence of alternative technologies	Dependent on alternative technologies	Follows emergence of suitable technology
Emulation	Established market	Relatively rare	Technology/inventor-dependent	Depends on market need
Nonworking, 'half-baked'	Desire to increase tally	Sporadic	Inventor-dependent	At any time

when, for example, a blocking patent is bypassed. Progress then reverts to the extrapolative or substitutional mode of advance.

Advances in a technology may be dependent on commensurate advances by a supplier. In such cases, there will be a pendulum effect in which impetus is transferred between the primary innovation and the supplier's innovation. Where a link of this nature develops, the cycle can become self-sustaining with a period which depends on the response times and the learning curves of both components. Such a system is ultimately constrained by physical parameters such as the minimum dimensional limits in optical lithography imposed by diffraction, but the timing of changes is not necessarily determined by such limits. In the semiconductor industry, this mode of advance led to a doubling of the density of components on a chip every eighteen months, a relationship which was encapsulated in Moore's Law. In many cases, premature obsolescence will be engendered by the desire to influence competitors' cash flow in order to preserve, or create, a dominant position. The framework, which is akin to an electronic relaxation oscillator, is unstable or, at best, quasi-stable. Because it needs an expanding market to drive it forward, so it must, ultimately, collapse like a pyramid selling scheme.

The influence of control parameters is time-dependent, both at the micro-economic and at the macroeconomic level. In the initial phase of an innovation, patent protection, obtainable at relatively little cost, can exert a major influence on the development. A disproportionate gain may be attained by combining several contiguous, weaker monopolies, the whole being greater than the sum of the parts. At a later stage in the evolution of an innovation, a whole raft of patents is necessary for control of the market. Military procurement, or direct intervention by agencies such as the Japanese Ministry for International Trade and Industry (MITI), will, at this stage, upset the delicate balance of market forces. *De facto* standards, which often arise from expedient solutions adopted early in the life of an innovation, potentially provide an advantage for their originator since they constrain the freedom of choice for competitors. (They may also constrain freedom of choice for the path of future development, as did Intel's original eight-bit microprocessor architecture.)

As an innovation matures, progressively greater effort is needed to achieve a dominant position – whole companies must be acquired to obtain access to their intellectual property or large cash payments made for the transfer of know-how.

In the short term, the control parameters remain essentially constant. Judicial interpretation of legislation follows a common path, largely governed by precedent. Seminal inventions set a pattern which, typically, may take thirty years to bring to fruition. Certainly, the laws of physics do not change and the same may be said of the properties of materials – although the development of new materials which may be substituted for the existing ones and increasing knowledge of the characteristics of the latter are equivalent to a change in this parameter.

In the long term, there are noticeable changes in some control parameters. Public attitudes alter and this is reflected in the way that judges interpret statutes. New laws are introduced and existing ones modified in reaction to a changing environment. The end to the cold war resulted in the dissolution of the 'Star Wars' strategic defence initiative which was responsible for great pressure for innovation in electronics and military procurement. A change of president in the USA and the incidence of the al-Qaida terror campaign resulted in its reinstatement. Emergence of the tiger economies introduced a new dynamic in world trading patterns.

12.8 CONCLUSION

Analysis of a system is assisted by the process of model building. This permits relationships between the components to be developed using established mathematical methods to gain a greater understanding of the process and, possibly also predictability of its future course.

The principal hypothesis was that it was not possible to treat the components of innovation separately. This therefore set an objective of creating an holistic model which took into account the need to consider the collective influence of all of the elements.

Like the evolution of biological species, innovation has a phylogenetic tree structure. Methodologies appropriate for biological systems are, therefore, also applicable for innovation. In the process of analysis, formulation of a problem is followed by qualitative description. Input–output diagrams are then used to illustrate signal flows and develop equations for the model.

Innovation may be regarded as a singular system which interacts with the socio-economic environment by means of a series of flows. Subsystems are identified, together with the relevant variables and control parameters.

As certain variables are inaccessible, the system may be treated as a black box. In such a model, the practice used in accountancy may conveniently be followed – revenue flows are distinguished from transfers of capital. Dimensional integrity is maintained through the separation of these flows into elementary constituents such as cash, materials and know-how. Variables comprise infrastructure, work-in-progress and market structure and control parameters include the laws of physics, facilitators and the legal regime. Not all of these components are measurable using currently available metrological techniques.

Timing *is* important. Invention occurs in cycles – the wheel *is* re-invented at periodic intervals. Its success at a particular genesis will, however, be entirely dependent on the then current environment. Innovation is a socio-economic process which follows a binary decision tree. Progress is contingent on the existence of enabling technologies and potential demand, both of which may be time-sensitive. An invention which is before its time cannot succeed – Lilienfeld's proposal for the transistor failed because semiconductor materials' technology was immature; the carbon filament lamp succeeded because, not only did Edison (in the words of James Swinburne) 'make a noise about it', (Swinburne 1886) he also set up the necessary infrastructure to meet the pent-up demand which had been created by the imperfections of the luminous flame as a light source. An invention which emerges successfully today may be irrelevant at a later date and would fail if it were to be introduced then. Inventions which succeed as solutions to a current problem are no longer required when that problem goes away. Success in innovation arises from maximisation of the capital flows. This is a consequence of the optimisation of the revenue flows which result from interactions between the state variables and control parameters of the individual system.

Within this model, individual innovations emerge, wax and wane. During their existence, they influence the evolutionary path of other innovations as well as contributing to the general accretion of wealth. If the innovation is treated as a black box, a number of system variables will exhibit temporal changes in characteristics over the innovation's lifetime. These variables will be influenced by intrinsic and extrinsic control parameters as well as their mutual interaction. Some parameters, such as the laws of physics and the properties of materials, are immutable, although efficiency of exploitation of those properties may improve as experience is gained. Other parameters, such as patent monopolies, will be ephemeral and, indeed, their propensity to control will be different at various stages in the innovation life cycle.

The logistic equation of each innovation is unique. It must therefore be constructed individually on the basis of observation. Since many variables are incommensurable, relationships can only be established qualitatively. Curve fitting will permit the derivation of a degree of mathematical predictability, but the associated uncertainty will be great.

Analysis of the effects of an innovation is complicated by the fact that, initially, at least, its influence is small and will be obscured by much greater socio-economic changes in the environment which are taking place concurrently.

13. Empirical Rules, OK?

... if I throw a ball to you, you don't go off and try to solve a set of differential equations to calculate its motion. You just catch it.
Chris Winter, *Personal Computer World*, May 1997

Don't touch this business. Not one man in a thousand ever succeeds in it.
Thomas Edison (to an aspiring inventor), 12 May 1885

Any intelligent corporation strategy must have innovation at its very heart
Walter Kunerth, Executive VP of Siemens, *Financial Times*, 22 Jan 1996

It had the right degree of difficulty. It was seven years before we had competition – that gave us a chance to expand in a vacuum.
Gordon Moore, *Electronics Weekly*, 26 March 1997

Moreover, most new technologies take off when consumers feel comfortable with them, not when they are first introduced. Remember the slow initial take-up of compact discs and mobile phones? Only when the shock of the new wears off and prices fall to consumer levels does the critical mass appear.
Andrew Emmerson, *Electronics World*, August 1997, p619

Dans les champs de l'observation le hasard ne favorise que les esprits préparés.
Louis Pasteur, 7 December 1854

13.1 INTRODUCTION

The previous chapter proposed a rudimentary black box model of innovation and described its characteristics in qualitative terms. Such a model cannot exist in isolation, but must interact with its environment. This environment is not the normal, four-dimensional world of space–time, but a multi-dimensional phase space, which not only includes space and time, but also possesses further variables such as know-how and market structure which cannot be measured in a conventional manner.

The nature of the prevailing relationships places further difficulties in the way of quantifying a model for the purpose of predicting the path which an innovation will take. Firstly, the signal representing the effects which it is desired to analyse is submerged in a sea of noise generated by the events of unrelated socio-economic activities. Secondly, in many instances, the outcome has a sensitive dependence on initial conditions, a symptom of systems which possess chaotic dynamics (Cullis 2004, Appendix 10). Thirdly, the time scales over which the effect of significant influences may be identified are usually to be measured in decades. Finally, many successes appear to be dependent on luck – euphemistically described as serendipity.

Most innovatory developments are unique. For this reason, it is impossible to construct a stochastic model since the sample sizes will be inadequate. However, the behaviour of the variables in the examples presented in the foregoing chapters has revealed a number of general characteristics. Although these are insufficiently refined to permit the construction of a rigorous mathematical relationship, they may be developed into a set of algorithms or, at least expressed as empirical rules which constitute a guide for predicting a trajectory in the multidimensional phase space of innovation.

Saviotti states (1991),

> Closely related to imperfect knowledge are the concepts of *search activities* of *routines* and of *decision rules*. Firms will follow established routines and decision rules as long as their targets (e.g. percentage return on capital) are exceeded and switch to new routines/decision rules when they are not. The kind of new routines/decision rules which emerge will depend upon the nature of the firm's search activities, that is, on its capacity to learn. Here routines and decision rules function essentially as information ordering and knowledge saving devices. In evolutionary terms the survival of the firm in the face of major environmental changes depends on its ability to learn how to change these internal decision rules.

Devising of empirical rules, which is the first step in defining a numeric model, will therefore, at least, yield a framework for the preliminary investigation into the way in which an innovation will influence future economic development. This chapter is concerned with such an assessment. Having proposed an interrogatory framework, this is then applied to the appraisal of an exemplary invention to test one of the initial hypotheses, namely, that it is possible to predict the prospects for success of an innovation.

13.2 THE NATURE OF THE PROBLEM

One difficulty with a model of innovation is that its components fall outside the bounds of conventional metrology. How, for example, may knowledge be measured? Goertzel (1993) proposed a mathematical model for the mind, but further research would be required to apply the methodology to the dynamics of innovation and thus it is beyond the scope of the present work.

Another difficulty will be that the boundaries between recognisable market structures are fuzzy – economists talk about *imperfect* competition; some oligopolies have a dominant member; multiplicity of patents means that competitors could have overlapping monopolies. How does one apportion flows for intersecting innovations or the cost of infrastructure which serves more than one industry? When does a derived invention from one innovation become a seminal invention for another? What is the know-how leakage in the sale of a finished product? How does one assess the value of a response-time monopoly? The best that can be achieved is a qualitative assessment of the interactions and changes which take place – it may not be feasible to measure knowledge in absolute terms, but it will usually be possible to determine whether there was a large or small relative increase and to make some conjecture about the temporal characteristics of any changes.

If the relevant variables (know-how or market structure, for instance) cannot be measured absolutely, they may be gauged by the effect they have on innovation rent. In other words, if you can't measure anything else, measure money – it is the universal criterion by which success is judged. The common denominator is 'What influence does a (qualitative) variation of a factor have on revenue flow?' Once this question has been answered, then the groundwork has been laid for the construction of a simulation, leading to the ability to pose the question 'What if ...?' and thereby to investigate the effect of altering individual control parameters.

In an evolving regime, a variety of influences determines the path an innovation will follow. The starting point is the current paradigm and the socio-economic environment in which it exists. The black box model discussed in the previous chapter provides a basis for an empirical appraisal of the innovation. The factors of the model and their inter-relationships, which have been examined in the earlier chapters, lay the ground rules, whilst the answers to a complementary series of questions will establish the specific contextual basis for an assessment of the prognosis for a new invention.

13.3 DOES THE INVENTION CONTINUE AN EXISTING PARADIGM OR START A NEW ONE?

A *seminal* invention forms the basis for a new paradigm and an evaluation of it will require polytechnic capability, to recognise opportunities and threats, and foresight, to balance one against the other. Almost certainly, lateral thinking will be involved. The more remote the returns, the greater will be the difficulty in convincing potential adopters that the risks are worth taking. Indeed the risks may not be readily apparent and, even if they can be identified, their magnitude may be hard to quantify. When the bipolar junction transistor was invented the prospect of 'deathnium' (the influence of deep-trap impurities introduced by contamination of the manufacturing machinery which greatly reduced minority carrier lifetime in the semiconductor) was not anticipated.

A *derived* invention will change the evolution of an existing paradigm, which will therefore define the boundaries of the risks and rewards. By the same token, the fact that there is an existing furrow to plough means that vested interests will have to be overcome to make the changes triggered by the derived invention. In other words, the NIH factor is likely to have a greater influence.

The boundary between these two types of invention is not rigid and will depend partly on the perspective. Thus a top-down approach may regard an invention as seminal whilst a bottom-up view will see it as derived. The substitution of a carbon filament for noble metal wires as the 'burner' in the early incandescent filament lamps was initially merely an attempt to take advantage of the properties of black-body radiation, which had not been realisable with platinum or iridium due to the relatively low melting points of these metals. However, the innovation created a paradigm which altered the development of the economy fundamentally and therefore, in retrospect, is recognisable as seminal. The succession of manufacturing processes in the Schumpeter A-phase of the transistor could also either be regarded as applications of existing technology or fundamental changes in fabrication techniques. In the words of (non-)Professor Joad, 'It all depends on what you mean by paradigm', suggesting an *ante*-preliminary question should be 'What is the paradigm?'

13.4 WHAT ARE THE PROSPECTS FOR THE INVENTION AND WHERE WILL THE CONSTRAINTS ARISE?

Having identified the nature of an invention by its effect, further insight may be gained by classifying it by the mechanics of its conception, since each category will have common characteristics.

Before attempting to categorise the invention in this way, again one should ask a preliminary question – what *is* the invention? Often an invention is *actually* the recognition of the fact that there is a problem to be solved. Examination of an invention in this manner will lead to a more fundamental appraisal of its essence.

Serendipitous inventions are the least predictable. They occur sporadically as a result of a chance observation or of a flash of inspiration following revelation of the existence of a problem. They may be made by anyone, so one cannot immediately make assumptions about the potential contribution of the invention. Enhanced thermionic emission in bright-emitter valves was the result of the inadvertent use, by an established manufacturer, of tungsten contaminated with thorium. The use of thorium-treated tungsten was subsequently adopted universally. Edison's technique of dropping a screwdriver on to a carbon filament lamp to increase its light emission, however, became a mere 'urban myth'.

Theoretical inventions (which may in due course yield a practical embodiment) can also occur at any time. The innovation rent is potentially large, but the investment likely to be required to realise this return will be commensurately great. However, unless the provenance of the inventor is well established, there is likely to be a high acceptance threshold to be surmounted. Tesla's alternating current machines, for example, completely revolutionised transmission of electricity. In his case, credibility was provided by his perspicacious product champion, George Westinghouse, who had already built a substantial reputation.

An *extrapolation* arises to overcome a deficiency in its precursor. The triode valve was followed in turn by the tetrode and the pentode, extra grid electrodes being added respectively to reduce the effect of anode capacitance and to reduce secondary electron emission. Such inventions are a logical, if not obvious, progression and will have easily quantifiable rewards. In consequence, acceptability of this type of invention is not likely to be an issue for lengthy discussion.

Product extension is a variant of the concept of extrapolation, adding fresh markets for an existing product. Its return is incremental since the larger aggregate market will give rise to a lower unit contribution to overheads. The high predictability equates to a low acceptance threshold. Flexible polyimide plastics film developed for the US space programme was stable at much higher temperatures than other extant plastics films. It would survive the application of soldered contacts to a superimposed copper layer and could therefore be used in the fabrication of a flat-diaphragm sound transducer. The Wharfedale Isodynamic hi-fi headphones made by this technique were a great and immediate success.

A *topological manipulation* is a relatively uncommon form of invention. By lateral thought, the shape or arrangement of an object or process may be adapted to solve a previously unrecognised problem or to address a new market. Thus, by modifying the rubber suspension used on the first Austin-Morris Mini, Alex Moulton was able to change the configuration of the conventional safety bicycle to produce a light-weight, folding version, with small wheels, which could be carried on a train or stowed in the boot of a car for use at a destination way beyond the range normally accessible by bicycle. By recognising that the application of the collector electrode to the same surface as the emitter and base electrodes of a bipolar transistor would add only marginally to the parasitic collector resistance, provided that a highly doped contact diffusion was made simultaneously with the emitter diffusion, the author was able to construct a 'flip-chip' transistor. This could then be mounted on a miniature printed circuit by direct soldering (GB Pat 1022366, GB Pat 1015588). Substitution of the base diffusion for the emitter diffusion, which was achieved by a minor alteration to the photolithographic masks used in fabrication, whilst preserving identical geometrical layout, yielded a four-layer, switching device (GB Pat 1039915). The value of the invention is therefore determinable by appraisal of the significance of the initial problem or of the market which can now be reached.

An *analogue* invention translates the concepts of an invention to a different paradigm. Nernst produced a lamp in which the glowing rare-earth materials of the Welsbach gas mantle were rendered incandescent by means of an electric current. Gordon Teal tamed the intransigent properties of silicon to fabricate a transistor with a structure similar to one produced from germanium, an element in the same group of the periodic table. The decision on whether to adopt such an invention will depend on whether the net present value of the innovation rent is sufficient to overcome the cost of the shift to the new paradigm.

An *emulation* uses a substitute mechanism to perform the same task as the precursor. Electronic engineers who designed circuits for the first transistors attempted to substitute them in circuits developed for valves, using the principle of 'duality'. Edison set out to produce an electrical light source which could be used in place of the luminous gas flame. Again the financial acceptance criterion is likely to be a straightforward one.

Finally, the *non-working* or *half-baked* invention will go nowhere for the obvious reason that it is based on a false premise or that its basis is inadequately thought out. Simply placing perishable foods in an evacuated glass container would not, as Edison suggested, preserve them because his proposal did not take any steps to prevent dehydration nor to sterilise the meat or vegetables against the action of anaerobic bacteria.

The success of an invention depends on the magnitude of the flows in the black box model. These, in turn, will be controlled by the current value of the state variables and constrained by the particular parameters which pertain to this invention. The objective of an appraisal of an innovation is, therefore, to establish which factors will have a particular influence in the individual case.

13.5 WHAT IS THE PRESENT AND POTENTIAL MARKET?

Table 12.1 summarises the flows and their contributory factors. The earlier analysis demonstrated that one of the most significant determinants of innovation rent is market structure. It is therefore important to develop an understanding of how this will be affected by the invention.

Development of an innovation is associated with complementary growth of a market, so that one reinforces the other. Initially, purchasers may not be sophisticated, but as the skills of the supplier become more refined, so the customer's requirements will also become more exacting. The linking of innovation and market, with increasing demand being matched by increasing ability to supply, will be associated with increasing revenue flows and, by inference, increasing innovation rent.

Symbiotic evolution of an innovation and its market reinforces the associated technological paradigm. Particularly if there are also statutory or informal monopolies, an innovator will be reluctant to move to a new paradigm and abandon his investment in the old one. By corollary, the stronger the protection surrounding a paradigm, the greater will be the propensity of competitors to attempt to circumvent the barrier to market entry by inducing a paradigm shift. The replacement for the carbon filament lamp came from Welsbach, von Bolton, Feuerlein and Just and Hanaman, not from Edison or Swan; Tesla, not Edison (who fought a rearguard action against them by using the electric chair as a marketing tool), pioneered the alternating current machines which made long-distance transmission of electricity feasible; Fairchild, not RCA, which had a heavy commitment to the use of alloying techniques, introduced the planar process for transistor manufacture.

The geographical *location* of the market is also important because it will, *inter alia*, influence the properties of the control parameters and state variables.

13.6 CONTROL PARAMETERS

13.6.1 Which Natural and Statutory Monopolies will be Applicable?

An innovator will, *ipso facto*, have an initial monopoly. At the very least, this will be a response-time monopoly, caused by the delay which occurs whilst competitors react and follow the innovator. Usually, there will also be some form of intellectual property monopoly because official policy sets out to encourage innovation.

Following the initial period of monopoly, other suppliers will appear and the market will become competitive or evolve into an oligopoly. In either case, the market will be shared and the innovation rent will be limited by the pricing policy imposed by market structure.

As new markets mature, they generate a resistance to change. This may, for instance, be due to the cost of creating a fresh standard to meet altered specifications. The effect of this interaction between market and innovator is the creation of *de facto* monopolies. These could give rise to legacy systems, such as the Edison screw fitting for light bulbs and the paging constraint of the Intel family of microprocessors, which create restrictions for later entrants.

The temporal phasing of the effect of these statutory and natural monopolies will vary. A *patent* exerts a strong influence early in its life, when the monopoly is absolute. It also has a sharp cut-off because the grant is for a limited period of time, although the pattern of trade which has been established will persist after expiry of the patent. As an innovation evolves, a multiplicity of patents on relatively minor features or developments of the innovation may achieve a similar blocking effect to that of the initial master patent. In the early days of the carbon filament lamp, Edison gained a monopoly of the UK market with a single patent – two decades later, the members of the lamp manufacturers' cartel pooled all of their patents and achieved the same dominance. In the development of the transistor, on the other hand, there was a time when patents were ignored, due to the difficulties of resolving the effects of intersecting monopolies within the time constraints imposed by rapid technological changes within the industry.

Trade marks have an effect over a longer time scale. Their power increases with the passage of time and with the associated trade reputation. The Rank Organisation built up the Bush trade marks for radio and television over a period of thirty to forty years. It sold them during the 1970s for £1.5m, which, at the time, was a substantial amount. *Copyright* subsists until seventy years after the death of the creator, an interval which, in the case of computer programs at least, is substantially longer than the typical product lifetime. *Response-time* delay will be reduced as competitors' skills increase. *De facto* monopolies will increase in strength as they become more established. However, unless they are reinforced by some form of intellectual property, they will become universal standards and cease to provide the differentiation necessary to establish a competitive advantage. As soon as Phoenix had cloned IBM's ROM BIOS to make the hardware compatible, anyone could purchase the MS-DOS operating system software from Microsoft and manufacture a machine which performed in a manner which was substantially identical to that of IBM's personal computer.

13.6.2 What Opportunities and Threats are Presented by the Laws of Physics and the Properties of Materials?

Innovation rent may also be influenced by the laws of physics and the properties of materials. The benign chemical and electrical properties of silicon laid the foundation for the semiconductor integrated circuit which underpinned the vast modern computing industry. On the other hand, the second law of thermodynamics places a precise limit on the efficiency obtainable from the internal combustion engine. Such factors set absolute boundary levels to what may be obtained from certain innovations. These limits are, however, approached asymptotically, the precise boundary being determined by the then current knowledge of how to overcome the physical constraints.

13.6.3 Who Will Be the Facilitators?

Facilitators play a significant role in the success or failure of embryonic inventions. At its conception, usually, the only person who has a view of its potential will be the inventor. Often this vision will be far from clear. If he loses faith before enthusiasm for its prospects has been passed on to others, or if he has an imperfect understanding of how to carry the invention through to that stage, failure will be the certain outcome. In an industrial environment, the period of vulnerability is likely to be extensive. Finance directors, the NIH-factor and take-overs are among the pitfalls which lie in wait for innovations.

13.6.4   Are there Regulatory Constraints Applicable to this Invention?

Physical regulation can exert an inhibiting influence. The 1882 Electric Lighting Act created a lacuna in the evolution of the British electricity industry, whilst the 1888 Act signalled a return to progress limited by the normal economic constraints of supply and demand. The draconian conditions which (probably justifiably) were imposed on the nuclear power industry have created a prejudice in favour of generation of electricity from fossil fuels to such an extent that no further nuclear power stations were currently being planned in the UK at the beginning of the current millennium.

13.6.5   Are there Military or other Government Intervention Implications?

Without military procurement for the space race in the time of the cold war, it is unlikely that the US semiconductor industry would have become the springboard for a huge expansion in the world economy in the short period of time after the invention of the transistor. By the same token, without the positive intervention of MITI in Japan and the injection of capital on a social scale by corresponding government agencies in Taiwan and South Korea, the USA would still be the dominant supplier of integrated circuits to the world.

13.7   STATE VARIABLES

13.7.1   What Infrastructure is Required to Put the Invention into Practice?

The nature of seminal inventions often dictates particular requirements for the infrastructure. Where this is of a specialist nature, and not shared by other inventions, there may be a delay whilst suppliers carry out any development which is necessary. This is certainly the case with bipedal markets – the period between successive generations of semiconductor integrated circuits is contingent on the time required to design and manufacture the corresponding next generation of photolithographic equipment required to fabricate them.

The size and complexity of the infrastructure provide an indication of the potential levels of innovation rent. It will be determined by the production and development needs, although, for some of these, it may be a shared resource. Innovations which attract large investment in infrastructure do so on the basis that they are likely to produce a commensurate return. The cost of infrastructure is a major component of the barrier to market entry and is therefore a pointer to likely competition and hence market make-up. At any given time, work-in-progress will provide an indicator of the current innovation rent. Subject to change only on account of pricing variation, the revenue cash flow will otherwise be proportional to the work-in-progress.

13.7.2 Are There Any Related or Enabling Inventions?

An *enabling* or *trigger* invention may be required to open up a new paradigm. Zone refining and levelling techniques, which purified germanium crystals, made the fabrication of the junction transistor possible. Faraday's theories of electromagnetism started the transition to the use of electricity as a viable power source.

Derived inventions result from down-stream development. They contribute to market maturity and signal the transition from the Schumpeter A-phase to the B-phase. Initially, they may introduce a fundamental change of direction, with a quantum step in operating economics. Such changes are unpredictable and may be short-lived if they are, in turn, supplanted by another paradigm shift. Manufacture of the point-contact transistor was cut short by the introduction of the grown-junction transistor, which was, in turn, replaced, in short order, by the alloyed-junction transistor, the double-diffused mesa transistor and the planar epitaxial transistor. The surface-barrier transistor, which was manufactured using complex automated plant, did not even get a look-in and was consigned to the trash can without recouping its capital investment. As an innovation reaches maturity, derived inventions will tend to be ones which improve efficiency whilst supporting progress in the established direction.

13.7.3 Are There Supply Side Constraints?

On the supply side, too, there are factors which may prevent an innovation from reaching its maximum potential. Market structure of suppliers, properties of materials and the laws of physics may all prove to be constraints. In the early days of the incandescent filament lamp, Edison was concerned about sources of platinum, which was the only satisfactory material then available to make electrical lead-in wires which would form a seal with the glass lamp bulb without its being vulnerable to cracking due to expansivity mismatch. The problem was surmounted in two ways. Firstly, the prospect of increased sales encouraged fresh suppliers to enter the market and, secondly, low-cost alloys of readily available materials with an appropriate expansivity were developed. A further consequence was that there was a modest increase in the price of platinum, albeit not to the level forecast by Edison.

13.7.4   What is the Cost of Market Entry and What are the Sources of Working Capital?

The need for working capital has an indirect influence on market structure. As successive improvements are introduced, plant becomes more sophisticated and the cost of market entry goes up. In the early stages of the semiconductor industry, anyone could throw together some rudimentary equipment and compete – nowadays, the cost of a manufacturing facility is of the order of $2bn and only companies with huge internal resources or access to government funding can join the club.

Working capital is a satisficing variable. It needs to be sufficient to service the production and R&D requirements and ensure an adequate supply of raw materials and facilitators. Beyond that threshold, the law of diminishing returns sets in rapidly.

13.8   WHAT IS THE HIERARCHICAL ARRANGEMENT OF THE FACTORS OF THIS INNOVATION?

Whilst certain parameters are contextually dependent, others have properties which follow directly from the innovation. In such an hierarchy the seminal invention must occupy the highest place, since its characteristics will determine the ultimate return. Second only to this are the laws of physics and the properties of materials which, at least in the short term, may be regarded as immutable. Intellectual property monopolies, however, have an impact which is innovation-dependent. Patents are not granted *ab initio*, but the mere threat of their existence may have an equivalent impact. Trade marks are of much greater significance in a consumer market than in sales for defence purposes, for example. Database rights will only be of value for innovations involving information technology and semiconductor mask protection will also be industry-specific.

13.9 ARE THERE PHASING CONSIDERATIONS UNIQUE TO THIS INVENTION?

In many instances, initial conditions have been major determinants of subsequent development. Fleming's academic leanings and, thus, his tendency to accept consultancies rather than develop his ideas entrepreneurially, led to Marconi's ownership of the diode valve patent because the consultancy agreement followed the English common law of master and servant and ownership of intellectual property arising during the course of employment was, therefore, vested in the employer. De Forest's impecuniosity, and his consequent failure to maintain his overseas rights, gave rise to a weak negotiating position with the triode valve patents, whilst his obstinate nature stopped him from reaching a compromise settlement and eventually resulted in his being sidelined in the development of the thermionic valve industry.

Phasing is extremely important. Application of a consent decree under US anti-trust law at the outset of the transistor industry shaped its structure. IBM's fear of anti-trust action at its launch of the personal computer inhibited it from imposing on its suppliers conditions which would restrict sales to third parties, thus opening the door to the creation of an industry based on clones of the IBM PC. Ingenuous action by the Justice Department, which was still at the stage of developing anti-trust litigation, permitted the well-established General Electric Company to negate the effect of the 1911 proceedings. After investigation by the UK Monopolies Commission, the mature valve manufacturing industry just blinked and carried on much as before. When IBM wanted to purchase operating system software, it sent representatives to visit Gary Kildall, proprietor of Digital Research. Kildall was out, flying his aeroplane, and could not be bothered to see them. His wife and corporate lawyer stumbled over the wording of the proffered confidentiality agreement and refused to sign. IBM then approached Bill Gates who, having no suitable software, went out, purchased a system which had been developed by a local supplier, and licensed it to IBM. That deal was the basis of the success of Microsoft, now one of the world's largest companies. In the early days of the carbon filament lamp the harsh local authority buy-back provisions of the 1882 Electric Lighting Act, which led to a six-year hiatus in the development of the British electricity supply industry, permitted German and American companies to draw ahead.

When they made their major breaks-through on the incandescent lamp, both Edison and Swan had considerable experience of the patent system. Edison had struck deals on the quadruplex telegraph and founded his Menlo Park laboratory using the proceeds from selling the British rights to his telephone patents. Swan had developed the carbon process of photography, made improvements in leather tanning and won a prize for a novel way of preparing opium, all of which he had patented. Edison's attitude was to file a patent application immediately, and then see if his idea worked. Swan's approach was more cautious – first analyse the idea and see if it is inventive (in the patent sense) and, if so, apply for a patent. These attitudes were instrumental in deciding the outcome of their relative positions in exploiting the new technology. Swan vacillated, decided that his ideas did not contain sufficient quantum of invention to support a patent, and then hesitated to file. Edison threw all of his ideas into the pot and, although he started his development later, beat Swan to the door of the Patent Office. Eventually, when his patent was put to the test, Edison hired eminent counsel who, by dint of eloquent argument, convinced the judge that the mere collocation of known integers was patentable.

Alliance with IBM at the genesis of the personal computer industry laid foundations for Intel's dominance of the microprocessor market. At a later stage, when the industry had matured, IBM, Motorola and Apple came together to create the Power PC in an attempt to loosen Intel's stranglehold on the personal computer industry. The initiative failed and Intel carried on, unbloodied.

Military procurement and the suspension of the US patent system in the first world war established the major manufacturers in the thermionic valve industry. It concentrated market power in the hands of the makers of incandescent lamps, who possessed the requisite skills to make valves. It prevented de Forest from converting his lead with the Audion into dominance of electronic component manufacture. By the time that world war II came along, valves were purchased from existing manufacturers and no change in the pattern of trade took place.

All of these illustrations demonstrate that, whilst a relatively minor act at the outset will set the course for an industry, for example by establishing a *de facto* standard, when an innovation has matured, even such elephantine measures as competition law may be brushed aside or their effects neutralised.

13.10   APPRAISAL OF AN EXEMPLARY INVENTION – THE EDFA

The questions posed in the previous sections are collated in Table 13.1. They provide a basis for an iterative appraisal of a new invention. As an example, the questionnaire may be applied to an assessment of the erbium-doped fibre amplifier (EDFA), which was one of the most important

Table 13.1   Invention appraisal questionnaire

1.	What is the paradigm?
1.1	What is the problem to be solved?
1.2	What is the invention?
1.3	Does the invention start a new paradigm?
2	What are the prospects for the innovation and where will the constraints arise?
2.1	Is the invention seminal or derived?
2.1.2	How was it conceived?
2.2	What is the present and potential market?
2.2.1	Who are the participants?
2.2.2	Is there a possibility of superseding technologies which cannot be controlled and thus enable others to take over the lead?
2.2.3	Is there prospect of continual advance or is this a 'one-off'?
2.2.3.1	Is there an asymptotic limit?
2.2.4	Is there a complementary developing paradigm?
2.2.4.1	What is the time constant of this?
2.3	What are the control parameters?
2.3.1	Which natural and statutory monopolies will be applicable?
2.3.1.1	Intellectual Property?
2.3.2	What opportunities and threats are presented by the laws of physics and the properties of materials?
2.3.3	Who will be the facilitators?
2.3.3.1	Inventors?
2.3.3.2	Who owns the invention?
2.3.3.3	Are there other agents?
2.3.4	Are there regulatory constraints applicable to this invention?
2.3.5	Are there military or defence implications?
2.4	What is the status of the variables? How may deficiencies be corrected?
2.4.1	What infrastructure is required to for the invention?
2.4.2	Are there any related or enabling inventions?
2.4.3	Are there supply-side constraints?
2.4.4	What is the cost of market entry and what are the sources of working capital?
3	What is the hierarchical arrangement of the factors of this innovation?
4	Are there phasing considerations unique to this invention?

inventions of the twentieth century (Digonnet 1993, Conti 2007). The EDFA, which was first announced in 1987 (Mears 1987), was conceived by a team of physicists working in the Opto-electronics Research Centre of Southampton University.

13.10.1 What is the Paradigm?

The invention is a development in the field of cable communications, the early history of which has already been considered (Cullis 2004, Case Study 2). Using rope-making techniques, electrical conductors were bound together to make a medium through which signals could be transmitted from one point to another. Initially, this communication was by means of telegraphy. An electric current flowing in a conductor was interrupted and the pattern of interruptions conveyed the desired message. To transmit more than one message simultaneously, it was necessary to increase the number of wires (electrical conductors) in the cable or to resort to some system of combining the signals (duplex and quadruplex systems). Such techniques had only limited possibilities. A further limitation of these cable systems was that the electric current was attenuated by the resistance of the conductor and this set a limit on the distance that telegraph signals could be sent. To send a message over greater distances, operators who would receive the messages and re-transmit them were placed at intermediate stations.

The first major change was the introduction of voice communications, using telephony. This removed the need for skilled operators. As with telegraphy, electrical signals modulated with the desired message were carried by an electric current between the transmitting and receiving stations. Instead of repeater stations staffed by telegraphers, compensation for attenuation of the current was achieved by placing amplifiers incorporating thermionic valves at intervals throughout the cable to restore the signal to its initial level. As with telegraphy too, multiplexing techniques were employed to transmit more than one signal simultaneously. The physical characteristics of the cable, the amplifiers and the transmitted signal set a limit on the number of signals which could be sent in this way – the so-called bandwidth limit.

Thermionic valves are inherently unreliable and have a short lifetime. They therefore need to be replaced at intervals. With submarine cables, replacement of the valves in the repeater amplifiers presented a particular problem because the cable had to be raised from the sea bed to permit this operation to be performed. The development of the highly reliable silicon planar transistor, which had a much greater lifetime (see chapter 6), presented an opportunity to surmount this difficulty (Cullis 1965a).

The next breakthrough in cable communications was the invention of the fibre-optic light guide. Based on the principle that a light beam may be totally reflected at the interface between a medium of high refractive index and one of low refractive index, an optical signal can be constrained to pass down glass fibres having an inner core of glass with a high refractive index and an outer sheath of glass having a low refractive index. This transmission technique has a much greater bandwidth than one using electrical signals, so many more signals could be transmitted simultaneously. However, optical signals are also attenuated as they pass down the fibre because the light guide is not perfectly transparent. It was therefore still necessary to amplify the optical signal to restore it to its original level. Repeaters for this purpose were placed at intervals of about forty kilometres.

13.10.1.1 What is the problem to be solved?

In order to restore the attenuated optical signal to its initial value, it was necessary to convert it to an electric current by means of an opto-electronic transducer, amplify the electric current using a transistor amplifier and then re-convert the amplified electric current to an optical signal using a radiation-emitting diode. This regeneration process imposed several constraints on an optical system. It imported all of the limitations of an electronic system – relatively narrow bandwidth, reduction in reliability due to multiplicity of electrical interconnections and susceptibility to cross-talk resulting from non-linearity of electronic devices – in addition to the inefficiencies of the opto-electronic conversion processes.

13.10.1.2 What is the invention?

Reduced to its essential features, the EDFA is an optical device which will regenerate a signal propagating in a fibre-optic light guide, without the need to convert it to an electric current to carry out the required amplification. Its operation is based on the principle of quantum physics that a system can exist only in certain pre-defined energy states.

An analogy can be drawn with a pumped-storage hydroelectric system. In this, water is pumped from a lower reservoir to an upper reservoir using energy from the electricity supply. At periods of peak electricity demand, the water is allowed to return to the lower reservoir, driving generators to supply electricity to the grid in the process. In the corresponding quantum mechanical system, optical radiation is absorbed by a medium, such as a crystal or block of glass, raising the medium to an excited energy state. When triggered by an appropriate stimulus, the medium returns to its original level, the so-called ground state, emitting a burst of radiation. This is the principle underlying the laser – Light Amplification by Stimulated Emission of Radiation. At the time of the invention of the EDFA, laser systems were well understood and were used in many applications. Indeed, proposals had even been made for the incorporation of lasers in fibre-optic

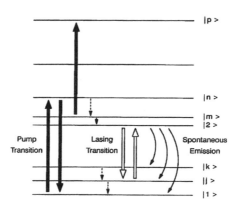

Source   France 1991

Figure 13.1 Energy level transitions in laser systems

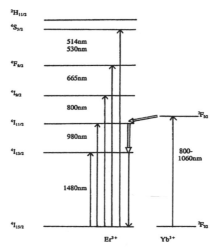

Source   France 1991

Figure 13.2 Energy level transitions in an erbium-based optical amplifier

systems (Snitzer 1968). The difficulty was that these systems were based on materials which were difficult to integrate into fibre-optic communication systems, which were predominantly constructed from fibre light guides of high-purity silica-glass.

Figure 13.1 is a schematic diagram outlining the quantum mechanical energy levels involved in the stimulated emission process underlying fibre lasers and amplifiers. An optical pump raises the active medium to an excited energy level from which it decays by a non-radiative process to a quasi-stable energy level. When triggered by an incoming photon, the medium decays spontaneously to a lower energy state, emitting radiation of the incoming wavelength, thereby amplifying the incoming signal.

The rare-earth element erbium, when incorporated at concentrations of less than about 1000 parts per million in communications-grade silica-glass optical fibres, absorbs radiation at the wavelength emitted by a standard gallium arsenide radiation-emitting diode and serves as a three-level, stimulated-emission amplifier for optical radiation at the standard 1.5μm wavelength used for telecommunications (Figure 13.2). The low concentration is critical, since, at higher amounts, so-called impurity clustering occurs (Namikawa 1982). This gives rise to the phenomenon of concentration quenching, which reduces amplification efficiency. Using a monomode optical fibre of around 40m in length it is possible to construct an amplifier which gives a gain of 30-40dB, a value which permits it to serve as a terrestrial or sub-oceanic booster without creating instability. These phenomena were discovered by Mears, Payne, Poole and Reekie at Southampton University when they were characterising fibres produced by a new, modified-chemical-vapour-deposition (MCVD) process which they had developed to incorporate low levels of rare-earth dopants in silica-glass fibre pre-forms (Mears 1985).

13.10.1.3 Does the invention continue an existing paradigm or start a new one?

When the EDFA was announced, high-reliability transistor amplifiers had been in use for around a quarter of a century and their failure mechanisms were well understood. Prospects for improvement in repeaters for fibre-optic communications systems depended either on enhancing the performance of existing opto-electronic transducers or on discovering conversion mechanisms based on new physical principles. Progress with the former was likely to be slow, since the invention was already well within its Schumpeter B-phase, whilst prospects for the latter were completely unpredictable.

The EDFA represented the start of a new phylogenetic branch, with a corresponding new learning curve. It therefore offered the opportunity of a paradigm shift in the overall evolution of cable communications. This was analogous to the development of the incandescent filament lamp in the field of artificial lighting.

13.10.2 Prospects for the Innovation and Potential Constraints

13.10.2.1 Is the invention seminal or derived?

The classification of an invention as seminal or derived will often depend on whether a bottom-up or top-down approach is adopted. In the case of the EDFA, it may be argued that the device was derived from the neodymium fibre laser developed by Stone and Burrus in 1973 (Stone 1973). However, until the paper by Mears *et al* (Mears 1987) it was not appreciated that an optical amplifier compatible with current silica-based fibre-optic light guides could be constructed. (Millar 1991, p229) The Mears publication stimulated great activity in this field. As with the transistor and the carbon filament lamp, the invention may therefore be regarded as seminal and thus a potential source of innovation rent in its own right.

13.10.2.1.1 How was it conceived? The felicitous properties of the EDFA were discovered by meticulous attention to detail during the fibre characterisation – an example of Pasteur's 'luck favouring the prepared mind'. Like Edison and Swan's carbon filament lamp, Mears' EDFA was a collocation of features which were already part of the state of the art – a gallium arsenide light-emitting diode (LED) used as an optical pump, a rare-earth-doped medium, with an appropriate quasi-stable energy level gap, to emit radiation when stimulated, a carrier material (silica-glass) with optical transmission characteristics useful for communications purposes, and a three-port fibre-connector to permit injection of radiation for end-pumping the active length of fibre which would give the right amount of amplification (30-40dB). As with Edison's and Swan's 'running on the pumps', the key step to success was a trigger invention – the Southampton team's development of a method of introducing dopant at the desired levels into the silica-glass fibre to produce a three-level laser/amplifier system (Poole 1985).

13.10.2.2 What is the present and potential market?

Like the carbon filament lamp, which provided a superior substitute for the gas flame, there was an immediate market for the EDFA. Although, with rapidly advancing technology, it would not be practicable to retro-fit EDFAs into existing fibre-optic communications systems, the techniques could readily be incorporated into new systems. Market prognostication for EDFA-based systems could therefore confidently be made using existing data for opto-electronic systems. The only change in the forecasts was that the market was likely to be larger due to the superior performance of the all-optical system.

Projections of the markets for various communications systems suggested there would be a twenty-fold increase in the traffic on fibre-optic systems during the last decade of the twentieth century (Cochrane 1991).

13.10.2.2.1 Who are the participants?   Once the enabling invention had been made, anyone with the current skills to manufacture fibre-optic communication systems was able to incorporate EDFAs into them in place of opto-electronic repeaters. All existing manufacturers had the requisite technological capability and were likely to continue unless there were to be a sea change brought about by new intellectual property rights. However, the probability of patents, for example, altering the market structure was low because the time-honoured practice in the industry, since the standoff between de Forest and Marconi, was either to offset the effect of new patents by means of licences or simply to ignore them.

13.10.2.3 Is there a possibility of superseding technologies which cannot be controlled?

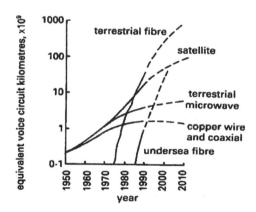

Source   Cochrane 1991

Figure 13.3   Temporal change in global transmission capacities

Figure 13.3 illustrates market projections for the different communications paradigms which were current when the EDFA was invented. One property

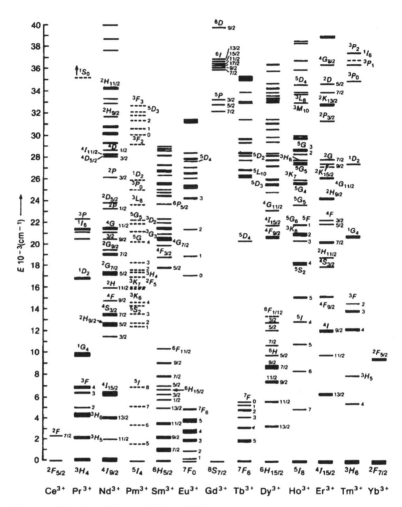

Figure 13.4   Energy levels for rare-earth dopant materials

Source   Hannah and Tropper in France 1991

which determined the prospects for the individual technologies was the bandwidth they would support. Copper cable, which had been in existence for over a hundred years, was reaching the limit of its development and had a bandwidth of around 1GHz. The corresponding value for microwave radio was 300GHz, but for an optical fibre system the potential bandwidth was 40000GHz. To place this in context, George Gilder, in a BBC broadcast in 1993 (Gilder 1993), stated that a single strand of optical fibre could carry simultaneously all the telephone calls made in the USA at peak time on Mothers' Day. On this basis it is unlikely that the existing alternative paradigms would have the capability of replacing optical fibre. Indeed, the contrary was likely to apply.

Figure 13.4 shows the energy levels for various rare-earth dopant materials in a silica-glass host medium. Many of the transitions support stimulated emission and therefore have the potential to replace the EDFA if they could be shown to have better properties in an optical communications system. However, the characteristics of the erbium-based amplifier provide an almost perfect match to the transmission characteristics of silica-glass optical fibres. Furthermore, the gallium arsenide LED, a mature-technology semiconductor device, has a radiation emission wavelength which makes it an ideal optical pump for the EDFA.

13.10.2.4 Is there prospect of continual advance or is this a 'one-off'?

The first EDFA-based systems could exploit less than 1 per cent of the available bandwidth of a monomode optical fibre. It was therefore the start of a learning curve comparable to that of the transistor. In the case of the latter, devices were, in 1950, crafted individually by hand. Half a century later, microprocessors and memory devices incorporated many million transistors in a single silicon chip which had been processed by photolithography. Extension of techniques, such as wavelength division multiplexing, which were currently used in radio communications, could ensure that the increased capacity of optical fibre was progressively exploited. Historic experience suggests that, as with the transistor, new applications of the EDFA will also be devised.

13.10.2.4.1 Is there an asymptotic limit? The ultimate bandwidth limit of an optical amplifier could not be realised using the technologies which were available when the EDFA was developed. However, the increase which *was* immediately accessible gave sufficient economic motivation to induce the necessary paradigm shift from hybrid opto-electronic systems. Furthermore, since an optical fibre light guide is comparable in diameter to a human hair, its small physical size meant that there was no significant penalty to be incurred by simply increasing the number of light guides to enlarge the capacity of an optical communications system. This strategy could create breathing space for the development of new technologies which would permit more efficient use of the fibre's capacity.

As the immediate prospects for the EDFA were not constrained by its own physical limitations, a considerable period was likely to elapse before such limits would come into play because further techniques would have to be devised to permit full exploitation of the bandwidth potentially available in the fibre-optic light guides.

13.10.2.5 Is there a complementary developing paradigm?

The EDFA is a simple device – a length of active, erbium-doped silica-glass fibre, an optical pump to raise the fibre to an excited energy state and a three-port connector to permit the pump radiation to be injected into the active fibre region. Even the very early EDFAs could be fabricated to give the optimum gain of around 40dB. The potential for refinement was not great. Possibly a fibre-based radiation source could be developed to replace the gallium arsenide radiation-emitting diode – one could envisage that new materials might permit the topography to be simplified – but even that would require ancillary electronics, so there would be no great motivation for introducing such a change. The EDFA was, proportionately, a low-cost component in a high-capital-value system. Whilst new systems would require new EDFAs, there was little prospect that improvements in the EDFA itself would create premature obsolescence and thus act as an innovation driver in a subservient paradigm in the way that the microprocessor did.

13.10.2.5.1   What is the time constant of this?   Since markets for the EDFA were dependent on the installation of new optical communication systems, any increase in innovation rent would have to await new applications for fibre optics. This, in turn, was a matter of waiting for organic growth and, ultimately, the creation of an information-based economy – a change comparable to the industrial revolution of the nineteenth century. However, the economic portents for such a paradigm shift were favourable, as they were for artificial illumination following the invention of the incandescent filament lamp. That change effectively was put in place during the decade commencing in 1880 and the expansion of fibre-optic communications could well follow this model because the need to communicate is a powerful economic driver (Cullis 2004, Case Study 2).

13.10.3 Control Parameters

13.10.3.1 Which natural and statutory monopolies will be applicable?

The methods used to fabricate the EDFA were straightforward developments of technologies which were currently in use. Once the key papers had been published (Poole 1985, Mears 1987) there was no technological barrier to market entry by competitors and hence no likelihood of response-time advantage. Furthermore, the invention of the device in an academic environment, with the accompanying pressure to publish, meant that there was no prospect of maintaining trade secrecy.

Early fibre-optic communication systems employed light guides of silica-glass. This *de facto* standard was the motivation for the adoption of the EDFA because it provided amplification at wavelengths at which silica optical fibres functioned most efficiently – the 1.5μm transmission window.

13.10.3.1.1 Intellectual property? The EDFA is a physical device rather than an intellectual concept. In consequence, patents rather than copyright or *sui generis* protection such as database rights are the appropriate vehicle for statutory protection of the innovation. Early market development is likely to depend on technological factors rather than promotion, so trade marks would be unlikely to have a significant role.

There are several issues relating to patents. Firstly, there is the question of the extent of a patent monopoly and its consequence for patenting strategy. The initial development by the Southampton University team was the use of a modified chemical vapour deposition (MCVD) method of producing a silica-glass optical fibre doped with rare-earth elements at a level of less than 1000 parts per million. They then employed a short length of this fibre to produce an optical amplifier which gave a gain of 30-40dB, a value which made it suitable for use as a repeater in an optical communication system.

A patent could certainly be gained for the novel method of making fibres. However, it would not be possible to ascertain from the end product that it had been fabricated by the novel MCVD method. All that analysis of the fibre would show was the level and distribution of the rare-earth (erbium) dopant element in the silica-glass. It would be necessary to gain access to proprietary information, which would not be readily accessible, to prove infringement of a patent for the method.

It would also be possible to patent the amplifier, though difficulties might arise because the device was a collocation of integers which, it could be argued, were either already known or were a development considered to be obvious.

A further point of significance to patenting strategy was that, although it is a component which is pivotal to the realisation of increased bandwidth in an all-optical communications system, the EDFA itself represented only a small proportion of the total capital cost of the system. For licensing purposes, it was therefore desirable to ensure that the patent monopoly for the EDFA also covered complete communications systems based on the EDFA.

When attempting to enforce EDFA patents, the capital value of optical communications systems is, *per se*, a likely stumbling block. It is usually straightforward to reach agreement to take a licence when the sums of money involved are not large. When the amounts are great, however, the incentive for a potential licensee to procrastinate is commensurately large. If, instead of paying royalties, the prospective licensee places the money on deposit, the interest earned thereby can be sufficient to finance a challenge to the validity of the patent. Those who have the resources to participate in the optical communications systems market will therefore also have sufficient resources to engage in patent litigation.

13.10.3.2 What opportunities and threats are presented by the laws of physics and the properties of materials?

Alternative transport mechanisms for communications are copper (or other conductive) cables, point-to-point microwave radio, extra-terrestrial satellite links and fibre-optic cables. Of these, only fibre has the bandwidth to provide virtually unlimited capacity. Its limitation is that it is suitable only for communication between fixed stations. If there is no direct link, a complementary technology, such as mobile radio or the copper-based local loop, must be used for final delivery to the end user. However, for the bulk transport of information over established routes, optical fibres have no competitor. There are the further advantages as optical signals are unaffected by electromagnetic radiation interference, meaning that communication is clearer and can be used in hostile environments, and that optical fibres do not radiate electromagnetic energy, and thus are secure and do not themselves interfere with other signals.

When the EDFA was invented, communications-grade optical fibres were manufactured from silica-glass. Shortly afterwards, glasses fabricated from fluorides were found to have suitable properties for communications. Specifically, their intrinsic losses were significantly lower than those of silica (France 1991, p183). In consequence, fluoride fibres would support a greater distance between repeater amplifiers. The most satisfactory fluoride-based optical fibre was a mixture of zirconium, barium, lanthanum, aluminium and sodium fluorides (known as ZBLAN after the initial letters of their chemical symbols). The fluoride glasses also possessed the right quantum mechanical energy states for the fabrication of lasers and amplifiers. Indeed, an erbium-doped fluoride fibre amplifier was demonstrated in the $1.34\mu m$ communications window as well as the $1.53\mu m$

one of silica-glass, so fluoride glasses had the potential not only to replace silica, but also to improve on it.

In the manufacture of semiconductor devices, silicon became the material of choice, even though some III-V compounds had more favourable electrical properties, because it possessed a stable glassy oxide and could be readily processed. By analogy, it is probable that, even if one of the quantum mechanical energy transitions of an alternative rare-earth dopant proves to be more efficient for optical amplification purposes, erbium will not be supplanted as the active element because of its ideal match to the ancillary components of the complete fibre-optic system. By the same argument, it would be difficult to supplant silica-glass as the material of choice for the optical fibres, even though the superior transmission characteristics of fluoride fibres provide a powerful driver in its favour. What can be stated definitively is that silica-based systems are more advanced, by about a decade, on the technological learning curve and that this factor would inhibit a paradigm shift to fluoride glass fibres.

13.10.3.3 Who will be the facilitators?

13.10.3.3.1 Inventors?   Four scientists contributed to the invention of the EDFA.   Three of these were academic staff of the University of Southampton and one was a post-graduate research student, working on his doctorate. Although one of the academics had peripheral involvement with a spin-off company, the main focus of their activities was research in opto-electronics.

13.10.3.3.2 Who owns the invention?   The academic staff were employees of the university and had normal contracts of employment granting the university rights to inventions made by them in return for a share of any revenue earned from those inventions. The research student was funded by a grant from the Science Research Council. A condition of this funding was that rights in his inventions should be assigned to the National Research Development Corporation, a UK government organisation which had been established in 1949, to exploit inventions made in the public sector. There had been a change in practice during the 1980s and this provision was not invoked at the time the EDFA was invented.

13.10.3.3.3 Are there other agents?   During the 1980s, under an initiative of the UK Department of Trade and Industry, funds for academic research in opto-electronics were provided by industrial partners under the Joint Opto-Electronics Research Scheme (JOERS). A consortium of British Telecommunications, Standard Telephones and Cables, the British General

Electric Company and Plessey had financed part of the development which led to the EDFA. As a result of this partnership, the industrial companies were granted a licence for the EDFA patent (EP 0269624), but did not receive a licence under the associated optical fibre manufacturing patent (EP 0272258).

This arrangement will have created a conflict of interest. Manufacturers and service suppliers make their greatest return from their mainstream activities. Licensing provides only incremental income. They are therefore primarily interested in obtaining freedom to use an invention. Gaining licensees ties up scarce technical and management resources and may even involve litigation with its associated delays, uncertainty and costs. A university is driven by the twin needs of enhancing its academic reputation and raising funds to continue its research programme. Academic staff and research students' first motivation is to publish ground-breaking papers; earning income from inventions is not usually a main objective, although some academics have an entrepreneurial motivation and may become involved in spin-off activities.

Another issue in this particular case may be inferred from the information set out in the case studies. All of the companies, or their predecessors, involved in the industrial sponsorship had been active during the early or middle part of the twentieth century. The drive for freedom to use inventions meant that they all had extensive cross-licensing agreements with competitors. They were obliged, under many of these agreements, to pass on rights which they obtained. This legacy gave rise to a considerable reduction in the potential patent monopoly for the EDFA.

13.10.3.4 Are there military or other government intervention implications?

Two factors are likely to excite military interest – the increased bandwidth and hence speed of communication and the lack of extraneous radiation from the fibre-optic cable, which means that the communications are more secure. A counter-factor arises because the fibre-optic cable needs to be installed before communications can flow. The cable could be destroyed as were cables in the first world war, but this drawback may be, at least partially, negated by construction of a network of cables, which is entirely feasible with fibre optics.

13.10.4   State Variables

13.10.4.1   What infrastructure is required for the invention?

The infrastructure used in existing hybrid electronic-repeater-based fibre-optic systems requires very little modification for all-optical systems based on the EDFA. The only change is the use of the EDFA in place of an electronic amplifier. The EDFA is readily constructed in existing fibre-optic manufacturing plant. This creates a prejudice in favour of existing suppliers and also puts up the cost of market entry for newcomers since they will have to compete in the established market.

13.10.4.2   Are there any related or enabling inventions?

The enabling invention was the use of the MCVD process to obtain consistent rare-earth doping levels of less than a thousand parts per million. Although this process is patentable, it is not possible to prove from examination of the finished fibre that the patented method has been used.

13.10.4.3   Are there any supply-side constraints?

Supply-side constraints are the costs and logistical problems involved in the installation of high-capital-value systems underneath oceans and between territories with different political regimes. The actual manufacture does not create difficulties, but the full exploitation of the EDFA is contingent on further expansion of optical communications systems.

13.10.4.4   What is the cost of market entry and what are the sources of working capital?

Manufacture of fibre for construction of the EDFA is ancillary to manufacture of mainstream fibre for long-distance optical cables. There would be no incentive to set up a separate plant to fabricate the required rare-earth-doped fibre, since most of the steps involved may be performed in pre-existing facilities. For an established manufacturer, the costs involved would simply be those associated with an incremental activity but, for a newcomer, a complete plant would have to be commissioned. In the former case, organic growth would supply the working capital. In the latter, the larger capital requirement would be subject to the further risk that the new plant would be competing with existing suppliers in an established market.

13.10.5 What Is the Hierarchical Arrangement of the Factors of this Invention?

The EDFA is a seminal invention, the characteristics of which are uniquely determined by the properties of the materials used in its fabrication. It is a substitute for an existing product (the transistor-based opto-electronic repeater amplifier), the market for which will determine the initial prospects for the new invention.

Intellectual property rights will not play a significant part because the effect of patents on the device is neutralised by prior licensing agreements and because infringement of a patent on the method of fabrication cannot be ascertained by examination of the finished product and it is therefore necessary to engage in litigation without certainty of a successful outcome.

Military applications are not sufficiently imperative to drive the innovation forward – they will provide only an incremental market.

The infrastructure is already in existence because the innovation will use the facilities already created for existing fibre-optic communications systems. For the same reason, facilitators are not required – the benefits of the invention are immediately apparent and easily realised. The road map of the substituted product may be followed.

13.10.6 Are there Phasing Considerations Unique to this Invention?

The involvement of the industrial partners at an early stage pre-empted the use of patents as a key tool in the development of the market because the consideration they received for providing research funding was the grant of a licence to use the device. It should be stated that this consideration provided the licensees with a serendipitous and disproportionate return on their investment. The situation was exacerbated by delays in the European and Japanese Patent Offices which meant that a patent was not available in those territories when the potential market was young.

13.10.7 Summary and Prognosis

This appraisal has been carried out on the basis of knowledge current in 1991, some four years after the EDFA was first announced to the world.

The invention contributed to the well-established paradigm of cable communications. It addressed a significant need by eliminating the step of converting an optical signal into an electronic one in order to amplify it, because, at the time, there was no means of amplifying the optical signal by means of an all-optical mechanism. The new process, which was based on proven physical principles, was made feasible by a trigger invention which provided improved materials that had not been fabricated hitherto. These improved materials themselves overcame an obstacle (concentration quenching) which had prevented the quantum mechanical process underlying stimulated-emission devices in optical fibres from operating at full efficiency. The result of the change was that it became feasible to construct an optical amplifier with characteristics which matched perfectly those required for the purpose of a repeater in a fibre-optic communications cable. The new amplifier was an ideal substitute for one which had reached the asymptotic limit of its development potential and was thus ripe for replacement.

The announcement of the EDFA generated great excitement and stimulated much activity. Market projections could be made using existing data and had only favourable indications. The potential for several orders of magnitude improvement in performance meant that the new invention could underpin optical communications systems for several product life cycles. No known technique was likely to displace fibre optics for point-to-point communications. All of the participants in the existing market would wish to continue and, in particular, would not be inhibited by intellectual property considerations.

The EDFA itself had a serendipitous, optimal combination of properties. The probability of finding a substitute which provided as good a match to the requirements of the application was therefore extremely low. EDFA-based optical communications were right at the start of their learning curve. Potential for growth was, therefore, high and likely to continue indefinitely. There was no significant retro-fit market, so growth would be dependent on the market for new systems. Nevertheless, the device was likely to become ubiquitous with the advent of the information-based economy.

Response time and diffusion of information were unlikely to cause delays, whilst existing *de facto* standards created a prejudice in favour of the EDFA. Although the device and its method of fabrication were patentable, there would be problems in attempting to enforce these patents because of the financial power of infringers and of difficulties in detecting infringement.

The laws of physics and the properties of materials gave strongly positive indications. The only cloud on the horizon was fluoride-glass-based systems, which were, however, some way behind on the learning curve.

The inventors were unlikely to make a major contribution to commercial development because their resources were very small in relation to the size of the operations required. Title was complicated and had been muddied by the history of the invention's conception. In consequence, intellectual property rights were unlikely to inhibit market evolution. Specifically, there was an unquantifiable leakage of rights, which would dilute any monopoly.

Military applications would not greatly enhance the market. On the other hand, infrastructure was in place and would not, therefore, cause delays. The market was a high-capital-value one with accompanying logistical constraints on growth. This, in turn, was counter-balanced by a strong demand for increased communications.

Because the EDFA was a superior substitute product for an established market, there was no NIH-factor to be overcome. For the same reason, a product champion would not be required. Furthermore, as a consequence of the conditions of the funding of the research which led to the invention of the EDFA, intellectual property considerations would not inhibit growth of the market. Risks associated with the EDFA's adoption were therefore minimal and the device had the prospect of a large innovation rent which would continue to increase for the foreseeable future.

13.10.8 Feedback

In 1999, KMI Corporation, (http://kmi.pennnet.com) an organisation which provides market intelligence in the field of optical communications, published a series of maps showing existing and planned fibre-optic cables, all of which require EDFA-based amplifiers. These maps provided confirmation of the positive result of the predictions made on the basis of the foregoing questionnaire.

13.11 CONCLUSION

Using the black box model of the previous chapter as a starting point, the underlying empirical relationships were deconstructed as a series of questions which may be employed to develop a prognosis for an invention. This questionnaire, which is applied iteratively as fresh information is acquired, was then tested on an invention which was sufficiently recent and of such significance that it was possible to utilise, for the purpose, the state of knowledge in the public domain shortly after the invention was conceived. The prospects were evaluated using this knowledge base and, using data published later, the resulting predictions were compared with subsequent market developments. The actual progress of the innovation was found to be in accordance with the prognosis. This result is, however, subject to the caveat that one swallow does not make a summer!

Analysis of the influence of various engineering innovations exemplified in this study reveals that, in each case, there was one factor which was dominant. Usually this was the laws of physics and the properties of the materials involved, particularly in the Schumpeter A-stage of the evolution. Thus the invention of the transistor was made possible by single-crystal germanium purified by new methods of zone refining and doped with significant impurities by zone levelling. Felicitous metallurgy heralded the paradigm shift to alloyed junctions. High-segregation-coefficient dopants improved emitter efficiency and hence transistor amplification factor. Suitable combinations of segregation and diffusion coefficients at high temperature led to the post-alloy diffused transistor, whilst silicon's ability to form a stable glassy oxide on its surface gave rise to the change from germanium to silicon as material of choice for the planar transistor.

With the thermionic valve, electron emission was enhanced by using low-work-function thoria for the cathode and the change in construction from triode to tetrode to pentode was stimulated by the need to improve control of the internal electric fields which determined electron trajectories within the device.

The EDFA came into being because a novel materials-processing technology made possible the fabrication of a host glass capable of supporting the quantum mechanical energy transitions which would give rise to stimulated emission of radiation at wavelengths suitable for optical communication. The fibre light guides themselves functioned because light is reflected at the interface between materials of differing refractive index.

In the development of the incandescent filament lamp, the Stefan-Boltzmann law of black body radiation led to the choice of carbon. Then patent monopolies and the nature of the legal code in the respective territories determined which companies would achieve dominance.

With the microprocessor and the transistor, the *indirect* influence of anti-trust law led respectively to Intel becoming market leader and Bell *not* becoming market leader.

In each of these cases, the development of the market was subservient to the influence of these initial determinants, thus supporting the original hypothesis that the influence is hierarchical. It is, however, not possible by logical argument to prove a positive premise. Furthermore, many of the innovations depended on luck for their success – silicon not only had a forbidden band-gap and minority charge carrier mobilities suitable for electronic device fabrication, it also possessed a stable glassy oxide which could be used to passivate the surface; erbium, when used as a dopant in fibres of the material used almost universally for optical communication, could be pumped by a commonly available light-emitting diode to induce a three-level quantum mechanical transition which provided amplification of the radiation transmitted by the light guide; Gary Kildall preferred to go flying rather than talk to the representatives of IBM, so Microsoft rather than Digital Research became a market leader; accidental contamination of tungsten with thorium led to the development of the more efficient dull-emitter thermionic valve.

A roulette wheel is a deterministic system in which the ultimate resting place of a ball depends precisely on the physical parameters of its initial trajectory and those of the motion of the wheel. However, the financial returns are influenced by many other factors, such as the personality of the gambler, the management policy of the casino and the regulatory regime under which it operates, together with the success of a liaison with Lady Luck.

Likewise, the economic rent of engineering innovation is governed, *inter alia*, by the laws of physics, chemical properties of materials, the timing of inventions and the stimulus and countervailing action provided by intellectual property monopolies, competition law and direct regulation, as well as the idiosyncratic contribution of the inventor's personality, all leavened by the unpredictable advent of serendipity.

14. *Post scriptum*

'Tis better to be fortunate than wise.

John Webster, *The White Devil* (1612)

14.1 SERENDIPITY

... he had formed it upon the title of the fairy-tale *The Three Princes of Serendip*
the heroes of which were always making discoveries, by accident and sagacity, of
things they were not in need of.
Horace Walpole (1754)

Luck, which is a major determinant of innovation, is unpredictable. How
then should one take account of it? As with the wise men of old,
enlightenment comes from the orient. In the highly developed Japanese art
of garden design, there is a technique, known as *shakkei*, in which a distant
view is revealed through a gap in the planting or the perimeter fence, and is
thereby incorporated in the overall structure of an individual garden.
Concepts and methodologies which are part of completely separate
disciplines may likewise be harnessed to give an insight into the dynamics
of innovation. Phenomena as diverse as dripping taps, laser optics,
epidemiology, stock market economics, meteorological forecasting and
plant taxonomy have been found to have common topological
characteristics. Solutions to multi-disciplinary problems may therefore be
taken from any field where an appropriate analogue is to be found. Cross-
correlation techniques, borrowed from seismology and signature
verification, deal with the identification of significant information
submerged in a sea of background noise, computer simulations assist in
compressing time, chaos theory gives guidance for the phase space analysis
of multi-variate influences found in innovations, whilst the observation of
Louis Pasteur provides a helpful strategy for improving the odds of success.
Methodological assistance may even be obtained from politicians by
adapting their stock in trade – if you can't answer the question that has been
asked, answer one that you can. Prevaricate and eventually an appropriate
solution will emerge.

Pasteur stated, and Shockley reiterated, the aphorism 'Fortune favours
the prepared mind.' – if you look in the right place then you are more likely
to be successful than if you are wandering blithely to and fro with no sense
of direction. It was Fleming, with advancing deafness and the need for a
visual wireless detector, who harnessed the Edison Effect, rather than
Edison and Upton, who observed, and then passed over, what was, to them,
a mere scientific curiosity. Nobel laureates Bardeen and Brattain
discovered the point-contact transistor whilst probing the surface of a
germanium crystal to characterise its electrical properties – Shockley, the
theoretician of the team, failed to predict the phenomenon because he was
struggling to explain the observed field-effect measurements which were
orders of magnitude less than his predictions.

Newton taught us that for every action there is an equal and opposite reaction. Likewise, in the analysis of the dynamics of innovation, for every guideline there is a corresponding caveat. Pasteur's advice needs to be tempered with the caution the science fiction writer and visionary Arthur C. Clarke gave in 1973 – 'The mind has an extraordinary ability to "see" things that are hoped for.' Nevertheless, as Thomas Edison and Bill Gates have shown, the rewards can be great. Success in innovation is the key to survival, whilst the alternative to striving for understanding is consignment to an eternal limbo.

Innovation is a fragile process. Particularly in its early stages, it is vulnerable to extraneous influences. Events such as the discovery of new materials or the appearance of an unexpected side-effect in the testing of a new drug are entirely outside the control of the innovator. Although steps may be taken to mitigate the effects of bad fortune or to take advantage of good luck, in the words of Miguel de Cervantes, 'Heaven's help is better than early rising' and of Victor Hugo, 'Have but luck and you will have the rest; be fortunate and you will be thought great.'

15. Epilogue

Well, I can see about as far ahead as I've ever been able to see. I can see how we can do the next two generations, and the people who are doing it can see how to do the next three. That takes us out about ten years. Beyond that, things look like they get very difficult, but things have looked that way before. I suspect that in the next twenty years we're going to run up against something fundamental, but that's well beyond my tour of duty – someone else can worry about that.

Gordon Moore, founder of Intel, *The Guardian*, 27 March 1997

...Dr Chris Winter, of BT's Martlesham Heath labs, said his group has made so much progress that self-programming computers could be commonplace within ten years. They may even replicate improved versions of themselves using programmable analog circuits and gate arrays.

One of the new techniques involves inventing a new set of sexes. The idea was first explored when lab director Dr Peter Cochrane asked why nature stuck with just two. Researchers tried evolving code using up to six sexes. 'The results have proven fascinating. Depending on the problem and the environment, four or even six sexes can work much better,' Winter said. This does not mean nature is 'wrong' in using two, because this number appears to favour resilience which, in living systems, is more important than the speed of evolution.

Breaking nature's rules works in other ways too. One of BT's fastest new algorithms, called virtual children, involves parents killing their offspring until they achieve the perfect child. The new biological software will bear more relation to cellular organisms than today's programs, so that computer crashes will be as likely as brain crashes.

Clive Akass, *Personal Computer World*, May 1997

Barnsley's central insight was this: Julia sets and other fractal shapes, though properly viewed as the outcome of a deterministic process, had a second, equally valid existence as the limit of a random process. 'If the image is complicated, the rules will be complicated,' Barnsley said. 'On the other hand, if the object has a hidden fractal order to it – and it's a central observation of Benoit's [Mandelbrot's] that much of nature does have this hidden order – then it will be possible with a few rules to decode it. The model, then, is more interesting than a model made with Euclidean geometry, because we know that when you look at the edge of a leaf you don't see straight lines.' His first fern, produced with a small desktop computer, perfectly matched the image in the fern book he had had since he was a child. 'It was a staggering image, correct in every aspect. No biologist would have any trouble identifying it.'

James Gleick, *Chaos – Making a New Science*, p236

From the initial observation that the process of technological advancement is not a uniform progression, this investigation set out to produce a model by means of which an innovator could optimise his use of resources and speed the achievement of his goals, whilst governments could apply its lessons to attain more effective implementation of public policy.

Rejecting the more customary approach that it was sufficient to study the dynamics of innovation from a unilateral viewpoint, the chosen starting premise was that many contributory factors should be taken into account. The value of this contention has been demonstrated by multifarious examples of interactions between system variables and parameters to control capital and revenue flows between an innovatory system and its environment. These showed that, not only are there many elements which are part of the equation, but that the timing of the interactions is also significant.

A consequence of coming from a multidisciplinary standpoint was that it led to the conclusion that methodologies developed to solve problems in other fields of endeavour could be applied to analogous problems in the study of the development of innovation. Mathematical analyses and modelling techniques which are useful in biology were chosen because innovation, too, is a process of survival of the fittest, with paradigm shifts taking the place of genetic mutation to create the phylogenetic tree structures which are characteristic of the evolution of biological species.

A series of case studies, in which the factors of innovation were examined iteratively over a period of two centuries, provided insights into macroeconomic changes. Notable amongst the observations was the vacillation of public policy towards private monopoly. During the latter part of the nineteenth century, opinion was strongly against private ownership of utilities which existed to serve the public. This resulted in legislation which, whilst recognising the right of private capital to introduce innovations, took the assets into public ownership when they became commercially viable. These attitudes persisted for around half a century, giving rise to such laws as the 1847 and 1871 Gasworks Clauses Acts, the 1868 and 1869 Telegraph Acts, the 1870 Tramways Act and the 1882 and 1888 Electric Lighting Acts, and judicial decisions, such as *Attorney-General* v. *Edison Telephone Company of London* (6 QBD 244), which put the public policy into practice.

By the end of the 1800s, cartels were beginning to emerge. The reaction was one of opposition in the United States but one of official approval in Germany. In Britain the cartels initially remained covert, but there were later attempts to justify their existence (BEAMA 1927) (*quaere* – why was Germany in favour of cartels, but antipathetic to patents?) In the United Kingdom, opinions which were hostile at the end of the nineteenth century changed to such an extent that, by the 1930s, judicial approval was given to dominant suppliers in a series of High Court decisions on the compulsory licensing of patents relating to the manufacture of tungsten filament lamps, thermionic valves and wireless broadcast receivers ([1915] RPC 202, [1929] RPC 457, [1938] RPC 479). Even whilst this was happening, the next swing of the pendulum in the other direction was commencing.

In the New World, embryonic opposition to cartels had emerged in the shape of the 1887 Interstate Commerce Act and the Sherman Anti-Trust Act of 1890. At first, the electrical industry was able to render this legislation nugatory. General Electric and thirty-four other companies circumvented the effects of a 1911 prosecution by re-grouping and producing mere paper acquiescence. By the latter half of the twentieth century, however, a number of anti-trust cases had given rise to Consent Decrees which re-shaped the progress of development and caused industry to be much more circumspect in its conduct (see chapter 9). However, British industry has, until the present time, still been cocking a snook at authority and continuing along its own sweet way, despite adverse Monopolies Commission reports (Geddes 1991, p318).

The influence of regulatory, intellectual property and competition laws was subservient to the driving force of market economics and the constraints and opportunities presented by the properties of materials. As the case studies show, Edison, General Electric and Microsoft support the proposition that, if your purse is deep enough, you can circumvent the will of the legislators, whilst the fates of Swan and IBM are a cautionary tale of the dangers of paying too much attention to the *perceived* interpretation of statutes. On the other hand, the delays of the legal process (as in the case of Fleming's invalid US diode detector patent and Intel's filibustering), the consequences of legal etiquette or an inexperienced judge in creating precedents in a common law system (Edison's UK litigation), an inappropriate legislative precedent (the Tramways Act 1870) or suspension of the patent system during hostilities (USA in world war 1 – Tyne 1977, p120) can have the effect of changing the structure of an industry.

The mechanics of invention also changed, partly as a result of Edison's development of the concept of an industrial research laboratory. In the nineteenth century, solitary inventors were *de rigueur*, but by the end of the twentieth century many, if not most, patents had multiple inventors. With the effective demise of the heroic inventor as part of the ever-increasing trend towards collaborative research, this is a change which is not likely to be reversed.

When Edison and Swan first invented the incandescent carbon filament lamp, the need for a cheap and reliable source of artificial lighting was universal. However, although communications were reasonably good, each pursued the development along his own lines. In particular, Edison constructed his lamps from bamboo fibres, whilst Swan quickly moved to structureless filaments fabricated from extruded cellulose. Separate companies were set up in each territory and, despite the fact that they combined forces in Britain for pragmatic reasons concerned with the conduct of patent litigation, the partnership was not pursued elsewhere.

In the Victorian economy, trade was highly protectionist, jealously guarded by means of tariff barriers and the Imperial Preference. During the first half of the twentieth century, major companies operated internationally, but this was done through the medium of individual subsidiaries in each country. Towards the end of the 1960s, triggered by liberalisation of trade through the agency of the General Agreement on Tariffs and Trade (GATT), and by the establishment of new technologies which required huge investment and operated to universal standards, industries began to organise on a global basis. Led by the semiconductor integrated circuit and the automobile industries, manufacturers set up plant in territories chosen because labour costs were low, they were convenient for their markets or individual national governments created incentives which distorted the normal economic rules of supply and demand. A political parallel to the classic structures of market economics evolved and the world technological scene moved from a regime dominated by America to one in which Japan, Europe and the tiger economies of the Pacific Rim played a major role. Again, this change is unlikely to be reversed because the economies of scale resulting from global operations preclude the establishment of industries which operate solely on a national basis.

The time taken for changes in laws to follow socio-economic developments is measured in decades and for international harmonisation of legislation in centuries. Intellectual property law has been in the vanguard, but the movement which began with the Paris Convention in 1883 has still not achieved complete unison, partly due to American reluctance, for constitutional reasons, to adopt measures which are readily accepted elsewhere. The stand-off, in the first part of the twentieth century, between Marconi and de Forest, with the Fleming thermionic diode and the de Forest Audion patents, arose because the USA did not, at that time, have renewal fees for maintenance of patent rights and thus the impecunious de Forest's patents in America did not lapse for non-payment as they had overseas. Edison and Swan dominated the US and British markets for incandescent lamps because the common law system gave them strong patents which they were not able to obtain in territories with inquisitorial legal codes which took into account inventive merit in the determination of patentability.

With the current pressures for harmonisation of laws and the development of global industries, it is unlikely that any country will henceforth diverge significantly from the common path. The reason for this is that, if a country attempts to do something which is out of line, economic pressures will place it at a disadvantage. Of course, there will be the occasional aberrant judicial decision, as in the Raytheon case on patentability of software-related inventions ([1993] RPC 427), but such divergence will only be transitory. (Commercial interests immediately started lobbying for a change in the law to negate the effect of this judgement.)

The overall trend to universal harmonisation will be followed more strongly in the future. The main intellectual property laws of patents, trade marks and copyright had diverse national origins and therefore needed to be brought into mutual conformity. New intellectual property laws to protect developments in technology, such as semiconductor masks and databases, are enacted as *sui generis* rights in internationally agreed format, or, at least, following a common precedent, so that, in the future, there will be no delay whilst laws are aligned, although there will still be uncertainties resulting from differing judicial opinions and national prejudices.

The main limitation of this study is that it attempts to devise stochastic rules by analysis of what are, essentially, unique deterministic systems. Although certain state variables and control parameters have been taken as a basis for model building, their selection was predominantly an intuitive choice rather than a generalisation from first principles. There was, however, an underlying objectivity, since the model construction was based on an extensive case study analysis. In support of the choice, there is no counter-indication to suggest that the conclusions reached are not broadly applicable. Because it is based on socio-economic needs, innovation in biotechnology, for instance, will be governed by the same financial incentives and general constraints as innovation in electronics. It is merely the relative importance of the variables and parameters which will differ. Patents for chemical compounds, for example, create an absolute monopoly, whereas, in electronics, patent monopolies intersect; pharmaceuticals are manufactured under stringent regulatory regimes which have the effect that they take around eight years or more before they reach the market place, whereas in the brown goods market, *caveat emptor* and product liability laws, which are only useful against gross misdemeanours, provide the protection for consumers.

A major problem in the analysis of the dynamics of innovation is the length of the time scales involved. It takes about thirty to forty years for a new development, such as digital television or the transistor, to become an essential part of the everyday life-style. In radio, for example, amplitude modulation broadcasting began in the second decade of the twentieth century, frequency modulation started to take over in the 1950s and we are just now making the changeover to digital standards. With such slow evolution and with so many variables and interactions in an innovatory system, it is very difficult to identify contemporary causes and effects. Retrospective analysis is simpler, but a changing macroeconomic environment, with different time scales for different control parameters, means that history will not repeat itself exactly, even if there is a cyclic element to the temporal dependency.

A unique aspect of this work is that the initial hypotheses were based on the author's personal experience of making inventions which satisfied the statutory criteria of novelty and non-obviousness, pre-requisites for the grant of patents. Viewed four decades later, which permits them to be assessed contextually, this provided a special insight into the process of invention.

Although the finding might be expected, because many natural phenomena have a skewed gaussian distribution, it was interesting to observe from their patent filings that heroic inventors have a propensity to invent which changes throughout their lifetimes in such a manner. Within the overall gaussian envelope, there were individual spurts of activity as new projects and ideas occupied the inventors' minds. There was also a dip during early middle age, possibly due to the conflicting demands of other interests at that time of life.

The semiconductor industry provided an excellent exemplification of the influence of innovation on the ebb and flow of market dynamics. Different phases of economic development were well illustrated – the Schumpeter A-stage passed through characteristic changes as the different dominant technologies evolved. In 1959, the transition to the B-stage took place. The basic manufacturing technologies of planar diffusion, epitaxial deposition and ion implantation were then adopted universally and have only undergone improvements in details ever since. During this evolution, various market characteristics were apparent. Using a biological analogy, markets were identified as having lion, hyena and vulture phases, with the rich feast of exclusive access to a fresh invention, the shared spoils of a mature market and the picked bones of a superseded product. On occasion, there was even a phoenix stage when a market rose from the ashes, as did gas lighting when von Welsbach's invention of the gas mantle caused the postponement of the paradigm shift to electric lighting. In an expanding market, such as the one which existed immediately after the invention of the transistor, at any given moment in time, individual companies operated in an instantaneous oligopoly, but, in the long term, emerged, prospered and failed – surfers and sinkers in a market which emulated an ocean wave. The forward progress was inexorable, but the participating firms waxed and waned as their proprietary technological contribution first found universal favour and then was abandoned. In this environment, patents were ignored because the technology moved on before legal disputes were resolved or even initiated. Technological decisions were often a compromise, with non-optimal performance being accepted because a particular raw material was easier to work – silicon with its lower charge carrier mobility but stable oxide was adopted in preference to germanium for integrated circuit manufacture.

As well as the statutory intellectual property monopolies, informal response-time and *de facto* monopolies were important in the creation of ultimate market structures. Feedback in this process had a stabilising effect in oligopolies, where initiatives tend to elicit a countervailing response from other market participants. In markets with a bipedal structure based on two advancing technologies, such as personal computer hardware and software or integrated circuits and photolithography, the possibility of overall positive feedback was identified. This gave rise to characteristics similar to those of a relaxation oscillator and created an 'anti-duopoly' or 'flip-flopoly'. In the analogous electronic circuit, output grows until limited by the impedance of the feedback loop. With the VLSI integrated circuit, consumer demand for 'killer' software applications controls growth, and the magnitude of the charge on the electron and size constraints of photolithographic imaging will provide the asymptotic limit.

The concept of Moore's Law, which was expounded by Gordon Moore on the basis of extrapolation of three empirical observations of successive generations of integrated circuits, was demonstrated to be a special case which arose in the evolution of bipedal markets. The relationship was generalised and a new 'Moore's Parameter' introduced. In software development, an effect similar to Parkinson's Law was identified, where the size of programs expands to fill the computer memory available.

The emergence of global markets gave rise to the political analogues of monopoly and oligopoly – the terms monocracy and oligocracy were used to describe their characteristics. The USA practises a form of technological imperialism. Its government forced semiconductor mask protection rights on its trading partners and refused to grant export licences for 128-bit encryption software in an endeavour to retain an ability to maintain surveillance of communications on the internet, whilst its companies colonised the world with products such as Microsoft Windows software, Intel integrated circuits and Ford cars. ('You can paint it any color, so long as it is black.')

In constructing a model of the innovation system, a key perception was that derived inventions have a separate character from that of seminal inventions. The former play the part of state variables, whilst the latter are parameters controlling the envelope which constrains the potential development.

A start has been made on a holistic approach to understanding the dynamics of innovation. How may this be carried forward? In terms of the existing model, many of the variables are, at present, incommensurable. Application of the principles of artificial intelligence may provide a metric tool by which this contribution to innovation can be assessed. Would development be better considered in the context of temporary synaptic links between ephemeral systems, rather than the serial progression of a deterministic ensemble? Can the biological analogue be developed? Would the results of research on the organisation of insect colonies and varying the number of sexes in evaluating the dynamics of evolving systems yield useful insights? In computing, the transition from von Neumann architecture to neural networks removed a major logistic constraint.

Aspects of the present model merit closer study. Chaos theory, self-similarity and cross-correlation techniques (Cullis 2004, Appendix 12) could lead to a greater understanding of this model. The techniques of auto- and cross-correlation, which are used, *inter alia*, in cryptography, seismology, electronic speech recognition and military surveillance to identify signals submerged in noise, might be adapted to highlight patterns in matching the demands of the environment to the supply of innovation. Construction of a cross-correlation matrix of innovations and their markets is one potentially fruitful area because it holds out the prospect of an objective success criterion. In certain systems, chaos theory (Cullis 2004, Appendix 10) provides strategic guidance through the use of concepts such as the butterfly effect, basins of attraction, trajectory plots in phase space and mode locking. Other questions to be considered are the nature and influence of noise in chaotic systems – how does it perturb? Will it induce trajectory flipping between adjacent attractors? What constitutes a basin of attraction in the multi-variate phase space of innovation? What, indeed, is noise in the context of such a system? The answers to these questions could improve the effectiveness of innovation as a business tool.

The databases which have been constructed for the present research also have the potential to yield more information. Did the change from individual inventors to multiple inventors lead to more inventions or different types of invention or more valuable inventions? The comment was made at the outset that 'It is a remarkable observation and a tribute to the nineteenth century economy that the gestation of the electricity industry took less than a decade.' Has the period of gestation of ideas changed during the last two centuries? Why and how were the nineteenth century electricians able to introduce their new ideas so quickly? What is the relative significance of seminal and derived inventions?   Can the semiconductor and valve databases provide an insight into the sailing-ship effect?   Would it be *fruitful* to investigate the sailing-ship effect in greater depth?

A detailed aspect of the case study on the incandescent lamp could be developed further. Gas discharge lamps had their origins in the Geissler tubes which emerged during the nineteenth century, but were not adopted widely because they were mechanically unwieldy and did not offer a luminous efficiency advantage to counterbalance this drawback.   The fluorescent tube which was developed between the two world wars became the *de facto* standard for illuminating industrial and commercial premises where the demand for high ambient lighting levels overcame antipathy to its awkward construction. Finally, the high-efficiency fluorescent lamp, which is a direct plug-in replacement for the incandescent filament lamp and offers a significant advantage in running costs, albeit at higher initial cost, has recently begun to make inroads into the general lighting market.   An investigation of the factors of these innovations could yield further insights.

Further work on bipedal markets should be undertaken because they hold the potential for faster growth than single-technology innovations.   In particular, the strategies employed by Intel, following its initial felicitous development of the microprocessor, led to its domination of this section of the semiconductor market.   Its finances exhibit underlying chaotic characteristics, which Intel has managed to harness to its advantage.   The progress of Motorola in the microprocessor market and of the semiconductor-memory-chip manufacturing oligopoly are tied to the technological features of Intel's strategy. A further aspect to such a study would be an investigation of the ancillary role of Cyrix and AMD as alternative suppliers in the mainstream microprocessor market – could AMD jump ahead of Intel, with the early introduction of devices such as the K6 processor, or must it, because of Intel's market power, remain a follower? The demise of Mostek – an early pioneer – and the relegation of Zilog, which had a product (the Z80) superior to that of Intel's first viable eight-bit processor (the 8080), to the role of supplier to niche markets are also worthy subjects.

Lessons may be learned from the decline and fall of the industry giants. On the back of demand for computing, IBM grew to be one of the world's most powerful companies. It was slow to adapt to the emergence of the personal computer and the rise of networking, which moved products more quickly but had far lower profit margins. Apple came to prominence as a result of the development of the spreadsheet. It prospered because Steve Jobs opportunistically exploited the graphic user interface which was developed by the Xerox Palo Alto Research Centre, but not recognised as a potential winner by Xerox's management at the East Coast headquarters. It withered because it attempted to retain a proprietary hold over its operating system when the Windows system of its rival was accessible to all. Although the successful launch of the Ipod has provided a period of resurgence, Apple's attempts to retain exclusive proprietary control show that it has not learned from its earlier activities.

This study set out to provide a basis for an understanding of the dynamics of innovation. Whether or not that quest has achieved its goal, it is apparent that it *has* revealed an underlying question. The progress of innovation takes the form of a phylogenetic tree. Is there a fractal order to its dynamics?

Figure 15.1   The fractal structure of a diffusion limited aggregate

TABLE OF CASES

REFERENCES

Arthur 1989   Arthur WB, 1989
Competing technologies, increasing returns and lock-in by historical events
Economic Journal **99** 116-131

Bardeen 1956   Bardeen J, 11 Nov 1956
Semiconductor research leading to the point contact transistor
Les Prix Nobel pp77-99

Basalla 1988   Basalla G, 1988
The evolution of technology
Cambridge University Press, Cambridge

Beale 1957   Beale JRA, Nov 1957
Alloy-diffusion; a process for making diffused base junction transistors
Proc Phys Soc **B70** pp1087-1089

BEAMA 1927   British Electrical and Allied Manufacturers Asscn.,
Combines and trusts in the electrical industry; the position in Europe in 1927
BEAMA, 1927

Bowers 1982   Bowers B, 1982
A history of light and power
Peter Peregrinus

Bright 1949   Bright A, 1949
The electric lamp industry: 1800-1947
MacMillan

Cavalli-Sforza 1981   Cavalli-Sforza CC and Feldman MW, 1981
Cultural transmission and evolution: a quantitative approach
Princeton NJ: Princeton University Press

Christie 1995   Christie A, 1995
Integrated circuits and their contents: international protection
Sweet and Maxwell

Clark 1977   Clark RW, 1977
Edison the man who made the future
Macdonald & Jane's

Cochrane 1991   Cochrane P and Heatley DJT, 1991
Future directions in long-haul optical fibre systems
Br Telecom Eng J **9** (4) pp268-280

Conot 1979   Conot R, 1979
                         ThomasA. Edison: A Streak of Luck
                         Da Capo
Conti 2007   Conti JP, Feb-Mar 2007
                         The 10 greatest communications inventions
                         IET Communications Engineer, pp14-21
Cringely 1992   Cringely RX, 1992
                         Accidental empires
                         Penguin
Cringely 1996   Cringely RX, 1996
                         *The triumph of the nerds – three television
                         programmes*
                         Channel 4 TV
Crompton 1928   Crompton RE, 1928
                         Reminiscences
                         Constable
Cullis 1965a   Cullis R, 01 Jul 1965
                         *An initial design study of transistors for 10Mc/s
                         bandwidth submerged repeater operation*
                         Standard Telephones & Cables Ltd   –
                         Internal Report
Cullis 1966a   Cullis R, May 1966
                         Semiconductor devices - British patent situation
                         Proc ITT Pat Conf 1966
Cullis 1966b   Cullis R, Sep 1966
                         *Manufacture of transistors and integrated
                         circuits. Part 1*
                         IEE - Students Qtly J **145**   p6
Cullis 1966c   Cullis R, Dec 1966
                         *Manufacture of transistors and integrated
                         circuits. Part 2*
                         IEE - Students Qtly J **146**   p59
Cullis 1973   Cullis R,   Sep 1973
                         *Management of intellectual property in the
                         commercial enterprise*
                         Polytechnic of Central London — DMS
                         dissertation
Cullis 1985b   Cullis R,   Oct 1985
                         Cambridge 32016 coprocessor
                         Practical Computing Oct 1985 pp 68-69

Cullis 1986   Cullis R,   Oct 1986
                         Keep it simple – RISC technology
                         Practical Computing Oct 1986 pp 92-93

Cullis 2004   Cullis R,   Jan 2004
                         *Technological roulette – a multidisciplinary
                         study of the dynamics of innovation in the
                         electrical, electronic and communications
                         engineering industries*
                         University of London — PhD thesis

Davenport 1979   Davenport N, 1979
                         *The United Kingdom patent system — a brief
                         history*
                         Mason

Davy 1836   Davy J, 1836
                         Memoirs of the Life of Sir Humphry Davy, Bart.
                         Longmans

de Forest 1950   de Forest L, 1950
                         *Father of radio: the autobiography of Lee de
                         Forest*
                         Wilcox & Follett

Digonnet 1993   Digonnet M, ISBN: 0-8247-8785-4, 1993
                         Rare earth doped fiber lasers and amplifiers
                         Marcel Dekker, Inc, 1993

Dugan 2000   Dugan S and Dugan D, ISBN: 0752218700, 2000
                         *The day the world took off. The roots of the
                         Industrial Revolution*
                         Channel 4,   London,   2000

Elliott 1993   Elliott M, 27 Oct 1993
                         STM goes multi with smart IC technology
                         Electronics Weekly   (No. 1657) p16

Flaschen 1966   Flaschen S, May 1966
                         Technical trends in components
                         Proc ITT Pat Conf 1966

Fleming 1883   Fleming JA, 1883
                         *On a phenomenon of molecular radiation in
                         incandescent lamps*
                         Proc Phil Soc **7**   pp283-284

Fleming 1896   Fleming JA, 1896
                         *A further examination of the Edison effect in
                         glow lamps*
                         Phil Mag **42**   p99

Fleming 1905   Fleming JA,   1905
                        *On the conversion of electric oscillations into
                        continuous currents by means of a vacuum
                        valve*
                        Proc Roy Soc Lon **74**   pp476-487

Fleming 1921   Fleming JA, 1921
                        Fifty years of electricity
                        The Wireless Press

Fleming 1924   Fleming JA,   1924
                        *The thermionic valve and its development in
                        radio-telegraphy and telephony*
                        The Wireless Press   1924

Fleming 1934   Fleming JA,   1934
                        Memories of a scientific life
                        Marshall Morgan & Scott

France 1991   France PW ed.   ISBN 0-216-93157-6 1991
                        Optical fibre lasers and amplifiers
                        Blackie

Friedel 1986   Friedel R & Israel P, 1986
                        Edison's electric light
                        Rutgers UP

Fürst 1926   Fürst A, 1926
                        *Das elektrische Licht: von den Anfängen bis zur
                        Gegenwart, nebst einer Geschichte der
                        Beleuchtung*
                        Albert Langen

Geddes 1991   Geddes K & Bussey G, 1991
                        *The Setmakers - a history of the radio and
                        television industry*
                        BREMA   p52

Gilder 1993   Gilder G,   May 1993
                        In business – the illumination of dark fibre
                        BBC Radio 4 broadcast

Goertzel 19935   Goertzel B,   1993
                        *The structure of intelligence –   a new
                        mathematical model of mind*
                        Springer Verlag   ISBN 0-387-94004-9

Gold 1977   Gold HJ, 1977
                        *Mathematical modeling of biological systems -
                        an introductory guide book*
                        Wiley

Goldschmidt 1940   Goldschmidt R,   1940
The material basis of evolution
Newhaven CT: Yale University Press

Gould 1987   Gould SJ,   1987
Time's arrow, time's cycle: Myth and metaphor in the discovery of geological time
Harvard University Press, Cambridge Mass.

Goodwin 1995   Goodwin WD, 1995
One hundred years of maritime radio
Brown, Son and Ferguson

Grayson 1995   Grayson L, 1995
Scientific deception
British Library

Hall 1950   Hall RN & Dunlap WC, 01 Nov 1950
P-N junctions prepared by impurity diffusion
Phys Rev **80** pp467-468

Hazen 1988   Hazen R,   May 1988
Superconductors: the Breakthrough
Simon and Schuster

Heerding 1986   Heerding A tr Jordan, 1986
The history of NV Philips Gloeilampenfabrieken
Cambridge UP **1**

Heller 1994   Heller R, 1994
The fate of IBM
Little, Brown

Hilsch 1938   Hilsch R & Pohl RW,   8 Dec 1938
Steurung von Elektronenströmen mit einem Dreielektrodenkristall und ein Modell einen Sperrschicht
Z Phys **11** pp399-408

Houston 1894   Houston EJ,   May 1894
Electricity - one hundred years ago and today
McGraw Publishing Co.

Houston 1915   Houston RA,   1915
A treatise on light
Longmans, Green and Co.

Hull 1916   Hull AW,   Jan 1916
Negative resistance
Phys Rev **7** pp141-143

Hutcheson 1996   Hutcheson GD and Hutcheson JD,   January 1996
                          Technology   and   economics   in   the
                          semiconductor industry
                          Scientific American   pp40-46

Jarvis 1955a   Jarvis CM,   Jan 1955
                          The rise of electrical science
                          JIEE   pp13-19

Jarvis 1955b   Jarvis CM,   Mar 1955
                          Towards the new light
                          JIEE   pp145-152

Jehl 1937   Jehl F,   1937
                          Menlo Park reminiscences
                          Edison Institute 1

Jewkes 1969   Jewkes J, Sawers D and Stillerman R   1969
                          The sources of invention
                          2nd Edition   MacMillan,   London

Johnson 1890   Johnson J and Johnson J.H.,   1890
                          The patentees manual – a treatise on the law
                          and practice of patents for inventions
                          Longmans, Green   London

Josephson 1961   Josephson M,   1961
                          Edison
                          Eyre & Spottiswoode

Kennedy 1990   Kennedy WP,   1990
                          Capital markets and industrial structure in the
                          Victorian economy
                          in *Capitalism in a mature economy: financial*
                          institutions, capital exports and British
                          industry, 1870-1939
                          Aldershot

Kingston 1977   Kingston W,   1977
                          Innovation - the creative impulse in human
                          progress
                          John Calder

Kingston 1984   Kingston W,   1984
                          The political economy of innovation
                          Martinus Nijhoff

Koestler 1964   Koestler A, 1964   ISBN 0140171919,
                          The act of creation
                          Hutchinson,   London

Kuhn 1970	Kuhn T, 1970 *The structure of scientific revolutions* Intl Encl of Unifd Scie **2** (2)
Kuznets 1930	Kuznets S, 1930 *Secular movements in production and prices* Houghton-Mifflin
Kynaston 1994	Kynaston D, 1994 *The City of London* **1** Chatto & Windus
Manners 1995	Manners D & Makimoto T, 1995 *Living with the chip* Chapman and Hall 0 412 61690 4
Manners 1996a	Manners D, 17 July 1996 *Report on the silicon chip industry* Electronics Weekly p14
Manners 1996b	Manners D, 18 September 1996 *Lust for life: interview with Dr. Federico Faggin* Electronics Weekly p19-20
Manners 1996c	Manners D, 25 September 1996 *God's own job: interview with Dr. Masotoshi Shima* Electronics Weekly
Martin 1996	Peter Martin 12 December 1996 *Branded by Success* Financial Times p18
Maynard Smith 1988	Maynard Smith J, 1988 *Did Darwin get it right* New York: Chapman and Hall
Mayr 1988	Mayr E, 1988 *Towards a new philosophy of biology* Cambridge MA: Belknap
Mears 1985	Mears RJ, Reekie L, Poole SB and Payne DN, 1985 Electronic Letters **21** pp738-740 (1985)
Mears 1987	Mears RJ *et al*, 1987 *Low-noise erbium-doped fibre amplifier operating at 1.54μm* Electronic Letters **23** (19) pp1026-1028 (1987)
Millar 1991	Millar CA, ISBN 0-8493-7716- 6 1991 *Future directions in Optical fibre lasers and amplifiers* ed. France PW pub. Blackie 1991

MRCP 1951   Monopolies & Restrictive Practices Commission,
Report on the supply of electric lamps
HMSO, London, 1951

MMR 1968   Monopolies Commission,   1968
Second report on the supply of electric lamps
HMSO, London, 1968

Mokyr 1990   Mokyr J,   1990
The lever of riches
Oxford University Press

Moore 1965   Moore GE,   1965
Cramming more components onto integrated circuits
Electronics **38** No.8 pp114-117 (19 Apr 1965)

Moore 1975   Moore GE,   1975
Progress in integrated electronics
International Electron Devices Meeting, 1975

Moore 1995   Moore GE,   1995
Lithography and the future of Moore's Law
Proceedings of the SPIE, 1995 Optical/laser lithography VIII (20 Feb 1995)

Morton 1952   Morton JA,   1952
Present status of transistor development
Bell System Tech J,   **31**   pp411-442

Mouton 1890   Mouton JT,   1890
Vragen des Tijds **2**   93-116

Namikawa 1982   Namikawa H, Arri K, Kumata K, Ishi Y and Tanaka H 1982
J.App.Phys **21** pp360-362 (1982)

Nelson 1982   Nelson R and Winter S,   1982
Evolutionary theory of economic change
Belknap Press, Cambridge MA

Nishi 1995   Nishi Y,   Nov 1995
Silicon faces the future
Physics World   pp29-33

O'Neill 1944   O'Neill JJ,   1944
Prodigal genius: the life of Nikola Tesla
Ives Washburn

Petritz 1962   Petritz RL,   May 1962
Contributions of materials technology to semiconductor devices
Proc IRE   pp1025-1038

Pickworth 1993	Pickworth G May 1993 *Germany's imperial wireless system* Electronics and Wireless World pp427-432
Pole 1888	Pole W, 1888 *The life of Sir William Siemens, FRS* John Murray
Poole 1985	Poole SB, Payne DN and Fermann ME Electron. Letts **21** (1985) pp737-8
Rossman 1931	Rossman J, 1931 *The psychology of the inventor* Inventors Publishing
Sahal 1981	Sahal D, 1981 *Patterns of technological innovation* Addison-Wesley Reading, Mass
Salter 1960	Salter WEG, 1960 *Productivity and technical change* Cambridge UP pp133-134
Saviotti 1991	Saviotti P and Metcalfe JS eds., 1991 *Evolutionary theories of economic change* Harwood Academic Press
Schmookler 1966	Schmookler J, 1966 *Invention and economic growth* Harvard UP
Schumpeter 1934	Schumpeter JA, 1934 *The theory of capitalist development* McGraw-Hill, New York
Schumpeter 1939	Schumpeter JA, 1939 *Business cycles* McGraw-Hill **1**
Schumpeter 1950	Schumpeter JA, 1950 *Capitalism, socialism and democracy* Harper and Row
Shockley 1957	Shockley W, Mar 1957 *On the statistics of individual variations of productivity in research laboratories* Proc IRE **45** 3 pp279-290
Shockley 1976	Shockley W, 1976 *The path to conception of the junction transistor* IEE Trans on Electron D **ED-23** pp597-620

Snitzer 1968   Snitzer E and Young CG,   1968
                          Glass lasers
                          Advances in lasers   **2**   ed. Levine A pub.
                          Dekker (1968)

Souriau 1881   Souriau ,   1881
                          Théorie de l'invention
                          Hachette, Paris

Stokes 1982   Stokes JW,   1982
                          70 years of radio tubes and valves
                          Vestal Press

Stone 1973   Stokes J and Burrus CA,   1 October 1973
                          *Neodymium-doped silica laser in end-pumped
                          geometry*
                          App. Phys Letts. **23** (No.7) pp 388-389,

Sturmey 1958   Sturmey SG,   1958
                          The economic development of radio
                          Duckworth

Swan 1929   Swan ME and Swan KR,   1929
                          *Sir Joseph Wilson Swan FRS, Inventor and
                          Scientist*
                          Oriel Press, reprinted 1968

Sweet 1988   Sweet W,   May 1988
                          *American Physical Society establishes major
                          prize in memory of Lilienfeld*
                          Physics Today (May 1988) pp87-89

Swinburne 1886   Swinburne J,   6 Aug 1886
                          The Edison filament case
                          The Telegraph Journal and Electrical Review (6
                          Aug 1886) pp129-432

Sylos-Labini 1957   Sylos-Labini P,   1957
                          Oligopolie e progresso technico

Taton 1957   Taton R,   1957
                          Reason and chance in scientific discovery
                          Hutchinson

Taylor 1973   Taylor CT & Silberston ZA,   1973
                          The economic impact of the patent system
                          Cambridge UP

Teal 1976   Teal GK,   July 1976
                          Single crystals of germanium and silicon
                          IEEE Trans ED **ED-23**   pp621-639

Tyne 1977   Tyne GF,   1977
                          The saga of the vacuum tube p597-620

Von Hippel 1988 von Hippel E,   1988
The sources of innovation
Oxford U.P.

Weber 1981 Weber S (ed) ,   1981
An age of innovation – a special issue comemorating the 50th anniversary of Electronics *magazine*
McGraw Hill, New York

Wolf 1912 Wolf J,   1912
Die Volkswirtschaft der Gegenwart und Zukunft
Leipzig   p11

Wong 2005 Wong H. and Iwai H.,   Sep 2005
The road to miniaturization
Physics World **18** (No.9) pp40-44

Wyatt 1986 Wyatt G,   1986
The economics of invention: a study of the determinants of inventive activity
Wheatsheaf Books

Zipper 1990 Zipper S,   28 Aug 1990
TI's patent blitz: keeping the wolf from the door
Electronic News

PATENTS INDEX

NAME INDEX